INSPIRE / PLAN / DISCOVER / EXPERIENCE

CHILE
AND EASTER ISLAND

DK EYEWITNESS

CHILE
AND EASTER ISLAND

CONTENTS

DISCOVER 6

Welcome to Chile
and Easter Island............................ 8

Reasons to Love Chile
and Easter Island........................... 10

Explore Chile and Easter Island...........14

Getting to Know
Chile and Easter Island............................16

Chile and Easter
Island Itineraries............................... 20

Chile and Easter
Island Your Way................................26

A Year in Chile
and Easter Island............................ 42

A Brief History........................... 44

EXPERIENCE SANTIAGO 50

Plaza de Armas
and Santiago Centro........................62

West of Santiago Centro.............. 84

Northeast of
Santiago Centro 98

EXPERIENCE CHILE 112

Central Valley....................................114

Norte Grande
and Norte Chico..............................150

Lake District and Chiloé...............194

Northern Patagonia 228

Southern Patagonia
and Tierra del Fuego......................248

Easter Island and
Robinson Crusoe Island..............264

NEED TO KNOW 280

Before You Go.. 282

Getting Around..284

Practical Information..............................288

Index.. 290

Phrasebook 299

Acknowledgments................................... 302

Left: Vibrant apartments in Valparaíso
Previous page: Salt mountains in the Atacama Desert
Cover: Panoramic views of Torres del Paine

DISCOVER

The sun cloaking the streets of Santiago

Welcome to
Chile and Easter Island............................8

Reasons to Love
Chile and Easter Island...........................10

Explore Chile and Easter Island...........14

Getting to Know
Chile and Easter Island...........................16

Chile and Easter
Island Itineraries.......................................20

Chile and Easter
Island Your Way...26

A Year in
Chile and Easter Island...........................42

A Brief History...44

WELCOME TO
CHILE AND
EASTER ISLAND

From arid deserts to icy fjords, tropical beaches to snow-covered mountains, Chile's landscapes are diverse and beautiful. Yet the modern cities, provincial towns, and remote villages are also deserving of exploration. Whatever your dream trip entails, this DK Eyewitness travel guide is the perfect companion.

① Moai statue looking out to sea from Easter Island.

② Curious and friendly penguin on Punta Arenas.

③ Hikers viewing the breathtaking Glacier Grey.

④ Buzzing and bustling streets of Valparasio.

Stretching more than 2,653 miles (4,270 km) north to south, with the Andes to the east and the Pacific to the west, the long and thin country of Chile has something for everyone. It is particularly famous for its dramatic scenery and myriad opportunities for hiking, rafting, diving, and other adventure sports. But the country also has a fascinating history, evident in its ancient sites, architecture, and impressive museums, not to mention fantastic seafood, world-class wine, and strong artistic, literary, and musical traditions.

Northern Chile is dominated by the volcanoes, lagoons, salt flats, and sand dunes of the dusty Atacama Desert, while in the heart of Chile, the buzzing and vibrant capital Santiago lies within striking distance of the bohemian port of Valparaíso and the vineyards of the fertile Central Valley. More than 2,182 miles (3,512 km) off the coast, the tiny and beautiful Easter Island is home to a dazzling array of monolithic statues. In the far south, meanwhile, Patagonia's many national parks rank among the world's finest places to hike.

With so much to see and do in Chile, it can be hard to know where to start. We've broken the country down into easily navigable chapters, with detailed itineraries, expert local knowledge, and colorful, comprehensive maps to help you plan the perfect visit. Whether you're staying for a week, a fortnight, or longer, this DK Eyewitness guide will ensure that you make the most of all that the country has to offer. Enjoy the book, and enjoy Chile.

REASONS TO LOVE
CHILE AND
EASTER ISLAND

Framed by the Andes, the Atacama Desert, and the Pacific Ocean, Chile's mesmerizing scenery, captivating cities, and beautiful landscapes are just a few of the reasons to love the country. Here are our favorites.

1 PATAGONIA

Patagonia is home to endless plains, icy fjords, heaving glaciers, and raucous penguins, not to mention one of the world's great drives, the Carretera Austral.

VALPARAÍSO *2*

"Valpo" is spread across a multitude of hills overlooking the Pacific. It boasts beautiful architecture, a bohemian vibe, and an array of excellent places to eat, drink, and dance.

3 WHITE WATER RAFTING ON FUTALEUFÚ RIVER

The "Futa" is one of the best white-water rafting rivers in South America, with more than 40 Class IV-V rapids, including the "Terminator" and the "Perfect Storm."

STARGAZING *4*
Northern Chile's lack of light pollution and cloud-free days ensure it offers the clearest skies – the best places for stargazing are San Pedro de Atacama and the Valle de Elqui.

EASTER ISLAND *5*
Easter Island – known locally as Rapa Nui – is one of the remotest inhabited places on earth, with a distinct Polynesian culture and a collection of monolithic statues.

SOAK IN THE LAKE DISTRICT HOT SPRINGS *6*
After a day's trekking, rafting, or kayaking in the adventure hub of Pucón, there are few better ways to relax than one of the hot springs in the region.

DIVERSE LANDSCAPES 7

From Atacama Desert's salt flats, geysers, and surreal rock formations to the icy reaches of Tierra del Fuego, Chile encompasses an incredible array of landscapes.

SANTIAGO 8

The rapidly developing capital has some of Chile's best museums and galleries, and an enviable food scene, plus some fantastic ski resorts within easy striking distance.

9 VISITING CHILOÉ'S WOODEN CHURCHES

Chiloé has more than 150 beautiful wooden churches and chapels that date back to the 19th century – 16 of the finest examples are UNESCO World Heritage Sites.

10 SURFING IN PICHILEMU

A laid-back town on the Central Valley coast, Pichilemu is the best place in Chile to learn to surf, hone your skills, or simply kick-back and watch the pros in action.

WINE TASTING IN CENTRAL VALLEY 11

Chilean wine has earned a world-class reputation. Many vineyards in the Central Valley offer tours and tasting sessions amid gorgeous rural scenery.

PARQUE NACIONAL TORRES DEL PAINE 12

With a series of soaring peaks, Torres del Paine is Chile's most famous national park and a haven for hikers. Set out on one of the beautiful routes, such as the Circuit and the W.

EXPLORE
CHILE

This guide divides Chile into seven color-coded
sightseeing areas, as shown on this map.
Find out more about each area on
the following pages.

*Easter
Island*

*P a c i f i c
O c e a n*

SOUTH AMERICA

VENEZUELA

GUYANA

COLOMBIA

ECUADOR

*Pacific
Ocean*

PERU

BRAZIL

BOLIVIA

*Easter
Island*

PARAGUAY

EASTER ISLAND
AND ROBINSON
CRUSOE ISLAND
p264

CHILE

*Robinson
Crusoe Island*

URUGUAY

ARGENTINA

*Atlantic
Ocean*

GETTING TO KNOW
CHILE AND
EASTER ISLAND

Unusually narrow and stretching for almost a third of the length of South America, Chile is a country packed with a diverse range of climates, ecosystems, and terrains. From the arid Atacama Desert to the terraced vineyards of the Central Valley, expect superlative landscapes at every turn.

PAGE 50

SANTIAGO

The modern Chilean capital makes quite an impression. This buzzing metropolis is flanked in the east by the towering, snow-dusted Andes, while high-rise buildings in the financial district give way to forested hillsides. Locals flock to the bustling commerce of Colonial downtown or sip Chilean wine in bars along tree-lined boulevards. Pulsing with a ceaseless energy, the city's keynotes are its thriving culinary scene, where long-forgotten indigenous gastronomy is embraced, and its world-class museums celebrating ancient cultures.

Best for
Museums, culture, food and drink

Home to
Museo Chileno de Arte Precolombino, Parque Quinta Normal, Parque Metropolitano de Santiago

Experience
Dining in some of Chile's finest restaurants

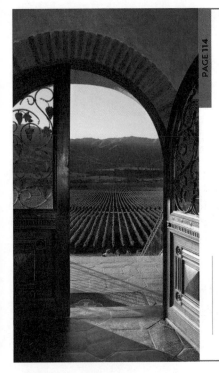

CENTRAL VALLEY

The Pacific Ocean licks sun-soaked, white-sand beaches along the full length of the Central Valley. The regional jewel is hillside Valparaíso, whose vibrant streets are a canvas for the country's finest artistic expression and accommodate rickety, turn-of-the-century funiculars and Nobel Prize-winning poets. Inland, fertile valley plains are dotted with sandy, Colonial towns where vine-lined wineries tantalize the taste buds with carménères and cabernet sauvignons. Eastward, the ever-present, snow-dusted Andes promise high-adrenaline skiing and astonishing valley views.

Best for
Historic cities, wine tasting, skiing

Home to
Valparaíso, Casa Museo Isla Negra, Colchagua Valley wineries

Experience
Riding Valparaíso's funiculars

NORTE GRANDE AND NORTE CHICO

The arid Atacama Desert spreads over the Chilean north, delivering stark, otherworldly landscapes. High-altitude plateaus, pitted with flamingo-flecked lagoons and geysers, are lit up at night by the dazzling arc of the Milky Way, while the wave-scoured beaches of Iquique offer visitors a place to surf huge, impressive waves. Further south, the calm, sweeping bay of picturesque La Serena has a swashbuckling legacy of pirates and privateers.

Best for
Otherworldly landscapes, stargazing, beaches

Home to
San Pedro de Atacama, Parque Nacional Lauca, Iquique, La Serena, Valle de Elqui

Experience
Stargazing in the Atacama desert

→

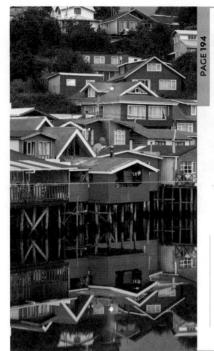

PAGE 194

LAKE DISTRICT AND CHILOÉ

A place of lush forests of araucaria (monkey puzzle) and towering alerce, the Lake District is Chile's adventure playground. Hikers are lured to Pucón to trudge up snowcapped volcanic craters or sink into inviting thermal spring waters. Separated from mainland Chile by a narrow channel, the sleepy fishing villages of the bucolic Chiloé archipelago charm photographers and culture vultures. Here, find whimsical, technicolor-painted wooden churches and indigenous seafood recipes dating back centuries.

Best for
National parks, sports, historic churches

Home to
Parque Nacional Conguillío, Parque Nacional Villarrica, Valdivia, Parque Nacional Vicente Pérez Rosales

Experience
Sampling curanto in Chiloé

PAGE 228

NORTHERN PATAGONIA

Careering through leafy temperate rain forests and glaciers that cling dizzyingly to cliff sides, the Carretera Austral extends through Northern Patagonia. Delving into the Patagonian hinterland, the mostly unpaved highway draws road-trippers and hikers. En route, the foam currents of the Río Futaleufú promise unparalleled white-water rafting, while national parks are awash with wind-blasted steppe and cobalt lakes. Head here to see the country's most mesmerizing terrain.

Best for
Dramatic Andean scenery, epic drives, whitewater rafting

Home to
Parque Nacional Pumalín, Futaleufú, Parque Nacional Queulat, Parque Nacional Laguna San Rafael

Experience
Driving the Carretera Austral

PAGE 248

SOUTHERN PATAGONIA AND TIERRA DEL FUEGO

The three granite towers of Torres del Paine soar in the clouds, casting a spell on every visitor to southern Patagonia. Excursions by boat into thepristine channels of the fjords stippling the coast reveal just some of the region's secrets. Hikers are guaranteed lofty mountains and lumbering glaciers, while photographers and wildlife lovers revel in glimpses of guanaco, chattering penguins, and even puma.

Best for
Glaciers and mountains, trekking, wildlife

Home to
Parque Nacional Torres del Paine, Punta Arenas, Puerto Williams

Experience
Cruising along the wonderful Beagle Channel

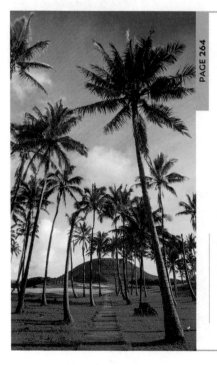

PAGE 264

EASTER ISLAND AND ROBINSON CRUSOE ISLAND

A far-flung outpost some 2,300 miles west across the Pacific, Easter Island is best known for stoic *moai*, who stare across the ages from their plinths. On the streets of Hanga Roa, modern Rapa Nui culture pulses through rhythmic dance and grueling sporting festivals. Closer to mainland Chile, Robinson Crusoe and the Juan Fernández Islands harbor a World Biosphere Reserve with hummingbirds and exotic endemic animals.

Best for
Ancient sites, indigenous cultures, diving

Home to
Ahu Tongarik, Rano Raraku, Ranu Kau and Orongo

Experience
The bustling Tapati Rapa Nui festival

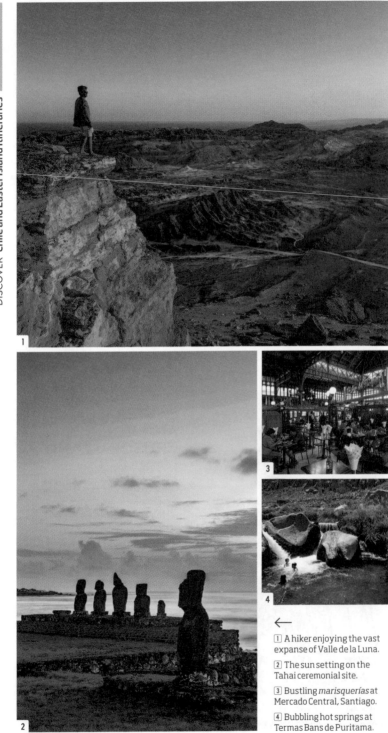

←

1 A hiker enjoying the vast expanse of Valle de la Luna.

2 The sun setting on the Tahai ceremonial site.

3 Bustling *marisquerías* at Mercado Central, Santiago.

4 Bubbling hot springs at Termas Bans de Puritama.

Chile is impossibly diverse. Spend your time hiking one of the world's driest deserts, visiting the icy expanses of Patagonia, and wandering around vibrant and bustling cities. Here we select some of the highlights to help you plan your stay.

2 WEEKS

Day 1

On the first day in San Pedro de Atacama you can take a guided tour of the Salar de Atacama *(p185)*, a vast, gleaming salt flat that contains glorious lakes, including the flamingo-populated Laguna Chaxa. The *salar* can be combined with several other sites, such as the beautiful Miscanti, Miñeques, and Lejía *lagunas*, and the scenic villages of Toconao, Peine, and Socaire *(p185)*. In the evening, head over to Café Adobe *(p185)* for dinner.

Day 2

Get up in the early hours for another full-day guided tour around San Pedro de Atacama. The first stop is the Geisers del Tatio *(p161)*, the world's highest geo-thermal field, excursions to which are often combined with a dip in a hot spring, such as the Termas Baños de Puritama *(p183)*. Tours also include visits to places like the oasis villages of Caspana and Chiu-Chiu, and the pre-Inca ruins of the Pukará de Lasana *(p182)*. Back in San Pedro de Atacama, try Tierra Todo Natural *(p185)* for dinner and then Chela Cabur *(p185)* for drinks.

Day 3

In the morning, take a guided tour of the ALMA observatory *(p160)*, the world's biggest astronomical project. After lunch, visit Pukará de Quitor *(p160)*, a ruined

pre-Inca fortress, and watch the sunset in the otherworldly Valle de la Luna *(p184)*. Then go for an early dinner at Pizzeria El Charrúa *(p159)* before taking a stargazing tour *(p160)*.

Day 4

Drive or take the bus for roughly an hour from San Pedro de Atacama to the city of Calama and catch a flight to Santiago. In the afternoon, look round the city center and the Museo Chileno de Arte Precolombino *(p66)*, one of the finest museums on the continent. In the evening, head over to the Lastarria neighborhood *(p79)* for dinner and drinks at Bocanáriz *(p78)*.

Day 5

In your first morning in Santiago, look round the Museo de la Memoria y los Derechos Humanos *(p90)*, which offers a powerful insight into the human rights abuses of the Pinochet dictatorship. After, reflect on your visit in the neighboring Parque Quinta Normal *(p88)*. For lunch, try one of the *marisquerías* (fish and seafood restaurants) at the Mercado Central *(p81)*, such as Richard El Rey Del Mariscal *(p69)*. In the afternoon, take the funicular to the summit of Cerro San Cristóbal *(p102)* and enjoy the vistas. Spend the evening in the Bellavista neighborhood, taking dinner at Galindo *(p109)* or Barandiarán *(p58)*.

Day 6

In the morning, take a flight to Easter Island, which will take five hours. After looking around the town of Hanga Roa *(p274)*, stroll to the Museo Antropológico Sebastián Englert for an introduction to Rapa Nui history and culture. Then find a vantage point near the Tahai ceremonial site *(p276)* and enjoy the sunset. Finish the day with dinner at Au Bout du Monde *(p275)*.

Day 7

Take a guided tour to Ahu Tongariki *(p272)* and watch the sun rise behind 15 monumental *moai*. Head to Rano Raraku *(p268)*, where the island's statues were carved. In the afternoon, swim, sunbathe, and stroll at Anakena beach *(p276)*, where the first settlers are believed to have landed. In the evening, head to Te Moana *(p275)*, a prime spot for drinks and dinner.

Day 8

Spend the day hiking up to the spectacular Rano Kau *(p274)* volcanic crater and looking round the ruins of Orongo village *(p274)*, which was closely associated with the Birdman cult. In the evening, watch one of the cultural shows in Hanga Roa, which often feature a traditional feast of *curanto* (meat, fish, and vegetables baked over hot rocks).

Day 9

Fly back to Santiago first thing. In the late afternoon, head to the upmarket Las Condes district for a well-mixed cocktail and panoramic views at the W hotel's swish rooftop bar *(p111)*. Then go for dinner in one of nearby Providencia's many restaurants, such as Bar Liguria.

Day 10

Drive or take the bus to one of the Casablanca Valley wineries *(p130)* for a tour, tasting session, and lunch. Head on to Valparaíso *(p118)* and spend the afternoon exploring the city's most atmospheric *cerros* (hills), Concepción and Alegre. Both are covered with cobbled streets and historic, European-style townhouses and churches, as well as

1 Restaurants of Providencia, Santiago, illuminated at night.

2 A hiker looking out at the Rano Kau crater, Easter Island.

3 Vibrant street art by Aibar of La Sebastiana.

4 Soaring peaks of Torres del Paine.

5 Casablanca wineries.

6 Hikers at the foot of the Valle del Francés.

plenty of places to eat, drink, and enjoy the sweeping views. For dinner, try Ápice (p120) or Le Filou de Montpellier (p120), followed by an *helado* (ice cream) at Amor Porteño (p120).

Day 11

Look around the crumbling architecture of the Barrio Puerto, before taking the *ascensor* (funicular lift) up to the Museo Naval y Marítimo (p118), which offers an insight into Chile's turbulent history. After lunch at Bar Inglés or La Playa (p120), take bus "O" (p118) up to Nobel Prize-winning poet Pablo Neruda's former home, La Sebastiana, which is now a museum (p118). Check out Valparaíso's innovative street art scene at the Museo a Cielo Abierto (p126). After dinner at Pasta e Vino (p121), head down to Bar Cinzano (p125) for drinks and live music.

Day 12

Drive, catch the bus, or take a taxi to Santiago airport for a flight to Puerto Natales (p258). Take it easy in the afternoon by exploring the town center

and the Museo Histórico Municipal, which offers a snapshot of Puerto Natales' history. Then stop off at Afrigonia (p257) for dinner, which offers a fusion of Chilean and Zambian flavours.

Day 13

Get up early and drive, catch the bus, or take an organized tour to Parque Nacional Torres del Paine (p252). Spend the day hiking along one of the park's trails, for example to Mirador las Torres (p254), which takes you to views of the park's iconic peaks. Stay at the campsites or *refugios* (huts that offer intriguing dorm-like accommodations), or splash out on a luxury lodge, such as Tierra Patagonia (p255).

Day 14

Spend your final day in the park soaking up the dramatic Patagonian landscapes of mountains, glaciers, waterfalls, and lagoons at Parque Nacional Torres del Paine. Two good trails to attempt are the ones to Mirador Zapata and Mirador Ferrier (p254).

7 DAYS

in Southern Patagonia

▌ *Day 1*

Spend the first day exploring Punta Arenas, the largest city in Chile's far south *(p256)*. Start in the main square, Plaza Muñoz Gamero, which has as its center-piece a statue of Ferdinand Magellan. Then look round the Palacio Sara Braun and the Museo Regional Braun Menéndez, both of which provide a glimpse into the city's heyday in the late 19th and early 20th centuries. After lunch at one of the cafés in the city center, visit the Museo Naval y Marítimo to see fascinating exhibits on Chile's naval history. Then meander around the Cementerio Municipal Sara Braun. Afterward, head for dinner at Damiana Elena *(p257)*.

▌ *Day 2*

Begin the day by joining a guided tour to the Isla Magdalena *(p257)*, a small island reserve northeast of the Punta Arenas that is home to a colony of 100,000 Magellanic penguins. Then head back to the center of Punta Arenas for a delicious lunch and take a trip south to Puerto Hambre (Port Famine; *p256*), site of one of the earliest

Spanish settlements on the Magellan Strait. In the evening, have some drinks at the charming La Taberna del Club de la Unión *(p257)*; if you fancy staying for din-ner, it also serves up tasty Chilean dishes.

▌ *Day 3*

In the morning, head to Puerto Natales *(p258)*. After lunch, drive, take a taxi, or go on a tour to the Cueva del Milodón *(p258)*, a massive cave north of Puerto Natales in which the remains of the giant sloth were discovered in 1890. Cueva del Milodón is also the location that provided inspiration for Bruce Chatwin's famous English travel book, *In Patagonia*. As well as exploring the wonderful cueva, visitors can check out displays on some of the interesting prehistoric creatures of Patagonia. Finish off with some dinner at El Living *(p257)*.

▌ *Day 4*

Drive or take the bus to reach the spectacular Parque Nacional Torres del Paine *(p252)*, a UNESCO World Biosphere Reserve and a trekker's paradise. Check

1 Plaza Muñoz Gamero, Punta Arenas.

2 Sunset over Punta Arenas.

3 Magellanic penguins.

4 View from the Cueva del Milodón.

5 The ice-blue Glacier Grey.

6 Horseback-riding in Parque Nacional Torres del Paine.

into the luxurious Explora Patagonia (p255), an upmarket hotel that offers spectacular views of the park's soaring granite peaks. Enjoy a light lunch in the restaurant, then make your first foray into the park on one of the hotel's horseback riding tours. Spend the rest of your afternoon trotting past aquamarine lakes and though ancient beech woods, keeping your eyes peeled for a glimpse of the region's diverse wildlife, including condors and guanacos.

Day 5

Rise early and grab a big breakfast in the hotel – you'll need it to tackle one of the park's best day-hikes, which ends at the base of the granite needles known as Los Cuernos ("The Horns"). This route – which is in fact the first section of the popular multi-day W trek – meanders through varied scenery, including grasslands, forests, and scrubland, passing by teal-hued lakes and sheer-sided mountains. Eventually, your legs tired, you'll reach Los Cuernos, whose shard-like prongs pierce the sky above. Take a minute

to soak in this magnificent sight, before heading back to your hotel for an evening of well-deserved relaxation in the spa.

Day 6

Today, it's time to explore Lago Grey; bordered to the north by a mighty glacier and to the west by the twisted peaks of the Cerro Paine Grande, this is one of the park's most beautiful lakes. Paddle over its shimmering, ice-berg-filled expanse on a kayaking trip with the excellent Kayak en Patagonia (www.kayakenpatagonia.com), whose full-day tours let you explore both the lake and gently winding Río Grey. Famished by a day in the great outdoors, head to El Living (p257) for tasty veggie dishes.

Day 7

In the morning, travel back to Puerto Natales and spend the rest of the day looking around the town. Make sure you stop off at Museo Histórico Municipal (p258), a museum that showcases some of Puerto Natales' pioneering history. Finish with dinner at Afrigonia (p257).

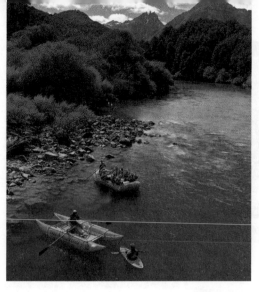

Grab a Paddle

The many rivers, channels, lagoons, and fjords of the Lake District and Patagonia are best explored in a raft or a kayak. Río Futaleufú *(p234)* is particularly great for those interested in white water rafting. A less adrenaline-charged but equally memorable experience is kayaking across the waterways of Parque Nacional Laguna San Rafael *(p238)* amid icebergs, glaciers, and sea lion colonies.

←

Rafters enjoying a rare calm spot on the Río Futaleufú

CHILE AND EASTER ISLAND FOR
THRILL SEEKERS

Chile's reputation as an adventure-sports hub is well deserved. There is a multitude of electrifying activities to try throughout the country, including some truly epic paddles, climbs, dives, and glides.

Head to the Skies

On the arid coast of northern Chile, the city of Iquique *(p162)* has the ideal combination of geographic and climatic conditions for paragliding: The sun shines year round, it rarely rains, the skies are largely cloud free, and air currents whistle off the Pacific. Moreover, the views from the air – notably of Cerro Dragón *(p164)*, the huge sand dune that looms over the city - are superb. Puro Vuelo *(www.purovuelo.cl)* is a popular local paragliding operator.

> **INSIDER TIP**
> **Where to Stay**
>
> Calling all outdoor enthusiasts. Not sure where to stay? The Lake District town of Pucón *(p214)* is the country's adventure-sport capital. Here you'll find various companies offering sports and excursions, including skydiving and white-water rafting.

Landing in the desert just outside the town of Iquique, northern Chile ↑

↑ Hiking the impressive
Villarrica, and *(inset)*
the volcano from afar

Scale a Volcano

Chile has more than 2,900 volcanoes, and several
agencies offer guided hikes, ranging from day
trips to technical climbs for experienced mountaineers. In the Lake District, Summit Chile *(www.
summitchile.org)* takes hikers up Lanín, Villarrica,
and Quetrupillán, all in Parque Nacional Villarrica
(p202). Soaring above Parque Nacional Vicente Pérez
Rosales *(p204)*, snowy Volcán Osorno can be explored
with Huella Andina Expeditions *(www.huellandina.com)*.

Dive into the Blue

Two of the world's largest
marine reserves surround
Easter Island *(p264)* and
Robinson Crusoe Island *(p278)*.
The former protects around
140 species and offers divers
the chance to see under-
ground caves and submerged
moai statues, while the latter
has reserves similarly rich in
marine life. Mike Rapu *(www.
mikerapu.cl)* is a dive centre
based in Hanga Roa *(p274)* and
Refugio Náutico Eco Lodge
(www.islarobinson crusoe.cl)
arranges trips on Robinson
Crusoe Island.

→

Snorkeling in waters
near Ahu Tongariki,
Easter Island

Culinary Cities

Santiago is fast becoming one of the continent's most delectable spots, with many of its restaurants ranking high among the world's best places to eat. Don't miss Boragó *(p59)*, an innovative eatery with a strong focus on sourcing indigenous ingredients, or Bocanariz *(www.bocanariz.cl)*, whose menu complements its extensive collection of Chilean wines. Beyond the capital, Valparaíso beckons gourmets with inventive restaurants; try Ápice *(p121)*, a stylish spot serving creative seafood dishes.

→

One of the many inventive restaurants found in Valparaíso

CHILE AND EASTER ISLAND FOR
FOODIES

Compared to other countries in Latin America, notably Peru and Mexico, Chile's cuisine remains under the radar. But with some of the world's finest fish and seafood, a burgeoning wine industry, an array of traditional dishes, and fabulous restaurants, Chile has plenty to offer the foodie traveler.

Sweet and Sour

From wine to pisco, Chilean drinks are famous around the world. Central Valley has vineyards offering tours and tasting sessions; many have been linked into wine routes, including in the Casablanca *(p130)* and Colchagua *(p148)* valleys. Although not as well-known as Chilean wine, pisco is not to be missed. It's often served in a pisco sour, where it's mixed with lemon, bitters, and sugar, and topped with egg whites. Valle de Elqui *(p172)* in Norte Chico is the heart of the pisco industry. Distilleries are open to visitors *(p172)*.

←

Pisco sour, an unmissable and delicious South American cocktail

Lush and Local

Although separated by more than 2,180 miles (3,508 km), Chiloé (p220) and Easter Island (p264) have a delicious dish in common: curanto. Traditionally, curanto is made by digging a pit, filling it with hot rocks, layering on fish, shellfish, meat, and starchy vegetables (and dumplings in Chiloé), covering everything with leaves, and allowing it to slow-cook for hours or even days. The result is worth the wait. As well as playing a key role in curanto, fish and seafood are staples throughout Chile. The Littoral Central (Central Coast) is known for its marisquerias (fish and seafood restaurants): keep an eye out for razor clams topped with a cheesy crust, conger eel stew, and super-fresh ceviche.

←

Curanto cooking amid hot rocks in the ground

→

Bustle and barter at Santiago's Mercado Central

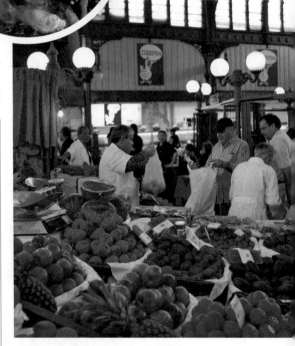

TOP
5 CHILEAN DISHES NOT TO MISS

Asado
A barbecue featuring a variety of cuts of beef (or lamb in the south), sausages, and sides.

Pastel de choclo
A minced-meat pie with a blitzed-corn topping.

Cazuela
A soupy stew with vegetables and a piece of meat on the bone.

Humitas
Steamed corn cakes.

Chorrillana
A heaped plate of strips of steak, eggs, onions, and chips.

Tale of Two Markets

It's easy to lose yourself for a few hours in either of Santiago's bustling markets: the Mercado Central (p81), which is housed in an elegant building that dates back to the mid-1800s, and the more rustic and less touristy La Vega, a few blocks away (p106). Both are buzzing hives of activity, with stalls piled high with fresh produce from across the country. They are also home to an array of low-cost fish and seafood restaurants.

Mapuche statues at the ↑
Museo Chileno de Arte
Precolombino

CHILE AND EASTER ISLAND FOR
ART LOVERS

From ancient crafts dating back thousands of years to cutting-edge fashion, indigenous jewelry to hard-hitting street art, Chile has something to suit every artistic taste.

Hit the Streets

Chile has a long tradition of creative, large-scale, and often highly political street art, murals, and graffiti, something that is evident across the country. The scenes in Santiago *(p50)* and Valparaíso *(p118)* are particularly interesting. Bellavista, Brasil, and Yungay neighborhoods in the capital are excellent places to start. Valparaíso, meanwhile, is home to the Museo a Cielo Abierto *(p126)*, an open-air gallery of works by some of Chile's best-known street artists. A number of agencies, such as Santiago Street Art Tours *(www.stgostreetart. com)*, offer tours, which are worth taking as works are often left unsigned.

Modern Art in Santiago

Chile's capital is home to one of South America's finest museums, the Museo Chileno de Arte Precolombino (p66), which has a remarkable and extensive range of exhibits. The Museo Nacional de Bellas Artes (p79), a fine arts museum featuring predominantly Chilean artists, also impresses, as does the Museo de Arte Contemporáneo (p80). Other venues include the Estación Mapocho (p80), a former railway station turned into a cultural venue, and the Museo de la Moda (p110), a fashion museum with a collection of more than 10,000 pieces.

← Exterior of the Museo Chileno de Arte Precolombino

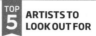

TOP 5 ARTISTS TO LOOK OUT FOR

Roberto Matta
Seminal figure in 20th-century surrealism and abstract expressionism.

Rebeca Matte Bello
Sculptor particularly known for her work *Icarus and Daedalus*.

Carlos Sotomayor
Leader of Neo-Cubism in South America.

Gracia Barrios
Painter who developed a style known as "informal realism."

Nemesio Antúnez Zañartu
Painter, engraver, and founder of Workshop 99.

💬 INSIDER TIP
Bellas Artes

Fine art meets street art at Bellas Artes metro station. Check out famous street artist Inti's work before heading to the Museo Nacional de Bellas Artes (p79).

A Mapuche woman working on beautiful textiles ↑

↑ A work by Gonzalo Matiz showing Santiago's vibrant street art scene

Indigenous Art

The Mapuche people (p207) are Chile's largest indigenous group: Roughly ten percent of the population have Mapuche heritage. In the face of long-standing discrimination, they have retained a distinct culture and way of life. From an artistic perspective, the Mapuche people are known for impressive textiles, metalworking, and silver jewelry. Museums in the Lake District, the Museo de Volcanes (p207) and the Museo Regional de la Araucanía (p206) have collections of Mapuche artworks and jewelry.

ROUTE OF PARKS

Launched in 2018 following a donation of land from Tompkins Conservation *(p233)* to the Chilean state, the spectacular Ruta del los Parques (Route of Parks; *www.rutadelos parques.org*) stretches 1,700 miles (2,736 km) from Puerto Montt to Cape Horn and connects 17 parks. It aims to use sustainable tourism to drive conservation efforts in Patagonia and Tierra del Fuego – including significant rewilding schemes – and provide various economic opportunities for what are often remote and underserved communities.

Hiking through Parque Nacional Torres del Paine ↑

CHILE AND EASTER ISLAND FOR
HIKERS

Few countries can compare with Chile when it comes to hiking. Its many national parks – which cover landscapes as diverse as deserts, rain forests, and ice fields – are home to a wide range of trails, with options to suit virtually every traveler, regardless of levels of fitness and aptitude.

Multi-Day Treks

Chile's two best-known multi-day treks can be found in Parque Nacional Torres del Paine *(p252)*: the W and the Circuit. Both routes showcase the park's three iconic peaks, and are extremely popular, which means you need to book accommodations in advance. South of Parque Nacional Torres del Paine, Puerto Williams *(p261)* – the southernmost town on earth – is the jumping-off point for the Dientes de Navarino circuit, a tough but truly spectacular four- or five-day expedition through the majestic mountain wilderness of Tierra del Fuego.

Glacier Grey in Parque Nacional Torres del Paine ↓

Hiking for Beginners

After a simple stroll? Parque Nacional Pumalín *(p232)* has the answer, with a wide range of impressive short hikes, including the Sendero Laguna Tronador, with views of the Michinmahuida volcano. Parque Nacional Queulat *(p236)* offers the 2-mile (3 km) Sendero Ventisquero Colgante hike, while Parque Nacional Patagonia *(p243)* has walks that take half a day or less. On Easter Island *(p264)*, you can hike up Rano Kau crater and the ruined Orongo village *(p274)*.

TOP 4 WAYS TO HIKE RESPONSIBLY

Plan ahead
Ensure that you have equipment suited to the environment.

Respect wildlife
Do not touch or approach the animals.

Dispose of waste
Retain rubbish and use the appropriate disposal points.

Leave what you find
Do not take what belongs to nature.

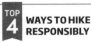

↑ Andean gull on the rocks in Parque Nacional Lauca

One-Day Hikes

Cochamó Valley in the Lake District has many trails that take a day or less. The 7-mile (12-km) La Junta trek follows an old logging route and passes through rain forest. The Norte Grande's Parque Nacional Lauca *(p166)* is a high-altitude region of volcanoes, brightly colored lakes, herds of vicuñas, and more than 140 species of birds. There are several one-day trails in the park. Before setting off, take time to acclimatize properly .

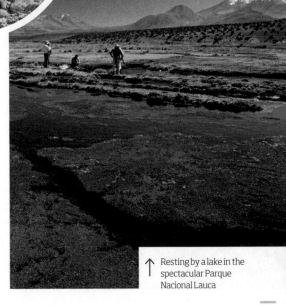

↑ Resting by a lake in the spectacular Parque Nacional Lauca

Chill with Penguins

From November to March, Isla Magdalena *(p257)* in the Strait of Magellan is home to a rookery of penguins. Day trips to the island run from the city of Punta Arenas. In the same region, and also easy to visit, Seno Otway *(p257)* attracts 2,500 pairs of Magellanic penguins. Alternatively, head for Bahia Inutil in Tierra del Fuego, which has king penguins, or Reserva Nacional Pinguino de Humboldt *(p191)* in the Norte Chico to see Humboldt penguins.

→

King penguins socializing in Tierra del Fuego

CHILE AND EASTER ISLAND FOR
WILDLIFE

From raucous penguin rookeries in Patagonia to skittish herds of camelids in the Atacama Desert, not to mention circling condors in the Lake District and breaching whales in the Stait of Magellan, Chile simply abounds with wildlife. Here we round up some of the most characterful critters.

Catch Sight of Condors

The sight of an Andean condor high in the air against a backdrop of Andean peaks lives long in the memory. One of the world's largest flying birds, with a wingspan of 10 ft (3 m), they are found in many of the Lake District's national parks, including Conguillío *(p198)* and Tolhuaca *(p208)*. Chile's national bird can also be spotted in places like Termas de Cauquenes *(p138)*, the Reserva Nacional Altos de Lircay *(p143)*, and the Parque Nacional Laguna del Laja *(p147)*, as well as in Parque Nacional Pan de Azúcar *(p189)* in the Norte Chico.

←

A condor surveying the scene in Parque Nacional Torres del Paine

Go Whale-Watching

The Strait of Magellan *(p260)*, which separates Southern Patagonia from Tierra del Fuego and links the Pacific to the Atlantic, is a breeding ground for an array of marine species, including humpback whales. To get the chance to catch a glimpse of these majestic creatures, take a boat trip on the waters of Parque Marino Francisco Coloane; Punta Arenas-based operator Whalesound *(www.whalesound.com)* runs tours, and has an eco-camp inside the reserve on Isla Carlos III. Blue whales, the world's largest mammals, can be seen off Melinka *(p240)* in Northern Patagonia, and in Reserva Nacional Pinguino de Humboldt *(p191)*, where sperm and humpback whales also visit.

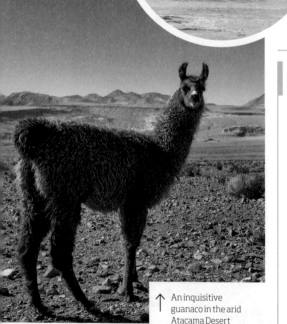

← Humpback whale jumping in Parque Francisco Coloane Marino

SAVING THE BLUE WHALE

Chile has a truly impressive track record when it comes to protecting endangered marine life, especially its approach to saving the blue whale. The world's largest animal was close to extinction and so it was with much excitement that a blue whale nursery was discovered off the coast of Chiloé, in 2003. In 2008, Chile decided to ban whale hunting along its entire coast, and then, in 2014, the country set up a sanctuary for declining marine life. This protected area is the size of Santiago and further welcomes dolphins and endangered otters. In 2017, two more protected marine parks opened.

↑ An inquisitive guanaco in the arid Atacama Desert

Keeping up with the Camelids

Four species of camelids – llamas, alpacas, guanacos, and vicuñas – can be spotted in Chile, predominantly in the high Andean regions. All four are found in Parque Nacional Lauca *(p166)* in the Norte Chico; the shy, elegant vicuña tends to be the most elusive. Also keep an eye out for the vizcacha, a long-tailed member of the chinchilla family seen in Parque Nacional Nevado Tres Cruces *(p190)* and Parque Nacional La Campana *(p137)*.

Step Back in Time

Some of Chile's finest architecture dates back to the colonial period. Santiago offers plenty of examples: highlights include the Palacio de la Real Audiencia and the Catedral Metropolitana *(p68)*. Similarly impressive are Chiloé's Jesuit churches *(p224)*. All the surviving churches are built from wood and typically face out to sea. 16 of them have been named UNESCO World Heritage Sites.

→

Interior of Santa María, one of 16 UNESCO World Heritage Sites

CHILE AND EASTER ISLAND FOR
ARCHITECTURE

Encompassing desert ghost towns and late 19th-century mansions, churches dating back more than 400 years and brightly colored fishermen's houses raised on stilts, the architecture in Chile is vibrant and diverse.

Picturesque Palafitos

Castro, capital of the Chiloé archipelago, is home to some beautiful *palafitos (p222)*, colorfully painted wooden homes raised above water. Many *palafitos* were destroyed in the 1960 Valdivia earthquake, but fortunately some survived. In recent years, *palafitos* have been turned into guesthouses, hostels, and restaurants.

→

Vibrant and charming *palafitos* in Castro

Valparaíso's Heyday

Spread across Valparaíso's many rolling cerros (hills) are wonderful examples of late 19th- and early 20th-century architecture, testament to a period in which the city was a commercial hub. Cerro Alegre and Cerro Concepción are the most attractive areas, once home to a community of European traders and businessmen. They lined the steep, cobbled streets with townhouses with bucolic gardens – many are now hotels or restaurants – as well as sober churches and promenades with views out to the Pacific.

ALEJANDRO ARAVENA

Founder of the architecture firm Elemental, Aravena (born 1967) is Chile's most famous contemporary architect. Known for his pioneering work on social housing across Latin America, he won the prestigious Pritzker Architecture Prize in 2016 for his work reinventing low-cost housing.

↑ Hotel in Valparaíso built from shipping containers

Like a Ghost Town

In the 19th century, huge nitrate reserves made the Atacama Desert one of the most profitable places on earth. Echoes of the period reverberate around two former nitrate oficinas, Santa Laura and Humberstone (p178), now atmospheric ghost towns. The crumbling machinery of the former seems straight out of a steampunk novel, while the latter is more intact, with abandoned houses, a theatre, church, and hotel.

↑ Abandoned factory at Humberstone and (inset) the outside of the ghost town.

The Craft of Neruda

"He who does not travel, who does not read, who does not listen to music, who does not find grace in himself... dies slowly," wrote Pablo Neruda, who remains one of Chile's most significant writers. He was just 19 when his second poetry collection was published. It sold more than 20 million copies and won him the Nobel Prize for Literature. Three of Neruda's homes – La Chascona (p105) in Santiago, La Sebastiana (p124) in Valparaíso, and Isla Negra (p128) in the place of the same name – are now museums.

→

Isla Negra, the Central Valley home of Pablo Neruda

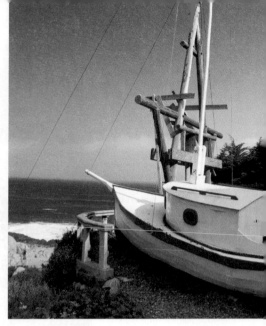

CHILE AND EASTER ISLAND FOR
BOOKWORMS

With a pair of Nobel Prize-winning poets and some of the most influential Latin American novelists of the 20th and early 21st centuries, Chile punches well above its weight in literary terms. The country has also inspired ground-breaking works by eminent scientists and travel writers.

The Magic of Gabriela Mistral

The first Latin American to win a Nobel Prize for Literature, Gabriela Mistral's poetry was deeply influenced by the beautiful Valle de Elqui (p172), which she described as a "heroic slash in the mass of mountains." She was born in this very valley, in the sleepy town of Vicuña, today home to a wonderful museum dedicated to her life and work. Mistral later moved to the village of Montegrande; seek out her tomb on a peaceful hillside just south of the village.

←

Chilean Nobel Prize-winning poet Gabriela Mistral

Follow in Bruce Chatwin's Footsteps

Southern Chile features heavily in Bruce Chatwin's seminal travelog In Patagonia. His quixotic journey was strangely inspired by a giant sloth skin that was found in the Cueva del Milodón (p258) near Puerto Natales. As well as exploring the cave, Chatwin also visited Punta Arenas (p256), where his distant relative Charlie Milward lived. In his collection What Am I Doing Here? Chatwin writes about the wooden churches, the rain-soaked landscapes, and the "tormented mythologies" of the archipelago of Chiloé (p220).

← Eminent travel writer Bruce Chatwin

TOP 4 LITERARY WORKS

The House of the Spirits, Isabel Allende (1982)
A family struggles through Chile's political upheavals.

The Savage Detectives, Roberto Bolaño (1998)
Two poets search for another poet.

Pinochet in Piccadilly, Andy Beckett (2002)
The book unpicks the arrest of the dictator in London, in 1998.

The Motorcycle Diaries, Che Guevara (1992)
An account of Guevara's travels through South America.

Retrace the Route of Charles Darwin

In the course of his journey on the HMS Beagle, Darwin explored many parts of Chile, including the San Rafael glacier (p238), Chiloé (p220), Concepción (p146), and Valparaíso (p118). He climbed the trail up the northern flank of Cerro La Campana and later wrote: "We spent the day on the summit, and I never enjoyed one more thoroughly. Chile, bounded by the Andes and the Pacific, was seen as in a map."

→ Viewing breathtaking Glacier Alley, once visited by Charles Darwin

Browsing an exhibit at the
Museum of Memory
and Human Rights ↑

CHILE AND EASTER ISLAND FOR
HISTORY BUFFS

Chile's myriad historic sites, museums, and ruins take visitors on a journey through 8,000 years of human history. The country is home to the oldest mummies ever discovered, pioneering Patagonian settlements, and 450-year-old cities, to mention just a few of its historical attractions.

Historic Cities

La Serena (p168), Chile's second-oldest city, is home to some truly beautiful churches, including the soaring Neo-Classical Catedral de La Serena and eye-catching Iglesia Santo Domingo. The city of Valdivia (p206), founded eight years after La Serena in 1552, is also worth a visit; stroll along its riverside to spy spectacular 19th-century Teutonic architecture. Don't forget to admire the ruins of three epic forts – Fuerte de Niebla, Fuerte de Mancera and Fuerte de Corral – found just outside of the city.

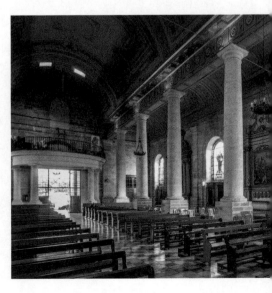

→

Beautiful interior
of the Catedral de
La Serena

Museums of Memory

Santiago is home to a pair of groundbreaking museums that rank among the finest on the continent. In the city center, the Museo Chileno de Arte Precolombino (p66) has a vast collection of artifacts from pre-Hispanic and indigenous cultures across Latin America. West of the center, in a glass building, the Museo de la Memoria y los Derechos Humanos (p90) uses multimedia, personal items, poetry, archival materials, and other exhibits to tell the stories of some of the estimated 3,000 people who were killed or "disappeared" by the Pinochet dictatorship.

Museum of Memory and Human Rights

GEOGLYPHS

Geo-glyphs are formed by elements of the landscape, such as clastic rocks, trees, or earth. Ancient geo-glyphs carry cultural significance and give visitors a glimpse into the past. They are often shrouded in mystery, leading to theories regarding origin. Chile hosts some of the world's most famous geo-glyphs, including the Atacama Giant, the largest prehistoric anthropomorphic figure in the world.

INSIDER TIP
Ride Around

A bike path runs through vibrant La Serena, passing by its many historic churches and cathedrals. Rent a bike from one of the city's guesthouses and get exploring.

Chinchorro mummies at the Museo Arqueológico San Miguel de Azapa ↑

Mummies Return

Chinchorro people (6000–2000 BC) used various complex techniques to mummify the dead, who were at the time buried in collective tombs in the Atacama Desert. Some of the mummies survived and are now considered the oldest examples of the process on earth, predating even the more famous examples from Ancient Egypt. The Museo Arqueológico San Miguel de Azapa (p157), just outside the city of Arica, provides a home to some of the Chinchorro mummies.

A YEAR IN
CHILE AND EASTER ISLAND

JANUARY

△ **Festival Internacional Teatro a Mil**
(Jan–early Feb). A major theater, dance, and performing arts festival that takes place in Santiago every year. It is the country's largest festival and aims to promote arts in Chile.

FEBRUARY

△ **Tapati Rapa Nui** *(early Feb)*. A two-week celebration of Rapa Nui (Easter Island) culture.
Festival Costumbrista Chilote *(mid-Feb)*. A celebration of Chiloé's culture, folklore, and traditional cuisine.

MAY

△ **Glorias Navales** *(May 21)*. Military ceremonies commemorate the 1879 Battle of Iquique. Expect parades and speeches.

JUNE

△ **Fiesta de San Pedro** *(Jun 29)*. Fishermen take statues of their patron saint out to sea to wish for good fortune.
Pride *(mid/late Jun)*. Chile's biggest LGBT+ Pride march held in Santiago.

SEPTEMBER

△ **Fiestas Patrias** *(Sep 18)*. Chile's Independence Day sees various celebrations, including street parties, dancing, music, and plenty of eating and drinking.
Festival de Cine Internacional *(mid-Sep)*. Viña del Mar's film festival.

OCTOBER

Festival de los Mil Tambores *(first weekend in Oct)*. The arrival of spring is marked by Valparaíso's Thousand Drums Festival.
Dia de la Raza *(Oct 12)*. Once commemorating the "discovery" of the Americas by Columbus, the festival now celebrates Chile's indigenous peoples.
△ **El Ensayo** *(late Oct/early Nov)*. An important horse race at Santiago's Club Hípico.

MARCH

△ **Festival de la Vendimia** *(throughout Mar)*. The grape harvest is marked in many of the wine regions with tastings, grape-crushing, and various other events. The festival is hugely popular with visitors.

Lollapalooza *(mid-Mar)*. The popular music festival comes to Chile, with celebrations taking place in Santiago's Parque O'Higgins.

APRIL

Semana Santa *(Mar/Apr)*. Holy Week (Easter) features church services and vibrant street processions, as well as huge numbers of Chileans heading off for a much-deserved weekend away.

△ **Fiesta de Cuasimodo** *(first Sun after Easter)*. After mass, priests travel in beautifully decorated carts, motorbikes, or bikes, accompanied by *huasos* (cowboys).

JULY

△ **Festival de La Tirana** *(Jul 12–16)*. Honors the Virgen de la Carmen in a major fiesta that blends pre-Columbian and Catholic traditions.

Fiesta de la Virgen del Carmen *(Jul 16)*. Military parades celebrate armed forces, the independence struggle, and the patron saint.

Carnaval de Invierno *(third weekend)*. Punta Arenas' carnival has parades and fireworks.

AUGUST

Santiago Fashion Week *(Aug 2–3)*. The biggest fashion event in Chile takes place in the capital. It celebrates designers from across South America.

△ **Jesús Nazareno de Caguach** *(Aug 21–31)*. One of Chiloé's key religious festivals, featuring rowing competitions, church services, and processions.

DECEMBER

△ **Fiesta Grande de la Virgen de Rosario** *(late Dec)*. Thousands travel to Andacollo to worship the patron saint of mining.

Noche Buena *(Dec 24)*. Chileans meet extended families for dinner and midnight mass.

Navidad *(Dec 25)*. Christmas Day is typically spent at home with the family.

Fin de Año/Año Nuevo *(Dec 31)*. Fireworks displays mark the end of the year.

NOVEMBER

△ **Dia de Todos los Santos** *(Nov 1)*. Chileans tend to family graves on All Saints' Day.

Feria del Libro *(early Nov)*. Book festival at Santiago's Centro Cultural Estación Mapocho, with various exhibits and readings from writers from across the continent and beyond.

A BRIEF
HISTORY

It was a rocky road to becoming South America's most stable economy and democracy. Ferocious earthquakes, violent clashes between indigenous peoples, colonizing empires, and a 17-year dictatorship have left their mark on what is now a modern and culturally rich country.

The First Pioneers

Excavations at Monte Verde, just north of Puerto Montt in the Lake District, date the arrival of humans to Chile around 15,000 years ago. These pioneers crossed the Bering Strait 2,000 years before, finding their way overland or by boat south through the Americas. Over the next 10,000 years, these semi-nomadic, hunter-gatherer cultures domesticated native camelids for transportation and practiced complex funerary rites; the Chinchorro began mummifying their dead around 7,000 years ago. South in the hinterlands of Patagonia, canoe-faring cultures used bone harpoons and vegetable fibre nets to hunt.

1 An early map of Chile.

2 Pioneers approaching the shores.

3 Painting of Easter Island.

4 Portrait of Ferdinand Magellan.

Timeline of events

13,000 BC

Establishment of Monte Verde, Chile's first-known settlement.

1200

Polynesians settle on Easter Island.

1520

Magellan reaches Tierra del Fuego and the Strait of Magellan.

1528

Francisco Pizarro and Diego de Almagro first land in Peru.

The Polynesian Colonizers

Hotu Matu'a and his people – Polynesians from the now unknown land of Hiva – sailed 1,200 miles (1,930 km) and settled in Rapa Nui (Easter Island), landing in 1200 AD. An organized society soon emerged, based on kinship and ancestor worship, with Hotu Matu'a as the *ariki mau* (supreme chief or king). The next 550 years were spent carving monolithic stone statues, before clan warfare sent the island into disarray.

The Arrival of the Europeans

The first European to discover Chile – reaching the archipelago of Tierra del Fuego – was Portuguese explorer Ferdinand Magellan in 1520. A few decades later, in 1541, a Spanish expedition from newly colonized Peru, led by Pedro de Valdivia, brought Chile under Spanish control, founding Santiago as capital. But the indigenous Mapuche prevented Spanish forces from penetrating south beyond the Río Bíobío in a 350-year conflict, with sporadic fighting lasting into the 18th century. Failing to make fortunes, the Spanish divided Central Valley into *encomiendas*, enslaving the indigenous population.

INDIGENOUS CULTURE AND HERITAGE IN CHILE

Chile is home to a rich array of indigenous cultures. The Mapuche is the largest, with 1,745,000 Chileans identifying as Mapuche today. Many Mapuche still live in small patri-lineal communities.

1574
Juan Fernández discovers islands in Pacific Ocean.

1704
Alexander Selkirk, inspiration for *Robinson Crusoe*, is marooned on uninhabited Juan Fernández Island

1774
Captain James Cook visits Rapa Nui.

1541
Pedro de Valdivia founds city of Santiago.

1722
Jacob Roggeveen is the first European on Rapa Nui, landing on Easter Sunday.

The Battle for Independence

As the long, narrow territory of Chile was being brought under central rule, the ties that bound the colony with the Spanish Crown were weakening. When Napoleon marched into Spain in 1808, Chile's independence campaign began in earnest. Spearheaded by Chilean Congressman and wealthy landowner Bernardo O'Higgins, the bitter and furious display of arms between republicans and royalists lasted until 1818, when O'Higgins was installed as the first head of state of an independent Chile.

The War of the Pacific

The nation's economy grew rapidly over the next century. Mining camps in the Norte Chico produced vast quantities of copper, making Chile the largest global producer. In 1879, an argument about Chilean investors paying export taxes for the nitrate deposits in the Atacama Desert – a region owned by Peru and Bolivia – provoked the three-year-long War of the Pacific. Chile emerged victorious, expanding its territory by one third to include the lucrative nitrate fields.

↑ Horace Castelli's depiction of boats near Easter Island

Timeline of events

1808
Napoleon invades Spain.

1818
Chile declares independence after ten years of conflict between royalists.

1826
Remaining Spanish troops on Chiloé surrender, ending Spanish presence.

1834
Charles Darwin sails along Chile's coast aboard HMS *Beagle*.

46

Indigenous Repression

Two years later, the country expanded further, this time into the south. The indigenous Mapuche had fiercely resisted Spanish rule since the 1500s. This came to a head between 1861 and 1883, when the government launched an offensive known as the Pacification of the Araucanía. Some 100,000 Mapuche – around 90 percent of the population – were killed and most Mapuche ancestral lands were ceded to the Chilean government.

The Annexation of Easter Island

In 1888, Chile annexed Easter Island. The population had been devastated by smallpox, which was introduced by European explorers, and by Peruvian slave raiders who had abducted 1,500 Rapa Nui - around 50 percent of the islanders at the time. Over the next 50 years, the Scottish-owned Williamson-Balfour Company turned the island into a sheep ranch, confining the indigenous population to its eastern corner. This continued until 1954, when the island came under the control of the Chilean Navy. It took another 12 years before the Rapa Nui were given citizenship and the right to vote in mainland elections.

[1] Clashes during the Battle of Independence.

[2] The three-year-long War of the Pacific.

[3] A Mapuche village.

Did You Know?

"Chile" most likely comes from the Mapuche word "chili," which means "where the land ends."

1849
California Gold Rush, with Valparaíso a key port.

1879
War of the Pacific begins as Chileans occupy the port city of Antofagasta.

1888
Easter Island annexed by Chile.

1883
The Pacification of Araucanía forces the Mapuche from their lands.

47

Economic Turbulence and Salvador Allende

By the mid-1900s, economic woes threatened stability. The Chilean nitrate industry collapsed, while copper prices hit rock bottom. In 1970, socialist Salvador Allende was elected president. He nationalized copper and confiscated land for redistribution. Strikes, runaway inflation, and shortages of basic commodities brought the country into chaos. On September 11, 1973, army commander-in-chief Augusto Pinochet launched a military coup. As the air force began bombing the presidential palace in Santiago, Allende killed himself rather than surrender.

The Pinochet Dictatorship

The following 17 years saw political parties banned and over 80,000 political opponents imprisoned, tortured, and executed. The economy was transformed using free-market strategies; regulations were eliminated and state assets sold off, while a new constitution expanded Pinochet's powers. But protests forced a plebiscite in 1988, with the electorate voting emphatically against Pinochet. In 1989, center-left politician Patricio Aylwin became the first president of a newly democratic Chile.

[1] Salvador Allende delivering a speech. ↑

[2] Protests against Augusto Pinochet.

[3] Michelle Bachelet, Chile's first female president.

1945

Gabriela Mistral is the first Latin American and the fifth woman to win the Nobel Prize for Literature.

Timeline of events

1966
The Rapa Nui are granted full Chilean citizenship and the right to vote.

1970
Salvador Allende elected as president.

1973
Military coup deposes Allende.

1988
Pinochet loses plebiscite; Chile starts returning to democracy.

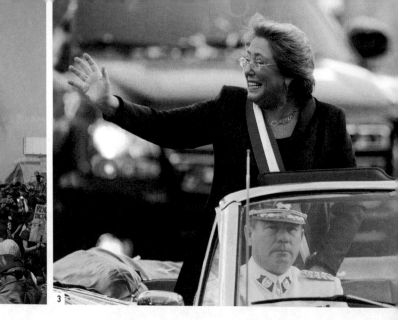

3

The After-Effects of Dictatorship

After the return to democracy, center-left presidents continued Pinochet's economic course, which created a stable economy but expanded the wealth divide. Over these years, there were national and international calls to investigate the human rights abuses of the dictatorship, but Pinochet held immunity. However, following an extradition request by Spanish judge Báltazar Garzón, Pinochet was charged with crimes against humanity and put under house arrest in 2001. He avoided conviction and died in 2006, aged 91.

Chile Today

In 2006, history was made when Michelle Bachelet was elected as Chile's first female president. She was replaced in March 2010 by right-wing billionaire Sebastián Piñera. Four years later, Bachelet succeeded Piñera. This back-and-forth continued when Bachelet was again replaced by Piñera in 2017. There was immediate issues, however, when Piñera appointed Pinochet and Nazi sympathizers and country-wide protests emerged over indigenous rights. In 2019, there were major anti-government protests *(p106)* across Chile, fueled by anger over rising inequality and high living costs.

(p106)

> **MICHELLE BACHELET (1951–)**
>
> Born into a military family, Bachelet was detained by Pinochet's secret police in 1975 because her father had worked for Allende. She went into exile in Australia, returning to Chile in 1979. In power, she has been lauded for her progressive political stance and, in 2018, she was appointed to the position of UN High Commissioner for Human Rights.

2006

Michelle Bachelet elected president; Pinochet dies in December.

2010

Sebastián Piñera elected president; central Chile struck by a major earthquake.

2010

A billion people watch the rescue of 33 trapped Chilean miners.

2018

Police kill an unarmed Mapuche man, leading to protests.

2019

Over a million Chileans protest government over inequality and high living costs.

EXPERIENCE
SANTIAGO

Relaxing in the Providencia district

Plaza de Armas
and Santiago Centro....................................62

West of Santiago Centro.........................84

Northeast of Santiago Centro.............98

EXPLORE
SANTIAGO

This guide divides Santiago into three sightseeing areas, as shown on the map below. Find out more about each area on the following pages.

RECOLETA

INDEPENDENCIA

Cementerio General

Museo de Arte Decorativas

BARRIO PATRONATO

La Vega

BALMACEDA

PLAZA DE ARMAS AND
SANTIAGO CENTRO
p62

Museo de la Memoria y los
Derechos Humanos

Museo Chileno de Arte
Precolombino

Cerro Santa
Lucía

Parque Quinta
Normal

BARRIO
BRASIL

Biblioteca de
Santiago

Palacio de La Moneda

Plaza
Bulnes

WEST OF
SANTIAGO CENTRO
p84

Basílica de los
Sacramentinos

BARRIO
REPÚBLICA

SAN
DIEGO

Club Hípico

Parque Bernardo
O'Higgins

0 kilometers   1
0 miles   1

N

VICTORIA

BARRIO
EL SALTO

Parque
Metropolitano
de Santiago

BARRIO
VITACURA

Club de Golf
Los Leones

LAS
CONDES

NORTHEAST OF
SANTIAGO CENTRO
p98

Gran Torre
Santiago

BARRIO
EL GOLF

Parque
Metropolitano
de Santiago

BARRIO
SUECIA

Santuario
Inmaculada Concepción

Zoológico
Nacional

PROVIDENCIA

BARRIO
BELLAVISTA

Patio
Bellavista

LOS
ESTANQUES

CHILE

BARRIO
ITALIA

DALMACIA

SANTIAGO

GETTING TO KNOW
SANTIAGO

Ever since it was founded in 1541, Santiago has been Chile's political, economic, and cultural hub. Home to more than 7 million people, the city is green, well connected, and constantly evolving. Most of its attractions are found in three main areas, each of which has its own distinct vibe.

PAGE 62

PLAZA DE ARMAS AND SANTIAGO CENTRO

The heart of downtown Santiago, the Plaza de Armas is a wonderful place for an idle stroll and a spot of people-watching. The surrounding area is an architectural treasure trove, with the cathedral and the presidential palace among its many emblematic buildings. Another must-see is the captivating Museo Chileno de Arte Precolombino, which has a remarkable collecton of indigenous Latin American art. For a change of pace from the museum, visit the bustling shopping streets and lively food markets.

Best for
Historic architecture, world-class museums, and colorful food markets

Home to
The Museo Chileno de Arte Precolombino

Experience
A seafood lunch at one of the marisquerías in the Mercado Central

PAGE 84

WEST OF SANTIAGO CENTRO

After a long period of decline, the area west of the city center has been rejuvenated. Historic and beautiful neighborhoods such as Brasil, Yungay, and Concha y Toro have blossomed into trendy and hip places to live, socialize, and have fun, while many opulent *palacios*, once the homes of Santiago's elite, have been restored to their previous glory. The area also has several worthwhile museums, notably the powerful Museo de la Memoria y Derechos Humanos.

Best for
Elegant palacios, hip neighbourhoods and insightful museums

Home to
Parque Quinta Normal

Experience
Learning about the victims of the brutal Pinochet regime at the Museo de la Memoria y Derechos Humanos

PAGE 98

NORTHEAST OF SANTIAGO CENTRO

As it stretches toward the foothills of the Andes, Santiago becomes greener, more modern, and residential. Much of the city's middle- and upper-classes live in this area, which is also home to Parque Metropolitano de Santiago, one of the world's largest urban green spaces, and the Gran Torre Santiago, the tallest skyscraper in Latin America. It is well-known for its array of restaurants, bars ,and clubs, many of them located in buzzing Bellavista.

Best for
A vibrant culinary scene and expansive green spaces

Home to
Parque Metropolitano de Santiago

Experience
Immersing yourself in the city's street art scene on a guided graffiti tour

←

1 Santiago as seen from Cerro San Cristóbal.

2 Statue at the center of Plaza de Armas.

3 Food from one of Mercado Central's *marisquerías*.

4 Vibrant buildings in the Bellavista neighborhood.

Chile's capital and biggest city offers visitors an appealing mix of architectural gems, insightful museums, peaceful green spaces, and top-class restaurants. Here we pick a few of the highlights to help you plan a two-day stay.

2 DAYS

in Santiago

▌Day 1

Morning After breakfast, walk over to the Plaza de Armas *(p62)*, Santiago's main square and the perfect place to start an exploration of the city's historic core. Keep an eye out for impressive buildings, such as the Catedral Metropolitana and the Ex Congreso Nacional, which was formerly home to the Chilean Congress. Make sure you also take a stroll down the pedestrian Ahumada, Bandera, and Huérfanos streets, bustling places lined with shops, arcades, and cafés.

Afternoon For an atmospheric lunch, head over to the Mercado Central *(p81)*, which is home to numerous *marisquerías* (fish and seafood restaurants), including Richard El Rey del Mariscal *(p69)*. Then walk back into the city center and spend the rest of the afternoon in the Museo Chileno de Arte Precolombino *(p66)*. This excellent museum has an exhaustive collection of artifacts from Latin America's pre-Columbian cultures. If you are looking for an afternoon snack, try a freshly baked empanada from nearby El Rápido *(p69)*.

Evening Head over to the lively, cosmopolitan Lastarria neighborhood *(p79)*, just east of downtown, for an evening stroll before drinks and dinner at Bocanáriz *(p78)*. Finish the night with an ice cream from Emporio La Rosa *(p69)*.

▌Day 2

Morning Start the day by heading west of the city center to the thought-provoking Museo de la Memoria y los Derechos Humanos *(p90)*, which commemorates the thousands of victims of the brutal Pinochet dictator-ship. Afterward take a stroll in the neighboring Parque Quinta Normal *(p88)*, one of the most tranquil green spaces in the city.

Afternoon For lunch, head over to the Bellavista neighborhood, a short walk west of downtown and home to scores of restaurants, including Galindo *(p109)* and Barandiarán *(p58)*. Next, visit the wonderful La Chascona *(p105)*, one of Nobel Prize-winning poet Pablo Neruda's former homes, which has now been turned into a quirky museum. Then take the funicular up to the summit of Cerro San Cristóbal for superb, sweeping views of the city and the Andes beyond. If the weather proves hot, take a dip in one of the two swimming pools that can be found on the hilltop.

Evening Take the metro or jump in a taxi to the fantasticProvidencia neighborhood for drinks at Baco Vino y Bistro *(p109)*. Afterward, stay for dinner at Le Flaubert or Bar Liguria.

Livin' La Vida Local

No visit to Santiago is complete without sampling some of the country's favourite dishes. El Rápido *(p69)* serves the best empanadas (deep-fried, filled pastries) in the city, while Galindo *(p109)* offers up classics like *pastel de choclo* (beef pie with a sweetcorn crust). One must is Confitería Torres *(p92)*, birthplace of the *barros luco*, a steak-and-cheese sandwich loved by the former president of the same name.

→

The *chacerero* sandwich, filled with steak, tomatoes, and green beans

SANTIAGO FOR
FOODIES

With historic food markets, world-famous wineries, local joints serving Chilean classics, and swish restaurants that rank among the best in Latin America, Santiago is a wonderful place to eat and drink.

EAT

Barandiarán

In the Patio Bellavista complex, Barandiarán serves some of the best Peruvian food in Santiago. The menu features dishes like *ceviche*, *parihuela* (seafood soup), and *seco de cordero* (lamb stew).

🏠 Constitución 74
📞 (02) 27370725
🕐 Mon-Thu 12:45pm-midnight, Fri-Sat 12:45pm-12:45am, Sun 1pm-4:30pm

$$$

Onces in a Lifetime

Chile's version of afternoon tea, *onces* is typically eaten between 5 and 7pm. At home, it is a simple affair, consisting of tea or coffee, a sandwich or toast, perhaps a biscuit or cake. *Onces* at a *salon de te*, however, are fancy occasions, with sandwiches, cakes and pastries – head to Café San Isidro *(San Isidro 53)* to indulge.

→

The quirky interior of Café San Isidro

Pinot and Pisco

On the outskirts of Santiago are some of Chile's oldest vineyards, most of which offer tours and tastings, such as Viña Cousiño-Macul (*www.cousinomacul.com*). Closer to the city is Baco Vino y Bistro (*p109*), perhaps the best wine bar in Santiago. For something different, head to El Hoyo (*p91*) for a terremoto (earthquake), an earth-shaking blend of sweet, fermented pipeño wine and pineapple ice cream.

$\rightarrow$

A selection of
red wines at
Toro Vineyards

Santiago in Style

The city's culinary scene is fast gaining global renown, with many of its restaurants regarded as the best in Latin America. One highlight is Boragó (*www.borago.cl*), which offers locally sourced dishes that draw on Chile's indigenous culture. Another is Ambrosia (*www.ambrosia.cl*), whose menu is inspired by the continent's diverse cuisines.

$\leftarrow$

Plate of food at Boragó, one of Chile's
most prestigious restaurants

Fish and Fruit

Dating back to 1872, Mercado Central (*p81*) is home to *marisquerías* (fish and seafood restaurants), which serve mouthwatering dishes such as ceviche and *paila marina*. Nearby La Vega (*p106*) is the city's main fruit-and-vegetable market. It offers a truly authentic experience, with simple restaurants providing hearty meals, such as *cazuela*, a stew packed with vegetables and a piece of meat on the bone.

$\rightarrow$

Plenty of fresh
produce on offer
at La Vega market

Showtime in Santiago

There are countless places in Santiago to watch a show, concert, or performance, from Neo-Classical *teatros* to indie venues. The Teatro Municipal *(p76)* is the city's premier theatre and opera house, while the Centro Cultural Gabriela Mistral *(p90)* has an innovative program of dance, theater, and music events, as well as film screenings and art exhibitions. Other notable venues include Matucana 100 *(p92)*, a multifunctional arts complex, and the Centro Cultural Estación Mapocho *(p80)*, which hosts everything from theater to film.

→

Former railway station Estación Mapocho has been refitted for cultural events

SANTIAGO FOR
CULTURE

From art-filled museums and kaledoscopically colorful graffiti tours to independent film screenings and energetic live performances, Chile's capital has a thriving art and cultural scene.

Writing on the Wall

Santiago street art is some of the best in the world. Works can be found throughout the city, but the Bellavista and Yungay neighborhoods have strong reputations. Check out San Miguel, home to the Museo a Cielo Abierto, a collection of 40 murals. Take a guided tour with an agency such as Santiago Street Art Tours *(p107)* to learn about the artists and the complex political, social, and historical background of the art.

Vibrant and daunting street art in Bellavista ↑

Art for Art's Sake

Santiago is awash with incredible artworks. The Museo Nacional de Bellas Artes (p79) and the Museo de Arte Contemporaneo (p80) might both be based in the same building – a spectacular Art Nouveau *palacio* over-looking the Parque Forestal – but they have very different focuses. Head to the former to admire a wealth of art, including religious-focused works from around the colonial period, 19th-century paintings of landscapes and historical themes, and 20th-century pieces by Surrealists such as Roberto Matta. If you're after modern art, head to the latter – which is more commonly known as MAC – to see works by members of the influential Grupo Signo and Generación del Trece movements. It also regularly hosts temporary exhibitions, often by succesful Latin American artists.

← Experimental pieces at the Museo de Arte Contemporaneo

Silver Screen

Chile – and Santiago – has a strong cinematic tradition, and its movie-makers are increasingly making an impact on the international stage. In 2017, *A Fantastic Woman* – filmed in Santiago – became the first Chilean movie in history to win the Best Foreign Language Film Oscar. But Santiago isn't just a filming location; if you're visiting in October, you'll see movie stars descend for the Santiago Festival Internacional de Cine (SANFIC). Want to catch a movie showing instead? The city has some impressive cinemas, including the striking Matucana 100 (p92).

→ Colorful poster for award-winning film *A Fantastic Woman*

GANADORA DEL OSO DE PLATA AL MEJOR GUION EN EL FESTIVAL DE BERLIN

ESTRENO 6 DE ABRIL

UNA MUJER FANTASTICA

UNA PELICULA DE **SEBASTIAN LELIO**

PLAZA DE ARMAS AND SANTIAGO CENTRO

The Plaza de Armas, Santiago's bustling main square, has always been the focal point of the city. It dates back to 1541, when Santiago was founded by conquistador Pedro de Valdivia. The cathedral, the governor's palace, the court of law, and several luxurious mansions were swiftly built around the plaza, which has since played host to everything from public executions and bullfights to markets and festivals. Many of the original buildings fell victim to earthquakes or fires, with those that remain dating largely from the 18th and 19th centuries. Nevertheless, the palm-lined square and the blocks that fan out around it remain the most historic part of Santiago, with locals and visitors enjoying the vibrant atmosphere, and the city's most famous shopping streets.

PLAZA DE ARMAS AND SANTIAGO CENTRO

Must See

❶ Museo Chileno de Arte Precolombino

Experience More

❷ Catedral Metropolitana
❸ Correo Central
❹ Palacio de la Real Audiencia
❺ Municipalidad de Santiago
❻ Paseos Ahumada and Huérfanos
❼ Ex Congreso Nacional
❽ Palacio de los Tribunales de Justicia
❾ Casa Colorada
❿ Cancillería
⓫ Palacio de La Moneda
⓬ Palacio Alhambra
⓭ Centro Cultural Palacio La Moneda
⓮ Plaza Bulnes
⓯ Barrio París-Londres
⓰ Iglesia y Convento de San Francisco
⓱ Bolsa de Comercio
⓲ Teatro Municipal
⓳ Biblioteca Nacional
⓴ Iglesia San Agustín
㉑ Basílica y Museo de la Merced
㉒ Club de la Unión
㉓ Cerro Santa Lucía
㉔ Museo de Artes Visuales
㉕ Barrio Lastarría
㉖ Museo Nacional de Bellas Artes
㉗ Museo de Arte Contemporaneo
㉘ Iglesia de Santo Domingo
㉙ Centro Cultural Estación Mapocho
㉚ Posada del Corregidor
㉛ Mercado Central

Eat

① El Rapido
② Bar Nacional
③ Blue Jar
④ Emporio la Rosa
⑤ Richard El Rey del Mariscal

Drink

⑥ Bocanáriz

Stay

⑦ Hotel Vegas
⑧ Andes Hostel
⑨ Río Amazonas
⑩ Luciano K

Shop

⑪ Libreria Inglesa

MUSEO CHILENO DE ARTE PRECOLOMBINO

⊙ E7 🏠 Bandera 361 Ⓜ Plaza de Armas 🕙 10am–6pm Tue–Sun
🌐 precolombino.cl

This Aladdin's cave of curiosities is arguably one of the city's – and the country's – best museums. The encyclopedic Museo Chileno de Arte Precolombino is dedicated to the artistic and symbolic legacy of cultures throughout Chile and Latin America, housing all manner of items and relics relating to the Incas, Aztecs, Mayans, and other ancient peoples.

Inaugurated in 1981, the museum is housed in the impressive Neo-Classical Palacio de la Real Aduana, which was built between 1805 and 1807 as the Royal Customs House, and which later served as the National Library and Court of Law. The museum housed 1,500 exhibits when it opened – today it's double this number.

The first floor's three temporary exhibition halls feature in-depth displays which focus on particular cultures. Galleries on the museum's second floor feature fascinating collections divided into cultural areas across Mesoamerica, Intermediate, Amazonian, the Caribbean, and Central and Southern Andes. Of special interest is the valuable collection of textiles and excellent ceramics. There is a café and a space for outdoor events at the museum's entrance patio. Tours are also available by prior arrangement.

> **🔍 HIDDEN GEM**
> **Cut from the Same Cloth**
>
> Don't miss the Sala Textil (Textile Gallery), which has some remarkable exhibits from across Latin America. In its holdings is a scrap of cloth from the Chavín culture (from what is now Peru) that is almost 3,000 years old.

SERGIO LARRAÍN GARCIA-MORENO

Hailed as a visionary advocate of Latin American and European art, Sergio Larraín Garcia-Moreno (1905–99) was the founder of the Museo Chileno de Arte Precolombino. An architect with a passionate interest in archaeology and ancient American cultures, Larraín traded modern art to buy pre-Columbian relics. He convinced the Santiago Municipality and the city mayor to let him convert the old, fire-damaged Royal Customs House into a museum, and employed experts to procure artifacts from private collections located across Europe and the Americas.

←
The museum's collection of *Chemamulles* – wooden funerary statues

1 A colorful woolen hat, which was worn by the Aymara people of the Altiplano region.

2 The striking exterior of the museum. The building was originally built as a palace in the 19th century.

3 A Mayan ceramic vase, thought to depict a hunchback. It dates from around 600–900 AD.

EXPERIENCE MORE

②

Catedral Metropolitana

📍E7 🏛Plaza de Armas 🚇Plaza de Armas 🕐11am-7pm Tue-Sat, 9am-7pm Sun 🌐iglesiadesantiago.cl

Set on the western side of the Plaza de Armas, the Catedral Metropolitana was inaugurated in 1775 and is the fourth church to be built on this site, after previous structures were destroyed in earthquakes. The cathedral is considered the most important in Chile, and is the seat of the Archdiocese of Santiago de Chile. The original design was conceived by Bavarian Jesuits, whose influence can still be seen in the cathedral's imposing woodwork, despite the church having undergone an endless series of renovations.

The grand interior is 295 ft (90 m) long and divided into three naves. The right nave holds an urn that guards the hearts of war heroes who fought the Concepción battle during the War of the Pacific (1879–83). Highlights in the central nave include the organ,

imported from London in 1850; the cathedral's original 18th-century pulpit; and the central altar, constructed in Munich in 1912. Behind the altar is the crypt where Chile's past cardinals and archbishops are buried. The left nave is the Iglesia de Sagrario (Tabernacle Church), a national monument and site of the first parish that was founded in the country. The cathedral's Capilla del Centesimo Sacramento (the Hundredth Sacrament Chapel) is covered in beautiful silverwork crafted by Jesuits.

The cathedral houses Jesuit artwork and other religious imagery in the Museo de Arte Sagrado, a small museum reached through the church.

---

③

Correo Central

📍E7 🏛Plaza de Armas 983 🚇Plaza de Armas 🕐9am-6pm Mon-Fri 🌐correos.cl

Historically known as the site of the first house built in early Santiago, the Correo Central (Central Post Office) was initially the residence of the

city's founding father, Pedro de Valdivia. Later it served as the Governing Council, and then as the presidential residence until 1846. In 1881, a fire destroyed part of the edifice. Soon after, the government planned a grand post office on the Plaza de Armas, enlisting the help of architect and musician Ricardo Brown, who adapted his design using parts of the existing building. In 1908, architect J. Eduardo Ferham renovated the facade in Renaissance style.

Today, the Correo Central has a small postal museum and stamp collection on the first floor to memorialize the history of Correos de Chile (Post Office of Chile).

---

④

Palacio de la Real Audiencia

📍E7 🏛Plaza de Armas 951 🚇Plaza de Armas 🕐10am-6pm Tue-Sun 🌐museo historiconacional.cl

Built between 1804 and 1808, the Neo-Classical Palacio de la Real Audiencia has been

← The Catedral Metropolitana, fronted by the bustling Plaza de Armas

INSIDER TIP
Plaza Life

Although busy during the day, the Plaza de Armas really comes alive in the early evening. To see how the locals live, arrive early, grab a seat on one of the benches, and settle down for a spot of people-watching.

witness to some of the most important events in Chile. In 1811, the palace was the site of Chile's first National Congress, and later it housed the governmental offices of Chile's first president and liberator, Bernardo O'Higgins. During the 20th century, the edifice also housed the City Hall.

Located in this old palace, the Museo Histórico Nacional charts Chile's history through a chronological display of exhibits from the Colonial period to the military coup of 1973. Exhibit rooms are spread around a central courtyard and feature rare 18th-century paintings and furniture, such as a sacristy wardrobe. Reproductions of home interiors depict daily life in Colonial Chile, as do traditional

← An old piece of machinery on display in the Museo Histórico Nacional

clothing and agricultural instruments. There are also sections dedicated to transportation and education. The temporary exhibit hall, called Sala Plaza de Armas (Heritage Square), features displays about Chilean culture and customs.

5

Municipalidad de Santiago

⊙ E7 🏛 Plaza de Armas s/n ⊞ Plaza de Armas ⏰ To the public 🌐 municipalidad desantiago.cl

Although Santiago's municipal building is closed to the public, its exterior architecture is easily appreciated from the Plaza de Armas. Originally founded in 1548 as the *cabildo*, or Colonial town hall, this was also the site of the city's first jail. Three buildings on the site were subsequently destroyed by earthquakes or fire. In 1785, Italian architect Joaquin Toesca, who had already put his signature Neo-Classical stamp on many of Santiago's buildings, rebuilt the city hall.

The city hall offices were expanded in 1883, following the transfer of the jail to new premises, but within a decade the edifice succumbed to a major fire. Renovations began apace and by 1895 the Santiago Municipality was installed in the restored building. This still maintained the previous structure's Neo-Classical style, but now displayed touches of Italian Renaissance, in the form of arched doorways and three enormous frontal windows framed by columns. Today, the front facade bears a coat of arms given by Spain.

EAT

El Rapido
A wallet-friendly joint with a concise menu. The freshly baked empanadas are delicious.

⊙ E7 🏛 Bandera 3471 ⏰ Sun 🌐 elrapido.cl

$ $ $

Bar Nacional
A reliable – if a little old-fashioned – spot in the city center, serving hearty portions of Chilean classics.

⊙ E7 🏛 Huérfanos 1151 ⏰ Sun 🌐 barnacional.cl

$ $ $

Blue Jar
This bustling café-restaurant is good for coffee, light meals, and alcoholic drinks. The reservation-only dinner on the first Thursday of each month is superb.

⊙ D8 🏛 Profesora Amanda Labarca, 102 ⏰ Sat, Sun 🌐 bluejar.cl

$ $ $

Emporio la Rosa
A delightful ice cream parlor with an inventive range of flavors.

⊙ F7 🏛 Merced 291 🌐 emporiolarosa.cl

$ $ $

Richard El Rey del Mariscal
One of Mercado Central's best *marisquerías* (seafood restaurants), with great service.

⊙ E6 🏛 Mercado Central, San Pablo 943 📞 (02) 2269-6255 ⏰ Mon

$ $ $

6 🍴 🍷 🛍

Paseos Ahumada and Huérfanos

📍E7 🚇 Plaza de Armas

Pedestrianized in 1977, Paseo Ahumada and Paseo Huérfanos are two walkways flanked by numerous shopping galleries, restaurants, electronics stores, and commercial businesses. Catering to a bustling downtown population, the *paseos* take on a lively ambience, with thousands of people walking to and fro all day. Street performers add to the excitement of a stroll here.

Paseo Ahumada stretches from Avenida del Libertador Bernardo O'Higgins, popularly called Avenida Alameda, to the Mercado Central *(p81)*. It is cut across by a number of streets, most notably by Agustinas, whose junction with Ahumada is the site of the former Hotel Crillón. The first story of this edifice is occupied by Galería Crillón, one of many downtown *galerías* – labyrinthine shopping centers brimming with stores selling everything from handicrafts to designer wear.

Paseo Huérfanos runs parallel to Agustinas and crosses Paseo Ahumada near the historic Banco de Chile. Built in 1921–25 by Viennese architect Alberto Siegel, the bank features ornate interiors and old-fashioned teller windows that are worth a look.

7

Ex Congreso Nacional

📍E7 🏛 Catedral 1158
📞 (02) 2674-7800 🚇 Plaza de Armas 🕙 10am-5:30pm Mon-Fri

The Ex Congreso Nacional, an imposing Neo-Classical structure with massive columns, was designated a National Monument in 1976. Beginning in 1858, the building's construction experienced a series of delays and was only completed in 1876, under the direction of architect Manuel Aldunate. In 1895, the building nearly burned to the ground and was rebuilt by architect Emilio Doyere in 1901.

Congressional sessions were held in this building until the dissolution of the Congress by former dictator Augusto Pinochet in 1973. Today, it houses the Santiago offices of the Senate as well as the Chamber of Deputies.

The edifice is surrounded by lush, exotic gardens that are open to the public. The statue of the Virgin that dominates the grounds was placed in memory of the 2,000 people who were killed in a fire at the Iglesia Compañía de Jesús in 1863, which was located nearby.

8

Palacio de los Tribunales de Justicia

Q D7 **⌂** Compañía de Jesús, esq Morandé **C** (02) 2412-5700 **M** Plaza de Armas **O** 9am–2pm Mon–Fri (IDs to be left at the front desk)

Constructed between 1905 and 1930, the Palacio de los Tribunales de Justicia (Supreme Court) exhibits both Neo-Classical and Greco-Roman features. The colossal building stretches from calles Morandé to Bandera, covering an area of around 43,000 sq ft (4,000 sq m). Designed by the French architect Emilio Doyere, the building is entered through a marble stairway that is flanked by two fine caryatids. Although the edifice has a somber facade, its interior offers a stunning example of 20th-century architecture. An open three-story central hall is encircled with wrap-around interior balconies and topped with a vaulted glass-and-metal ceiling. Located above the entrance is a bas-relief of a condor clutching a book

←

The Ex Congreso Nacional, set amid immaculately landscaped gardens

inscribed with the letters LEX, the Latin term for Law.

Today, the palace houses Chile's Supreme Court, the Court of Appeals, the Military and Police Courts, as well as the Supreme Court Library.

9

Casa Colorada

Q E7 **⌂** Merced 860 **M** Plaza de Armas **O** Noon–6pm Mon–Fri **W** santiago cultura.cl

One of Santiago's few remaining Colonial structures, the Casa Colorada (Red House) is regarded as a pristine example of Colonial architecture designed for the bourgeoisie of Chile. Built in 1770, it was the home of Don Mateo de Toro y Zambrano (1727–1811), a wealthy entrepreneur and the first Count of the Conquest, who went on to serve as a senior military leader and Royal Governor during Spanish rule. On September 18, 1810, he was elected the first president of the newly formed government junta during Chile's fledgling struggle for independence. In 1817, after the Battle of Chacabuco, revolutionaries José San Martín and Bernardo O'Higgins stayed at the

↑ Casa Colorada's front, dotted with wrought iron balconies

Casa Colorada, followed by Lord Cochrane.

The Casa Colorada is unique in that it has two floors, which was unusual at the time. The family originally lived on the second floor and rooms on the first floor were used as Don Mateo's offices. The building was built with a brick facade painted red (hence the name) and reinforced with decorative stone along the base, arched windows, and a central patio.

> **COFFEE WITH LEGS**
>
> You're likely to stumble across one of these bizarre Chilean establishments: a *café con piernas*, or coffee with legs. These seedy cafés, which date back to the 1960s, are served by scantily clad waitresses. The clientele is older and overwhelmingly male. Two of the most famous, Café Caribe *(Paseo Huérfanos 796)* and Café Haiti *(Paseo Ahumada 140)*, remain unfeasibly popular.

↑ The stately, white-pillared facade of the Cancillería

⑩ Cancillería

📍 D7 🏛 Teatinos 180
🚇 La Moneda
🌐 minrel.gob.cl

Chile's Ministry of Foreign Relations, or Cancillería, is located in an impressive 17-story building that was formerly the Hotel Carrera. Open from 1940 to 2003, this was the grandest hotel of its time. It was designed by architect Josué Smith Solar, who was already well known for his design of the Club Hípico (p96). The hotel's guests included Fidel Castro, Henry Kissinger, Charles de Gaulle, Nelson Rockefeller, and Neil Armstrong, among others.

The hotel was most famous for its proximity to the Palacio de La Moneda during the 1973

Did You Know?

New Year's Eve fireworks take place at the Torre Entel, near the Palacio de La Moneda.

coup d'état, when it acted as a temporary home for nearly every international journalist reporting in the country. Most of the images of the presidential building being bombarded were taken from the hotel's windows and rooftop. The hotel itself was slightly damaged by the shelling.

In 2004, the hotel was sold for US$24 million and renovated to accommodate the Ministry of Foreign Relations. Today, most of the building's interiors, other than the lobby, are unrecognizable from its hotel era. The lobby features beautiful marble columns and a striking mural made of opal glass – a depiction by Spanish artist Luis Egidio Meléndez of the discovery of the Americas.

⑪ 🅿️ Palacio de La Moneda

📍 D8 🏛 Avenida Alameda, between calles Morandé & Teatinos 🚇 La Moneda
🕙 9am–5pm daily 🌐 visitas guiadas.presidencia.cl

The immaculately preserved Palacio de La Moneda is Chile's presidential headquarters. Built between 1784 and 1799 by the Spanish, it was inaugurated in 1805 as the Casa de Moneda, the nation's mint. From 1845, it housed the republican government offices, and also served as the presidential residence until 1958. The palace was the largest building erected in any of Spain's colonies during the 18th century, and is considered one of Chile's finest examples of Neo-Classical architecture.

At its northeastern side is the Plaza de la Constitucíon, an expansive grassy space crisscrossed by walkways. Visitors can present their passports here to enjoy a stroll through the palace's patios (although you must also email in advance). The plaza was designed in the 1930s to create Barrio Cívico, the country's administrative and

political center. At the plaza's southern corner is a statue of Chile's former president Salvador Allende, who perished here during the coup d'état of 1973. A ceremonial changing of the guard takes place at the plaza at 10am every other day. Visitors can also enter the palace's interior courtyards that comprise the Patio de los Cañones – named for the two 1778 cannons that are on display here – and the Patio de los Naranjos, named for its pleasant orange trees.

⑫ Palacio Alhambra

📍 D7 🏛 Compañia de Jesús 1340 📞 (02) 2698-0875
🚇 La Moneda 🕙 9am–2pm & 6–9pm Mon–Fri

This extraordinary architectural gem stands out in a neighborhood dominated chiefly by Neo-Classical structures and modern storefronts. It was built in 1860–62 by the architect Manuel Aldunate, who traveled to Granada, Spain, to study the original Alhambra Palace. Upon his return, he created a smaller version of it with elaborate plaster ceilings and a replica lion fountain. Following the original owner's death, the *palacio* was bought by Don Julio Garrido Falcón, a wealthy Chilean philanthropist, who donated it to the National Society of Fine Arts in 1940.

Today Palacio Alhambra operates as a cultural center, offering art classes and hosting a variety of exhibitions.

Centro Cultural Palacio La Moneda

📍 E8 🏛 Plaza de la Ciudadanía 26 🚇 La Moneda 🕐 9am–7:30pm daily 🌐 ccplm.cl

A pet project of former president Ricardo Lagos, the cutting-edge Centro Cultural Palacio La Moneda was inaugurated in 2006 as part of the 2010 Bicentennial Project that introduced new museums and improved road infrastructure in Santiago. It is located in what once served as the Palacio de La Moneda's basement. Designed by noted Chilean

> **Today Palacio Alhambra operates as a cultural center, offering art classes and hosting a variety of exhibitions.**

architect Cristián Undurraga, the center features three subterranean floors that surround a spacious central hall. Three large salons host international traveling expositions and shows by well-known Chilean artists. The Centro Cultural also houses the Arts Documentation Center library; the National Film Archive; a number of cafés and restaurants; and a superb *artesanía* store that showcases arts and crafts from the length of Chile. The Plaza de la Ciudadanía, landscaped with walkways and reflecting pools, acts as the roof for the underground center.

14
Plaza Bulnes

📍 E8 🏛 Northern end of Paseo Bulnes 🚇 La Moneda

Plaza Bulnes was the site of military and patriotic celebrations during the years of the Pinochet dictatorship, as well as a center for dissident protests that continued long after the return to democracy.

In 1975, General Pinochet established the controversial Eternal Flame of Liberty at the plaza. The flame was regarded by many as a visible monument to the dictatorship, and dissidents regularly attempted to extinguish it in protest.

In 1979, the remains of Chile's first president, Bernardo O'Higgins (*p259*), were moved from the Cementerio General (*p104*) to the plaza by the Pinochet regime, in an attempt to create a patriotic altar that symbolized a return to traditional historical values.

Plaza Bulnes was renovated in 2005 and now features an underground crypt holding the remains of O'Higgins that can be viewed through a glass window. The Eternal Flame of Liberty was finally put out during the renovations.

↑ Centro Cultural Palacio La Moneda's cavernous main hall

STAY

Hotel Vegas

Conveniently located in the quaint París-Londres neighborhood, this mid-range hotel does the basics well: well-equipped rooms, competitive prices, and efficient service.

📍 E8 🏠 Calle Londres 49 🌐 hotelvegas.net

$$

Andes Hostel

As well as clean four- and six-bed dorms, this handsome central hostel has private rooms and apartments that surpass those in many more expensive hotels. There's a communal roof terrace and bar, too.

📍 F7 🏠 Monjitas 506 📞 (02) 2632-9990

$$

Río Amazonas

Located just 10 minutes from Bellavista, this delightful guesthouse is an place for travelers of all ages. There's a great vibe and lots of information on offer.

📍 G7 🏠 Vicuña Mackenna 47 🌐 hostal rioamazonas.net

$$

Luciano K

This boutique hotel is an architectural gem, with gorgeous 1920s Art Deco fittings, generous en suites, and a superb restaurant-bar on the roof terrace.

📍 F7 🏠 Merced 84 🌐 lucianok.com

$$

15 🎨

Barrio París-Londres

📍 E8 🏠 Londres and París 📞 (02) 2325-037 🚇 Universidad de Chile

With small, artful mansions, the tiny neighborhood known as Barrio París-Londres (because the two neighborhoods intersect) is an architectural oasis in an area full with parking garages and utilitarian buildings from the 1960s and 1970s. Laid out in 1922, the *barrio* was constructed over the gardens of the Convento de San Francisco. It was conceived by the architect Ernesto Holzmann, who believed that downtown Santiago lacked attractive neighborhoods that were within walking distance of services and shops. After purchasing the gardens of the Convento de San Francisco, he enlisted architects to create what he envisioned as a "model block residence," one he hoped to reproduce in other parts of the city.

Today, the neighborhood is well preserved, with an elegant ambience, courtyards, and cafés. Within a four-block radius of winding, cobblestone streets are styles such as French Neo-Classical (Londres 70), and Italian Renaissance and Neo-Colonial (Londres 65).

The building at Londres 38 was infamous during the dictatorship years (1973–90) as a torture center. Visitors can explore the exhibits pertaining to the repressions of the Pinochet years here.

---

16 🎨

Iglesia y Convento de San Francisco

📍 E8 🏠 Londres 4 🚇 Universidad de Chile 🕐 9:30am-1:30pm & 3-6pm Mon-Fri, 10am-2pm Sat & Sun 🌐 museosanfrancisco. com

This church, which is the oldest surviving building in Santiago, is a national

1951

The year that the Iglesia y Convento de San Francisco became a national monument.

←

A pretty street in the Barrio París-Londres neighborhood

monument with distinct architectural details from various eras. Pedro de Valdivia first erected a chapel here in the 16th century in honor of the Virgen del Socorro, whose image he had brought with him and who, he believed, had protected the conquistadores against attacks. In 1618, the Franciscan Order established a church of stone walls and coffered ceilings, expanding the complex to include cloisters, gardens, and an infirmary. With the exception of the church's bell towers, the structure survived two major earthquakes. The current tower was designed by Fermín Vivaceta in 1857 in Neo-Classical style.

The giant stones used to build the walls of the original church are still visible, as are the nave's intricately carved woodwork and the grand doors carved from cedar. The convent's lush and tranquil patio and tiled roofs are early examples of the traditional architecture of Chile (p36). Set in the church is the Museo San Francis, with an extremely valuable series of 17th-century paintings that narrate the life of St. Francis of Assisi. Also on display are antique locks; paintings representing the life of the Virgen del Socorro; a graph indicating the lineage of the Franciscans; and the Salon Gabriela Mistral, which houses the poet's Nobel Prize medal (p38).

---

17 🔄

Bolsa de Comercio

📍 E8 🏛 La Bolsa 64
Ⓜ Universidad de Chile
🕐 Mar-Oct: 9:30am-4pm Mon-Fri; Nov-Feb: 9:30am-5pm Mon-Fri 🌐 bolsade santiago.cl

Launched in 1884 with only 160 incorporated companies, Chile's stock market expanded rapidly to include twice the number of companies within a decade. The early years of the 20th century continued to be a time of tremendous good fortune for the Chilean economy, mostly due to the boom in metal and nitrate mining in the northern deserts.

Today this area – the financial nerve center of the capital – is a micro-district comprising charming cobblestone streets and historic buildings. At the heart of this economic hub is the Bolsa de Comercio, Santiago's lively stock exchange. It is housed in a French Renaissance-style triangular structure, with Roman pillars and a slate roof with a cupola. This elegant old building was built in 1917 by Emilio Jecquier, who was already famous for his design of the Museo Nacional de Bellas Artes (p79).

Visitors are required to show their passports or IDs in order to enter the interiors of the building and witness the hustle and bustle of the stock market business.

Although there has been considerable modern technology installed, the interiors of the Bolsa de Comercio retain their original splendor.

→

The striking Bolsa de Comercio, housing Santiago's stock exchange

↑ The gleaming marble interiors of the Teatro Municipal

18

Teatro Municipal

📍 E7 🏛 Agustinas 794 🚇 Universidad de Chile 🌐 municipal.cl

Built between 1853 and 1857, the Teatro Municipal is Chile's most important venue for classical music, opera, and theater. The theater was originally designed by architect Claude François Brunet des Baines in an elegant, French Neo-Classical style with a lovely symmetrical facade. Its first ever performance was an Italian production of Verdi's *Ernani*. Soon the theater became the cultural and social center of Santiago's elite, who contributed heavily to the production of important opera performances. In 1870, a raging fire nearly razed the theater. However, architect Lucien Henault successfully restored the building to its earlier splendor, and it was reopened in 1873.

The theater foyer, La Capilla, features two sculptures by Nicanor Plaza – *Prólogo* and *Epílogo*. The main concert hall has a capacity of 1,500, not including the private Sala Arrau salon that has space for 250. The interior hall was designed after the Paris Opera house with lateral viewing boxes and a large ceiling cupola, whose grand crystal chandelier dates from 1930. Throughout the theater there are costume workshops, rehearsal studios, dressing rooms, and set design studios. The Philharmonic Orchestra, Santiago Ballet, and Municipal Theater Chorus are all permanent residents. Many great artistes have graced this stage, including Igor Stravinsky, Anna Pavlova, and Chilean pianist Claudio Arrau.

Tours take place Tuesday through Saturday.

19

Biblioteca Nacional

📍 E8 🏛 Avenida Alameda 651 🚇 Santa Lucía ⏰ 9am-7pm Mon-Fri, 9:15am-2pm Sat 🌐 bibliotecanacional.cl

An imposing building that occupies a whole city block, the Biblioteca Nacional was built 1914–27 by architect Gustavo García Postigo in the style of the French Academy in Paris. Its interiors have marble staircases, bronze balustrades, painted murals, and carved wood detail in a highly ornamental style, unusual in a 20th-century building. The library is home to one of Latin America's most valuable collections of Colonial-era literary works – it is estimated that 60 percent of everything printed during this period can be found in the second-floor Medina Library. Key works include *Mística Teología* from Mexico (1547), *La Doctrina Cristina* from Peru (1584), and chronicles of explorers such as Sir Francis Drake.

20

Iglesia San Agustín

📍 E7 🏛 Agustinas 828 🚇 Universidad de Chile ⏰ 9am-6pm Mon-Fri 🌐 iglesiadesantiago.cl

The construction of the Iglesia San Agustín, formerly known as Templo de Nuestra Señora de Gracia, marked the founding of the Catholic Augustinian mission in Chile. Reaching Chile from Peru in 1595, Augustinians erected their first church here in 1625. In 1647, an earthquake destroyed the church, along with most of the city. After being rebuilt in 1707, the church was toppled by another earthquake in 1730. It was restored by architect Fermín Vivaceta, who added columns to the facade and bell towers.

A curious aspect of San Agustín is the *Cristo de Mayo* statue. After the 1647 earthquake, priests salvaged the

> Soon the Teatro Municipal became the cultural and social center of Santiago's elite, who contributed heavily to the production of important opera performances.

HIDDEN GEM
Mystery Tablet

The Basílica y Museo de la Merced contains some remarkable Easter Island exhibits, such as a rare tablet covered with the undeciphered *rongorongo* script – a system of glyphs used by the Rapa Nui.

intact statue to find that Christ's crown of thorns had fallen around his neck, which seemed miraculous given that the diameter of the crown was smaller than that of the head. Priests paraded through the rubbled streets of Santiago to celebrate this event, and in the ensuing decades the commemoration of May 13 grew into the city's most venerable religious festival. Today, followers still

The Basílica y Museo de la Merced, standing in a leafy square ↓

celebrate May 13, but on a much smaller scale.

---

21 ⬙

Basílica y Museo de la Merced

♀ E7 🏛 Mac Iver 341 Ⓜ Plaza de Armas ⏱ 10am–1pm & 3–7:30pm Mon–Fri 🌐 mercedarios.cl

Established by the Order of the Blessed Mary of Mercy – who arrived with the first expedition to Chile – the Basílica de la Merced was built in 1566. During the city's early years, it was patronized by the elite, some of whom are buried within its walls. These include Governor Rodrigo de Quiroga and his wife Inés de Suarez, the first Spanish woman to arrive in Chile. The present-day basilica was built in 1760 and later adorned with Neo-Classical touches by architect Joaquín Toesca. On the second floor of the basilica is the Museo de la Merced, an interesting

collection of Easter Island artifacts, Colonial art, and 18th-century figurines.

22

Club de la Unión

♀ E8 🏛 Avenida Alameda 1091 Ⓜ Universidad de Chile 🌐 clubdelaunion.cl

The exclusive Club de la Unión is an architectural gem. It was constructed between 1917 and 1925 by noted Chilean architect Alberto Cruz Montt (1879–1955) in French Neo-Classical style. Inside, the club's gleaming marble walls and antique furnishings line spacious dining rooms, halls, a private art gallery, and the longest carved oak bar in the country. It operated as a men's-only association until 2006, when it invited its first female member.

The club's on-site restaurant is open to non-members, though visitors should be aware that entry to the club itself is by invitation only.

23

Cerro Santa Lucía

F7 **Avenida Alameda 499** **Santa Lucía** **9am-7pm daily**

Rising above the bustle of Santiago, the Santa Lucía hill is a lush park that was once the strategic defense point for conquistador Pedro de Valdivia, who founded Santiago at this very spot in 1541. Following the conquest, local Mapuches named the hill Huelén, meaning Sadness or Pain. In 1871, Mayor Benjamin Vicuña Mackenna transformed the 226-ft (69-m) denuded outcrop into a veritable Eden, with dense foliage, Gothic-style iron balustrades, stone walkways, statuary, fountains, and lookout points. Vicuña was buried here in the tiny chapel, Capilla la Ermita. Other historical curiosities include a 6-ft (2-m-) high stone carved with a passage chronicling the land features of Chile that was taken from a letter sent to Charles V,

The ornate Plaza
↓ Neptuno staircase,
on Cerro Santa Lucía

Holy Roman Emperor, by Pedro de Valdivia. There is a statue representing the Dissidents Cemetery that was once part of Cerro Santa Lucía; dissidents referred to non-Catholics or to those who had committed suicide. At the summit sits Castillo Hidalgo, built by Royalists in 1816 during the Chilean War of Independence.

The principal access point to the hill from Avenida Alameda is at the monumental Plaza Neptuno staircase, or up a cobblestone road across from Calle Agustinas. Visitors can also take the glass elevator from Calle Huérfanos, but that only operates occasionally. There is a cannon boom at noon every day, a tradition dating from the 18th century.

24

Museo de Artes Visuales

F7 **José Victorino Lastarría 307** **Universidad Católica** **11am-7pm Tue-Sun** **mavi.cl**

Opened in 1994, the Museo de Artes Visuales is the ideal place to view contemporary Chilean sculpture, painting, photography, and conceptual art. The museum's permanent collection comprises more than 1,500 works by artists such as Samy Benmayor, a Neo-Expressionist painter; Gonzalo Cienfuegos, who uses a variety of media, including oil and acrylic; and Rodrigo Cabezas, best known for his three-dimensional assemblies. Located on the second floor, the Museo Arqueológico de

---

DRINK

Bocanáriz
This is the city's best dedicated wine bar, with hundreds of bottles, and dozens available by the glass. It also has a good food menu, friendly French ownership, and pleasant, contemporary surroundings.

F7 **Lastarría 276** **bocanariz.cl**

Santiago is a compact salon with over 3,300 artifacts from pre-Columbian Chile, including a Chinchorro mummy, hallucinogenic tablets from Atacama, everyday utensils and tools, and decorative finery from the Aymara, Mapuche, Fuegino, and Rapa Nui cultures.

Barrio Lastarría

⑨F7 ⊕José Victorino Lastarría ⊜Universidad Católica ⊌barriolastarria. com

Also known as Barrio Parque Forestal, the charming Barrio Lastarría is a fashionable neighborhood for artists, actors, and other young creatives. On Calle Lastarría and the narrow streets that branch off it, there are cafés, restaurants, high-end *artesanía* shops, galleries, bookstores, and a couple of boutiques, which together provide a wonderful atmosphere for shopping and strolling. In the middle of Calle Lastarría is the serene and sober Iglesia de Vera Cruz, dating from 1858.

Barrio Lastarría's prime attraction is the tiny **Plaza Mulato Gil de Castro**. Named for the famed 19th-century portrait painter José Gil de Castro who lived in the *barrio*, the plaza was once the patio of a former house. A small, outdoor book and antiques fair is held here Thursday through Saturday.

The **Centro Gabriela Mistral** art center, named for the first Latin American Nobel Prize

↑ Attractive interiors and vaulted glass ceiling of the Museo Nacional de Bellas Artes

winner for literature, regularly hosts concerts, theater and dance performances. It is set in a remarkable building and is a maze of little plazas and cafés. The center also has airy exhibition spaces on the first floor where Chilean artists display their works. Free tours in Spanish can be requested at the information desk.

Plaza Mulato Gil de Castro

⊕Mecred, esq Lastarría
⊙11am-midnight Mon-Fri

Centro Gabriela Mistral

⊕Avenida O'Higgins 227
⊙10am-9pm Tue-Sat, 11am-9pm Sun ⊌gam.cl

Museo Nacional de Bellas Artes

⑨F7 ⊕Palacio de Bellas Artes, Parque Forestal ⊜Bellas Artes ⊙10am-6:45pm Tue-Sun ⊌mnba.cl

First established in 1880 as the Museo de Pintura Nacional and housed in the Parque Quinta Normal *(p88)*, the Museo Nacional de Bellas Artes is the oldest and one of the most important art

museums in South America. The lovely palace in which it is housed today was built to celebrate Chile's centennial in 1910. It was designed by French-Chilean architect Emilio Jéquier, who created a French Neo-Classical edifice with Art Nouveau details, including a facade modeled after the Petit Palais in Paris. In front of the museum is a large bronze sculpture by Chilean artist Rebeca Matte, *Unidos en la Gloria y la Muerte* (United in Glory and Death), from 1922.

The museum's permanent collection numbers 2,700 works and is divided according to aesthetic, historic, and thematic criteria. Early works include Colonial art – which principally centered on religious themes and the fusion of Spanish and indigenous cultures; 19th-century paintings of landscapes; and portraits of major figures in Chilean history, the most famous of which are by José Gil de Castro. The most valuable paintings here are by Roberto Matta, the 20th-century Surrealist. Since 1990, the museum has drawn major traveling expositions from artists including Damien Hirst and David Hockney.

🔍 HIDDEN GEM
Visual Artistry

South of Barrio Lastarría is the intriguing Museo Violeta Parra, celebrating the first Chilean artist to have a Louvre exhibition *(www. museovioletaparra.cl)*.

↑ Exhibits within Santiago's Museo de Arte Contemporaneo

 27

Museo de Arte Contemporaneo

⊠ F7 🏛 Palacio de Bellas Artes, Parque Forestal Ⓜ Bellas Artes Ⓒ 11am–7pm Tue–Sat, 11am–6pm Sun Ⓦ mac.uchile.cl

The Museo de Arte Contemporaneo (MAC) is housed in the Palacio de Bellas Artes, but is accessed via a separate western entrance. The museum, along with its auxiliary branch at Parque Quinta Normal, features over 2,000 works in its permanent collection, and there are also monthly exhibits highlighting international and local artists. The collection features Latin American art, including works by members of Chilean artists' collective groups Generación del Trece and Grupo Signo. The influence of Europe in the creation of Chilean artwork is vividly apparent, though the art features indigenous viewpoints. This is seen in the work of Chilean Hugo Marín, who has melded European technique with pre-Columbian influences. The grounds house a sculpture by Colombia's famous artist Fernando Botero.

28

Iglesia de Santo Domingo

⊠ E7 🏛 Santo Domingo 961 Ⓒ (02) 698-5933 Ⓜ Plaza de Armas

The present-day Iglesia de Santo Domingo is the fourth church of the Dominican Order to be built on this site. The existing building was designed by architect Juan de los Santos Vasconcelos. Its construction began in 1747 in a Doric Neo-Classical style that is distinct from other structures in downtown Santiago. In 1795–99, Italian architect Joaquín Toesca intervened to complete the church's interiors and added Bavarian Baroque brick towers. The church was finally inaugurated in 1808. Today, worshipers pray to the Virgin of Pompeii, whose statue occupies the central altar.

29

Centro Cultural Estación Mapocho

⊠ D6 🏛 Plaza de la Cultura s/n, Balmaceda and Independencia Ⓜ Cal y Canto Ⓒ 11am–8pm daily Ⓦ estacionmapocho.cl

Now a cultural center, Estación Mapocho was built in 1913 as a grand terminal for trains that connected Santiago to northern Chile and Argentina. The station was designed by renowned French-Chilean architect Emilio Jéquier, who had studied in France and returned greatly influenced by the Beaux-Arts movement and the teachings of Gustave Eiffel, architect of Paris's Eiffel Tower. The Beaux-Arts style can be readily appreciated in the details of the station's stunning facade and the columns in the access hall. The station's vast steel roof and skeleton were produced in Belgium, and its interior vaults were designed by a Paris-based company. All were later shipped to Chile and assembled there.

Estación Mapocho was one of several public works projects to celebrate the country's centennial in 1910, and construction lasted from 1905 to 1912. It was declared a national monument in 1976. The station closed in 1987 when train services were suspended. Abandoned, the building fell into disrepair. Eventually, the government converted it into a cultural center, and it reopened as the Centro Cultural Estación Mapocho in 1994.

During the restoration, architects rescued the station's facade and preserved most of the edifice's ornate details, so visitors today can marvel at the splendor of its architecture and decor. The center now hosts all manner of events, including music concerts,

→ Packed restaurants in the beautiful Mercado Central

theater performances, and cinema. Many of the original salons have been converted into galleries, but the building is worth a visit in its own right.

The signature event at the center is the austral spring's Feria Internacional del Libro de Santiago. Held in October or November, this fortnight-long book fair attracts Chilean and foreign authors from throughout the Spanish-speaking world and beyond. See www.camaradellibro.cl for up-to-date information on forthcoming book fair events.

---

30 (M)

Posada del Corregidor

📍 E7 🏛 Esmeralda 749 Ⓜ Bellas Artes ⏰ 10am–1:30pm & 2:30–5:30pm Mon–Fri 🌐 santiagocultura.cl

A national landmark dating from 1750, the Posada del Corregidor is one of the few Colonial adobe buildings left in Santiago. Its thick walls, stone foundations, and second-story wraparound balcony are outstanding examples of urban architecture in 18th-century Chile. In the 1920s, the *posada* became a social center for Santiago's bohemian set.

Today, it operates as an art gallery featuring exhibits of emerging artists, but it once served as a dance hall of dubious reputation known as the Filarmónica. The *posada* suffered significant damage in the 2010 earthquake, but has since been restored.

---

31 (M) (Y)

Mercado Central

📍 E6 🏛 San Pablo 967 ⏰ 6am–5pm daily (to 8pm Fri & to 6pm Sat) 🌐 mercadocentral.cl

Built in 1872 for the National Exposition in Chile, Mercado Central (Central Market) stands on the site of the burned ruins of Plaza de Abasto, which had been set up in the early 1800s. Designed by self-taught architect Fermín Vivaceta, the

🔍 HIDDEN GEM
Empanadas

If you're heading for the Mercado Central, and hankering for an empanada, try Zunino. The family business has been running since 1930 and they've perfected their recipe *(www. empanadaszunino.com)*.

market is considered one of the most beautiful public structures of its era.

After the 1872 Exposition, Mercado Central became Santiago's major wholesale fish and vegetable market. Although it has since moved elsewhere, the Mercado is still an important commercial center. It is popular with both locals, who come to see and buy fresh produce, and tourists, who come to eat lunch at one of its many atmospheric seafood restaurants. Guided bicycle tours *(www.labicicletaverde. com)* take in the site.

A SHORT WALK
PLAZA DE ARMAS

Distance 1 mile (1.5 km) **Time** 20 minutes
Nearest metro Bellas Artes

The symbolic heart of Santiago, the Plaza de Armas (Arms Plaza) was designed to suit the Spanish norm of leaving one block of a city grid empty for use as a parade ground. Government offices ringed the plaza during the Colonial years, and in the 17th century it became a thriving commercial area with shopping galleries stretching around the perimeter. In 2000, the square was cleared to create more open spaces. Today, it is a vibrant social center, drawing people who come here to rest on park benches, play chess, or enjoy the lively atmosphere and street performances.

The venerable **Ex Congreso Nacional** *(p70) edifice was constructed 1858–76 in the Neo-Classical style, with striking Corinthian columns.*

MORANDÉ

COMPAÑÌA DE JESÚS

CATED

Chile's Supreme Court, **Palacio de los Tribunales de Justicia** *(p71), occupies a Neo-Classical building with French influences. Its vaulted glass-and-metal ceiling runs the length of the edifice.*

BANDERA

Housed in the Palacio de la Real Aduana, the **Museo Chileno de Arte Precolombino** *highlights the arts and symbols of pre-Columbian cultures in the Americas.*

PASEO HUÉRFANOS

PASEO AHU

Paseos Ahumada *and* **Huérfanos** *are lined with shopping centers, cafés, and restaurants.*

←
Neo-Classical facade of Palacio de los Tribunales de Justicia

Locator Map
For more detail see p64

↑ The vibrant colors and lively atmosphere of Plaza de Armas

Consecrated in 1775, **Catedral Metropolitana** *(p68) is the fourth church to be built on this site. It was designed by Jesuits, but received a Neo-Classical makeover from 1780 to 1789.*

Chile's **Correo Central** *(Post Office p68) occupies a French Neo-Classical edifice built in 1882 on the site of Pedro de Valdivia's residence.*

Dating from 1785, the Neo-Classical **Municipalidad de Santiago** *(p69) served as the city jail before housing Santiago's municipality.*

The **Palacio de la Real Audiencia** *(p68) served as Chile's Supreme Court until independence in 1810. The Museo Histórico Nacional within offers a walk through Santiago's Colonial past.*

PASEO PUENTE

PLAZA DE ARMAS

MONJITAS

PLAZA DE ARMAS

SAN ANTONIO

PASEO ESTADO

0 meters 60
0 yards 60
N ↗

One of the last 18th-century structures left in Santiago, **Casa Colorada** *(p71) features a second story, uncommon in its day.*

WEST OF SANTIAGO CENTRO

Stretching west from Santiago Centro to verdant Parque Quinta Normal are some of the city's oldest residential neighborhoods, notably *barrios* Brasil, Concha y Toro, Yungay, and Dieciocho. This was once where the city's wealthier classes lived, as the opulent Neo-Classical and French-style *palacios* on and around the Alameda testify. As the 20th century wore on, however, the area fell into serious decline, as many residents decided to leave for the fast-developing, more suburban neighborhoods northeast of the city center. Over the last 20 years, the situation has changed. The area has become increasingly gentrified, with *barrios* such as Brasil and Yungay now among the hippest in the city. Few Colonial-era buildings have survived, but there is an array of handsome 19th- and early-20th- century architecture, much of it renovated and home to various restaurants, bars, and boutique hotels. Founded in 1841 to cultivate a variety of plants, the Parque Quinta Normal now provides an open green space for visitors to relax in the heart of the city.

WEST OF SANTIAGO CENTRO

Must See

1. Parque Quinta Normal

Experience More

2. Museo de la Memoria y los Derechos Humanos
3. Museo Pedagógico Gabriela Mistral
4. Biblioteca de Santiago
5. Museo Artequín
6. Confitería Torres
7. Matucana 100
8. Planetario USACH
9. Barrio Brasil
10. Fantasilandia
11. Museo de la Solidaridad Salvador Allende
12. Palacio Cousiño
13. Barrio Concha y Toro
14. Barrio Dieciocho
15. Basílica de los Sacramentinos
16. Club Hípico
17. Parque Bernardo O'Higgins

Eat

1. El Hoyo
2. Boulevard Lavaud
3. Ocean Pacific

Stay

4. Happy House Hostel

Strolling around the beautiful Parque Quinta Normal ↑

❶

PARQUE QUINTA NORMAL

📍 A7 🏠 Avenida Matucana 520 📞 (02) 2689-0119 🕐 9am–7pm daily

Stroll alongside beautiful trees, take a pedal boat around an artificial lake, picnic on expansive lawns, explore fascinating museums, or listen to soapbox rants – experience them all and so much more at Parque Quinta Normal.

HISTORY IN THE PARK

Quinta Normal has long been associated with learning. It hosted the Chilean International Exhibition in 1875-76, an event that featured scientfic, artistic, and agricultural exhibits. One venue built for the fair was turned into the Museo Nacional de Historia Natural.

Set up in 1842 to propagate foreign plants, Parque Quinta Normal is famous for its wide varieties of tree species. Many of the different variety of trees were planted by French naturalist Claudio Gay, whose extensive pioneering studies of Chilean flora and fauna gave birth to the city's Museo Nacional de Historia Natural and to the actual park itself. In its early years, Parque Quinta Normal was also used for agricultural studies and in 1928 it was incorporated into the University of Chile as the School of Agronomy and Veterinary Sciences. Today, the park is only a mere fraction of its earlier size, but it nonetheless remains popular owing to its large and expansive lawns, and its mature and beautiful trees. The park is also home to a handful of scientific museums, an art museum, picnic areas, and an artificial lake.

Museo de Ciencia y Tecnología

▶ Set up in 1985, the Museo de Ciencia y Tecnología was the first interactive museum in Chile designed to engage children in science and technology. The museum is housed in a building called the Parthenon, a Greco-Roman-style edifice built in 1884 by Naples-born artist Alejandro Cicarelli and inaugurated by Chilean painter Pedro Lira, who sought to create a permanent exhibition hall for art. Interactive displays are offered on astronomy, geology, technology, and many more. In 1887, the Unión de Arte opened the city's first Fine Arts Museum here. It later became the Museo de Arte Contemporaneo (MAC), then in 1974 it was transferred to its current location in Parque Forestal, in the center of Santiago.

MAC Espacio Quinta Normal

◀ Housed in the Neo-Classical Palacio Versailles, built in the early 1900s, and declared a national monument in 2004, Espacio Quinta Normal is a branch of MAC (p80). In 2005, MAC briefly relocated here while its salons in the Palacio de Bellas Artes were renovated. Since then, this building has been retained by MAC for shows. With 12 spacious salons surrounding a central plaza, the museum hosts large expositions of up-and-coming national artists and large international expositions such as Germany's Fluxus and the Sao Paulo Biennial.

Museo Ferroviario

Housing one of the most important collections of steam locomotives in Latin America, the Museo Ferroviario is spread across 5 acres (2 ha) in the southwest corner of the Quinta Normal. On display are 16 locomotives and three wagons. Locomotive type 20, made by the now defunct Sociedad de Maestranza y Glavanizaciones from Caleta Abarca, is a pristine example of a locally built machine. Also on display is a Kitson-Meyer locomotive built in 1909 in Leeds, UK. This served the Ferrocarril Transandino that, until 1971, connected Los Andes (p135) in Chile with Mendoza in Argentina – a distance of 154 miles (248 km) across the precarious peaks of the Andes. In all, there were nine locomotives used for the Andean passage, of which only two remain. Visitors can also view the restored 1923 presidential carriage used by former presidents Arturo Alessandri (1868-1950) and Carlos Ibáñez del Campo (1877-1960).

Museo Nacional de Historia Natural

▶ Santiago's museum of natural history was built in 1875 for the city's first International Exposition. The main hall is dominated by the skeleton of a juvenile fin whale. Displays are divided into 12 categories, including insects and flora. There is a salon dedicated to the native forests of Chile, with wood slabs showing the age of such giants as alerce, the world's second-oldest tree. The building was restored after it was damaged in the 2010 earthquake.

TOP 3 ACTIVITIES FOR KIDS

Museo de Ciencia y Tecnología
Offers plenty of child-friendly, hands-on exhibits, experiments, and activities.

Pedal Boats
Rent one of the retro pedal-powered boats and head out for an adventure on the lake.

Open-Air Pools
Go for a swim in the park's open-air *piscina* (swimming pool) or splash around in the fountains.

EXPERIENCE MORE

②

Museo de la Memoria y los Derechos Humanos

📍A7 🏛Matucana 501 🚇Quinta Normal ⏰10am–6pm Tue–Sun 🌐museode lamemoria.cl

The Museum of Memory and Human Rights opened in 2010 as a memorial to the victims of Chile's brutal military dictatorship (1973–90), during which an estimated 3,000 people were killed or "disappeared," and many others were tortured, detained, or exiled. Among the items on display are personal letters, official documents, and government propaganda, alongside information on torture methods and some of the implements used, offering grisly testimony to the horrors of the time, as well as the historical background that led to the rise of the dictatorship.

The vast, spacious glass building utilizes its interior for multimedia exhibits on the notorious regime and its survivors, with the objective of encouraging reflection and debate on human rights. Although sobering, a visit here is essential for anyone who wants to gain an understanding of Chile's past and present.

---

③

Museo Pedagógico Gabriela Mistral

📍B8 🏛Chacabuco 365 🚇Quinta Normal ⏰10am–5pm Mon–Fri, 10am–3:30pm Sat 🌐museodelaeducacion. gob.cl

Housed in the Escuela Normal Brígada Walker, the Museo Pedagógico Gabriela Mistral tracks the history and development of education in Chile. The museum is named for Nobel laureate and literary artist Gabriela Mistral (p38), who was an educator throughout most of her life in spite of having left school at the age of 12. Self-taught and born with a natural verbal dexterity, Mistral became an advocate for education in response to the lack of opportunities for schooling in Chile.

This education museum was launched in 1941 as an exposition by the Museo Nacional de Bellas Artes (p79) to celebrate Santiago's 400th anniversary. Its exhibitions explored the history of education from the Colonial period onward. Following the popular success of the exposition, director Carlos Stuardo combed through grade schools and even industrial and mining schools in search of material and furniture to establish a permanent collection. Today, the exhibits consist of more than 6,500 historical pieces, including antique maps, school desks, skills-based teaching apparatus such as sewing machines, abacuses, and more. There is also an extensive library of some 40,000 texts covering education, as well as a photo library of 6,000 digitalized images that track the history of education in the country.

↑ Visitors examining an exhibit at the Museo de la Memoria y los Derechos Humanos

↑ The colorful Pabellón París, housing the cool Museo Artequín

4 📺

Biblioteca de Santiago

📍 B8 🏛 Avenida Matucana 151 Ⓜ Quinta Normal 🕐 11am-8:30pm Tue-Fri, 11am-5pm Sat & Sun 🌐 bibliotecasantiago.cl

Opened in 2005, this was Chile's first major public library. It was built near Quinta Normal *(p88)* in an effort to create a center of cultural and educational development. Housed in a 1930s warehouse, the Biblioteca has given the people of Santiago access to a vast range of literature, lectures, and children's books.

5 🖌 📺

Museo Artequín

📍 A8 🏛 Avenue Portales 3530 Ⓜ Quinta Normal 🕐 9am-5pm Tue-Fri, 11am-6pm Sat & Sun 🚫 Feb 🌐 artequin.cl

This offbeat museum features reproductions of the world's greatest painters. It is located in the gorgeous Pabellón París, which was designed to represent Chile at the 1889 Universal Exposition in Paris. The Pabellón's Art Nouveau facade and interiors are the work of French architect Henri Picq, who used iron, steel, and zinc in a clear reference to the Industrial Revolution. Built in Paris, taken apart, and then reassembled at Parque Quinta Normal, the Pabellón housed a museum, and also featured works by contemporary figures such as writer and artist Pedro Lira (1845–1912). It became a national monument in 1986, and in 1992, the Pabellón was renovated and reopened as the present-day Museo Artequín. The purpose of the museum is to inspire and educate visitors about art through a "real" version of the world's best paintings. On display are prints of some of the world's greatest artists, each represented by a piece for which he or she is best known. Among the most recognizable international names are Goya, Dalí, Kahlo, and Kandinsky.

EAT

El Hoyo

This restaurant may look modest, but it delivers delicious meaty dishes. To drink, try the *terremoto* (earthquake), a potent Chilean cocktail mix of white wine and pineapple ice cream served in a glass jug.

📍 B9 🏛 San Vicente 375 🚫 Sun 🌐 elhoyo.cl

⑤⑤⑤

Boulevard Lavaud

A restaurant with an attached barbershop sounds unlikely, but somehow it works at Boulevard Lavaud. The tasty menu is vaguely French with specialities such as *Confit de Pato a la Naranja (*orange duck confit*)*, and there's often live music, too.

📍 B7 🏛 Compañía 2789 🚫 Sun 🌐 boulevard lavaud.cl

⑤⑤⑤

Ocean Pacific

Decked out with maritime memorabilia and waiters dressed as sailors, Ocean Pacific serves delicious first-rate fish and seafood. The restaurant can get very busy, so try to book ahead.

📍 C8 🏛 Avenida Ricardo Cumming 221 🌐 oceanpacific.cl

⑤⑤⑤

The Biblioteca has given the people of Santiago access to a vast range of literature, lectures, and children's books.

6 🍽 🖥
Confitería Torres

📍 D8 🏛 Avenida Alameda 1570 🚇 Quinta Normal ⏰ 10:30am-midnight Mon-Sat 🌐 confiteriatorres.cl

The Confitería Torres opened in 1879 and is Santiago's oldest café. Located close to the government buildings of the Palacio de la Moneda *(p72)*, the café served the capital's politicians, intellectuals, and elite society when the Barrio Dieciocho area was still considered fashionable. After a period of declining popularity, lengthy renovations began in 2002 that salvaged the old red-leather booths, French doors, and long oak bar, and the café reopened in 2004 with its antique ambience still quite palpable. The Confitería is steeped in history and has produced several emblematic elements of Chile's culinary repertoire. Perhaps the most famous item on the café's menu is the *barros luco*, a beef sandwich with melted cheese that is named after former president Ramón Barros Luco, who ordered one every time he visited. The *cola de mono* aperitif of alcoholic *aguardiente*, with milk and coffee was also invented here. The restaurant can be parti cularly popular at lunchtime, so it's best to book in advance.

7 🖥
Matucana 100

📍 A8 🏛 Avenida Matucana 100, Estación Central 🚇 Quinta Normal ⏰ 11am-3pm & 4-8pm Mon-Wed, 11am-3pm & 4-9pm Thu & Fri, 5-9pm Sat & Sun 🌐 m100.cl

Matucana 100 is set in a huge brick warehouse built in 1911 for the state railway company. The gallery was designed in 2001 to create a space in which a variety of art forms could participate simultaneously – whether cinema, theater, artwork, photography, or music. Over time, the center has grown to include a large art gallery and a concert hall. It now focuses solely on contemporary works principally by national artists.

8 ⛷ 🎿
Planetario USACH

📍 A9 🏛 Avenida Alameda 3349, Estación Central 🚇 Estación Central ⏰ 11:30am-7pm Mon-Wed, 10am-5pm Thu, 1:30-5pm Sat & Sun 🌐 planetario chile.cl

The University of Santiago's planetarium is one of Latin America's most prominent astronomy education centers.

↑ White tablecloths and a checkered floor inside the Confitería Torres

Its projection dome, the Sala Albert Einstein, has an unusual conical design. Made of copper, it is 72 ft (22 m) in diameter, and has a Carl Zeiss model VI projector that uses 160 lenses, allowing visitors to observe the moon and the solar system, and over 5,000 stars in both hemispheres. Of particular interest are the special expositions that highlight discoveries by Chile's top astronomical observatories. The planetarium offers workshops, audiovisual salons, and exhibitions for both children and adults.

9
Barrio Brasil

📍 C7 🚇 Cumming, Santa Ana

During the early 20th century, Barrio Brasil was a posh residential neighborhood. By the 1940s, wealthy residents began migrating eastward, toward the Andes. Later, the

→ *The girl graffiti* by izak and Henruz, in the Barrio Yungay neighborhood construction of the Norte-Sur Highway severed the neighborhood from the rest of the city, and Barrio Brasil was by and large forgotten. Thanks to this, the area escaped development and many of its grand early 20th-century Gothic and Neo-Classical mansions have been left intact. As a result, Barrio Brasil is now one of the most picturesque areas in Santiago. It has also experienced a cultural and architectural resurgence, due to the presence of many universities nearby. Artists and musicians have moved in, drawn by the neighborhood's eclectic ambience. Today, trendy lofts and funky restaurants sit alongside traditional *picadas* and bars.

The streets of nearby Barrio Yungay are especially well preserved, with two of the most beautiful being Pasaje Adriana Cousiño between Huérfanos and Maipú, and Pasaje Lucrecia Valdés off Compañia between Esperanza and Maipú. Both are cobblestone walkways that exude a strong European feel. Other vestiges of Barrio Yungay's past can be seen at the restaurant Boulevard Lavaud *(p91)*.

🔟 ♿ 🍴 🖥 🛍
Fantasilandia

📍 C10 🏠 Beaucheff 938
Ⓜ Parque O'Higgins
🕐 Noon–7pm Sat & Sun
🌐 fantasilandia.cl

The third-largest amusement park in South America, Fantasilandia is sometimes dubbed the Chilean Disneyland. It opened in 1978 as the brainchild of entrepreneur Gerardo Arteaga, who felt that Santiago had grown insufferably boring for families who were seeking amusement during their spare time.

The park offers plenty of knee-trembling rollercoasters and stomach-churning rides such as Xtreme Fall, Raptor, and Boomerang. There are also more tranquil attractions for younger children, including a carousel, the Kids' Zone, and Villa Mágica, with music jamborees and magic acts. The amusement park is set in leafy surroundings and a variety of dining options are available.

TOP 5 RIDES AT FANTASILANDIA

Tsunami
You'll definitely get soaked on this giant wave-themed ride.

Boomerang
A stomach-churning rollercoaster that features a "cobra roll" and a "vertical loop."

Xtreme Fall
This ride lifts you up to a great height, lets you stew for a few moments, and then plunges you back to earth.

Kamikaze
Passengers are spun back and forth to build up momentum before some 360-degree spins.

Raptor
A classic, fast-paced rollercoaster with multiple loops.

⑪ 🏛️ 🏛️ 🏛️

Museo de la Solidaridad Salvador Allende

📍 C9 🏠 República 475 Ⓜ República ⏰ Mar-Nov: 10am-6pm Tue-Sun; Dec-Feb: 11am-7pm Tue-Sun 🌐 mssa.cl

Set in the former head-quarters of DINA, the secret police during the Pinochet military dictatorship *(p48)*, the Museo de la Solidaridad is the only museum in Latin America that consists entirely of works donated by artists. In an act of solidarity with the government of Salvador Allende *(p48)*, artists in 1971 founded this museum with a collection of more than 400 pieces by such names as Joan Miró, Alexander Calder, Víctor Vasarely, and Roberto Matta. After Salvador Allende was overthrown in the 1973 coup d'état, the works were hidden in the Museo de Arte Contemporaneo *(p80)*. The museum's administration moved to Paris, where artists continued to donate until the collection reached some 1,500 pieces. The works date from 1950 to 1980, and many of them evoke the social struggle of Latin Americans. In 2005 the Fundación Allende bought and remodeled this townhouse, where the works are now displayed.

---

⑫ 🏛️ 🏛️

Palacio Cousiño

📍 D9 🏠 Calle Dieciocho 438 Ⓜ Toesca ⏰ 9:30am-1:30pm & 2:30-5pm Tue-Fri, 9:30am-1:30pm Sat & Sun 🌐 santiagocultura.cl

Built between 1870 and 1878, the Palacio Cousiño was Santiago's most extravagant mansion of the day. It was designed by French architect Paul Lathoud for the Cousiño family, who had made a fortune in mining and shipping. The Cousiños imported many of their materials from Europe: walnut and mahogany parquet floors, brocade tapestries, Italian marble, and French embroidered curtains. They also employed some European artisans to install these fineries.

The mansion also housed the country's first electric fittings and included the first elevator in Chile. The palace was auctioned off to Santiago's mayor in 1940, who donated it to the city. Subsequently, the building was used to house visiting dignitaries such as Golda Meir, Charles de Gaulle, and Belgian king Baudouin. In 1968, the mansion was converted into a museum that preserved the house as it was during the 19th century.

Following the renovations after the 2010 earthquake,

CITY CENTER PALACIOS

As well as the Palacio Cousiño, there are several other historic *palacios* in this part of Santiago. These include Edificio Íñiguez at the corner of the Alameda and Calle Dieciocho, which dates to 1908 and houses the Confitería Torres *(p92)*. The Palacio Irarrázabal, next door, was built two years later and has a distinct French style. Palacio Errázuriz, at Alameda 1656, was built in 1872 and was once home to the Brazilian embassy – it's looking a little worn these days, but a restoration is reportedly in the pipeline.

Palacio Cousiño is now restored and holds exhibitions througout the year.

⑬ Barrio Concha y Toro

❏ C8 ⓜ República

Dating from the 1920s, Barrio Concha y Toro is one of Santiago's best-preserved neighborhoods, comprising mansions built by the flourishing upper class in the early 20th century. The area was initially owned by engineer-entrepreneur Enrique Concha y Toro and his wife Teresa Cazotte, who reaped a fortune in mining in the late 1800s. They sought to replicate European towns with sinuous cobblestone streets, closely grouped buildings behind a continual facade, and a tiny plaza. The best Chilean archi-

The stately exterior of Palacio Cousiño, and *(inset)* the intricate ↓ detail of the gate

tects of the time – Larraín Bravo, Siegel, González Cortés, Machiacao, and Bianchi – were entrusted with the design. They created a cohesive style that incorporated influences such as Neo-Gothic, Neo-Classical, Baroque, and even Bauhaus. Highlights include the Teatro Carrera, built in 1926 by Gustavo Monckeberg. The former home of poet Vicente Huidobro is now the popular Zully restaurant. The picturesque Plazoleta de la Libertad de Prensa, often used as a set for television productions, was named in 1994 in honor of the World Press Freedom Day.

⑭ Barrio Dieciocho

❏ D9 ⓜ Los Héroes

During the turn of the 20th century, Santiago's upscale neighborhood was centered around Calle Dieciocho. Wealthy families erected opulent mansions here as

a means of flaunting their new-found fortunes from shipping and mining. The constructions clearly reflect the influence of European styles, principally French.

Santiago's elite has since moved uptown but the architectural gems their ancestors built can still be seen, in spite of the fact that the neighborhood now looks a little worse for wear. Among its best are the Subercaseaux Mansion at No. 190, Residencia Eguiguren at No. 102, and the Palacio Astoreca at No. 121. The grand buildings are now occupied by university groups, libraries, and other similar associations.

15

Basílica de los Sacramentinos

Q E9 **A** Santa Isabel 1127
C (02) 2638-3189 **M** Toesca
O 10am-7pm daily

Designed by architect Ricardo Larraín Bravo, the Basílica de los Sacramentinos was built as an imitation of the Sacré-Coeur in Paris, between 1919 and 1931. The church is notable for its Roman Byzantine architecture and the crypt, a 4,925-ft- (1,500-m-) long burial chamber that runs underneath. The parquet floors are the first of their kind to be made in Chile. The wooden pulpit, confessionals, and seats were all hand-carved by Salesians, a Roman Catholic order. Also of interest are the French stained glass and the organ, which was imported from Germany. The church suffered significant damage in the 2010 earthquake, but has since been restored. The exterior is also striking, and made more pleasant by Parque Almagro, which stretches out before it.

↓ The splendid exterior of the Basílica de los Sacramentinos

16 🍽

Club Hípico

Q C10 **A** Avenida Almirante Blanco Encalada 2540
M Unión Latinoamericana
O For races; schedules vary, check website
W clubhipico.cl

Founded in 1870, Club Hípico is Chile's preeminent racetrack and home to South America's oldest stakes race, El Ensayo (*p42*), which takes place in late October/early November every year. It is part of the Triple Corona together with Hipódromo Chile and Valparaíso Derby.

The current racetrack was designed by architect Josué Smith and opened in 1923, the previous track house having succumbed to fire in 1892. The club building is a fine example of early 20th-century architectural grandeur, a result of Chile's economic boom during the late 1800s. Club Hípico features stylish terraces and viewing platforms, restaurants, formal gardens, and a picnic area, set amid the faded elegance of the old República neighborhood. In the distance, the looming bulk of the Andes provides a backdrop to the racetrack.

In total, there are about 1,500 races held here annually, including the famed Alberto Vial Infante and the Arturo Lyon Peña. The club has also hosted major music concerts, including performances by Iron Maiden, Jonas Brothers, and Linkin Park. Despite the racetrack's roots as an elite social club, it is now visited by people from all backgrounds.

↑ Pedaling along one of the wide avenues in Parque Bernardo O'Higgins

17 🍽 🎭

Parque Bernardo O'Higgins

📍 D10 🏛 Between Avenida Beaucheff & Autopista Central Ⓜ Parque O'Higgins 🕐 6am–8pm daily

The capital's second-largest park is a popular recreation area for families and a major staging area for the Fiestas Patrias celebrations (p42). The park was inaugurated in 1873, at which time it was originally named Parque Cousiño after the Chilean millionaire Luis Cousiño who commissioned it. Some 100 years later the park's name was changed to honor Bernardo O'Higgins, one of Chile's founding fathers. Sprawling Parque Bernardo O'Higgins is home to tennis courts, soccer fields, an artificial lake, Santiago's largest indoor music stadium, and a public pool. Perhaps the most curious aspect of the park is the Campo de Marte, a gigantic strip of concrete that resembles a landing strip. Military parades take place here every September 19 – known as the Day of the Glories of the Armies – which

draw thousands of spectators.

Among the park's attractions is El Pueblito, a mock Colonial village with simple restaurants serving traditional cuisine. There are also two museums located here. The Museo de Huaso is especially popular with families, and depicts the culture and history of the cowboys of the Central Valley (p114); while the Museo de Insectos y Caracoles houses a collection of butterfly and insect displays. There are also artisan workshops and fairs held at the Plaza de las Artesanías. During the Fiestas Patrias, the grounds are bloated to capacity with revelers who come for the *fondas*, or festival centers tents – a hallmark of this popular park. For days, a veritable patriotic bacchanal takes over the park with nonstop *cueca* music, smoking barbecues, and excessive drinking. Another hugely busy event is the Lollapalooza Chile music festival – the first version of the popular Chicagoan festival to take place outside the United States.

Lollapalooza Chile has been held in the park since 2011, mixing popular Chilean acts with international headliners, and takes place in late March or early April each year. Fantasilandia (p93), one of the biggest amusement parks in South America, is located on the side of the park bordering Avenida Beaucheff.

> Sprawling Parque Bernardo O'Higgins is home to tennis courts, soccer fields, an artificial lake, Santiago's largest indoor music stadium, and a public pool.

NORTHEAST OF SANTIAGO CENTRO

For the first 400 years of Santiago's existence, the area northeast of the city centre was largely undeveloped, home to only a scattering of country houses surrounded by large plots of land, as well as a number of slums. Things started to change in the 1950s, as Santiago's population grew and many middle- and upper-class residents abandoned neighborhoods like Brasil, Concha y Toro, and Yungay, and headed towards the foothills of the Andes. They settled first in Providencia – which includes the bohemian Barrio Bellavista at the foot of Cerro San Cristóbal – and slowly pushed east. Today, leafy Providencia has a thriving dining scene and an exciting selection of buzzing bars, though it is relatively short on tourist attractions. To the northeast are the skyscrapers of Las Condes, home to the city's financial district, high-end restaurants, and luxury apartments, while to the north is the similarly exclusive but more residential neighborhood of Vitacura.

NORTHEAST OF SANTIAGO CENTRO

Must See

❶ Parque Metropolitano de Santiago

Experience More

❷ Cementerio General
❸ Museo de Artes Decorativas
❹ Museo Ralli
❺ Casa Museo La Chascona
❻ La Vega
❼ Barrio Patronato
❽ Plaza Camilo Mori
❾ Patio Bellavista
❿ Parque de las Esculturas
⓫ Casa de la Ciudadanía Montecarmelo
⓬ Parque Balmaceda
⓭ Museo de Tajamares

⓮ Providencia
⓯ Pueblo Los Dominicos
⓰ Museo de la Moda
⓱ Gran Torre Santiago
⓲ Barrio Vitacura
⓳ Las Condes

Eat

① Galindo
② Etniko
③ El Huerto

Drink

④ Baco Vino y Bistro
⑤ La Casa en el Aire

Stay

⑥ The Aubrey

❶ 🛴 🚡 🍽 💻 🛍

PARQUE METROPOLITANO DE SANTIAGO

📍 G5 🏠 Pedro de Valdivia Norte ☎ (02) 2730-1331 Ⓜ Baquedano
🕙 10am–6pm daily (summer: to 9pm) 🌐 parquemet.cl

With rare and endangered animals roaming the National Zoo, cable cars climbing the summit of San Cristóbal, and open-air swimming pools providing respite from the heat, it is no surprise that Parque Metropolitano de Santiago attracts visitors all year round.

Covering some 3 sq miles (7 sq km) of vegetation-clad slopes, the Parque Metropolitano de Santiago was developed between 1903 and 1927 as the lungs of Santiago, encompassing the hills San Cristóbal, Pirámide, Bosque, and Chacarillas. Previously bare and dry, the park was reforested with native plants and trees from across Chile and further developed with trails, picnic areas, swimming pools, a cultural center, and a cable car. It is now the city's recreational center and home to the Zoológico Nacional, and offers sweeping views of Santiago and the Andes.

Did You Know?

The Statue of the Virgin is believed to be a reproduction of the "Virgin of Rome."

The 45-ft- (14-m-) high Statue of the Virgin was donated by France in 1904. It can be seen from most of Santiago Centro.

The 1925 cable car takes visitors to the top of Cerro San Cristóbal and past the park's zoo.

The Pío Nono entrance, leading directly to the Estación Funicular, forms part of the Plaza Caupolicán garden, with its medieval-style facade and souvenir stands.

The funicular station at Plaza Caupolicán is the main entry point to the park.

↑ The sun shines on the Statue of the Virgin at the top of San Cristóbal

Offering beautiful views of the city, Piscina Antilén is Santiago's highest swimming pool and a great respite from the summer heat.

Inaugurated in 1997 by Prince Hitachi of Japan, the Jardín Japonés features a lotus pond, water wheel, cherry trees, and Japanese maples.

Housed in the Camino Real restaurant, the Enoteca Wine Museum is a good spot for sampling some of Chile's best vintages.

The Jardín Mapulemu covers over 8 acres (3 ha) of diverse Chilean flora.

↑ Illustration of Parque Metropolitano de Santiago showing the main sights

 HIDDEN GEM
Piscina Antilén

For a "swim with a view," head for a dip in the Antilén and Tupahue pools, located on the summit of Cerro San Cristóbal.

EXPERIENCE MORE

② Ⓜ

Cementerio General

📍 E4 🏛 Avenida Alberto Zañartu 951 🚇 Cementerios 🕙 9am–5:30pm daily 🌐 cementariogeneral.cl

Santiago's principal cemetery is the final resting place for many of the country's historical figures. Most of the nation's past presidents are buried here, including Salvador Allende, whose remains were moved to this site from Viña del Mar (p130) in 1990. The cemetery opened in 1821 and was inaugurated by Chile's first president, Bernardo O'Higgins, who now rests in a crypt at Plaza Bulnes (p73). The area was designed as a "city" for the dead, with tree-lined streets and elaborate mausoleums. These run the gamut of styles from Gothic to Egyptian to Greek, and the cemetery's aesthetics are an integral part of its appeal.

Among those buried here are legendary folk singer

Violeta Parra; former Senator and leftist Orlando Letelier, who was murdered in Washington, DC; noted poet and singer Victor Jara, tortured and shot dead by the Pinochet regime in 1973; and, more recently, the Communist Party leader Gladys Marin. There is also a somber monument to the dictatorship era (p48) – a mural by sculptor Francisco Gazitúa called *Rostros* (Faces) that lists thousands of Chileans who were executed. On the west side of the cemetery is the Dissenters' Patio, a burial sector for the city's Protestants, who had been moved from their earlier burial site at Cerro Santa Lucía (p78) in the late 1800s.

---

③ Ⓜ

Museo de Artes Decorativas

📍 E5 🏛 Avenida Recoleta 683 🚇 Cerro Blanco 🕙 10am–5:30pm Tue–Fri 🌐 artdec.cl

In 1982, the very valuable Coleccion Garcés was donated to the Chilean government and established as the Museo

de Artes Decorativas. The pieces here (more than 2,500) are divided into 20 thematic displays and include beautiful examples of 18th- and 19th-century porcelain, crystal glasses and vases, ornate silverwork, marble and ceramic objects, jewelry, and Greek, Roman, and Oriental art.

The center houses two other collections of interest. The Museo Historíco Dominico displays 18th- and 19th-century religious objects,

↓ An Egyptian-style tomb in Santiago's Cementerio General

while the Biblioteca Patrimonial Recoleta Dominica is one of the largest private libraries in Latin America, with 115,000 historically important books, maps, and investigative papers covering science and religion.

④

Museo Ralli

🅟 M1 🅰 Alonso de Sotomayor 4110
🕙 10:30am–5pm Tue–Sun (Jan: Sat & Sun only) 🗓 Feb
🌐 museoralli.cl

One of Santiago's lesser-known museums, the Museo Ralli has a small yet impressive collection of Latin American and European art, which includes a handful of works by Salvador Dalí, Marc Chagall, and Joan Miró. This transnational museum – there are other branches in Spain, Uruguay, and Israel – was founded in 1992 by Harry Recanati, an art collector and retired banker who shuns any profit from it. The museum is spread across 32,290 sq ft (3,000 sq m) and is located on a residential street, where it occasionally hosts temporary exhibits by contemporary European and Latin American artists.

⑤

Casa Museo La Chascona

🅟 G6 🅰 Fernando Márquez de la Plata 192
Ⓜ Baquedano 🕙 10am–6pm Tue–Sun (Jan & Feb: to 7pm)
🌐 fundacionneruda.org

Built in 1953 on a steep slope of Cerro San Cristóbal in the Bellavista neighborhood, the entrancing Museo La Chascona is one of 20th-century poet Pablo Neruda's three homes. The home was named La Chascona (Woman with Unruly Hair) for Matilde Urrutia, Neruda's secret mistress, who lived here alone for a year; they eventually married in

1966. Neruda eschewed many of his architect's designs for the home, and instead used a deeply personal and notably whimsical layout, filled with winding staircases and secret doors. His love of the sea is evident in the house's maritime-influenced details, such as porthole windows, a dining area that was once fronted by a stream to give the illusion of sailing, and a living room that resembles a lighthouse. The interiors exhibit Neruda's vast collection of art and artifacts, bought during his travels around the world.

Neruda was both a friend of former president Salvador Allende and a Communist. After the Pinochet-led coup of 1973, military vandals damaged the house, and while it was declared that the poet's funeral would not be a public event, Chileans took to the streets in his memory nonetheless. The Fundación Pablo Neruda later restored La Chascona to its original state. It now contains household items rescued from the house, as well as furniture and personal objects from Neruda's office in France, where he served as ambassador between 1970 and 1973. The library holds Neruda's famous Nobel Prize medal along with various letters, photographs, books, and other publications. Audio-guided tours are available on a first-come, first-served basis.

↑ Street art by Gabriel Maulen outside Casa Museo La Chascona

PABLO NERUDA

Chile's most beloved poet was born Neftalí Ricardo Reyes Basoalto in 1904 *(p38)*. He took his pen name from Czech poet Jan Neruda, in part to hide his earliest works from his father, who did not consider writing a suitable career choice. Neruda found early success with the collection *Twenty Poems of Love and a Song of Despair*, after which he undertook a series of diplomatic posts abroad. He wrote his opus *Canto General* in 1950, and won the Nobel Prize for Literature in 1971, but died two years later.

6

La Vega

E6 Dávila Baeza 700
Cal y Canto, Patronato
4am–7:30pm Mon–Sat,
9am–2:30pm Sun
vegacentral.cl

Located just across from
Mercado Central *(p81)*, La
Vega is the city's principal
fruit and vegetable market
and a must-see for foodies.
Amid its chaos of crates and
stalls, and the buying and
negotiating, La Vega offers
an earthy and colorful
experience. The market
occupies a purpose-built
structure that covers several
city blocks and is surrounded
by 100 or more vendors
selling items such as shoes,
electronics, and pet food. At
the center are the food stalls
that sell inexpensive meals
such as chicken soup *cazuela*.
This is an ideal place to look
out for local fruits such as
chirimoya (a custard
apple), *tuna* cactus fruit, and
lucuma, a butterscotch-
flavored fruit used in desserts
such as ice cream.

7

Barrio Patronato

E6 Between Loreto,
Bellavista, Dominica and
Recoleta sts Patronato
Shops: 10am–7:30pm
Mon–Fri, 10am–5:30pm Sat
tiendaspatronato.cl

Occupying over a dozen blocks,
Barrio Patronato is a bustling
shopping area dominated
by clothing stores
and small

eateries operated in large part
by immigrants from Korea,
China, and the Middle East.
During the Colonial period, the
barrio was a poor residential
neighborhood. It was then
called La Chimba, which means
Other Side of the River. The
area continues to be populated
by the working class and many
of the neighborhood's original
adobe houses still stand.

During the late 19th
century, Arab immigrants
from Syria, Lebanon, and
especially Palestine settled in
the Patronato neighborhood.
They established the city's
principal textile commercial
center here, selling imported
clothing and fabrics, as there
was little national production
of textiles at the time. Today,
Patronato heaves with
more than 10,000

Creative shops,
bars, and
↓ restaurants in
Patio Bellavista

shoppers per day, who pack the streets searching for T-shirts, shoes, ball gowns, suits, and trendy clothing at dirt-cheap prices.

8

Plaza Camilo Mori

📍 G6 🏠 Constitución, esq Antonia López de Bello 🚇 Baquedano

Located in the heart of the bohemian neighborhood of Bellavista, Plaza Camilo Mori is named for the well-known Chilean painter whose house and studio stood here. The triangular plaza is dominated by the Castillo Lehuedé, a striking mansion popularly known as the Casa Rosa (Red House) that is now a boutique

> 💬 **INSIDER TIP**
> **Walking Street Art**
>
> Bellavista is well known for its impressive array of street art. Several agencies offer guided walking tours that take in some of the finest examples, including Santiago Street Art Tours (*www. stgostreetart.com*).

hotel. This beautiful stone edifice was built in 1923 by architect Federico Bieregel for entrepreneur Pedro Lehuedé. The plaza is also home to trendy boutiques and restaurants, as well as the Centro Mori, which hosts offbeat theater performances.

9

Patio Bellavista

📍 G6 🏠 Constitución 30 🚇 Baquedano 🕐 10am-2am Sun-Tue, 10am-3am Wed, 10am-4am Thu-Sat 🌐 patiobellavista.cl

Inaugurated in 2006 as an urban renewal project, the charming Patio Bellavista is a large collection of shops and restaurants that are spread around an interior square. This central plaza was originally a *cité* – a housing facility for the working class in the 19th century. Today, well restored, Patio Bellavista features over 80 stores selling high-end *artesanía*, or crafts, around two dozen restaurants and bars, bookstores, art galleries, jewelry shops, as well as the boutique Hotel del Patio. For those souvenir shopping, this is an excellent place to pick up some jewelry featuring lapis lazuli – a blue, semi-precious

TOP 3 **LGBT+ VENUES IN BELLAVISTA**

Fausto
🏠 Avenida Santa María 832
🌐 fausto.cl
A popular club that's been running for over 30 years. Expect great live music and a slightly more mature crowd.

Xlimon
🏠 Dardignac 142
One of the few local joints open throughout the week, this place has inexpensive drinks and a wide-ranging playlist.

Illuminati
🏠 Antonia López de Bello 131
This cool and welcoming bar-cum-club draws a varied crowd, and is a great place for drinks and a dance.

stone. Pretty pieces are sold by many of the shops and stalls in Bellavista.

There are a number of excellent outdoor cafés here too, which are popular with both locals and visitors. Patio Bellavista also hosts a variety of open-air cultural programs that include dance performances, live music shows, as well as rotating exhibitions of paintings and photography.

10

Parque de las Esculturas

📍J5 🏠Avenida Santa María 2205, between Avenue Pedro de Valdivia and Padre Letelier 📞(02) 2335-1832 🚇Los Leones 🕐10am-7:30pm daily

Laid out after a massive flooding of Río Mapocho in 1982, Parque de las Esculturas was a creative response to the need to reinforce this area of the river shore. The park was landscaped between 1986 and 1988 by architect Germán Bannen, and offers views of the snowcapped Andes. Serene walking paths meander through the area, which is dotted with some 40 sculptures by Chilean and international artists, including *Pachamama* by Marta Olvín, *La Pareja* by Juan Egneau, and *Conjunto Escultorico* by Federico Assler.

> **Serene walking paths meander through the area, which is dotted with some 40 sculptures by Chilean and international artists.**

11

Casa de la Ciudadanía Montecarmelo

📍G6 🏠Bellavista 594 🚇Salvador 🕐9am-7pm Tue-Fri 🌐cultura providencia.cl

Barrio Bellavista's primary cultural center, the Casa de la Ciudadanía Montecarmelo, is located in the building of the former Montecarmelo Convent. In the late-19th century the covent belonged to the nuns of Carmelitas de Santa Teresa – an order that was known for its humility, with its members being referred to as *descalzos* (barefoot). The convent's doors reopened as a beautifully renovated cultural space in 1991, and today the center – operated by the Corporación Cultural de Providencia – conducts workshops and classes in music, photography, art, and dance. There is an impressive year-round calendar of concerts, cinematic events, and theater productions that take place on an outdoor stage, surrounded by the picturesque brick walls of the old convent. Montecarmelo also provides a place for Chilean authors to showcase new works of fiction and poetry.

12

Parque Balmaceda

📍G7 🏠Avenida Providencia, between Baquedano and Del Arzobispo 🚇Baquedano, Salvador

Built in 1927 following the canalization of Río Mapocho, Parque Balmaceda is named for José Manuel Balmaceda, Chile's former president and a central figure in the country's short-lived Civil War of 1891. A statue commemorating this national hero stands at the western end of the park.

Parque Balmaceda's central attraction is the new Fuente Bicentenario – a fountain shooting out graceful arcs of water that are lit up at night in a rainbow of colors. Standing at the foot of the fountain is the Monumento de Aviación, an abstract sculpture installed during the Pinochet dictatorship.

The Café Literario, located at the center of the park, opened in 2001 as the city's first literary café, and is well stocked with newspapers and books. An enjoyable place for a stroll, Balmaceda attracts locals from the Providencia and Bellavista neighborhoods, and from downtown Santiago.

A sculpture in the Parque de las Esculturas, with the Gran Torre Santiago glinting behind

13 Museo de Tajamares

📍 G7 🏛 Avenida Providencia 222 ☎ (02) 2223-2700 Ⓜ Baquedano 🕐 10am–5pm Tue-Sat

Santiago's *tajamares* were a complex series of underground dikes and brick walls that held back Río Mapocho during the 18th century, as the river is prone to periodic flooding. The mortar used for their construction was a mixture of egg white, limestone, and sand called *cal y canto*. Designed by master architect Joaquin Toesca, the tajamares protected 33 blocks and prevented the city from flooding until the modern canal system was developed in the late 19th century.

A portion of Santiago's old *tajamares* was rediscovered during excavations in the Providencia neighborhood in the late 1970s. The Museo de Tajamares, created in 1980, features well-preserved examples of these archaic thick walls and arched dikes. The museum suffered considerable damage during the 2010 earthquake, which led to years of renovations, and has also been subject to severe flood damage in both 2016 and 2019.

14 🍴 🍽 Providencia

📍 J6 🏛 Ave Providencia Ⓜ Baquedano, Salvador, Manuel Montt, Pedro de Valdivia and Los Leones

The pleasant, leafy district of Providencia is a good place for visitors to base themselves. Although there is only a handful of tourist attractions, there are many mid-range hotels, an array of cafés and restaurants, and a lively nightlife scene (although you're advised to skip the bars and clubs in the rather tacky Suecia neighborhood). Good transport connections also make it easy to travel to the rest of the city.

Relaxing at a café in the lovely neighborhood of Providencia

EAT

Galindo

Head here for rustic Chilean staples such as *pastel de choclo* (sweetcorn-topped pie).

📍 G6 🏛 Dardignac 98 ☎ (02) 2777-0116 🕐 Sun

$$⑤

Etniko

A swish spot with influences from all over Asia and South America, but the sushi is the real stand out. Etniko turns into a bar-club later on.

📍 G6 🏛 Constitución 172 🕐 Sun 🌐 etniko.cl

$$$

El Huerto

One of the city's best vegetarian restaurants, with plenty of vegan options and a tempting array of desserts.

📍 J5 🏛 Orrego Luco 054 🌐 elhuerto.cl

$$⑤

DRINK

Baco Vino y Bistro

A cross between a wine bar and a bistro, Baco serves Chilean and international wines by the glass, as well as French-inspired food.

📍 J5 🏛 Nueva de Lyon 113 🌐 elbaco.cl

La Casa en el Aire

Taking its name from one of Pablo Neruda's verses, The House in the Air is an appealing place for a drink.

📍 G6 🏛 Antonia López de Bello 125 🌐 lacasaenelaire.cl

Shopping along the tree-lined Pueblo Los Dominicos ↑

15 🍴 🥤 🛍

Pueblo Los Dominicos

📍M4 🏠 Ave Apoquindo 9085 🚇 Los Dominicos 🕐 10:30am–7pm daily 🌐 plosdominicos.cl

One of Santiago's best shopping areas for local arts and crafts, the Pueblo Los Dominicos is a rustic complex housed within the former grounds of the neighboring Iglesia Los Dominicos. In 1982, the *pueblo* was expanded and landscaped to resemble a Chilean Colonial village with whitewashed, low-slung adobe buildings. The area was originally a Mapuche settlement headed by chief Apoquindo, whose name was given to the grand avenue that ends here.

Today, the *pueblo* offers 160 small shops to independent artisans for selling wares such as ceramics, leather goods, jewelry, folk art, textiles, and even animals such as rabbits and birds. The shops double as workshops, allowing visitors a glimpse of the artistic process and a chance to interact with the artisans.

The ambience is truly idyllic, enhanced by trickling creeks and the sound of flute music wafting through the village. Saturday and Sunday are the best days to come here, when the Iglesia Los Dominicos holds Mass. The church is

featured on the Chilean 2,000 peso bill and is a historical monument that provided shelter to revolutionaries during the nation's battle for independence in the 1810s.

16 ⚡ 🎭 🍴

Museo de la Moda

📍M1 🏠 Avenida Vitacura 4562 🔒 For restoration 🌐 museodelamoda.cl

Built to honor a family legacy and love of fashion, the Museo de la Moda was established in 2007 by Juan Yarur, who converted his parents' Modernist home into one of the most important fashion museums in the world. Yarur scoured the globe for a decade in order to compile a nearly encyclopedic collection of more than 10,000 pieces of clothing. These range from the 18th century to modern day, from classic couture gowns by Chanel and Lanvin to modern frocks by Gaultier and celebrity memorabilia such as Madonna's cone bra and John Lennon's jacket from 1966. The utterly stylish museum rotates its collections in themes, with a special wing devoted to tennis, Yarur's sport of choice. The museum is also a tour through his family home, preserved as it was in the 1960s and 1970s and with

clothing once owned by Yarur's mother, Raquel Bascuñán, on display. There is also a restaurant occupying the family's former garage.

17

Gran Torre Santiago

📍K4 🏠 Ave Andres Bello 🚇 Tobalaba 🌐 skycostanera.cl

This is the tallest building in Chile – and in South America – at 984 ft (300m) high. It was designed by the Argentinian architect César Pelli (of Malaysia's Petronas Towers fame) and can be seen from almost every point in the city. On a clear day there are panoramic views of the capital and the Andes from the Sky Costanera viewing platform.

Did You Know?

The Sky Costanera within the soaring Gran Torre is the highest observatory in Latin America.

Barrio Vitacura

◉L2 🌐vitacura.cl

Named for the Mapuche chief Butacura (Big Rock) who lived here with his clan at the time of the conquistadores' arrival, Barrio Vitacura was expropriated in the mid-1500s as an *asentamiento* – Spanish settlements on indigenous land and developed into haciendas.

Vitacura lies under the shadow of Cerro Manquehue, which is a popular day-hike. Today, it is the residential neighborhood of the affluent, characterized by towering condominiums and upscale stores and restaurants.

The borough's sparkling new municipality building is part of a colossal urban renewal project that includes Parque Bicentenario, a grassy expanse with lagoons and trails that has renovated the banks of Río Mapocho. It is the staging center for outdoor festivals, especially wine galas and artisan fairs, and an important institution here is the headquarters of CEPAL, the Spanish acronym

GREAT VIEW
Sky-High Sips

For some of the finest views in the city - with drinks and music to match - head to the rooftop bar at the W hotel *(www.marriott. com)* in Las Condes.

for the United Nation's Economic Commission for Latin America.

Barrio Vitacura is also Santiago's epicenter of high-brow art galleries, with more than two dozen venues highlighting Chile's finest artists. The best-known is Galería Animal, the city's first cutting-edge gallery, which offers an extensive range of Chilean art, and frequently rotates temporary exhibits. Several heavyweight galleries are open to the general public, including the transnational AMS Marlborough Chile, Isabel Aninat (known especially for

new talent), Arte Espacio, and Patricia Ready.

Las Condes

◉M4 🏛Ave Apoquindo & Ave Las Condes Ⓜ️El Golf, Alcántara, Tobalaba, & Escuela Militar

East of Providencia *(p109)* is Las Condes, a large, upscale area home to many of the city's wealthier residents, foreign embassies, and the offices of major Chilean corporations. Tourist attractions are thin on the ground, but there are many four- and five-star hotels, plenty of good (though pricey) restaurants and bars, and several shopping malls. Within Las Condes and bordering Providencia, the micro-neighborhood of El Golf is often referred to as "Sanhattan," thanks to its glitzy skyscrapers and North American feel.

↑ Gran Torre Santiago, towering above the skyscrapers of the Las Condes neighborhood

EXPERIENCE CHILE

Hiking across the Perito Moreno Glacier

Central Valley...................................114

Norte Grande
and Norte Chico................................150

Lake District and Chiloé....................194

Northern Patagonia.........................228

Southern Patagonia
and Tierra del Fuego.......................248

Easter Island and
Robinson Crusoe Island...................264

CENTRAL VALLEY

Inhabited since pre-Columbian times, Central Valley is considered Chile's oldest region and a bastion of its traditions. Its original settlers were the Mapuche, who resisted assimilation into the Incan Empire. The Spanish arrived in 1541, founding Santiago at the foot of the Andes, Valparaíso on the coast, and, later, towns across the valley floor. Central Valley became the center of Colonial Chile: the womb from which the country's north and south grew, its wealthiest area, and the political hub. The hacienda system, by which old families controlled vast tracts of land, evolved around Central Valley, spawning Chile's legendary *huaso* (cowboys). Mining of silver, nitrates, and copper brought later wealth.

Agriculture, in particular viticulture, remains the greatest source of income, the dry climate and long summers making the region ideal for fine wine production of fine wines. The valley's world-class wineries , open for tours and tastings, are part of a tourism sector that offers an array of other other activities to locals and visitors alike. The cities still have well-preserved haciendas and mines, and towns full of Colonial charm.

CENTRAL VALLEY

Must Sees

① Valparaíso
② Casa Museo Isla Negra

Experience More

③ Casablanca Valley
④ Viña del Mar
⑤ Sewell
⑥ Cartagena
⑦ Quintay
⑧ Algarrobo
⑨ Cachagua
⑩ Papudo
⑪ Zapallar
⑫ Los Andes
⑬ Cristo Redentor
⑭ Portillo
⑮ Termas de Jahuel
⑯ Rancagua
⑰ Parque Nacional La Campana
⑱ El Teniente
⑲ Valle de Cachapoal
⑳ Termas de Cauquenes
㉑ Cajón del Maipo
㉒ Hacienda Los Lingues
㉓ Reserva Nacional Río de los Cipreses
㉔ Valle de Curicó
㉕ Santa Cruz
㉖ Pichilemu
㉗ Termas de Panimávida
㉘ Maule
㉙ Reserva Nacional Altos de Lircay
㉚ Parque Nacional Radal Siete Tazas
㉛ Lago Vichuquén
㉜ Chillán
㉝ Nevados de Chillán
㉞ Saltos del Laja
㉟ Concepción
㊱ Parque Nacional Laguna del Laja
㊲ Lota
㊳ Tomé

CENTRAL
VALLEY

*Pacific
Ocean*

Río del Sobrante

Petorca

Ingeniero Santa María

5

La Ligua

PAPUDO 10
ZAPALLAR 11
CACHAGUA 9

VALPARAÍSO

TERMAS DE JAHUEL 15

San Felipe

**PARQUE
NACIONAL
LA CAMPANA**

PORTILLO 14 13 **CRISTO
REDENTOR**

Quintero

12 **LOS ANDES**

60

Concón

17

57

VIÑA DEL MAR 4

Quilpué

Colina

VALPARAÍSO 1

El Colorado

QUINTAY 7

**CASABLANCA
VALLEY**

3

Curacaví

ALGARROBO 8

68

Santiago
International Airport

Santiago

CASA MUSEO ISLA NEGRA 2 6 **CARTAGENA**

San Antonio

78

Talagante

Puente
Alto

25

**CAJÓN DEL
MAIPO** 21

Melipilla

San José de Maipo

66

Paine

Navidad

METROPOLITAN

Vila Ahué

SEWELL 5

Litueche

Río Rapel

5

18 **EL TENIENTE**

RANCAGUA 16

20 **TERMAS DE
CAUQUENES**

VALLE DE CACHAPOAL 19

PICHILEMU 26

Rengo

66

LIBERTADOR

23 **RESERVA NACIONAL
RÍO DE LOS CIPRESES**

Cahuil

San Fernando

Paredones

**SANTA
CRUZ** 25

22 **HACIENDA
LOS LINGUES**

Chimbarongo

Volcán Tinguiririca
14,107 ft (4,299 m)

El Sosneado

LAGO VICHUQUÉN 31

Teno

24 **VALLE DE CURICÓ**

Licantén

Curicó

Los Quenes

Molina

Huaquén

MAULE

5

Lagunas
de Teno

40

Carrizal

Cumpeo

Malargüe

Constitución

Talca

**PARQUE NACIONAL
RADAL SIETE TAZAS**

MAULE 28

30

Lago
Colbún

29 **RESERVA NACIONAL
ALTOS DE LIRCAY**

Chanco

San Javier

Peluhue

126

Sauzal

27 **TERMAS DE PANIMÁVIDA**

145

Cauquenes

Linares

Cerro Campanario
13,284 ft (4,048 m)

Bardas
Blancas

Cobquecura

126

115

Quirihue

128

Parral

Camelia

Río Maule

Laguna
del Maule

ARGENTINA

Vegas de Itata

San Carlos

5

Coelemu

40

TOMÉ 38

152

CHILLÁN 32

San Fabián de Alico

Talcahuano

**Carriel Sur
International
Airport**

Pinto

Barrancas

CONCEPCIÓN 35

Bulnes

Recinto

Chiguayante

146

BÍO BÍO

**NEVADOS
DE CHILLÁN** 33

Andacollo

Coronel

Pemuco

N59

Volcán Chillán
10,538 ft (3,211 m)

Chos Malal

LOTA 37

Yumbel

Yungay

Polcura

Río Laja

Laguna de
la Laja

Llico

156

**SALTOS
DEL LAJA** 34

Antuca

Arauco

160

Laja

5

Los Ángeles

36 **PARQUE NACIONAL
LAGUNA DEL LAJA**

40

Lebu

Nacimiento

Santa Bárbara

Los Álamos

Río Bío Bío

Mulchén

Ralco

Cañete

Cayucupil

Río Renaico

Volcán Copahue
9,776 ft (2,979 m)

Quidico

Lago
Lanalhue

Lago
Lleulleu

**LAKE DISTRICT
AND CHILOÉ**
p194

0 kilometers   60

0 miles   60

N
↑

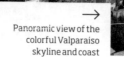

Panoramic view of the colorful Valparaíso skyline and coast

❶
VALPARAÍSO

🅐B7 🚗75 miles (120 km) NW of Santiago 🚌🚐🚢 ℹ️Plaza Sottomayor 233, piso 1; 9am–6pm Mon–Fri, 9am–5pm Sat; www.ciudaddevalparaiso.cl

Founded in 1543, the city of Valparaíso covers over 45 steep hills, each a jumble of winding streets lined with colorful houses, post-Colonial edifices, and 19th-century museums. It is a UNESCO World Heritage Site, and much of its rich architecture is beautifully preserved.

① Ⓜ
Edificio de la Aduana

🏠Plaza Wheelwright 144 🕘9am–5pm Mon–Fri 🌐aduana.cl

Built in 1855, the pink-painted Edificio de la Aduana (Customs Building) is a rare example of post-Colonial architecture. The institution's most famous employee was

> 💬 INSIDER TIP
> **City Tour**
>
> For an inexpensive sightseeing tour of the city, catch public bus "0" (also known as the "612"), which takes a scenic route from the port and winds its way up to La Sebastiana.

the Nicaraguan Modernist poet Rubén Darío, who worked here in the 1880s while writing his seminal work, *Azul* (1888). Guided tours visit a small museum, which displays objects from the building's history. Edificio de la Aduana overlooks Plaza Wheelwright, named for American industrialist William Wheelwright, who played a major role in building Chile's railroads and steamship fleet. His statue, raised in 1877, adorns the plaza.

②
Plaza Echaurren

🏠Calle Cochrane 253, esq Calle Serrano

The birthplace and historic heart of Valparaíso, Plaza Echaurren marks the spot where Spanish explorer Juan de Saavedra first made landfall in 1543. Today, it is fronted by crumbling yet elegant mid-19th-century structures such as the beautiful old market building of Mercado Puerto.

Overlooking the plaza is the Iglesia de la Matriz, notable for its octagonal steeple. This edifice was built in 1837 on the site of the city's first church.

(3) 🏛️ 🅿️ 💻 🛍️

Museo Marítimo Nacional

📍 Paseo 21 de Mayo 45, Cerro Artillería
🕐 10am–5:30pm Tue–Sun
🌐 museomar.cl

Chile's excellent Museo Marítimo Nacional is housed in a building dating from 1893, which offers great views of the city from its front lawns. It has 17 exhibition rooms, including salons dedicated to Chile's foremost naval heroes – Lord Thomas Cochrane, Arturo Prat, and Bernardo O'Higgins – and to Chile's key 19th-century naval battles. Exhibits include antique sabres and swords, pocket revolvers, bayonets, military plans, and models of battleships. Items salvaged from Prat's schooner, *Esmeralda*, such as the clock which stopped at the precise time the ship sank during the Battle of Iquique (1879), are also displayed.

The museum also has an interesting display that explores the remarkable rescue of 33 San José miners who were trapped underground for 69 days in 2010. The story of these miners was widely covered on international news and watched around the world.

Children will also love the large replica pirate ship in the Sala Hermandad de la Costa. Surrounding the ship are flags from countries all around the world.

THE TROLEBUSES

Valparaíso's fleet of electric *trolebuses* was imported from the US between 1946 and 1952, and includes the world's oldest trolleybuses in service. Trolleybus systems had deteriorated under the Pinochet regime, but in 1982 city businessmen acquired and renovated them. Today, they ply between Avenida Argentina and Edificio de la Aduana. Low on noise and air pollution, they offer an easy and charming way to see the city.

FUNICULARS OF VALPARAÍSO

Valparaíso's funiculars are the cheapest, easiest, and most fun way of traveling between the city's residential hill-sides and the port and financial districts of its El Plan (Lower Town). The funiculars were introduced between 1883 and 1912, and only eight are currently still in service. They rattle up and down Valparaíso's steep hills and spill out on to dramatic promenades with beautiful city and ocean vistas. Many also access historic sights and tourist attractions.

Towering far above the southern end of Plaza Sotomayor is the unique and elaborate facade of the Neo-Gothic Comandancia Jefe de la Armada. Built in 1910, its design was inspired by the Hôtel de Ville in Paris, and its interiors were multi-functional, serving both as a summer residence for various of Chile's former presidents and as the office of many of the city's mayors and regional governors. Expro-priated by the Chilean navy in the mid-1970s, it has since functioned as Chile's naval headquarters.

The Ministry of Culture, a Modernist building which dates back to1936, is open daily to the public and hosts various displays and art exhibitions. Adjacent to this edifice, the Compañía de Bomberos, which was built in 1851,is the site of the oldest volunteer fire service in Latin America, still helping across Valparaíso to the present day.

④ 🍴 Bar Inglés

🏠 Cochrane 851 ☎ (032) 2232874 🕐 1-9pm Mon-Sat

Bar Inglés evokes Valparaíso's halcyon days as the greatest port-city in the South Pacific. The bar was founded by English immigrants in 1926 and was saved from closure in 2017. It has since been refurbished and the interior remains in a traditional English style, with its familiar mix of polished wood, kitsch British memorabilia, intriguing model ships, and football pennants. A five-minute walk leads to **Bar La Playa**, which offers a bohemian vibe that is popular with both locals and tourists.

Bar La Playa

🏠 Serrano 567 ☎ (032) 2232874 🕐 11am-10pm, daily

⑤ Plaza Sotomayor

🏠 Calle Cochrane, esq Avenida Tomás Ramos

Valparaíso's main square is the stately Plaza Sotomayor, a large open space that holds parades on Glorias Navales or Navy Day *(see p41)*. The plaza is centered around the Monumento a los Heroes de Iquique, raised in memory of the crew of the *Esmeralda*, killed in the 1879 Battle of Iquique. The battle saw *Esmeralda*, the Chilean navy's oldest ship, fight the Peruvian fleet's most powerful vessel, *Huascar*, for 4 hours.

Although the former was sunk, and her captain, Arturo Prat, killed, the battle was a turning point in the War of the Pacific *(p46)*. Prat's bronze effigy crowns the monument and his body also lies buried in a crypt here.

> The plaza is centered around the Monumento a los Heroes de Iquique, raised in memory of the crew of the Esmeralda, killed in the 1879 Battle of Iquique.

People resting on benches in the vast Plaza Sotomayor ↑

⑥
Palacio de la Justicia

Plaza Justicia **To the public**

Built in 1939, the Palacio de la Justicia is Valparaíso's appeals court. The imposing edifice has a sober, rectilinear facade, with a 10-ft- (3-m-) high statue of Justitia (Lady Justice) at its entrance. The figure is curiously anomalous in that she wears no blindfold, her customary symbol of objectivity, and her scales of truth dangle forlornly at her side, rather than at the end of her outstretched arm. According to legend, it was an angry merchant who had the statue placed here to protest against a perceived injustice, though the statue has been subject to many different myths.

⑦
Muelle Prat

Avenida Errázuriz, in front of Plaza Sotomayor

A bustling and busy pier, Muelle Prat is the departure point for half-hour tours of Valparaíso's bay by water-taxi. Vendors on the pier are set up with various offerings, including small pieces of jewelry, face painting, and temporary tattoos. There are dozens of bobbing *lanchas* (small and often colorful boats) that are dwarfed by the much larger cargo ships in the area. The bobbing ships are often used to call out the departure times for the next tour that is leaving the pier. There are plenty of tours available, which offer tremendous views of Valparaíso's hillsides, densely built-up with rows of brightly colored houses. Boats wind a sinuous trail between gigantic cruise ships docked in the bay and the Chilean navy's battleships stationed offshore, before stretching out onto the open water. If you are very lucky, you may even get a close-up view of a sea lion colony. The port has a large amount of history and remains a significant and active commercial port today.

EAT

Amor Porteño
Come to this charming Argentine-style ice-cream parlour and coffee shop for a sundae, churros, or a *medialuna* (a sweet, doughy croissant).

Almirante Montt 418, Cerro Concepción
(032) 2216253

$$$

Pasta e Vino
An excellent Italian restaurant with eight different varieties of gnocchi on the menu. Make sure you book a table in advance.

Templeman 352, Cerro Concepción **pastaevinoristorante.cl**

$$$

Le Filou de Montpellier
This French restaurant serves excellent, moderately-priced food. Typical offerings include French onion soup, homemade pâté, and moules mariniére.

Almirante Montt 382, Cerro Alegre **(032) 2224663**

$$$

Ápice
This swish restaurant has a creative, regularly changing menu. Expect dishes like octopus with a chorizo emulsion, and oysters with goat's cheese. Reservations are required.

Lautaro Rosas 343, Valparaíso, Cerro Alegre
(032) 2089737

$$$

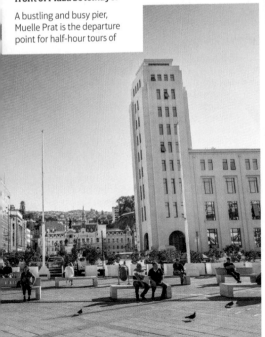

STAY

Palacio Astoreca

This historic hotel is the result of a Francophile union of two former residences. The rooms and restaurant all feature contemporary decor.

📍 Montealegre 149, Cerro Alegre
🌐 hotelpalacioastoreca. com

$ $ $

Hotel Somerscales

Experience history at this boutique hotel, which was once home to British-Chilean artist Thomas Somerscales.

📍 San Enrique 446, Cerro Alegre
🌐 hotelsomerscales.cl

$ $ $

Hostel Voyage

An attractive hostel in a great location. It offers dorms and private rooms, plus communal areas and regular film screenings.

📍 Leighton 229, Cerro Alegre
🌐 hostelvoyage.cl

$ $ $

⑧

Calle Prat

A narrow thoroughfare through the city's financial district, Calle Prat links Plaza Sotomayor and the monumental 1929 Reloj Turri (Turri Clock Tower), the city's Big Ben. Looming over both sides of the road are grand buildings of stone and black marble, constructed at the turn of the 20th century. Many include columns and pediments. Among these is the old Bank of London building, today the Banco de Chile (No. 698), which houses a monument built to commemorate the British soldiers that were killed in World War I. Another evocative edifice here is Valparaíso's stock exchange, La Bolsa de Valores, the oldest stock exchange in South America. The old bidding wheel still stands inside the building's cavernous, domed interior.

⑨

Plaza Aníbal Pinto

📍 End of Calle Esmeralda

Uniting Valparaíso's financial district and the commercial downtown area, Plaza Aníbal Pinto is a small, chaotic square fronted by beautiful buildings and the old Bar Cinzano. A sepia-tinted bar, the café was founded in 1896 and features live tango shows. The plaza is a busy spot, right on the edge of the historic district. On one side is the striking Librería Ivens building. Founded in 1891, it is one of the city's oldest bookshops. At the entrance to this building is

←

The fountain sculpture of Neptune in Anibal Pinto Square

The attractive exterior of Palacio Baburizza, now a historic monument ↑

the plaza's attractive public artwork – a street fountain that was sculpted as Neptune in 1892.

⑩

Calle Esmeralda

An extension of Calle Prat, Calle Esmeralda starts at the Turri Clock Tower, which is close to Ascensor Concepción (p130), and ends at Plaza Ánibal Pinto. The street's most beautiful construction is the El Mercurio building, which is home to the popular El Mercurio de Valparaíso newspaper. The ornate exterior of the edifice is crowned by an incredible bronze statue of Mercury pointing skyward. Adjacent to El Mercurio, a stairway climbs up to the mystical Cueva Chivito, a natural rock cave, which according to local folklore and legend was formed by and once inhabited by the devil.

⑪ Palacio Baburizza

🏛 Paseo Yugoslavo s/n, Cerro Alegre 🚠 Ascensor El Peral ⏰ 10am–6pm Tue–Sun 🌐 museobaburizza.cl

An elegant Art Nouveau mansion, the Palacio Baburizza was constructed in 1916 for Italian saltpeter tycoon Ottorino Zanelli. It was subsequently purchased by Pascual Baburizza, a Croatian immigrant and nitrates magnate, in 1925. Today, the structure houses Valparaíso's fine arts museum, whose displays include the Baburizza family's personal collection of 19th- and 20th-century European art.

The palace is situated on the summit of Cerro Alegre, from where it overlooks the lovely Paseo Yugoslavo. A leafy promenade and viewing point, the street offers breath-taking vistas of neighboring hillsides, the city's port, financial districts, and the blue Bahía de Valparaíso.

Now reopened after having been restored to something that perhaps even exceeds its original elegance, the museum features a new wing that showcases Chilean landscapes as depicted by expatriate painters. It also boasts original furnishings and an extra-ordinary Art Deco bathroom. The collection has been being gathered since 1895, and is considered to be one of the country's most important. It includes works by national and European artists. The garden annex includes a café that serves snacks and drinks and a museum shop.

⑫ Paseo Gervasoni

🏛 Cerro Concepción 🚠 Ascensor Concepción

Spilling out on to Paseo Gervasoni at the top of Cerro Concepción, this cobbled promenade edged with wildflowers affords splendid views across the Bahía de Valparaíso to Viña del Mar in the north. Along the street are the elegant Café Turri *(p293)*, the old Danish consulate building dating from 1848, and **Casa Mirador de Lukas**. The last is a 1900 house with a museum dedicated to the life and works of Chile's best-loved cartoonist, Renzo Antonio Pecchenino Raggi (1934–88), popularly known as Lukas.

Casa Mirador de Lukas

♿🅿👤♿ 🏛 Paseo Gervasoni 448, Cerro Concepción ⏰ 10:30am–6:30pm Tue–Fri, 11am–7pm Sat & Sun 🌐 lukas.cl

Did You Know?

The Valparaíso Painting Museum was destroyed in the 1906 earthquake.

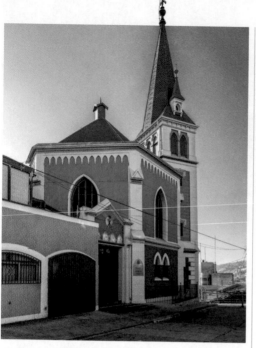

↑ The striking Iglesia Luterana de la Santa Cruz with its towering steeple

> **Inside, the nave fills with natural light and a sculpture of Christ on the cross, which is carved from a single pine trunk, hangs above the altar.**

Concepción and is visible from the city's lower sections. Inside, the nave fills with natural light and a sculpture of Christ on the cross, which is carved from a single pine trunk, hangs above the altar. A grand organ, which was brought over from England in 1884, stands opposite the altar.

---

⑮ Cementerios Católico and Disidentes

🏛 Dinamarca s/n, Cerro Panteón Cementerio Católica: 🕐8:30am-5:30pm daily Cementerio Disidentes: 🕐9am-1pm, 3-5:30pm Mon-Sat, 9am-1pm Sun

Spectacularly located high up on an overhanging hillside, the Cementerio Católico and Cementerio Disidentes are poignant evocations of this port-city's halcyon days in the 1800s as a melting pot of different cultures and creeds. The Cementerio Disidentes is the site of the simple, sometimes austere, graves of the city's non-Catholic communities, including American Mormons, English Anglicans, and German

⑬ Iglesia Anglicana San Pablo

🏛 Pilcomayo 566, Cerro Concepción 🕐10:30am-1pm Tue-Fri 🌐saintpaulchile.cl

The Neo-Gothic Iglesia Anglicana San Pablo was built in 1858 by British engineer William Lloyd. This church was established by Valparaíso's English community, but only after the city's Catholic archbishop imposed many conditions on what he considered a temple to a rival faith. Among the most curious was that this church's doors be smaller than those of the city's Catholic churches – and to this day visitors enter not via a grand portal, but by one of the two small side doors. The church's simple stone and wood interior houses a pipe organ, which was donated in memory of Britain's Queen Victoria in 1903.

⑭ Iglesia Luterana de la Santa Cruz

🏛 Abtao 689, Cerro Concepción 🕐10am-1pm Mon-Fri 🌐iluterana.cl

Built by the city's German community in 1898, the Iglesia Luterana de la Santa Cruz was South America's first Protestant church to be allowed a steeple and bell tower. Its beautifully austere facade tapers upward toward a slender, 115-ft (35-m) high steeple, which crowns Cerro

---

EL MERCURIO DE VALPARAÍSO

The oldest newspaper in continuous circulation in the entire Spanish-speaking world, *El Mercurio de Valparaíso* was founded in 1827 by Chilean journalist Pedro Felix Vicuña and the American typographer Thomas Well. Since the 1880s, it has been under the uninterrupted stewardship of Chile's eminent Edwards-Ross family, who continue to aspire to the newspaper's founding ideal that it be "adequate enough to moderate the extreme passions that divide men."

DRINK

Bar Cinzano

A Valpo institution, Bar Cinzano draws a loyal local crowd. The evening atmosphere is a real attraction – especially when there's live tango music on Fridays and Saturdays.

🏠 Plaza Aníbal Pinto 1182

Lutherans. Many of the gravestones are engraved with tales of war and shipwreck. Opposite the Cementerio Disidentes, a grand portal enters the Cementerio Católico, otherwise known as Cementerio N°1. Valparaíso's most illustrious sons and daughters lie here in grand, marbled mausoleums. Among the luminaries buried are members of the Edwards-Ross family, owners of the *El Mercurio de Valparaíso* newspaper; José Francisco Vergara, founder of the town Viña del Mar; and Renzo Pecchenino, a popular Chilean cartoonist.

⑯ 🏃 🖥 🛍

La Sebastiana

🏠 Ferrari 692, Cerro Florida 🚡 Ascensor Espiritu Santo 🕙 10am-6pm Tue-Sun 🌐 fundacion neruda.org

A must-see for devotees of Pablo Neruda (*p38*), La Sebastiana is the last of three houses that were bought by the poet in Chile. Neruda and two of his friends acquired the shell of this house in 1961 and named it for its architect and first owner, Sebastian Collado. The house was unfinished and had been abandoned for many years after the death of Don Sebastian in 1949. Neruda made extensive renovations to the structure, which resulted in an anarchic but interesting architecture that mirrored the city itself – the house became a jumble of narrow, twisting stairways and myriad nooks and crannies, painted in a range of colors.

The interesting interior of Pablo Neruda's house, La Sebastiana, and *(inset)* the colorful exterior ↓

In 1991, the structure was restored and converted into a museum that preserves the house as it was when Neruda lived there. It also contains a number of strange and wonderful objects bought by the poet, such as a Parisian carousel pony in the living room and an unfitted washbasin from England in the study. Pablo Neruda's rich imagination is also evident in the American oakwood stairway which was rescued from a demolition site, and a floor mosaic of uncut pebbles shaped into an antique map of Patagonia and Antarctica.

As with Neruda's other houses in Santiago and Isla Negra, La Sebastiana is open for audio-guided tours, which are avilable in a range of languages, and on a first-come, first-served basis. There is no need to book in advance.

A street mural by Sammy Espinosa in the open-air gallery of urban murals ↑

⑰
Museo a Cielo Abierto

🏛 Cerro Bellavista
🚟 Ascensor Espiritu Santo

A fascinating outdoor museum on Cerro Bellavista, the Museo a Cielo Abierto comprises a maze of winding streets and passageways painted with giant, colorful street murals by some of Chile's best-known contemporary artists. There are about 20 murals, ranging from highly abstract works to humorous depictions of daily life in the city, and a self-guided tour takes about an hour. There are many steps

Did You Know?

The open-air museum of graffiti and street art was a unique and pioneering project.

along the way, as well as steep inclines, so be sure to wear comfortable shoes. The greatest concentration of murals are on Calle Ferrari and on Pasaje Santa Lucía. The latter is a steeply stepped passageway and a whirl of kaleidoscopically vibrant motifs and figures.

The museum features works by Chilean artists, including surrealist Roberto Matta, Gracia Barrios, of the Grupo Signo, and Nemesio Antúnez, founder of Taller 99, an artists' collective.

Unfortunately, weather and vandalism have damaged many of the works, but they are undergoing restoration.

---

⑱
Palacio Lyon

🏛 Museo de Historia Natural de Valparaíso: Condell 1546 🕙 10am–6pm Tue–Sat, 10am–2pm Sun
🌐 mhnv.cl

Built in 1887, Palacio Lyon houses the Museo de Historia

Natural de Valparaíso, the city's natural history museum and Chile's second-oldest state museum. Built of stone, cast iron, and glass, this edifice evokes the 19th century as a golden age of exploration, scientific discovery, and public education. Displays include exhibits from the early 1900s that feature Chile's marine flora and fauna, stuffed animals from around the world, and rows of curiosities including bovine conjoined twins conserved in tanks of formaldehyde. The crypt in the basement features contemporary artworks by Chile's finest artists.

---

⑲
Iglesia de los Sagrados Corazones

🏛 Avenida Independencia 2050–2084 📞 (032) 2746728 🕙 daily

Dating from 1874, the impressive Iglesia de los

Sagrados Corazones was the first church built in the Americas for the French Order of the Sacred Hearts. Inside the church, a Gothic style predominates. Most of its striking architectural elements, including the elegant clock tower, the wooden altar, pulpit, and confessional boxes, were brought over from France. There is a stunning pipe organ that was made by Aristide de Cavalle-Coll, the most famous French organ maker of the time. Stained glass, a replica of the glass found in the Church of Santa Gúdula in Belgium, adorns the church's upper reaches and there are thousands of tiny gold-painted stars decorating its vaulted ceiling. The church was declared a national monument in 2003.

Adjacent to the church, the Colegio de los Sagrados Corazones dates from 1837 and is Chile's oldest private high school. Several former presidents were educated here.

㉒ 🖐

Iglesia y Convento de San Francisco

📍 Blanco Viel s/n, Cerro Barón 🕒 9am–1pm, 4pm–8pm daily 🌐 iglesiade santiago.cl

Established in 1846, the Iglesia San Francisco is one of Chile's most impressive examples of redbrick architecture. The church, designated a national monument in 1983, features an ornate facade topped with a distinct, rising bell tower, which used to be illuminated at night to guide ships to Valparaíso's port. The interior of the church is a study in beautiful simplicity, comprising modest whitewashed walls and a Spanish-tiled floor beneath an arched, dark-wood ceiling.

Entered from the side of the church, the Convento de San Francisco was established as a boarding house for visiting priests. In 2013, as both church and convent were undergoing a restoration, a fire struck the site, setting the work back for several years.

㉑ Ⓜ 🖥

Congreso Nacional

📍 Avenida Pedro Montt s/n 🕒 9:30am–12:30pm & 3–5pm Mon–Fri (reserve 24 hrs in advance) 🌐 camara.cl

In 1988, General Pinochet was obliged to return the country to democracy after 14 years of dictatorship *(see p52)*. In doing so, Pinochet chose Valparaíso, rather than Santiago, as the seat of the country's new

National Congress. Two years later, the starkly modern Congreso Nacional building, built on the site of one of Pinochet's boyhood homes, was inaugurated. The structure has been met with divided opinion ever since its construction – some see it as a powerful and vital symbol of democracy and of decentralized political power, while other people question its general aesthetic appeal.

Tours of its halls and salons guide visitors through the rich allegory and symbolism of this building's spectacular architecture. The tours, which are given in both Spanish and English, cover the National Senate, the Deputy chambers, and the Salón de Honor – the ceremonial hall where international statesmen, such as Mikhail Gorbachev and Bill Clinton, former Russian and US presidents respectively, have given speechs to dignitaries.

> ### VALPO'S BEST STREET ART
>
> Valparaíso is famous for its array of street art and graffiti, much of it political in nature and highly creative. The Museo a Cielo Abierto (Open Air Museum; see p30) on Cerro Bellavista is the best place to start: it has a collection of murals by some of the city's best-known street artists. For a deeper dive into the scene, head out for a guided walk with local agency Valpo Street Art Tours (*www. valpostreetart.com*).

> **The interior of the church is a study in beautiful simplicity, comprising modest white-washed walls and a Spanish-tiled floor beneath an arched, dark-wood ceiling.**

2 🛠️ 〽️ 🍴 ☕ 🛍️

CASA MUSEO ISLA NEGRA

🅰️ B6 📍 56 miles (90 km) S of Valparaíso; Poeta Neruda s/n, Isla Negra
📞 (035) 2461284 🕐 10am–6pm Tue–Sun (Jan–Feb: to 7pm)

Steeped in literary history, Museo Isla Negra offers visitors a charming insight into the life of Nobel Prize-winning author Pablo Neruda. Isla Negra is home to thousands of unique and eccentric objects collected by Chile's most famous writer, including figure heads, retort of sails, whale teeth, antique shoes, and smoking pipes.

Attracted by its location facing the Isla Negra beach, Pablo Neruda bought the original building from a Spanish sailor in 1939. Neruda extended the house, creating a structure whose long, thin shape mirrored the geography of Chile, and filled it with over 3,500 weird and wonderful objects from across the globe. Today, the house is a museum and remains exactly as it was when the poet lived here with his third wife, Matilde Urrutia, prior to his death in 1973.

Dining room

Neruda's bedroom

Ship figureheads, stained glass, and wooden angels adorn the living room. Neruda encrusted its floor with seashells to massage his feet.

The house bar conserves Neruda's comprehensive collection of surreal bottles. An array of colors, shapes, and sizes are displayed.

Named for its isolation and wild black rocks, Isla Negra beach is associated with the poet's love for the sea.

Did You Know?

Isla Negra gets heavy rains in winter, which inspired Neruda to write "Ode to the Storm."

→

The terrace of Pablo Neruda's house and *(inset)* an anchor statue by the sea

The reception area where Neruda entertained guests, including other writers. Eclectic collections fill its space.

Narrow wooden corridors like those on old ships run along the house. Neruda lined this one with African face masks.

Neruda's collection of seashells occupies an entire room. The long rapier-like tusk of a narwhal whale is also exhibited here.

The stable was built for a papier-mâché horse. Neruda called it "the world's happiest horse."

Neruda's study is crammed with miscellanea, such as model ships, butterfly collections, astrological charts, portraits, and an antique washbasin.

Two years after the museum's 1990 inauguration, Neruda was re-buried at Isla Negra. His third wife, Matilde Urrutia, is buried alongside him.

↑ Vineyards rolling across the hills of Casablanca Valley

EXPERIENCE MORE

③ Casablanca Valley

🅰B6

Located between Santiago and Valparaíso, the Casablanca Valley is home to a string of vineyards whose maritime-influenced climates produce crisp, refreshing white wines. Overlooked by the snow-topped Andes, most of the wineries offer tours, tasting sessions, and accommodations. Many are easy to visit independently (*www.rutadel vinodecasablanca.cl* for more information), or a trip can be booked with the excellent Wine Tours Valparaíso agency (*www. wine toursvalparaiso.cl*).

> **🔍 HIDDEN GEM**
> **Reloj de Flores**
>
> Planted in 1962 on a grassy slope facing the ocean, the Reloj de Flores (Flower Clock) symbolizes Viña del Mar's status as the "Garden City." The dial is a circular flower bed set with bright flowers.

④ Viña del Mar

🅰B6 🚂🚌 ℹ️ Avenida Libertad 250; www.visite vinadelmar.cl

Founded in 1874, Viña del Mar (Vineyard of the Sea) has its origins in a Colonial hacienda whose vineyards faced the ocean. The area became a city after the 1906 earthquake compelled Valparaíso's elite to relocate here. Its flatter topography was ideal for building the French-style garden palaces that were then fashionable and the town became a resort for the rich. Today, it is Chile's Ciudad Jardín (Garden City), with green spaces, great beaches, and fine palaces that house stunning museums.

Viña del Mar's elegant central square, Plaza José Francisco Vergara, is named for the city's founder, whose bronze statue stands on a marble plinth in one corner. The plaza is dotted with pools, statues, fountains, and shaded trees, as well as impressive buildings. Also of note is the **Palacio Vergara**, which houses the Museo Municipal de Bellas Artes. It is

home to over 150 artworks. Surrounding the palace are the parklands of the Quinta Vergara, which are planted with exotic trees. Dominating the grounds, the Anfiteatro Quinta Vergara is a modern amphitheater that hosts the

Festival Internacional de la Canción de Viña del Mar (p42).

Castillo Wulff, located on the city's coastal avenue, was constructed in 1908. A national monument and architectural landmark, it is built in the style of a typical medieval castle, with turrets, ramparts, a round tower, and a central courtyard. The courtyard stairs offer great ocean vistas, while the tower out the back has a fantastic view of the sea through its glass floor.

The **Museo de Arqueología e Historia Francisco Fonck** features displays of pre-Hispanic objects collected from across Chile and Latin America. Its standout collection was brought from Easter Island (p264) in 1951. Constructed after the 1906 earthquake, the **Palacios Rioja and Carrasco** are national monuments. The former was inspired by Versailles and is now a decorative arts museum that conserves the Rioja family home as it was a century ago. The Palacio Carrasco was built between 1912 and 1923 in the Beaux-Arts style, and houses the city's cultural center.

The **Jardín Botánico Nacional** is located 5 miles (8 km) southeast of the city. The park's well-kept grounds are home to more than 3,000 plant species.

Palacio Vergara

⊛ ⊛ ⓣ ⊜ ⌂ Errázuriz 563-596 🔧 For restoration 🌐 quintavergara.cl

Castillo Wulff

⌂ Avenida Marina 37 🕙 10am-1:30pm; 3-5:30pm Tue-Sun 🌐 patrimoniovina.cl

Museo de Arqueología

⊛ ⊛ ⓣ ⌂ Historia Francisco Fonck 4 Norte N 784 🕙 10am-2pm & 3-6pm Mon, 10am-6pm Tue-Sat, 10am-2pm Sun 🌐 museofonck.cl

Palacios Rioja and Carrasco

⊛ ⊛ ⌂ Palacio Rioja: Quillota 214 📞 (032) 2184693 🕙 9:30am-1:30pm, 3-5:30pm Tue-Sun; Palacio Carrasco: Avenida Libertad 250

Jardín Botánico Nacional

⌂ 5 miles (8 km) SE of Viña del Mar 🕙 9am-7pm daily 🌐 jbn.cl

EAT

Entre Masas

This bakery specializes in delicious, freshly made *empanadas* – try the chorizo and goat's cheese. There is also a branch in the Valparaíso Region.

🅰 B6 ⌂ 6 Poniente 235, Viña del Mar 📞 (032) 2979919

$$$

Divino Pecado

This upmarket spot offers Italian-influenced fish and seafood dishes in sophisticated surroundings. It's popular, so book ahead.

🅰 B6 ⌂ San Martín 180, Viña del Mar 📞 (032) 2975790

$$$

↓ Gulls flying above the shoreline in Viña del Mar

5

Sewell

🅰C7 🚗46 miles (75 km) SE of Santiago; Carretera al Cobre 🌐sewell.cl

Clinging to Cerro Negro at 7,215 ft (2,200 m) above sea level, Sewell – the City of Stairs – was established by the American Braden Copper Company in 1905 as a camp for workers of the nearby El Teniente mine. By 1960, it was a thriving metropolis, with around 15,000 inhabitants, a bank, a courthouse, a town hall, recreational clubs, and Chile's most advanced hospital. Sewell was slowly abandoned from the 1970s to 1999, but was declared a UNESCO World Heritage Site in 1998, and now remains an eerily beautiful preserved city of multistoried wooden buildings. A steep central staircase, the Escalera Central is the backbone of the abandoned city. Access paths and secondary stairs stem from it in a herringbone pattern. Worth a visit is the Museo de la Gran Minería del Cobre, occupying the Modernist building of the old Industrial School, which displays historical and geological exhibits from Sewell's past. The ghost town's pretty blue church dates from 1928.

6

Cartagena

🅰B6 🚗62 miles (100 km) S of Valparaíso 🚌
🛈Municipalidad, Plaza de Armas; www.cartagena-chile.cl

The delightful hillside town of Cartagena has narrow winding streets and colorful houses hanging from a hilltop overlooking a bay. The best time to visit is late spring or early fall, when the beaches are not as crowded as they are during summer.

From the palm-shaded Plaza de Armas in Cartagena's upper town, twisting streets and stairways wend down to Playa Chica, south of the plaza, and to Playa Grande, north of the plaza. Set on a hillside east of Playa Chica is the home and tomb of Vicente Huidobro (1893–1948), a great Chilean poet who lived for several years in Cartagena. Sadly rundown, the spot is still a popular point of pilgrimage for Chilean poets and artists. The house is under private ownership and closed to public view.

Did You Know?

A group of Humboldt penguins in water is known as a "raft," and on land, they're called a "waddle."

7

Quintay

🅰B6 🚗29 miles (47 km) S of Valparaíso 🚌

The fishing village of Quintay is an idyllic spot. Buses drop off visitors at its small plaza, from where sandy lanes wend down to the *caleta*. This is a horseshoe-shaped fishermen's harbor edged by a rocky beach and weatherboard seafood restaurants. Sea otters and birds congregate on the beach and fishermen unload their catch here from wooden boats.

Overlooking the *caleta* is the **Ballenera de Quintay**, Chile's biggest whaling station until its closure in 1967. Now a whaling museum, it includes the station's old and somewhat eerie whaling platform onto which the carcasses of 1,600 blue whale – the world's largest animal – were dragged year after year.

Quintay has two main beaches. From the plaza a 10-minute walk through cool pine and eucalyptus forest leads to the breathtakingly picturesque Playa Chica, a wave-pummeled beach ringed by high, rugged cliffs and wildflowers. North of the town center, Playa Grande is a long stretch of golden sand, spoiled slightly by condominiums. For activities in Quintay, diving schools at the *caleta* run scuba-diving and kayaking excursions. These are ideal for beginners and enthusiasts alike.

Ballenera de Quintay
⊛ 🅰 Caleta de Quintay
🕘 9:30am–6:30pm daily
🔲 fundacionquintay.cl

---

❽
Algarrobo

🅰 B6 🏁 43 miles (70 km) S of Valparaíso 🚌
🔲 vivealgarrobo.cl

The largest town along the section of Pacific coast south of Valparaíso, Algarrobo is a family-oriented resort that gets crowded in summer with families arriving from Santiago. This town has excellent tourist services as well as some 14 separate beaches where activities include scuba-diving, windsurfing, and horseriding. Its most popular beach, Playa San Pedro, is close to the town center and faces calm waters, ideal for swimming. Playa Grande is a more dramatic, big-wave beach. South of the town center is Playa El Canelo,

←
A small fishing harbor in Quintay, with traditional boats lining the sands

↑ Humboldt penguins perched on the rocky islet of nature reserve Cachagua

a stretch of fine sand washed by aquamarine waters, which backs onto thick pine forest. Playa El Canelillo is secluded and quieter. Reached by boat from Algarrobo, the Isla de Pájaros Niño is a rocky islet visited each September to April by nesting colonies of Humboldt penguins. Boats skirt the islet's shore, moving past birdlife such as pelicans, cormorants, and gulls.

---

❾
Cachagua

🅰 B6 🏁 45 miles (73 km) N of Valparaíso 🚌

A beautiful, rustic beach-town, Cachagua arrives as a welcome change along a stretch of coastline dominated by upscale resorts and condominiums. The town has a eucalyptus-shaded plaza from which sandy lanes flanked by thatched houses descend to the long, dramatic Playa Grande, Cachagua's main beach. Horseriding and surfing are popular activities here.

Visible from Playa Grande, the Monumento Natural Isla Cachagua is a rocky islet that is refuge to a wide variety of birdlife, including nesting colonies of Humboldt penguins from September to April. Boat trips take visitors near the islet and offer a

chance to observe this rare birdlife from a close range. Also of interest at Cachagua is Playa Las Cujas, a sheltered, rocky beach that is popular with divers and anglers.

→
Stone street in the coastal town of Papudo with street art by Izak

10

Papudo

B6 **56 miles (91 km) N of Valparaíso** **Chorrillos 9, 2nd Floor; www.municipalidadpapudo.cl**

Less exclusive than the neighboring beach-towns of Zapallar and Cachagua, Papudo is a small and unpretentious seaside town with great walks. A sweeping coastal boulevard runs parallel to the two main beaches: Playa Grande, a long open beach popular with surfers; and the smaller, sheltered Playa Chica, which is frequented by families. A number of attractive seaside walks strike out from both beaches, crossing sections of cliffs along the coast that are pitted with caves and caverns. On fine days, horses are available for those who wish to ride along the shoreline.

Among the buildings that line the main coastal boulevard, visitors will find the Iglesia Nuestra Señora de las Mercedes, a church and national monument that was built in 1918. Farther on, the honey-colored Chalet Recart, site of Papudo's town hall, is one of several alpine-chalet buildings that front the coast here.

11

Zapallar

B6 **50 miles (80 km) N of Valparaíso** **Municipalidad, Germán Riesgo 399; www.turismozapallar.cl**

An exceptionally picturesque coastal town and an erstwhile high-end destination, Zapallar is small, secluded, and ringed by steeply forested coastal mountains. The town sits on a wooded hillside that sweeps dramatically down to rocky cliffs and a half-moon-shaped sandy beach. A number of weatherboard holiday villas dot the coastal mountains around Zapallar.

Since the late 19th century, this town has been a favorite summer destination for the wealthy citizens of Santiago, and today Zapallar is only a two-hour drive from the capital along fast-moving freeways. From Zapallar's beach a 4-mile (6-km) coastal path skirts clifftops and has wide ocean vistas. Boat launches make daily departures in summer, taking bird-watchers and holiday-makers southward to the Monumento Natural Isla Cachagua (p133).

A sandy path up the hillside from the beach leads to Zapallar's white-sand plaza, which is fronted by a clapboard theaterhouse. This dates from 1908 and was originally the town church.

Did You Know?

La Ligua, just inland from Papudo, was home to La Quintrala, an infamous Chilean serial killer.

From the plaza, a number of lanes climb uphill to Zapallar's commercial center, which is filled with shops, eateries, and tourist information.

12 Los Andes

B6 **87 miles (141 km) NE of Valparaíso** **Avenida Santa Teresa 333; www.turismoaconcagua.cl**

Ringed by the vineyards of Aconcagua valley, at the foot of the Andean cordillera, Los Andes was founded in 1791 as a staging post on a Colonial trade route. Today, it is the first stop for many travelers making the road crossing of the Andes from Argentina into Chile's Central Valley. There's not a huge amount to see in the town itself, but there are two museums of interest here. The first, the **Museo Arqueológico de los Andes** is a small Colonial house with well-kept pre-Columbian displays. The **Museo Histórico Religioso del Antiguo Monasterio del Espiritu Santu** is a convent building dedicated to Santa Teresa de Los Andes, Chile's first saint. Visitors can wander about the convent's old workrooms, sleeping quarters, cloistered courtyard, and orchard. Next door, the Capilla Espiritu Santo is a Neo-Gothic chapel and shrine to the saint, who was a novice nun in Los Andes during her short life.

Also of note are the Neo-Classical headquarters of the regional government, which were built between 1888 and 1891 and overlook Los Andes' pretty Colonial plaza. At the edge of town, the Cerro de la Vírgen is a hilltop lookout point with fine views.

Museo Arqueológico de los Andes

Avenida Santa Teresa 396–398 **(034) 2420115** **10:30am–6pm Tue–Sun**

Museo Histórico Religioso del Antiguo Monasterio del Espiritu Santu

Avenida Santa Teresa 389 **(034) 242 1765** **9:30am–12:30pm, 3–5:30pm Mon–Fri, 10am–5:30pm Sat & Sun**

13 Cristo Redentor

C6 **130 miles (210 km) E of Valparaíso; Camino Cristo Redentor** **Dec–Mar**

The gigantic Cristo Redentor (Christ the Redeemer) marks one of the world's great frontier passes: the crossing of the central Andes between Chile and Argentina. Set against a backdrop of the snow-swathed Andes, the figure stands at a dizzying 12,539 ft (3,823 m) above sea level. The 23-ft- (7-m-) tall statue of Christ is set on a 20-ft (6-m) granite plinth weighing 8,800 lb (4,000 kg). Sculpted in 1904 in Buenos Aires, the Cristo Redentor was conveyed by train to the foot of the Andes, dismantled into various parts, and hauled up the mountains by mules. Its erection marked a historic signing of peace between Chile and Argentina, following decades of border disputes that pushed both countries to the brink of war. Tour buses and private cars that pass the Chilean customs post reach the monument by taking the Camino Cristo Redentor, a gravel turn off en route to the Túnel del Cristo Redentor, a 2-mile- (3-km-) long tunnel crossing of the Andes.

↑ Visitors taking photographs of the Cristo Redentor against its mountainous backdrop

14

Portillo

🅰C6 🏠126 miles (203 km)
E of Valparaíso; Renato
Sánchez 4270, Las Condes
📅 ⏰Mid-Jun-Sep 🌐ski
portillo.com

Spectacularly located at
10,000 ft (3,000 m) above
sea level, Portillo is South
America's oldest ski resort.
It has 17 runs for skiers and
snowboarders of all levels.
Expert and extreme skiers
will find fantastic opportunities on slopes that
descend from an altitude of
10,900 ft (3,270 m). Challenges
include 50-degree descents,
countless off-piste routes,
heli-skiing and night-skiing.
Views from the slopes are
tremendous, embracing
surrounding peaks and the
Laguna del Inca, a lake that
freezes in winter. The ski
center is a self-contained
resort with packages that
include hotel lodging, lift
tickets, and facilities such as
a cinema and a heated outdoor pool. Visitors can also
choose to stay in cheaper
mountain lodges or back-
packers' lodges. There is a
lively après-ski scene and
excellent family-oriented
services, including a ski camp
for children aged 4–6 years.

Ski slopes of Portillo,
where *(inset)* compe-
titions take place ↑

15

Termas de Jahuel

🅰B6 🏠87 miles (140 km)
NE of Valparaíso; Jahuel
s/n, San Felipe 🌐jahuel.cl

Set on the slopes of the arid
Andean foothills, overlooking
the fertile Aconcagua valley,
Termas de Jahuel is a modern,
luxurious spa retreat that
accepts both day and overnight
guests. Sophisticated natural
therapies are on offer; the spa's
signature massage treatment
is an olive-oil therapy that
uses organically grown plants.
There is also an outdoor pool
edged by palms and jasmine.

Jahuel's thermal properties
were recognized in Colonial
times when travelers crossing
the Andes came to rest here.
Today, guests reside in a
Colonial-style pavilion or an
exclusive boutique hotel with
en-suite thermal baths, and
activities include mountain-
biking and horseback riding.
Trails climb to a plateau with
fine views of the high-altitude
Aconcagua Valley wine district.
Facilities include children's
playrooms, tennis courts, and
a good range of restaurants.

16

Rancagua

🅰B7 🏠54 miles (87 km)
S of Santiago 🚉
ℹ️ Germán Riesgo 350;
www.rancagua.cl

Founded in 1743, Rancagua
lies deep in *huaso* (cowboy)
country and hosts the
Campeonato Nacional de
Rodeo *(p42)* each year.
Steeped in history, the city
was the site of one of Chile's
bloodiest conflicts – the 1814
Battle of Rancagua, in which
the patriot militia led by
Bernardo O'Higgins *(p258)*
fought against vastly superior
Spanish forces. The Monu-
mento a Bernardo O'Higgins
dominating the city's central
plaza is an equestrian memorial honoring Chilean soldiers
who were killed at this spot.

Just north of the plaza, the
Iglesia de la Merced is an
adobe church built in 1778.
O'Higgins directed his troops
from its bell tower, which was
rebuilt in 1857. It suffered
damage in the earthquake of
2010, and is still undergoing

restoration. Located south of the plaza, the Paseo del Estado is an old Colonial street lined with fine historic structures. The highlight here is the **Museo Regional de Rancagua**, housed in two buildings that date from 1790 and 1800. The museum has engaging exhibits on religious art and on the Central Valley's weaving traditions and mining heritage. It also re-creates typical Colonial-era living quarters. At the southern end of Paseo del Estado, another large Colonial building houses Rancagua's **Casa de la Cultura**. Built in the early 1700s, it was the base for Spanish forces during the Battle of Rancagua. Today it is a cultural center, fronted by shaded gardens.

Museo Regional de Rancagua

📍 Paseo del Estado 685 🕐 10am–6pm Mon–Fri (to 5pm Fri), 10am–2pm Sat 🌐 museorancagua.cl

Casa de la Cultura

📍 Avenida Cachapoal 90 📞 (072) 2226076 🕐 10am–6pm Mon–Fri (to 7pm Thu), 10am–2pm Sat 🌐 rancagua cultura.cl

A lofty Chilean wine palm in the Parque Nacional La Campana ↓

17

Parque Nacional La Campana

🅱 B6 🚗 37 miles (60 km) E of Valparaíso; Paradero 43, Avenida Granizo 9137 🕐 9am–5:30pm Sat–Thu, 9am–4:30pm Fri 🌐 conaf.cl

A UNESCO-recognized area, La Campana harbors a wilderness habitat that is considered exceptional for its biodiversity. The park's signature flora is a relict population of Chilean wine palms (*Jubaea chilensis*), the world's southernmost palm. The birdlife here is rich, while among mammals and reptiles, there is the vizcacha, a large burrowing rodent, as well as iguanas, snakes, and lizards. The park is named for its dominant natural feature, Cerro La Campana (The Bell Peak).

From the entrance in the Granizo sector, Sendero El Andinista is a popular 9-mile (14-km) day-hike that reaches the summit of this peak. Less visited, the park's northern Ocoa sector has its largest, densest concentrations of Chilean palms, which may live for several hundred years. This sector is accessed via the 5-mile (7-km) Sendero Amasijo, which is connected to the Sendero Los Peumos.

DARWIN AND LA CAMPANA

In August 1834, English naturalist Charles Darwin began a two-night ascent of Cerro La Campana on foot and horseback. With two cowboys, Darwin climbed the hill's northern flank and made camp at the Agua del Guanaco spring. Writing later in *The Voyage of the Beagle*, he noted, "the atmosphere was so clear the masts at anchor in the Bay of Valparaíso... could be distinguished as little black streaks." The group summited on the second morning, where a plaque commemorates their ascent.

18

El Teniente

C7 🚗 49 miles (79 km) SE of Santiago; Carretera al Cobre 🚌 **w** vts.cl

The biggest subterranean copper mine in the world, El Teniente comprises over 1,500 miles (2,400 km) of underground tunnels. In operation since the early 1800s, the mine produces around 485,000 tons (440,000 tonnes) of copper-ore each year. Guided tours take visitors through a maze of tunnels, past giant ore-crushing machinery and an underground cave of crystal that miners discovered while digging for copper.

19 🍽️

Valle de Cachapoal

B7 🚗 60 miles (96 km) S of Santiago **w** winesof chile.org

Located in Chile's agricultural heartland, Valle de Cachapoal is renowned for its production of two excellent red wine grapes, the cabernet sauvignon and the distinctive carménère. Most of the valley's wineries are nestled in its cool eastern sector and are open for tours and tastings. The ultra-modern Viña Altair, inaugurated in 2001, features a contemporary design that uses gravity to make wine rather than pumps, and offers moonlit tours. More traditional wineries include the Spanish-Colonial-style Viña Chateau Los Boldos.

Valle de Cachapoal lies in prime *huaso* territory and customized wine tours here include rodeo shows and horseback rides through the mountains. Although the valley can be covered on a day trip from nearby Rancagua, overnight travelers will find accommodations at Hacienda Los Lingues (*p140*).

20 🍽️

Termas de Cauquenes

C7 🚗 73 miles (117 km) S of Santiago 🕐 7:30am–6:30pm daily **w** htdc.cl

Nestled in the Andean foothills, Termas de Cauquenes has entertained such luminaries as English naturalist Charles Darwin and revered Chilean hero Bernardo O'Higgins. This historic spa complex is set amid dense eucalyptus forests with numerous guided walks to an appealing lookout, from where condors can be seen circling in the air. The 19th-century bathhouse of the spa

is cathedral-like in size and ambition, with a soaring ceiling, stained-glass walls, and a mosaic floor between rows of private bathrooms. Overnight guests are housed in a Colonial-style hotel constructed around a Spanish courtyard.

The resort also welcomes day visitors, who can luxuriate in the spa's thermal baths and enjoy a range of relaxing therapeutic treatments. Facilities include a heated outdoor pool, a children's playground, and a lovely gourmet restaurant.

21 🖋

Cajón del Maipo

🅰 C6 🚗 20 miles (33 km) SE of Santiago 🚌
ℹ Comercio 19788, San José del Maipo; www.cajondel maipo.com

Offering a gamut of outdoor activities, Cajón del Maipo is a popular weekend destination from Santiago. Independent visitors usually make their base at San José del Maipo, the largest of several small towns in the area. Founded in 1791, the town is an attraction in its own right for its Colonial church and adobe houses.

Southwest of Cajón del Maipo is **Reserva Nacional Río Clarillo**, an area of stunning natural beauty spread over some 40 sq miles (102 sq km). The reserve is ideal for hiking, bird-watching, horseback riding, and rafting excursions.

The ski resort of **Lagunillas** has 13 slopes attracting skiers of all levels during the winter months. It is also one of the few ski centers where night skiing is possible.

An adventure-tourism resort and sanctuary, **Santuario de la Naturaleza Cascada de las Animas** protects an area of rugged mountains, rivers, and waterfalls, and lures visitors with adrenaline-charged activities such as white-water rafting, hiking and horseback riding, and zip-lining. Accommodations include log-cabins set in the forest, a guesthouse, and a scenic campsite *(p140)*.

Monumento Natural El Morado embraces the 16,597-ft (5,060-m) high Cerro El Morado. This snowcapped peak is best viewed on the park's 3-hour trek to Laguna El Morado, an alpine lake from where a trail reaches the base of the Glaciar San Francisco. The Baños Morales area has

hot-spring pools that attract weekenders from Santiago.

The rustic hot-springs resort of **Termas Valle de Colina** sits at the eastern end of Cajón del Maipo. It comprises a series of natural clay pools that bubble and steam on the slopes of a mountain overlooked by snow-capped peaks. Access to the pools is difficult, as the road to the resort is closed to public transportation; however Santiago-based Expediciones Manzur runs round trips over weekends. Visitors can hire horses at the resort, and rides to the Argentine border can be arranged in advance.

Reserva Nacional Río Clarillo

⊛ ⊛ 🚗 25 miles (40 km) SW of San José del Maipo ⏰ Apr-Nov: 8:30am-6pm daily; Dec-Mar: 8:30am-7pm 🅦 conaf.cl

Lagunillas

⊛ 🚗 11 miles (17 km) NE of San José del Maipo ⏰ Jun-Oct 🅦 skilagunillas.cl

Santuario de la Naturaleza Cascada de las Animas

⊛ ⊛ ⊛ ⊛ 🚗 9 miles (14 km) SE of San José del Maipo; 31087 Camino al Volcán, San Alfonso 🚌 🅦 cascada.net

Monumento Natural El Morado

⊛ 🚗 26 miles (43 km) E of San José del Maipo 🚌 ⏰ Oct-Mar: 8:30am-6pm daily 🅦 conaf.cl

Termas Valle de Colina

⊛ 🚗 37 miles (60 km) SE of San José del Maipo ⏰ Oct-May: daily 🅦 termasvalledecolina.cl

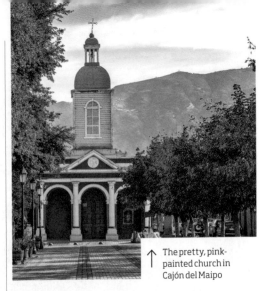

↑ The pretty, pink-painted church in Cajón del Maipo

STAY

Cascada de las Animas

A base from which to explore Cajón del Maipo, this lodge has camping, dorms, and private rooms. Horseback-riding and hiking are popular from here, with trails along short nature paths and tours through the mountains.

🅰 C6 🚗 Camino al Volcán Nº 31087, San Alfonso 🅦 cascada delasanimas.cl

⑤⑤⑤

←

Sun beaming on a Colchagua Valley vineyard

22

Hacienda Los Lingues

B7 **78 miles (125 km) S of Santiago; Panamericana Sur Km 124.5, San Fernando** **Daily** **loslingues.com**

One of Chile's oldest and most prestigious estates, Hacienda Los Lingues dates from the end of the 16th century when it was gifted by King Philip III of Spain to

Don Melchor Jufré del Águila. For over four centuries, it has remained in this Spanish nobleman's family, the current generation of which lives on the hacienda.

Overnight guests stay in sumptuous Colonial rooms that preserve the original architecture and furnishings. Antique family portraits hang from walls, and the sensation of staying at an old aristocratic home rather than simply at a luxury hotel is tangible – although contemporary amenities, such as a pool, have been added.

Visitors can also opt for the more economical day tour of the hacienda, which takes in the courtyard, parks, wine cellar, stables, and 1790-built chapel. Dating from 1760, the impressive stables breed gorgeous thoroughbred Aculeo horses, whose lineage can be traced back to Moorish Spain. Day tours also feature a delivious gourmet lunch, rodeo show, and even horseback rides.

The hotel is situated near the wine valleys of Cachapoal (p138) and Colchagua (p148), making it a perfectly placed stop-off for wine-tasting novices and oenophiles alike.

↑ Workers harvesting grapes in the vineyards of Los Lingues

23

Reserva Nacional Río de los Cipreses

C7 **81 miles (131 km) S of Santiago; Camino Chacayes s/n** **8:30am–5:30pm daily** **conaf.cl**

Created in 1985, Reserva Nacional Río de los Cipreses protects over 142 sq miles (367 sq km) of Andean wilderness, comprising river canyons and forests of mountain cypress. The reserve's popular northern sector has an administration center with displays on the area's wildlife. Starting at the center, paths cross the scenic Cajón Alto Cachapoal, from where the short Sendero Tricahues trail leads to a wildlife observation point. Here, colonies of the burrowing parrot, loro tricahue, can be seen nesting in the canyon wall.

The reserve's less-visited central and southern sectors can be reached by longer hikes and horseback rides that depart from the

---

TOP 3 **LOCAL SKI CENTERS**

El Colorado
elcolorado.cl
A popular, economical option, within easy reach of Santiago.

La Parva
(02) 2889-9210
Caters to both beginners and experts, offering good off-piste skiing.

Valle Nevado
vallenevado.com
Chile's biggest, most modern ski center, with heli-skiing and a snowboard park.

> One of the less-visited wine valleys of central Chile, the Valle de Curicó carries one significant advantages for wine enthusiasts - personalized, unhurried tours and tastings hosted by wine experts.

administration center. These trace the Cajón Río Cipreses that forms the spine of the reserve. Along the way, visitors traverse cypress forests and pass grazing guanaco herds. It is also possible to see pre-Hispanic petroglyphs and enjoy dramatic Andean vistas including views of the soaring 15,941-ft- (4,860-m-) high Volcán Palomo.

㉔
Valle de Curicó

🅰B7 🄰37 miles (60 km) S of Santa Cruz; Curicó 🄰🚌

While smaller than most other wine valleys of central Chile, the Valle de Curicó carries one significant advantage for wine enthusiasts – personalized, unhurried tours and tastings hosted by wine experts. Valle de Curicó produces fine white wines, especially sauvignon blanc, as well as cabernet sauvignon reds – some from 80-year-old vines. Its wineries (many of which are relatively small and family-owned) include the Spanish-owned Miguel Torres estate, the San Pedro, and Millamar vineyards. The wineries are visited on customized tours arranged by **Ruta del Vino Curicó**, which also organizes private tours. In the third week of March each year, the Fiesta de la Vendimia Curicó is held here – a unique celebration that elects a Queen of the Harvest alongside many wine-themed activities. The festival has been running since 1991.

Ruta del Vino Curicó
🄰 Prat 301-A, Curicó 🄰9am-2pm & 3:30-7:30pm Mon-Fri 🆆rutadelvinocurico.cl

㉕
Santa Cruz

🅰B7 🄰113 miles (182 km) SW of Santiago 🚌 🅸Plaza de Armas s/n

One of the larger towns of the Colchagua Valley (p148), Santa Cruz was founded in the 19th century. The town's most notable Colonial building is the Municipalidad (town hall), a reddish arcaded house. The undoubted highlight of Santa Cruz is the private **Museo de Colchagua**, owned by alleged arms dealer Carlos Cardoen. It houses over 5,000 objects relating to Chilean history. Displays range from rare objects that belonged to former president Bernardo O'Higgins to the Gran Rescate exhibit, which showcases objects relating to the rescue of 33 miners trapped in San José in August 2010, and 19th-century carriages.

Santa Cruz is the starting point for winery tours to Colchagua. A popular tour option is via the wine-themed 1920s steam train, **Tren Sabores del Valle**, which departs from San Fernando in the valley's north and ends at Santa Cruz in the south. At Santa Cruz visitors depart for two winery coach tours.

Museo de Colchagua
🈂🈯🄰 🄰Avenida Errázuriz 145 🄲10am-7pm daily 🆆museocolchagua.cl

Tren Sabores del Valle
🄰 🄰Plaza de Armas 298 🄲Sat 🆆rutadelvino.cl

> **CHILE'S RODEO**
>
> The rodeo arose in the 16th century, when cattle were gathered together and branded as a means of identification, before it evolved into Chile's national sport. Today *huasos* - or cowboys - steer the horses around a *medialuna*, a half-moon arena, in an attempt to pin down a calf. The sport is an integral part of Chilean life, but it is highly controversial and some organizations continue to seek a ban similar to the bullfighting ban in Catalonia, Spain.

↑ An antique horse carriage displayed at the Museo de Colchagua in Santa Cruz

EAT

El Viejo Rancagua

This spot is primarily a live-music venue that also offers set lunches and simple Chilean dishes in the evenings. Inside, the walls are covered with cool vintage adverts.

B7 ☐ Paseo del Estado 607, Rancagua ☐ (072) 2222130 ☐ Sun

$ $ $

---

26 Pichilemu

B7 ☐ 161 miles (259 km) SW of Santiago ☐ Angel Gaete 365; www. pichilemu.cl

Central Valley's surf capital, Pichilemu is a haven for surfers, bodyboarders, and hippies. Before the boarders arrived, Pichilemu was a luxury coastal resort, built in the 1900s by Chilean speculator Agustín Ross-Edwards. It was the site of Chile's first casino, but went into decline with the rise of Viña del Mar

(p130) in the north. Pichilemu retains many charming vestiges of its aristocratic past, however. The old casino building is now occupied by a cultural center.

Today, Pichilemu is a small laid-back town with several beaches, including the main Las Terrazas stretch, which has surf schools and is popular with novice boarders owing to its small waves. About 4 miles (6 km) south of the town center, the Punta de Lobos beach's long, 8-ft- (2-m-) high leg breaks attract expert surfers. A stop on the international surfing circuit, Punta de Lobos has excellent infrastructure. Located between the two is Infernillo, with its extremely dangerous lefts. It is recommended only for experienced surfers.

---

27 Termas de Panimávida

B7 ☐ 55 miles (88 km) SE of Talca; Panimávida s/n, Linares ☐ ☐ 9am-5pm Mon-Fri ☐ termasde panimavida.cl

Set in pastoral farmlands in the Andean foothills, this spa resort occupies an old Colonial-style edifice surrounded by statue-dotted gardens. There

are large indoor and outdoor thermal pools, as well as children's pools. Therapeutic treatments include massages, hot rooms, and Jacuzzis, as well as wine therapies and herbal, Turkish, and mud baths.

Slightly to the south, **Termas de Quinamávida** is a spa with similar facilities and services. Its therapies also include steam treatments in cactus wood baths. The resort is closer to the mountains and is a picturesque modern complex of honey-colored buildings set in century-old eucalyptus and pine forests.

Termas de Quinamávida

☐ Camino Linares-Colbún Km 16 ☐ 8am-1pm & 3-8pm daily ☐ termas dequinamavida.cl

---

28 Maule

B7 ☐ 47 miles (76 km) S of Santa Cruz

Offering an authentic Ruta del Vino that takes in eight of the region's wineries, Maule is one of Chile's top wine producing regions. The area around the city of Talca is renowned for its reds, but there are also a few refreshing white wines being produced here.

Viña Corral Victoria doesn't provide tours, but its restaurant pours its own carménère – the only wine its vineyard produces – and a selection from other Maule wineries. Serving traditional Chilean dishes focused on beef, it's open for lunch only.

Only 9 miles (15 km) south of Talca, the town of San Javier is home to **Viña Balduzzi**, a family-run winery that welcomes drop-ins. They produce a range of reds and whites, including a superb sauvignon blanc, but the truly premium wines are the cabernet sauvignon and the syrah.

To the west of San Javier, on the highway to Constitución, **Gillmore Winery** focuses on

↑ Preparing to ride the waves from the beach of Punta Lobos in Pichilemu

reds, with merlot, cabernet franc, and cabernet sauvignon, plus blends. It's open for tours and tastings on short notice, but call ahead. It also has its own exclusive spa that specializes in wine-based therapies.

East of San Rafael, **Via Wines** is based on the Fundo Las Chilcas. It is known for its sustainable approach and its terrific syrah and sauvignon blanc. Advance booking is mandatory for the organic winery tour.

HISTORY OF WINE IN CHILE

Chilean wine-making began in the 16th century for use in religious rites. Secular demand followed, and by the 19th century it was fashionable in elite circles for families to plant vineyards at their country estates. High-quality vines were introduced from France and Chile set up its first wineries. In the 1980s, foreign wine-makers and consultants built ultra-modern wineries. Chile rediscovered its signature carménère grape and a new wine-tourism industry emerged.

↑ Reserva Nacional Altos de Lircay, and *(inset)* one of the local birds

Viña Corral Victoria
🏠 Km 11, Camino San Clemente, Talca
🌐 corralvictoria.cl

Viña Balduzzi
🏠 Avenida Balmaceda 1189, San Javier 🕐 9am-6pm Mon-Sat 🌐 balduzzi.com

Gillmore Winery
🏠 Camino a Constitución Km 20 🕐 9am-5pm Mon-Wed, 9am-6pm Thu-Sat
🌐 gillmore.cl

Via Wines
🏠 K-409 🕐 9am-5pm Mon-Sat 🌐 viawines.com

---

29 🚶 Ⓜ

Reserva Nacional Altos de Lircay

🗺 B7 🏠 42 miles (67 km) E of Talca; Ruta Internacional Pehuenche, Cruce Vilches Alto 🚌 🕐 8:30am-1pm & 2-6pm daily 🌐 conaf.cl

Conserving a wilderness area of southern-beech forest and rugged river-canyon country, Reserva Nacional Altos de Lircay offers activities such as mountain-biking, hiking, and horseback riding. Birds can be spotted along nature-watching trails, including Andean condors and, in forests, the loro tricahue (an endangered native parrot), and Magellanic woodpeckers. The two most popular hiking trails strike out from the park entrance. The Sendero Laguna del Alto is an eight-hour return trek through southern-beech forests to the mountain-ringed Laguna del Alto. The Sendero Enladrillado is a seven-hour return trek, of similar difficulty, that ascends through native woods to the Enladrillado, a soaring platform of hexagonal basalt. A stunning vantage point, it overlooks a deep river canyon and has 360-degree vistas of an area that includes the peaks of three volcanoes – Cerro Azul, Volcán Quizapú, and Descabezado Grande (The Big Beheaded). The latter can be climbed on a 5-day circuit, organized through tour agencies such as Trekking Chile.

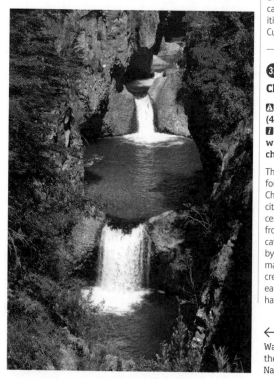

30 Parque Nacional Radal Siete Tazas

B7 **78 miles (125 km) SE of Santa Cruz** **8:30am–5:30pm daily** **conaf.cl**

This national park is named for its most striking natural feature, the Siete Tazas (Seven Bowls). Located in the western section of the park, these are seven connected rock pools formed by the erosive waters of the Río Claro that plunges down a narrow gorge here. Nearby are two breathtaking waterfalls: the 131-ft- (40-m-) high Velo de la Novia and the 82-ft- (25-m-) high Salto de la Leona. The trail linking Salto de la Leona with the Siete Tazas passes transition forest that features both Central Valley flora and temperate rain forest common to the Lake District farther south. A short distance from the pools, the Sector Parque Inglés has scenic walking, horseback riding, and mountain-biking trails. The Sendero El Bolsón offers visitors a full day's hike to a refuge; beyond, an unsigned trail continues to Reserva Nacional Altos de Lircay (p143). Nature-watching, swimming, and kayaking are all popular activities here.

31 Lago Vichuquén

B7 **60 miles (96 km) SW of Santa Cruz** **Manuel Rodríguez 315, Vichuquén; www.turismovichuquen.cl**

Central Valley's most beautiful lake, Lago Vichuquén is an intensely blue tongue of water ringed by green, pine-swathed hills. The lake and its surrounds attract birdlife, including species of swan, heron, and duck. In Colonial times, the rich suggestiveness of this area led to its notoriety as a supposed meeting place of sorcerers and witches. Today, it attracts bikers, anglers, windsurfers, water-skiers, horseback-riding aficionados, and nature-watchers.

Some 4 miles (7 km) east of the lake is the historical settlement of Vichuquén, built by the Spanish in 1585 on the site of an old Incan colony. Today, it preserves warrens of winding Colonial streets lined with orange trees and fronted by adobe houses. Both Vichuquén and its lake can be included on wine tour itineraries of the Valle de Curicó (p141).

INSIDER TIP
Surf's Up

Those looking to catch some waves should consider driving just beyond Vichuquén to the seaside town of Llico, popular for its surf. It also hosts surfing competitions in January and February.

32 Chillán

F1 **252 miles (405 km) S of Santiago** **18 de Septiembre 455; www.municipalidad chillan.cl**

The birthplace of Chile's founder Bernardo O'Higgins, Chillán is one of the oldest cities in the country. It is centered on a main square fronted by a Modernist cathedral that is supported by 11 giant parabolic arches made from reinforced concrete. Built after the 1939 earthquake, the cathedral has a tunnel-like interior.

← Water tumbling between the rock pools of the Parque Nacional Radal Siete Tazas

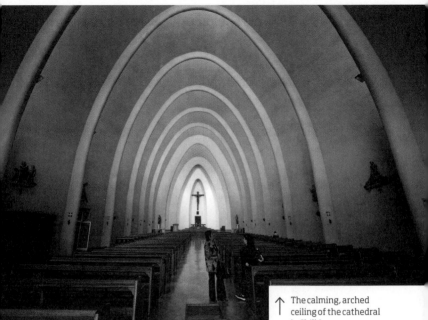

↑ The calming, arched ceiling of the cathedral in Chillán

Above its altar, on a wooden cross pulled from the quake's rubble, is a figure of Christ sculpted in Italy.

Also of interest in Chillán is the **Escuela de México** primary school, whose interior contains two giant murals painted in 1941–2 by Mexican artists David Alfara Siqueiros and Xavier Guerrero. Siqueiros' allegorical *Muerte al Invasor* (Death to the Invader) combines the bold Cubist and Impressionist styles to symbolize the struggle for independence of the Mexican and Chilean peoples. Guerrero's Realist *De Mexico a Chile* (From Mexico to Chile) depicts, among many scenes, a Mexican woman pulling a Chilean baby from rubble.

Another site worth visiting is Chillán's indoor food market, the **Mercado Chillán**, which is an absolute delight for foodies. Eateries here serve various regional specialties; in particular, don't miss out on the city's wonderful chorizo-esque *longaniza* sausages.

Escuela de México
⊛ ⌂ Ave. O'Higgins 25
☎ (042) 221 2012 ⊙ 10am–1pm & 3–6pm Mon–Fri, 10am–6pm Sat & Sun

Mercado Chillán
⌂ 5 de Abríl, Isabel Riquelme, esq El Roble ⊙ 8am–6pm daily

---

③③

Nevados de Chillán
⌂ F1 ⌂ 51 miles (82 km) E of Chillán ⊙ Daily
ⓦ nevadosdechillan.com

This year-round resort is best known for its skiing, but it also features a state-of-the-art thermal spa complex. The winter ski resort sits on the slope of Volcán Chillán and has 28 runs, including the longest one in South America. Expert skiers can enjoy the excellent off-piste skiing here, while the lower part of the mountain also offers great terrain for beginners. The spa complex has thermal pools and outdoor hot springs that rise from natural geothermal fissures. Treatments on offer here include massages, mud baths, aromatherapy, and hydrotherapy. There are several excellent hotels around the region, including the ski area's fantastic Hotel Nevados de Chillán and the posher Gran Hotel Termas de Chillán.

EARTHQUAKE OF 2010

In the early hours of February 27, 2010, an earthquake measuring 8.8 on the Richter scale struck central Chile, destroying homes and buildings, and flattening highways across the region. The quake's epicenter was Concepción, one of Chile's most densely populated cities. Nearby towns were the worst hit, but there was also widespread damage reaching as far as Santiago, 322 miles (518 km) away. Over 500,000 homes were destroyed or severely damaged and an estimated 500 people killed.

34 Saltos del Laja

F1 298 miles (480 km) SW of Santiago From Chillan & Los Angeles 8am-8pm daily saltosdellaja.com

Natural marvels at the southern end of the Central Valley, the Saltos del Laja are four waterfalls plunging into a rocky canyon ringed by green forest. Vapor-drenched trails lie at the base and top of the falls. Reaching 167 ft (51 m), Salto del Laja is the highest fall in the chain, and forms a curtain of white water. Facilities around the falls include hotels and camps.

35 Concepción

F1 322 miles (518 km) SW of Santiago Aníbal Pinto 460; www. concepcion.cl

A vibrant university city, Concepción was founded in 1550 as a frontier settlement on the banks of Río Bío-Bío, and in Colonial times acted as the springboard for Spanish attacks on the Mapuche-held Lake District south of the river.

Much of the city's architectural heritage was destroyed in the 19th century by earthquakes and tsunamis, which left behind a rather bland and empty metropolis. The historical highlight is the Mural Historia de Concepción, a huge mural in the regional government headquarters, the Edificio Gobierno Regional. Painted in the Socio-Realist style in 1945 by Chilean artist Gregorio de la Fuente, this mural is a stunning visual description of this region's turbulent history from pre-Hispanic times onward.

Opposite this building, Plaza España has many lively bars and restaurants, while to its north, Plaza Independencia is the historic square from where Bernardo O'Higgins proclaimed Chile's independence in 1818.

The city suffered severe damage in the 2010 earthquake, but it has since managed to rebuild.

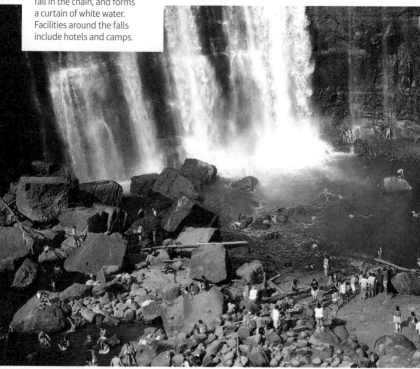

36 🏂 🍴

Parque Nacional Laguna del Laja

🗺 F1 📍 348 miles (561 km) S of Santiago ⏰ 8:30am–2pm & 3–5:30pm daily 🌐 conaf.cl

This compact park protects Chile's northernmost distribution of araucaria trees and mountain cypress. Its grandest natural feature is the Volcán Antuco, whose summit is reached by an undemanding eight-hour return trek. The trail has views of the glacier-covered Sierra Velluda range, just beyond the park's boundaries. A small ski center operates on the volcano between June and October. The park's namesake lake, the Laguna del Laja, was formed by a 1752 eruption. An easy trail skirts this lake and leads to two gorgeous falls: Salto las Chilcas and Saltos del Torbellino. Along the trails, hikers can see plenty of birdlife, as the park is refuge to over 50 bird species, including the Andean condor.

---

37 🏂

Lota

🗺 F1 📍 333 miles (537 km) SW of Santiago 🚌 ℹ Municipalidad, P. Aguirre Cerda 200; www.lotasorprendente.cl

For 150 years, Lota lay at the heart of the Central Valley's coal-mining industry. Its mines were owned by the Cousiño family, who oversaw their investment from a grand villa in town. An earthquake in 1960 destroyed the villa, but its magnificent gardens are open for visits. At their entrance, the **Museo Histórica de Lota** has historical displays on the Cousiño family. The now-closed mines can be seen on tours: visitors descend into the tunnels in a metal cage elevator, and take a look at *Pueblito Minero*, a re-creation of miners' houses that were used as a prop in the Chilean movie *Underground (Subterra)*.

Museo Histórica de Lota
🏂 🏂 📍 Avenida El Morro s/n, Lota Alto ⏰ 10:30am–5:30pm daily 🌐 lotasorprendente.cl

---

38

Tomé

🗺 F1 📍 293 miles (472 km) SW of Santiago 🚌 ℹ Municipalidad, Mariano Egaña 1115; www.tome.cl

A seaside town, Tomé was founded in 1875 as a port for shipping wine and maize from the Central Valley; it later became Chile's main textile port. Tomé's sandy beaches still attract visitors, but the 2010 earthquake and tsunami did severe damage here. Central El Morro is the most popular stretch of white sand, while Playa Bellavista is a family-oriented beach fronted by good restaurants. North of the center, Playa Cocholgüe features high sand dunes and waves for surfers.

← Cascading waterfalls of the Saltos del Laja and (inset) the view from the side.

A DRIVING TOUR
COLCHAGUA VALLEY

Length 47 miles (75 km). The tour needs at least two days.
Starting point San Fernando, 27 miles (43 km) E of Santa Cruz

Chile's premier wine-making region, the Colchagua Valley starts at the Andean foothills and sweeps westward toward the Pacific coast. The valley's fertile floor and rolling hills are home to many wineries that specialize in red wine; nearly all are open for tours and tastings. They feature various architectural styles ranging from ultra-modern designs to Colonial-style estates.

Visitors can make and label wines at **Viña MontGras.** *In March the winery hosts the annual grape harvest festival, Fiesta de la Vendimia.*

Población

FINISH ☐ Viña Los Vascos

Peralillo

Las Majadas

Río Tinguiririca

Owned by the French Rothschild family, **Viña Los Vascos** *runs group tours. It is notable for cabernet sauvignon and carmenere aged in French oak barrels.*

San José del Carmen

Viña Mont Gras ☐ San Rafael

At the center of Chile's leading wine-making region, **Santa Cruz** *is the springboard for Colchagua's wineries. The town ia also serves the terminal for the Tren Sabores del Valle.*

Isla de Yaquil

Palmilla

Villa E Cóndor

Santa Cruz

Viña Viu Manent

Founded in 1935, **Viña Viu Manent** *is housed in a Spanish-style hacienda. It offers vineyard carriage rides, an excellent handicrafts shop, and an equestrian club.*

0 kilometers   6

0 miles   6

N ↑

↑ Winding path down to Santa Cruz Vineyards

Locator Map

Viña Lapostolle is a state-of-the-art winery with a gravity-induced facility which descends six levels beneath ground. Its vineyards produce the award-winning Canto de Apalta wine.

→ Sorting grapes at the family-run Viña Casa Silva

Colchagua's oldest winery, the family-run **Viña Casa Silva** is housed in a Colonial-style building. Tours include carriage rides, polo matches, and rodeo shows.

Colchagua's smallest winery, **Viña Las Ninas** is run by three generations of women from a single French family. Activities here include picnics, walks, and bike rides amid lushly planted vineyards.

Viña Casa Silva

Quilapan Polonia

Cerro Corral
△ 3,842 ft (1,171 m)

START
San Fernando

Viña Lapostolle

Cerro Rukatalca
△ 3,891 ft (1,186 m)

San Jose de Reuelas

5

Viña Las Niñas

Río Tinguiririca

Viña Montes

Roma Arriba

Millahue de Apalta

90

San José de Apalta

Placilla

La Tuna

Nancagua

Tinguiririca

unaco

90

La Dehesa Abajo

890

San Gregorio

Puquillay Bajo

Chimbarongo

826

86

Auquinco

86

Designed along feng shui principles, **Viña Montes** grows only premium and icon wines. Tours include tractor-drawn trailer rides to a hilltop.

Did You Know?

The Colchagua Valley wine region has roughly 50,000 acres of vines.

NORTE GRANDE AND NORTE CHICO

The north is Chile's desert region: an epic landscape of sand dunes, ocher earth, and white-sand cliffs. The land rises from the coast to the altiplano, where camelids roam, flamingos fly, and volcanoes overlook brilliant blue lagoons. Port-cities line the coast, while indigenous hamlets and oasis villages with adobe churches bring the desert to life.

The ever-changing Atacama desert blankets much of the arid Norte Grande (Big North) and the semi-arid Norte Chico (Little North). The original inhabitants of this area belonged to the Diaguita, Aymara, and El Molle cultures, important pre-conquest societies ruled in the past by the Tiwanaku (AD 500–1000) and Incan (1450–1540) empires. The latter was supplanted by Spanish conquistadores and colonizers, who coveted the metal and mineral wealth of the desert, particularly gold, a symbol of power among pre-Hispanic peoples. Pirates of this time, most notably Bartholomew Sharp, sacked Colonial cities such as La Serena, and burnt down historic buildings, such as churches.

Today, mining in the Atacama is the bedrock of Chile's economy and port-cities have prospered from the growth in the industry. Workers have moved to the region, and universities are drawing on local expertise and experience to provide training to aspiring mining engineers.

NORTE GRANDE AND NORTE CHICO

Must Sees

1. Arica
2. San Pedro de Atacama
3. Iquique
4. Parque Nacional Lauca
5. La Serena
6. Valle de Elqui

Experience More

7. Iglesia de San Gerónimo de Poconchile
8. Putre
9. Reserva Nacional Las Vicuñas
10. El Gigante de Atacama
11. Humberstone and Santa Laura
12. Parque Nacional Volcán Isluga
13. Mamiña Hot Springs
14. La Tirana
15. Pica
16. Cerro Pintados
17. Caspana
18. Calama
19. Chiu-Chiu
20. Pukará de Lasana
21. Chuquicamata
22. Termas Baños de Puritama
23. Valle de la Luna
24. Geisers de Tatio
25. Salar de Tara
26. Salar de Atacama
27. Cerro Paranal Observatory
28. Antofagasta
29. La Portada
30. Copiapó
31. Caldera
32. Parque Nacional Pan de Azúcar
33. Parque Nacional Nevado Tres Cruces
34. Ovalle
35. Laguna Verde
36. Reserva Nacional Pinguino de Humboldt
37. Monumento Natural Pichasca
38. Monumento Nacional Valle del Encanto
39. Termas de Socos
40. Parque Nacional Bosque Fray Jorge

Pacific Ocean

PERU

Tacna

PUTRE 8

Chacalluta International Airport ✈

Azapa 4 **PARQUE NACIONAL LAUCA**

ARICA 1 7

9 **RESERVA NACIONAL LAS VICUÑAS**

IGLESIA DE SAN GERÓNIMO DE POCONCHILE

Codpa

Challapata

Camiña

Cuya

Enquelga

Oruro

4

TARAPACÁ

12 **PARQUE NACIONAL VOLCÁN ISLUGA**

Potosí

EL GIGANTE DE ATACAMA 10

13 **MAMIÑA HOT SPRINGS**

HUMBERSTONE AND SANTA LAURA

IQUIQUE 3 11 **LA TIRANA**

Diego Aracena International Airport ✈ 14 15 **PICA**

16 **CERRO PINTADOS**

Salar de Uyuni

Uyuni

Lagunas

Atacama Desert

BOLIVIA

Quillagua

Ollagüe

Tupiza

16

Volcán San Pedro 20,206 ft (6,158 m)

PUKARÁ DE LASANA

Tocopilla

CHUQUICAMATA 21 20

24 **GEISERS DE TATIO**

El Loa Airport ✈ 18 19 17 **CASPANA**

CALAMA

CHIU-CHIU

Pumahuasi

22 **TERMAS BAÑOS DE PURITAMA**

VALLE DE LA LUNA 23 2 **SAN PEDRO DE ATACAMA**

Mejillones

26 25 **SALAR DE TARA**

Humahuaca

LA PORTADA 29 ✈ Andrés Sabella Gálvez Airport

SALAR DE ATACAMA

ANTOFAGASTA 28

Socaire

Cerro Rincón 18,353 ft (5,594 m)

San Salvador de Jujuy

ANTOFAGASTA

9

△ *Volcán Socompa 19,786 ft (6,030 m)*

Salta

CERRO PARANAL OBSERVATORY 27

5

Atacama Desert

Paposo

Catalina

Volcán Azufre 18,635 ft (5,679 m)

La Viña

Taltal

43

40

ARGENTINA

El Peñón

9

PARQUE NACIONAL PAN DE AZÚCAR 32

El Salvador

Chañaral

San Miguel de Tucumán

Diego de Almagro

35 **LAGUNA VERDE**

CALDERA 31

△ *Volcán Ojos del Salado 22,609 ft (6,891 m)*

Desierto de Atacama Airport ✈ 30 **COPIAPÓ**

33 **PARQUE NACIONAL NEVADO TRES CRUCES**

Bahía Copiapó

Tierra Amarilla

Belén

Catamarca

38

Punta de Díaz

Juntas

Carrizal Bajo

ATACAMA

Huasco

Cerro del Potro 19,127 ft (5,829 m)

Vallenar

Alto del Carmen

Domeyko

Cerro del Toro 20,931 ft (6,379 m)

Chilecito

40

La Rioja

RESERVA NACIONAL PINGÜINO DE HUMBOLDT 36

Guandacol

Casa de Piedra

La Higuera

5

LA SERENA 5 ✈ La Florida Airport

Coquimbo

Vicuña

6 **VALLE DE ELQUI**

Patquía

38

OVALLE 37

PARQUE NACIONAL BOSQUE FRAY JORGE 40 34

MONUMENTO NATURAL PICHASCA

Chañar

38

TERMAS DE SOCOS 39 38

MONUMENTO NACIONAL VALLE DEL ENCANTO

COQUIMBO

Salamanca

San Juan

40

Los Vilos

5

CENTRAL VALLEY

p114

0 kilometers   150

0 miles   150

N ↑

1

ARICA

📍 B1 🚗 1,034 miles (1,664 km) N of Santiago ✈️🚌🚆
Aeropuerto Chacalluta ℹ️ Sernatur, San Marcos 101;
www.turismoenarica.com

The coastal city of Arica has palm-lined plazas and
a vibrant indigenous flavor. Grand Peruvian-era
buildings, including some by France's Gustave Eiffel,
are spread across this compact grid of streets and
plazas. Indigenous crafts and markets add bursts of
color, alongside sweeping beaches and outstanding
archaeological highlights.

① 🤿 Ⓜ️ 🖥️
Morro de Arica

📍 Camino Al Morro, off Colón
🕙 10am-8pm Tue-Sun
🌐 mmorro.rialis.cl

This 360-ft- (110-m-) high cliff
towers above the city center
and marks the end of Chile's
coastal cordillera. It stands as
a symbol of national glory,

←

Morenada dance group
performing during a parade
at the Carnaval in Arica

marking the site where, in
1880, Chilean forces stormed
Peruvian fortifications to win
possession of Arica in the War
of the Pacific. At the summit
sits the Museo Histórico y de
Armas, which houses objects of
war, plus a monument to the
unknown soldiers of Chile and
Peru and a 33-ft- (10-m-) high
bronze of Christ.

②
Catedral de San Marcos

📍 San Marcos 260
🕙 8:30am-9pm Mon-Fri,
11am-1pm Sat, 9am-1pm
& 7:30-9pm Sun

Built by French engineer
Gustave Eiffel, Arica's

💬 INSIDER TIP
Beaches

South of Arica center,
Playa El Laucho and the
pretty Playa La Lisera
have calm waters. North
of the center, Playa
Chinchorro is popular for
its big surfer waves, as is
the rustic Playa Las
Machas farther on.

↑ The Chile national flag marking the summit of the Morro de Arica

cast-iron, Neo-Gothic cathedral was prefabricated in France and assembled in Arica in 1876. Its latticed facade is a rich chocolate color, and the interior is notable for a delicate tracery that props up the cathedral's columns. The bell near the entrance is from 1729 and belonged to the basilica that stood on this site. Above the altar is a 17th-century sculpture of Christ.

---

③
Museo de Sitio Colón 10

🏠 Avenida Colón 10
📞 (058) 2205041
🕐 10am–6pm Tue–Sun

In 2004, during excavations for a residential project, construction workers found a host of mummies and skeletons from the pre-Columbian Chinchorro culture. Although many similar finds are already displayed at the museum in Azapa, archaeologists decided to leave them in situ, under glass, on the slope just before the Morro, where they now represent an unmissable sight.

---

④ 🍴 🛍
Poblado Artesanal

🏠 Hualles 2825 🕐 10am–1:30pm & 3:30–6:30pm Tue–Sun

On the outskirts of Arica, this craftspeople's village is the place to buy Quechua crafts such as weavings of alpaca and llama wools, ceramics, jewelry, and leather-ware. A walled space, the colony is built in the image of an altiplano village and includes workshops and lodgings that are occupied by local craftspeople. The village has a beautiful church with fascinating murals.

STAY

Hotel Casa Beltrán
A short walk from the beach, this mid-range hotel has comfortable and modern, albeit rather generic, rooms, as well as a good in-house restaurant-bar.

🏠 266 Rafael Sotomayor

$ $ $

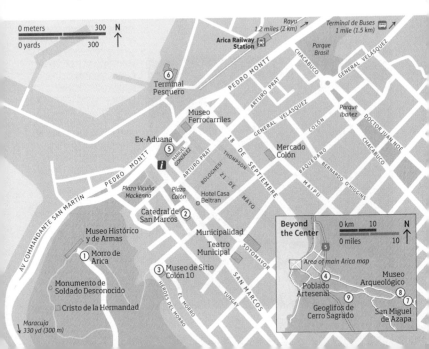

EAT

Rayu

A smart restaurant serving up Peruvian classics such as *ceviche* and *lomo saltado* (a combo of steak strips, onions, tomatoes, fries, and rice).

🏠 2590 Ingeniero, Raúl Pey
🕐 1pm-1:30am Mon-Sat, 1-6pm Sun

$$$

Maracuya

Restaurant specializes in fish and seafood. Its highlights include grilled *corvina* (fish similar to sea bass) with shrimps.

🏠 321 Avenida Comandante San Martín
🕐 12:30pm-3:40pm & 8:15pm-12:30am daily

$$$

⑤
Ex-Aduana

🏠 Manuel González 📞 (058) 2209501 🕐 9am-5:30pm Mon-Thu, 9am-6:30pm Fri, 10:30am-2pm Sat

Another building designed by Gustave Eiffel, the city's former customs house (officially called the Casa de la Cultura) was prefabricated in France and erected in Arica in 1874. This squat, brick building has an attractive pink-and-white striped exterior. Its interior, with cast-iron pillars and spiral staircase, houses art exhibitions. Photographs show pre-urban Arica, including shots of Morro de Arica with thousands of penguins.

⑥
Terminal Pesquero

🏠 Avenida Commandante San Martín 🕐 7am-3pm Tue-Fri, 7am-4pm Sat & Sun (boat tours)
🌐 terminalpesquero.cl

In Arica's port area, Terminal Pesquero (Fishermen's Port) is a smelly but colorful experience. Boisterous water birds and sea lions vie over discarded scraps, while fishermen clean and gut the day's catch at stalls. Frequent boat tours of the bay depart from here.

⑦
San Miguel de Azapa

🏠 Azapa Valley, 7.5 miles (12 km) east of Arica

A short drive from Arica, tranquil San Miguel de Azapa is a pleasant spot for a morning or late-afternoon stroll. Known for its enticing olive groves and beautiful tropical fruit trees, the village is home to a bright and colorful cemetery, which is situated dramatically in the desert, loomed over by a stark cliff-face.

⑧
Museo Arqueológico San Miguel de Azapa

🏠 Camino Azapa, Km 12
🕐 10am-6pm daily
🌐 masma.uta.cl

This outstanding and intriguing museum of archaeology displays objects ranging from up to 10,000 years ago and includes an exhibit showcasing the world's oldest known mummies, the Chinchorro mummies. This exhibit comprises a man, woman, and two children buried in mass graves by the Chinchorro people between 4,000 and 8,000 years ago. The site also includes a display of severed heads, part of a "cult of the head" that existed between 500 BC and AD 500. Museo Arqueológico San Miguel de

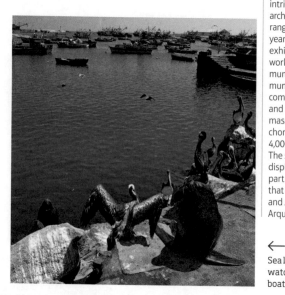

← Sea lions and pelicans watching over the fishing boats at Terminal Pesquero

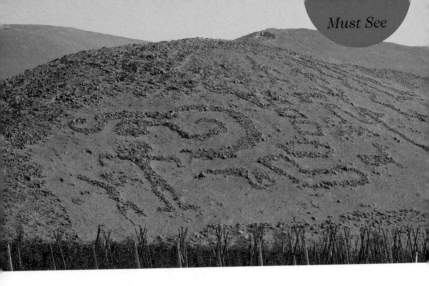

Azapa also has an intriguing exhibition that shows some of the utensils that were carved by the Tiwanaku people (AD 500–1000) to manufacture hallucinogens. Visitors can also explore a series of ancient petroglyphs, which are rock carvings made by chipping away directly on the surface of the rock, usually using a stone chisel, a hammerstone, or another similar tool. Also interesting the mummies an Incan fisherman and a baby.

---

⑨
Geoglifos de Cerro Sagrado

🏛 Alto Ramírez, Valle Azapa

The great stone mosaic on the Cerro Sagrado (Sacred Mount) hillside is the most eye-catching of several enormous geoglyphs in the Valle Azapa. A mosaic of anthropomorphic and zoomorphic motifs, it depicts giant human figures – adult and child – as well as mammoth lizards and llamas. The latter are composed in dynamic form, as if scaling up or bounding across this barren hillside. The geoglyphs date from this region's Incan period

(AD 1450–1500), when farmers settled this green valley. Close to Cerro Sagrado is the quaint and beautiful village of Pampa Alto Ramíre, which is still home to the remains of 30 dwellings, all of which are made of various lightweight materials. Geoglifos de Cerro Sagrado is also home to small llama corrals, some

↑ Geoglyphs cut into the hillside, Geoglifos de Cerro Sagrado

storehouses, a cemetery, and two fresh water springs that once provided the water needed for crop irrigation and consumption. Visitors can stroll around and explore all of these sites.

CHINCHORRO MUMMIES

The Chinchorro populated Norte Grande during 6000–2000 BC and their mummies, buried in the Atacama desert, are the oldest in the world. The Chinchorro method of mummification was complex - it entailed the removal of the skin, extraction of the internal organs and extremities, and filling in of cavities with mud, ash, and resinous substances. The mummies were then buried in the extended position in collective tombs, which comprised adults, children, and fetuses.

❷

SAN PEDRO DE ATACAMA

🅰 C2 📍 304 miles (490 km) SE of Inique ✈️ 🚌 ℹ️ Toconao esq Gustavo Le Paige; www.sanpedroatacama.com

Picturesque San Pedro de Atacama is northern Chile's traveler hub, the springboard for trips into an other-worldly region of dazzling salt flats, lunar valleys, soaring volcanoes, high-altitude lagoons and hot springs, and the ruins of pre-Inca forts.

① Iglesia de San Pedro de Atacama

🅰 Caracoles 362 🕐 10am-9pm Thu-Tue

Overlooking the town's pretty plaza, lined with algorrobo and pepper trees, the Iglesia de San Pedro de Atacama is a white adobe structure whose doors and ceiling are made from cactus wood bound together with llama leather. The roof is made of large rafters of algarrobo wood overlaid by slices of cactus logs.

The church was built after the town's first church was destroyed. The current structure dates from the 1740s, though the rustic bell tower was added in the 1800s and the surrounded white

Did You Know?

San Pedro de Atacama prohibits building above two stories, to enhance the town's oasis impression.

walls were renovated in the 1970s. Further restoration work occurred in 2009. Inside, visitors will find numerous religious icons, most notably one of San Pedro (St. Peter), from whom the town takes its name, and St. Mary and St. Joseph, both softly illuminated by a fluorescent lighting feature. The interior also contains an alterpiece that is delicately carved and painted in bright and vibrant colors, providing a contrast against the white walls.

② Casa Incaica

📞 (057) 2544734 🕐 Times vary; call ahead

Standing directly opposite the Iglesia de San Pedro de Atacama, the Casa Incaica (Inca House) is the oldest house in the town. Rickety and with a roof that is seemingly on the verge of collapse, the house was reputedly built for the founder of Chile, Pedro de Valdivia, back in 1540. Today, rather more prosaically, it is home to a shop selling local souvenirs, but it is still worth having a quick look inside. The range of souvenirs on offer include authentic alpaca knitware and Rica Rica, a common herb found in the region, characterized by its aroma and often praised for its various medicinal and digestive benefits.

←

A traditional street café found in the city center of San Pedro de Atacama

③

Museo Arqueológico Gustavo Le Paige

🏠 Gustavo Le Paige 380
🕐 For restoration
🌐 iaa.ucn.cl

Named after the Jesuit missionary and pioneer in archaeological research who was its founder, the Museo Arqueológico Gustavo Le Paige (Archeological Museum Gustavo Le Paige) is home to about 380,000 pre-Columbian artifacts and archaeological objects from the Atacameño culture. The vast collection includes stone paraphernalia sculpted with images of animalistic deities, which members of the Tiwanaku (AD 500–1000) culture once used to make hallucinogens. Unfortunately, at the time of writing, the museum is closed for renovations and is unlikely to open before late 2020.

EAT

Tierra Todo Natural
Housed in a building resembling a thatched Nissen hut, this restaurant is renowned for its extensive vegetarian menu.

🏠 Caracoles 271, San Pedro de Atacama
📞 (055) 2851585

$$$

Café Adobe
This large café serves skilfully presented versions of Chilean specialties. The space itself is an attraction, warmed by an open fireplace, and there is live Andean music.

🏠 Caracoles 211
🌐 cafeadobe.cl

$$$

ALMA Observatory, home to the largest radio telescope in the world ↑

④ 🥾 🏍

Museo del Meteorito

📍 Tocopilla 101
🕐 10am-1pm & 2-6pm Tue-Sun 🌐 museodel meteorito.cl

This is a little gem of a museum which, although quite small, tends to generate lots of interest from visitors. Based in a series of compact, interlinked geodesic domes just north of the center of San Pedro de Atacama, the Meteorite Museum is a great place to visit before embarking on a stargazing tour or a visit to the incredible ALMA Observatory, the biggest astronomical project on earth, comprising 50 antennae, each 39 ft (12 m) in diameter. As the name suggests, the museum has a

---

> 💬 INSIDER TIP
> **Keep Active**
>
> Beyond the normal 4X4 trips, there are plenty of other interesting activities on offer around San Pedro de Atacama, including hikes and climbs. Agencies like Rancho Cactus (www.rancho-cactus.cl) even offer horseback-riding trips through the desert.

---

collection of 80 different meteorites, most of which have been found in or around the Atacama desert. Visitors are invited to examine, and in some cases handle, the meteorites. There are useful explanatory and educational panels available, as well as interactive displays, including a great multilingual audio guide which is included in the admission price and can help visitors to better understand all the aspects of the museum that are on offer.

---

⑤

Catarpe

📍 5 miles (8 km) N of San Pedro de Atacama

From Pukará de Quitor, determined visitors can continue 3 miles (5 km) north to Catarpe, site of the ruins of a *tambo*, an Inca administrative center. Although the site is far less intact than the *pukará*, the journey to it traverses some breathtakingly wild canyon country and stretches through a difficult but nonetheless beautiful old road that leads to a tunnel built in 1930. The road offers visitors some amazing views of the Catarpe valley and the incredible surrounding rock formations.

---

⑥ 🏍

Pukará de Quitor

📍 2 miles (3 km) N of San Pedro de Atacama
🕐 8am-5pm daily
🌐 monumnetos.gob.cl

Accessible by taxi, mountain bike, or even on horseback from San Pedro de Atacama, the Pukará de Quitor gets its name from the Ayllu de Quitor, once locals whose fields were based at the foot of the site. Pukará de Quitor comprises the ruins of a red-stone pre-Inca fortress, built in the 12th century during a period of warfare. The *pukará* was attacked by the Spanish in the 1520s but remarkably its defenders managed to hold out for some two decades until they were finally defeated by conquistador Francisco de Aguirre and his band of men in 1540. In recent years, the fortress has been partially restored and it is easy to see why it was once so impregnable. The ruins sprawl across a steep hillside, which overlooks the stunning San Pedro river canyon and consist of an outer wall, narrow passageways, some living quarters, grain storehouses, herding pens, and a collection of communal squares. Visitors can take a walking trail and climb to the top of the fortress for fantastic views of the canyon, volcanoes, and the Valle de la Muerte. Pukará de Quitor was designated a national monument in 1982.

---

⑦ 🏍 🥾 🏛

Aldea de Tulor

📍 6 miles (9 km) SW of San Pedro de Atacama
🕐 Dec-Mar: 9am-7pm daily; Apr-Nov: 8:30am-5:30pm

Excavated in 1982, after being buried under sand for 1,500 years, the Aldea de Tulor comprises the 2,800-year-old red-clay ruins of one of Chile's first sedentary settlements.

The Atacameño abandoned this site in AD 500 owing to the encroaching desert. The remains of the settlement were eventually rediscovered in the late 1950s by an intrepid Belgian priest and amateur archaeologist, Gustavo Le Paige, who also founded the eponymous museum in San Pedro de Atacama (p159). Today the walls of their settlement and its doorways, passageways, and huge honeycomb-like patterns of rooms lie partially or fully exposed to view. Most visitors travel to Tulor independently by car via its sandy tracks, on mountain bike or even horseback, crossing the dusky Atacama desert in the dark shadows of impressive and towering volcanoes. Buggy safaris and guided archaeological tours take travelers around the sites of the ancient settlement.

⑧ 🖎
Valle de la Muerte

🅰 C2 🏠 6 miles (10 km) W of San Pedro de Atacama; Camino a Calama

An otherworldly spectacle of huge sand dunes and jagged red-rock pinnacles, Valle de la Muerte (Valley of Death) was thrust upward from the earth's crust 23 million years ago during the violent upheaval that created the Andes. Also known as Valle de Mart (Valley of Mars), this region's death tag is no misnomer – though rich in mineral deposits, it is one of the driest, most inhospitable places on the planet and no known life exists here. Guided tours to Valle de la Luna (p184) stop briefly en route, often at sunset. Travelers with more time can join horseback excursions, including full-moon rides.

> Excavated in 1982, after being buried under sand for 1,500 years, the Aldea de Tulor comprises the 2,800-year-old red-clay ruins of one of Chile's first sedentary settlements.

DRINK

Chela Cabur
This bar offers a great range of Chilean and imported beers and has a welcoming vibe.

🅰 Caracoles 212, San Pedro de Atacama
📞 (055) 285 1576

$$$

STAY

Tierra Atacama
This gorgeous boutique hotel on the edge of town features swish en suites and an excellent restaurant-bar serving innovative twists on Chilean cuisine.

🅰 Séquitor s/n, San Pedro de Atacama
🌐 tierrahotels.com

$$$

← The mighty Duna Mayor (Greater Dune) in Valle de la Muerte, Atacama desert

③

IQUIQUE

🅐 B2 📍 196 miles (316 km) S of Arica ✈🚌 ℹ️ Sernatur, Aníbal Pinto 436; 9am–6pm Mon–Fri, 10am–2pm Sat; www.iquique.cl

Originally part of Peru, Iquique was annexed by Chile during the War of the Pacific (1879–83) and emerged as its nitrate capital. Opulent buildings from the nitrate era stand testament to the city's decadent past, when Iquique is said to have consumed greater quantities of champagne per capita than any other city in the world.

① 🅜³

Palacio Astoreca

📍 O'Higgins 350 🕙 10am–6pm Mon–Fri, 11am–2pm Sat 📞 (057) 2526890

One of Iquique's extravagant mansions, Palacio Astoreca is a beautiful 27-room house that was designed in British Georgian style for a nitrate magnate in 1903. The building was constructed with Douglas fir that was shipped from the US. The house retains vestiges of a glorious past that include silk wallpaper, a grand staircase, and a stained-glass skylight in its reception hall. Today, this grand building serves as Iquique's cultural center, and hosts occasional art exhibitions and workshops.

The permanent exhibitions include re-creations of nitrate-era living quarters with original Art Nouveau furnishings. On display is a collection of seashells of varying sizes from around the world. The work of local and national artists is featured, including a fine collection of engravings by the Chilean painter Roberto Matta, who was considered one of the great representatives of Surrealism.

②

Cerro Dragón

Popular with parapente (paragliding) enthusiasts, the massive Cerro Dragón sand dune looms high above the city and acts as a launching point for paragliders. After a running start off the dune, soar above the city and get

Did You Know?

Iquique is one of only two free ports of Chile, the other one being Punta Arenas, in the country's far south.

↑ Iquique set below a vast sand dune popular for paragliding

propelled by the currents before landing on the beach. Paragliding here makes for a truly memorable experience. Stretching 2.5 miles (4 km), the coastal dune probably originated some 20,000 years ago.

③ 🪂

Teatro Municipal

🏠 Calle Thompson 269
📞 (057) 2544734
🕐 10am-6pm Mon-Fri, 10am-2pm Sat

Built in 1890 at the height of the Chilean nitrate boom, Iquique's Teatro Municipal is housed in a magnificent wooden structure, whose Neo-Classical facade is ornamented with female figures cut in stone, symbolizing various theatrical elements, such as costume and dance. The foyer, which is topped by a cupola, has a ceiling painted with cherubic allegories of music, dance, painting, and theater, as well as various depictions of famed literary and musical masters, including William Shakespeare, Frédéric Chopin, and Wolfgang Amadeus Mozart. A domed ceiling crowns the beautiful auditorium and is painted with more theatrical motifs, including musical instruments and theater masks that are said to symbolize comedy and tragedy. Adjacent to the stage is a set of stairs that descend to the bowels of this edifice, where century-old wooden pulleys and wheels still serve as stage machinery. The theater attracts some of the greatest international talent from around the world, in ballet, opera, and various forms and styles of music.

STAY

Hotel Terrado Suites
This high-rise hotel, based at Playa Cavancha, has various rooms on offer, including ones with balconies and sea views. There is a selection of nice restaurants based nearby.

🏠 Los Rieles 126
📞 (057) 2363901

$ $ $

↑ The historic Torre Reloj, a symbolic landmark of the city located on Plaza Arturo Prat

EAT

El Tercer Ojito

The menu features various options, including sushi, satay, pad thai, and curry.

🏠 1–5pm & 7pm–1am Mon–Sat, 1–4pm Sun

$$$

El Viejo Wagon

Packed with historical artifacts, this restaurant feels like a regional museum. Fortunately, the food is good, particularly the fish and seafood dishes.

🏠 Thomson 85
🕐 1–4pm & 8pm–2am Mon–Sat, 1–4pm Sun

$$$

④ 🍴 🖥 🛍

Plaza Arturo Prat

🏠 Between Calle Aníbal Pinto & Avenida Baquedano

Iquique's main square, Plaza Arturo Prat is located in the heart of the city's historic center. Dominating the plaza is the city's emblematic landmark, the flamboyant Torre Reloj. Built from Douglas fir by the English community in 1877, this clock tower is made up of three tapering tiers that are painted white and rise to 82 ft (25 m). The tower's arched base features a bust of Arturo Prat, considered Chile's greatest naval hero. He captained the *Esmeralda* schooner that was sunk by the Peruvian battleship *Huáscar* at the Battle of Iquique during the War of the Pacific. This battle

→

A mix of high-rise buildings and mountains creating the backdrop to Playa Cavancha

ended with the death of Prat and much of his crew, but proved to be the turning point in a war that secured possession of Iquique for Chile and dominion over this area's lucrative nitrate deposits.

⑤ 🍴

Casino Español

🏠 Plaza Prat 584
🕐 12:30am–4pm, & 8–11pm Mon–Sat, 12:30–4pm Sun
🌐 casinoespanoliquique.cl

Constructed by the city's Spanish community in 1904, the Casino Español occupies a Moorish-style wooden edifice with an arched, Arabesque facade. Its domed interior recalls the Moorish palaces of Andalusian Spain with every inch of floor, wall, and ceiling space decorated with glittering Moorish motifs, patterns, and inscriptions. Arabesque archways and columns divide the salons, and kaleidoscopically glazed tiles decorate floors overlooked by Spanish stained glass, mirrors, and statues.

There is also a public restaurant housed in Casino Español, the walls of which are embellished with eight giant oil paintings by well-known Spanish artist Antonio Torrecilla. Completed in 1907, these depict scenes from Miguel de Cervantes' famous novel *Don Quijote de la Mancha* (1605).

---

⑥

Beaches

🅰 **Along Avenida Arturo Prat**

Located within walking distance south of the city center, Playa Cavancha is Iquique's most popular beach for swimming. Further south lies Playa Brava, accessible via shared taxis, a favorite among sunbathers, but with treacherous rip currents. While it is possible to ride some waves toward the northern end of Playa Cavancha, serious surfers make their way further south to the exhilarating breaks of Playa Huaiquique.

⑦

Museo Regional

🅰 Baquedano 951
🕒 9am–6pm Mon–Thu, 9am–5pm Fri
🌐 registromuseoschile.cl

Orginally founded in 1960, the Regional Museum has been located at its current site since 1987, in the building that once housed the Courts of Justice. The museum traces the original cultures of the area, the emergence of the old city of Iquique, and its growth as a port city, through a series of photographs, while giving an insight into the nitrate industry.

The museum is divided into three areas. Among the important pieces on display are the Isluga ethnographic collection and an Inca mummy found on the Esmeralda Hill of Iquique, which provides evidence of the connection of the region with the great empire of the Incas.

> Constructed by the city's Spanish community in 1904, the Casino Español occupies a Moorish-style wooden edifice with an arched, Arabesque facade.

THE WAR OF THE PACIFIC

Until the outbreak of this conflict (1879–83), Chile's northern border territory extended only as far as Copiapó in the northern region of Atacama, a seven-hour bus ride from Iquique. The nitrate-rich lands of the Atacama belonged to Bolivia and Peru, though many were controlled by Chilean investors. A dispute over export taxes served to provoke a Chilean invasion of Bolivian territory in 1879 and Peru was soon sucked into the conflict on the side of Bolivia. The War of the Pacific ended with an overwhelming victory for Chile, which significantly expanded its territory and natural resources at the expense of both its adversaries; Bolivia, in contrast, was left landlocked.

④ Ⓜ ▢ 🛍 🍴

PARQUE NACIONAL LAUCA

🅰 C1 🏕 102 miles (165 km) E of Arica 🚌 🅸 CONAF, Putre; (058) 2585704

This is one of Chile's most popular national parks. Wherever you turn the scenery is spectacular – snow capped mountains, glistening lakes, and roaming wildlife. Looming over it all is Volcán Parinacota, a dormant volcano, whose brother Pomerape sits northeast on the Bolivian border.

Northern Chile's most scenic sanctuary, Parque Nacional Lauca protects around 532 sq miles (1,378 sq km) of altiplano wilderness. The park features a tiered ecology that starts at 10,500 ft (3,200 m) in its western zone and rises to over 20,700 ft (6,300 m) in the east. The accessible, high-altitude attractions include brilliantly colored lakes, snowy volcanoes, lava islands, stretches of high tableland, and tiny Aymara villages. There is also an abundance of wildlife. Over 140 bird species find refuge in this area, key among them the ostrich-like ñandu and three species of flamingo, which feed and nest on lakeshores. Wild populations of vicuña and viscacha are also easily spotted.

Exploring the Park

Parque Nacional Lauca can be reached via hired vehicles, organized tours, or the Arica-Bolivia international bus, whose route passes through this area. Within the park, the CH-11 international highway runs east to west, and walking trails link the popular sites of Parinacota, Lago Chungará, and Lagunas Cotacotani. There are CONAF stations at Las Cuevas, Parinacota, and Lago Chungará. The last of these has *refugio* accommodation and Parinacota has a visitors' center.

[1] A hiker crosses a bridge in Las Cuevas. This area marks the start of the Altiplano region and is a great place for spotting local wildlife.

[2] Llama are commonly sighted in Parque Nacional Lauca, as are it's relatives Vicuñas.

[3] Llareta is a cushion plant found at high altitudes.

> 💬 INSIDER TIP
> ### Altitude Sickness
>
> Avoid traveling to high altitudes from sea level. Instead ascend slowly, allowing time to acclimatise. The town of Putre, at 11,500 ft (3,500 m) is a good place to break the journey. Avoid alcohol, drink lots of water, and don't over-exert yourself.

STAY

Terrace Lodge
Just outside of the town of Putre – the best base for visiting the park – this small, friendly B&B has cozy rooms. Staff can arrange tours.

🏠 Circunvalación 25, Putre ⓦ terracelodge.com

Ⓢ Ⓢ Ⓢ

Hotel Kukuli
Clean, basic, and cheap rooms. Be sure to bring layers of warm clothes.

🏠 Baquedano 301, Putre
📞 (09) 9161-4709

Ⓢ Ⓢ Ⓢ

← Parinacota volcano reflected in the waters of Lago Chungará

⑤

LA SERENA

🅰 B5 🅰 435 miles (700 km) S of Antofagasta
🛫 Aeropuerto La Florida ℹ️ Sernatur, Matta 461;
www.turismolaserena.cl

Founded in 1544, La Serena is Chile's second-oldest city and one of its biggest coastal resorts. At La Serena's historical heart, the bell towers of Colonial churches ring out amid contemporary Spanish-style architecture. On the coast are beaches, white waves, and modern buildings lining avenues. At the mouth of Río Elqui, La Serena is the gateway to the lush Valle del Elqui.

① 〰️ 🎿 🍴 🖥️ 🛍️

Plaza de Armas

🏛️ Museo Histórico Gabriel González Videla: Matta 495 📞 (051) 2217189 🕐 10am-6pm Mon-Fri, 10am-1pm Sat 🌐 museohistorico laserena.cl

La Serena's central plaza marks the site of the city's second founding by conquistador Francisco de Aguirre (1507–81). Located here is the beautiful limestone Catedral de La Serena as well as the Neo-Colonial Tribunales de la Justicia (Law Courts) and Municipalidad (City Hall). The latter two date from the 1930s and have extravagant red-and-white exteriors. A Modernist fountain by the sculptor Román Rojas adorns the center of this square. On a corner of the plaza is the Museo Histórico Gabriel González Videla, housed in the 19th-century family home of the former Chilean president whose name it bears. The first floor displays personal objects which once belonged to the former president, and a regional historical museum that occupies the floor upstairs.

②

Catedral de La Serena

🏠 Plaza de Armas 📞 (051) 2216956 ⏰ 9am–1pm & 3–6pm Tue–Sun

The Neo-Classical facade and tower of La Serena's cathedral stand over the Plaza de Armas. Built under the direction of French architect Juan Herbage in 1844, this cathedral preserves the tomb of conquistador Francisco de Aguirre. The building stands on the site of a previous cathedral destroyed in 1680 by English pirate Bartholomew Sharp, who sacked the city over three days before razing it to the ground. Beautiful stained-glass windows from France ornament the cathedral's walls. Located on the grounds, the Museo Sala de Arte Religioso displays religious art and objects from the 17th to 19th centuries.

←

A charming Modernist fountain in Plaza de Armas

DESIERTO FLORIDO

Every 4–5 years, the rainfall on a section of the Atacama causes seeds to explode into life in a phenomenon called the Desierto Florido (Flowering Desert). The event can be seen from La Serena. The desert turns into a carpet of flowers of vibrant blues, reds, purples, and yellows that attract thousands of visitors. It is impossible to predict the year of Desierto Florido, but it occurs between September and November.

③ Iglesia de San Francisco

🏛 Balmaceda 640
📞 (051) 2224477
🕐 8am-1pm & 4-9pm Tue-Fri 🕐 10:30am-1pm & 3-6pm Mon- Fri, 10am-2pm Sat & Sun

Built between 1585 and 1590, the Iglesia de San Francisco is the oldest of La Serena's wonderful stone churches, and the only one of the city's temples to escape destruction at the hands of several pirates, most notably Bartholomew Sharp. Iglesia de San Francisco is crowned by a bell tower and cupola, and its exterior walls are flamboyantly carved with Baroque motifs a design that is considered mestizo for its South American influences. In the early years of the 20th century, part of the convent was sold and demolished to build the Barrio París-Londres. Adjacent to the church, the Museo de Colonial Iglesia San Francisco holds an interesting collection of religious art and imagery dating from the arrival of the Franciscan Order to Chile in the 16th century, including a Bible penned in 1538.

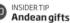

💬 INSIDER TIP
Andean gifts

La Recova is a bustling local market, which provides a perfect opportunity to find local gifts for friends and family. Options include rain sticks, artisan jewelry, and a range of Andean wool clothing.

④ Museo Arqueológico

🏛 Cordovez, esq Cienfuegos
📞 (051) 2672210
🕐 9:30am-6pm Tue-Fri, 10am-1pm & 4-7pm Sat, 10am-1pm Sun 🌐 museo arqueologico laserena.cl

Entered via an 18th-century Baroque portal, La Serena's archaeological museum displays various different pre-Columbian objects stemming from the regions of Norte Chico, Norte Grande, and Easter Island. Some of the artifacts include petroglyphs carved by the Molle civilization (AD 1–700) and ceramics painted by the Diaguita between AD 1000 and 1536. Perhaps the most remarkable exhibit at the Museo Arqueológico is the 1,500-year-old mummy dug up in the dusty Atacama desert near the village of Chiu-Chiu, which is essential viewing for people who are interested in pre-Colombian history. Also essential is the 10-ft- (3-m-) tall *moai* statue that came from Easter Island.

⑤ Museo Mineralógico

🏛 Benavente 980
📞 (051) 2204096
🕐 9:30am-12:30pm & 2-5pm Mon-Fri

Set in the grounds of the Universidad de La Serena, the museum of mining and metallurgy features over 2,000 mineral and rock samples, all of which were collected by the Polish mineralogist Ignacio Domeyko, who arrived in Chile at the height of its 19th-century mining boom. Displays include samples from each of Chile's major mining zones and exhibits of all their different minerals, ranging from gold to magnesium, which glitter and shine in beautiful glass display boxes. Arguably the most compelling exhibits are great boulder-sized, multi-colored crystallized rock samples, and the exhibit that displays a meteorite that crashed into the

↑ Fascinating moai statue at Museo Arqueológico

Atacama desert in 1861. Other displays include mineral samples from outside Chile, collected from Europe, Asia, and Africa.

The museum often assists with Chilean mineralogical, petrographic, and geological teaching, and also contributes to the preparation and training of mining engineers at the university.

Sands of Avenida del Mar and (inset) the Monumental Lighthouse ↑

⑥ 🍴 ☕ 🛍

Avenida del Mar

📍 Benavente 980
📞 (051) 2204096
🕐 9:30am–12:30pm & 2–5pm Mon–Fri.

La Serena's 4-mile- (6-km-) long coastal boulevard is the city's thriving restaurant and bar zone, where visitors can drink interesting cocktails before grabbing something to eat. The avenue, which is lined by sandy beaches and big white waves on one side and by modern hotels, apartment blocks, bars, and restaurants on the other, is a frenzy of day- and night-time activity in summer. In the offpeak season, it offers dramatic sea walks, especially at sunset. A 20-minute walk from the center, west along the city's main Avenida Francisco de Aguirre, leads to El Faro Monumental, a fascinating lighthouse marking the northern end of Avenida del Mar.

The lighthouse, which was built in between 1950 and 1951 at the request of President Gabriel González Videla, is one of the most popular tourist attractions in the area. Beaches around this area are rustic, with massive waves that attract surfers from across Chile. Just south of the El Faro Monumental lighthouse are the main bathing beaches, Playa 4 Esquinas and Playa Canto del Agua, which have plenty of bars and restaurants.

EAT

Casona del 900
The menu at the traditionally decorated Casona del 900 is extensive. Most people share mixed grills, but there's also a nice selection of seafood.

📍 Francisco de Aguirre 443
📞 (015) 2520767

⑤⑤⑤

Porota's
A beautiful setting for finely presented dishes such as ravioli, risotto, and Thai chicken.

📍 Avenida del Mar 900-B
📞 (015) 2210937

⑤⑤⑤

> Perhaps the most remarkable exhibit at the Museo Arqueológico is the 1,500-year-old mummy dug up in the dusty Atacama desert Chiu-Chiu.

6

VALLE DE ELQUI

◉ B5 🚌 From La Serena and Santiago 🌐 chile.
travel/en/where-to-go/north-and-the-atacama-
desert/elqui-valley

East of La Serena, the tranquil, slow-paced Valle
de Elqui (Elqui Valley) feels like another world. A
welcome contrast to the largely arid landscapes of the
Norte Chico, this lush valley is a famous stargazing
destination, home to Chile's finest pisco distilleries,
and has strong associations with Nobel Prize-winning
poet Gabriela Mistral, who was born and raised here.

① Vicuña

**🏠 39 miles (63 km) E of La
Serena** 🚌 **ℹ Gabriela
Mistral, esq San Martín;
www.turismovicuna.cl**

Set in the valley of Río Elqui,
Vicuña is a small town of adobe
houses ringed by rippled
mountains. The birthplace of
Chile's Nobel Prize-winning
poet, Gabriela Mistral (p38),
Vicuña is a popular pilgrimage
site for writers and artists. The
Museo Gabriela Mistral
displays personal items of

the celebrated poet, including
books, paintings, and awards.
At the center of town, sculptures inspired by Mistral's
works adorn Vicuña's plaza.
Overlooking the plaza is the
landmark Torre Bauer, an
incongruous yet charming
red Bavarian tower. It was
constructed in 1905 at the
behest of Vicuña's former
mayor of German descent,
Alfonso Bauer. Adjacent to
the tower, the *cabildo* (town
hall) dates from 1826 and
houses a small, historically
themed museum as well as
an information office for

visitors. Also bordering
the plaza, the Iglesia de la
Inmaculada Concepción was
built in 1909 and has a luminous interior with beautiful
frescoes on the ceiling. The
font here was used to baptize
Mistral in 1889.

Located two blocks east of
the plaza, the **Museo Casa El
Solar de los Madariaga** is a
restored adobe house from
1875 with period furnishings,
photographs, and artifacts.
At the edge of town is **Planta
Capel**, Chile's biggest pisco
distillery. Guided tours take
visitors to its vineyards, plant
facilities, and a pisco museum,
and end with tastings.

Museo Gabriela Mistral

⊗ 🏠 Gabriela Mistral 759
⏰ 10am–5:45pm Tue–Fri,
10:30am–6pm Sat, 10am–
1pm Sun 🌐 mgmistral.cl

△ GREAT VIEW
**View from
the Top**

It's well worth the climb
to the summit of the
Cerro de la Virgen, a hill
near Vicuña, where you
will see panoramic
views of the Valle de
Elqui and wonderful
photo opportunities.

→
An courtyard displaying
various sculptures at the
Museo Gabriela Mistral

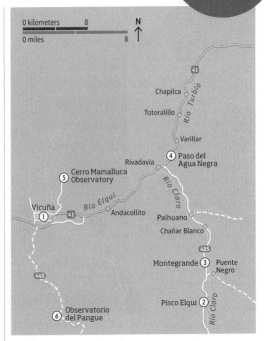

Museo Casa El Solar de los Madariaga

⊛ ⊛ ☐ Gabriela Mistral 683
🕐 Dec–Mar: 10am–2pm & 3–7pm Wed–Mon; Apr–Nov: 11am–1pm & 3–6pm Wed–Mon ⓦ vicunacapital astronomica.cl

Planta Capel

⊛ ⊛ ⓣ ⊜ ☐ Camino a Peralillo s/n 🕐 10am–6pm Fri–Tue ⓦ centroturisti-cocapel.gob.cl

---

② **Pisco Elqui**

☐ 65 miles (105 km) SE of La Serena ⊟ From La Serena & Montegrande ⓦ piscoelqui.com

Set 4,100 ft (1,250 m) above sea level, Pisco Elqui is one of the prettiest villages of Valle del Elqui. It was originally called La Unión by the Spanish, but was renamed in 1936 as part of a government initiative to boost the area's famous commodity, pisco. Among the best-known distilleries here is the **Destileria Pisco Mistral**. This facility has been making pisco for over a century. Tours cover its museum and the production, barreling, and bottling salons, and end with tastings.

Destileria Pisco Mistral

⊛ ⊛ ⓣ ⊜ ☐ O'Higgins 746 📞 (051) 2451358
🕐 10:30am–6pm Tue–Sun ⓦ piscomistral.cl

---

③ **Montegrande**

☐ 63 miles (101 km) E of La Serena ⊟ From La Serena & Vicuña

The tiny village of Montegrande lies at the eastern end of Valle del Elqui, at 3,600 ft (1,100 m) above sea level. Here, the valley narrows to a width of just 1,312 ft (400 m) and is surrounded by the steep slopes of the pre-cordillera, behind which the snowcapped peaks of the Andes form a backdrop.

The poet-diplomat Gabriela Mistral spent her childhood in Montegrande, having moved from Vicuña with her mother and stepsister when she was three years old.

The house in which Mistral grew up is preserved as the **Museo de Sitio Casa-Escuela Gabriela Mistral**. It doubled as a school when Mistral lived here and has furniture and personal belongings of the poet.

Prior to her death in 1957, Mistral had requested that she be laid to rest in Montegrande; her tomb lies on the crest of a low hill near the village plaza. Facing this tree-lined plaza is a church. Mistral took her first communion in its decorative interior.

Museo de Sitio Casa-Escuela Gabriela Mistral

🕐 10am–1pm & 3–6pm Tue–Sun

> The birthplace of Chile's Nobel Prize-winning poet, Gabriela Mistral, Vicuña is a popular pilgrimage site for writers and artists.

STAY

El Tesoro de Elqui

Delightful German-run establishment with dorms and private cabins surrounded by peaceful gardens, plus a swimming pool, hammocks, and a great little café. The property also offers various unique activities, including hot tubs under the starry night skies and therapy with Tibetan basins.

⌂ Arturo Prat s/n, Pisco Elqui
🅦 eltesorodeelqui.cl

$$$

Refugio Misterios del Elqui

A collection of thatched-roof cabins with stylish fittings and superb views are set in well-kept grounds, which are also home to a wonderful swimming pool and (unusually) a putting green.

⌂ Arturo Prat s/n, Pisco Elqui
🅦 misteriosdelelqui.cl

$$$

Cabañas Los Sauzales

This charming establishment is located next to the river, with handy private parking and surrounded by gorgeous fruit trees, these cabins offer visitors a taste of nature and tranquility.

⌂ Pisco Elqui, Paiguano
🅦 lossauzales.cl/

$$$

The Paso del Agua Negra snaking around the mountains, (*inset*) partly covered in snow

④
Paso del Agua Negra

📍 115 miles (185 km) E of Vicuña

The spectacular road, Ruta 41, is on the Chilean side of Paso del Agua Negra. It twists and turns through mountains and skirts the Andean border between Chile and Argentina The road rises to 15,633-ft (4,765-m) above sea level.

The views are made even more spectacular by the presence of *penitentes* (enormous snow pinnacles that are sculpted into unearthly shapes by the fierce wind); so called as they resemble hunched forms of penitent monks. The route also passes the turquoise reservoir known as La Laguna and leads to the hot-springs resort of Termas de Pismanta

in Argentina and to the provincial capital San Juan.

Note that Paso del Agua Negra is normally only open in summer – snows often close the route between May and October. If you're planning on crossing early or late in the season, check with the authorities beforehand that the road is still passable.

⑤
Cerro Mamalluca Observatory

📍 6 miles (9 km) NE of Vicuña ⏱ Tours are mandatory; contact the information center in Vicaña (051 2670330) for reservations & departures
🅦 turismoastronomico.cl

One of the valley's greatest attractions is stargazing. Opened to the public in

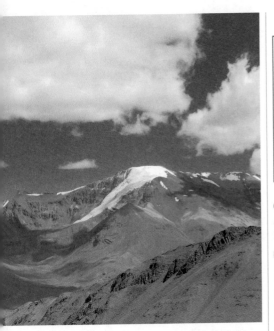

HIDDEN GEM
Cochiguaz

On the eastern edge of the valley, the village of Cochiguaz has a strong new age vibe and locals offer an array of therapeutic treatments and classes. It's also, reputedly, a good place to spot UFOs.

⑥ Ⓜ3

Observatorio del Pangue

📍 11 miles (17 km) S of Vicuña 🌐 odp-i. blogspot.co.uk

Run by French and Chilean astronomers, Observatorio del Pangue arranges nightly tours of the stars. The tours start at 8:30pm and have a maximum capacity of ten people. Visitors are shown the wonders of the universe in optimal conditions, using state-of-the-art telescopes.

The Observatorio del Pangue stands atop a hill in a mountainous landscape from where the views are stunning. Yet the most noticeable feature here is the quality of the sky, which is the result of a rare combination of an adjusted geology, a favorable local climate, and an absence of light pollution.

November 1998 as the first project of its kind, the fascinating Cerro Mamalluca Observatory provides the perfect spot to do so. It is a large complex of huge telescopes and white domed buildings that sit like giant golf balls on the mountainside.

The facility can only be seen by taking two-hour guided tours that are conducted in English and Spanish by specialized guides. Visitors are invited to participate in a cosmic journey through sounds and images, and to use the lens of a powerful 12-inch telescope to view stars and planets. The observatory's spherical roof slides open to reveal the Milky Way, constellations that are thousands of light years away, planets, nebulae, and clusters, as well as blue and red stars. Other highlights include watching the rings on Jupiter and Saturn, and craters on the surface of the moon, all of which appear with a photographic clarity in what is one of the clearest night skies in the world.

PISCO

Developed by Spanish settlers in the 16th century, *pisco* is an aromatic, fruity brandy made from distilled Muscat grape wine. The national drink of Chile (and Peru, which claims its version is superior) is commonly consumed neat, in a *pisco* sour (a refreshing aperitif that features lemon juice and sugar), or as a *piscola* (mixed with cola). The Valle de Elqui is the home of Chile's *pisco* industry and many distilleries offer tours and tastings, including Pisco Capel *(www.piscocapel.cl)*, Pisco ABA *(www. piscobaba.cl)*, Pisco Mistral *(www.piscomistral.cl)* and Los Nichos *(www.fundolosnichos.cl)*.

EXPERIENCE MORE

7
Iglesia de San Gerónimo de Poconchile

△B1 △22 miles (35 km) E of Arica; Poconchile

Located in the village of Poconchile, Iglesia de San Gerónimo is the oldest of northern Chile's early Colonial churches. It was built by Spanish priests in 1580, on a site along the old Camino del Inca (Inca Road), and served to evangelize the Aymara people of this area. The church's dazzlingly white exterior is faithful to the classic Spanish Colonial style – a thick adobe perimeter wall marks the boundary of this sacred site and twin bell towers flank its entrance. The restored interior is wooden and painted white. At the back of the church,

Did You Know?

Llamas and guanacos are the largest of the Andean camelids.

a desert cemetery contains old graves marked by pebbles and simple wooden crosses.

8
Putre

△C1 △90 miles (149 km) NE of Arica

The largest of the high-altitude settlements close to Arica, Putre is an oasis town ringed by the pointed peaks of several snow-swathed volcanoes. At 11,500 ft (3,500 m) above sea level, it is a stopover for travelers seeking acclimatization before continuing onward to higher altitude highlights such as the adjacent Parque Nacional Lauca and the more distant Reserva Nacional Las Vicuñas. Putre's roots lie in pre-Incan Chile, but the present town was founded by the Spanish around 1580 as a resting place for muleteers transporting silver from the mines of Potosí, in modern-day Bolivia, to the Pacific coast. The town's most attractive structure is the heavily restored Colonial church fronting the plaza. This edifice dates from 1670 and stands on the site of the original temple that was destroyed by earthquake, and which, according to Spanish

→
Vicuñas and alpacas grazing in the Reserva Nacional Las Vicuñas

chronicles, was completely clad in silver and gold. The rest of Putre is a compact grid of cobbled streets lined with relatively new concrete-and-zinc buildings and old Spanish adobe houses. A selection of hotels and restaurants dot this pleasant altiplano town; tour agencies are found on Calle Baquedano.

9
Reserva Nacional Las Vicuñas

△C1 △143 miles (230 km) E of Arica ⓘCONAF, Guallatire; www.conaf.cl

Spectacular and remote, the Reserva Nacional Las Vicuñas protects a vast wilderness of giant volcanoes, high-altitude tablelands, abandoned Aymara settlements, and diverse indigenous fauna. This reserve has a steppe landscape that rises from

←
Exploring the striking adobe buildings of a hamlet in Putre

13,120 ft (4,000 m) above sea level at its lowest elevation, to 18,370 ft (5,600 m) at its highest. It is overlooked by three 20,000-ft (6,000-m) volcanoes: Volcán Acotango, Volcán Capurata, and Volcán Guallatire. Vicuñas, for whose protection this park was founded in 1983, can be seen bounding across the puna region; ñandus, ostrich-like birds, sprint over open plains; pink flamingos congregate on the banks and vizcachas (large chinchilla-like rodents) scurry over rocks.

In the central sector of the reserve, the llama-herding hamlet of Guallatire has a couple of basic lodging options, the National Forest Corporation (CONAF) ranger post, and a 17th-century church. South of this hamlet, the Monumento Natural Salar de Surire is a dazzlingly white salt plain. Three different species of flamingo nest on its shores in the summer, and on its western bank a CONAF *refugio* offers rustic accommodations. The weather throughout the reserve resembles a desert, so expect drops in temperature at night.

⑩

El Gigante de Atacama

△ C1 **⌖ 50 miles (80 km) NW of Iquique**

Located 9 miles (14 km) east of the town of Huara, this 283-ft- (86-m-) tall geoglyph is the world's largest image of a human being. It rests on the west slope of Cerro Unitas hill, along the Huara-Colchane road. Although there is no public transportation to its location, tours of Humberstone (p178) from Iquique generally stop here.

> ### PUKARÁS AND THE CAMINO DEL INCA
>
> Northern Chile's pre-Incan fortresses, built between AD 1000 and 1450, are known as *pukarás*. In the 11th century, the reigning Tiwanaku empire collapsed, returning autonomy to the Norte Grande's Aymara and Atacameño peoples. However, the peace of empire was replaced by intermittent warfare as local warlords competed for resources. To protect ancestral trading routes, the warlords built *pukarás* on strategic hillsides. The *pukarás'* role as a powerbase continued until the 1450s, when Inca forces sacked them and incorporated their routes into the Camino del Inca (Inca Road), a 3,720-mile (6,000-km) highway that ran the length of the Incan empire.

↑ An abandoned school yard in the ghost town of Humberstone

⓫ Ⓜ Ⓐ

Humberstone and Santa Laura

🅰C1 📍30 miles (48 km) E of Iquique; Ruta A16, Km 3
🚌 🕐9am-7pm daily (tours Tue-Sat, on request)
🌐museodelsalitre.cl

In the 1930s, British investors built the towns of Santa Laura and Humberstone to provide housing and leisure for the workers and management of the area's nitrate mines. By 1960, the advent of artificial nitrates had closed the mines, leaving the two towns eerily abandoned. Today, these UNESCO-protected nitrate ghost towns have become popular visitor attractions. The more-visited Humberstone is a silent grid of named roads, empty plazas, creaking street signs, and shells of deserted buildings and facilities. These include quarters that once housed 3,700 employees, a hospital and school, an outdoor pool, sports fields, a marketplace, a church, clock tower, and a theater that could seat up to 800 people. Each of these desolate structures is signposted with panels bearing historical information that help visitors explore the town independently. Adjacent to these buildings stands the rusting machinery of the town's nitrate mine.

About one mile (1.5 km) east of Humberstone, the smaller ghost town of Santa Laura feels all the more abandoned for receiving fewer visitors. Its hulking processing facilities – which include giant chimneys and mills – are perfectly preserved.

⓬ Ⓨ Ⓓ Ⓐ

Parque Nacional Volcán Isluga

🅰C1 📍155 miles (250 km) NE of Iquique 🚌
🕐8:30am-7:30pm daily
ℹ CONAF; www.conaf.cl

Isolated from northern Chile's beaten path, Parque Nacional Volcán Isluga protects around 674 sq miles (1,741 sq km) of altiplano wilderness that embraces brilliantly hued lagoons, forgotten Aymara villages, and soaring volcanoes, including the 18,209-ft- (5,550-m-) high Volcán Isluga. Home to similar flora and fauna as Parque Nacional Lauca (p166) but much less visited, it's an excellent option for those looking to escape the tourist crowds. The park's highlights are clustered in its eastern sector, accessible via the paved A-55 international highway that connects Iquique with neighboring Bolivia. Close to the park entrance, Isluga is an Aymara village with a beautiful 17th-century church as well as the Pukará de Isluga, a ruined fortress dating from pre-Columbian times.

Also located in the eastern sector, the Aymara village of Enquelga is the gateway to the park's hot springs. This sector has two pristine lakes: Laguna Arabilla has a walking trail along its shore, while Laguna Parinacota is popular for sightings of

Did You Know?

Of the roughly 200 Chilean nitrate works in operation during the industry's heyday, only one still runs.

→

The vast desert landscape of Parque Nacional Volcán Isluga

wildlife, including pink flamingos, camelids, and the taruca, a mid-sized Andean deer.

13 🍴 📷 🛍️

Mamiña Hot Springs

🅰️ C1 📍 78 miles (125 km) E of Iquique; Mamiña 🚌 🌐 termasdemamina.cl

Located 8,860 ft (2,700m) above sea level, the Mamiña Hot Springs have historically been used to cure afflictions ranging from eczema to anxiety since the age of the Incas. They comprise a number of springs, such as Baños de Ipla with its sodium-rich waters and Baños Barros Chinos, famous for its mud baths. Adjacent to the springs you'll find the village of Mamiña, with stone houses, terraced fields, and Incan ruins. The village's restored Iglesia de San Marcos, dating from 1632, is unique among Andean churches for its twin bell towers.

14

La Tirana

🅰️ C2 📍 45 miles (72 km) SE of Iquique 🚌

A somnolent oasis village with adobe houses, La Tirana springs to life each July for the lively Festival de La Tirana, a religious celebration, drawing over 200,000 devotees to the village from across Chile.

The origins of the village can be traced to the 1500s when an Incan princess, notorious for killing Christians, ruled the area. The princess, who was known as La Tirana (The Tyrant), eventually fell in love with a Portuguese prisoner and converted to Christianity, only to have her irate subjects kill them both on their wedding day. In 1540, a Jesuit missionary found the cross marking the princess's grave and ordered the construction of a church on the site. Named the Iglesia de la Virgen del Carmen de la Tirana in honor of Chile's patron saint and the Incan princess, the church became the progenitor of the cult of La Tirana. The **Santuario de la Tirana** comprises the present-day wooden church; a sweeping plaza adorned with effigies of the Virgin and the princess; and the Museo de la Virgen de la Tirana, which displays costumes and masks from the Festival de La Tirana. Inside the church is a polychrome shrine to the Virgin.

Santuario de la Tirana

🕐 9:30am–1pm & 3:30–8pm Mon–Fri, 9am–8pm Sat & Sun 🌐 fiestadelatirana.cl

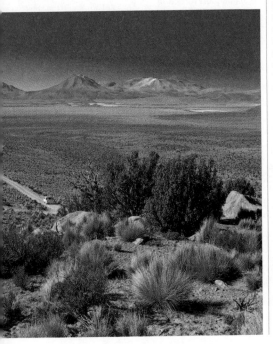

⑮
Pica

🄰C2 🄰71 miles (114 km) E
of Iquique 🚌 🚋Balmaceda
299; www.pica.cl

Known locally as the Flower in
the Sand, Pica is a pleasant
oasis village famed for its
orchards. Regional and local
varieties of fruit trees thrive in
Pica's micro climate, and
adobe houses line its sleepy
streets. Facing the main plaza,
the Iglesia de San Andrés was
built in 1886, and its polychrome interior holds a life-
size representation of the Last
Supper carved from wood.
Just east of the plaza, the
Museo de Pica displays
millennia-old preserved
Chinchorro mummies (p156).
At the edge of town, the warm
waters of **Cocha Resbaladero**
thermal pools have attracted
visitors since the 16th century.

Museo Municipal de Pica
🄰Balmaceda 178 🄲(057)
2741665 🕘9am–2pm & 3:30–
5:30pm Mon–Fri

> **Regional and local
> varieties of fruit
> trees thrive in Pica's
> micro climate, and
> adobe houses line its
> sleepy streets.**

→
The village of Caspana,
which is still home to a
number of traditional
sheep farmers *(inset)*

Cocha Resbaladero
🗺🏊 🄰Balneario Cocha
Resbaladero 🄲(057)
2741310 🕘8am–8pm daily

⑯ 🚶
Cerro Pintados

🄰C2 🄰59 miles (96 km)
SE of Iquique; El Cruce de
Geoglifos de Pintados, La
Panamericana 🕘10am–
4pm daily 🌐wmf.org

The barren hillsides of
Cerro Pintados are etched
with more than 420 gigantic
geoglyphs (p41). Dating from

AD 500–1450, when this region
was part of a caravan route to
the Pacific coast, the geoglyphs
comprise huge geometric
shapes as well as anthropomorphic and zoomorphic
figures including depictions
of fish, llamas, and the ñandu,
a native ostrich-like bird.
These are accessible via a
3-mile (5-km) long path that
skirts the base of the hills.

⑰
Caspana

🄰C2 🄰52 miles (84 km)
E of Calama

One of the oasis villages that
dot the high mountain pass
between Calama and San
Pedro de Atacama, Caspana is
spectacularly situated 11,870
ft (3,260 m) above sea level in
a steep gorge irrigated by a
tributary of the Río Salado.
The village is an adobe jewel,
with monochrome stone-
and-mud houses that were
inhabited by the Atacameño
people before the arrival of
the Incas and Spanish. Today,
it subsists on farming, and
sinuous rows of green terraces

↑ Interior of the church of San Andrés in Pica,
with its beautiful sky-blue ceiling

can be seen along the contours of the lower slopes of the gorge. These are planted with root vegetables, grown to be sold at the market in Calama. At the edge of the village, the adobe and cactus-wood Iglesia San Lucas dates from 1641 and backs on to a small cemetery. The village's **Museo Etnográfico** has archaeological and ethnographic exhibits. The tiny village plaza offers shaded benches and lovely vistas of the rocky gorge, pale houses, and verdant terraces.

Museo Etnográfico

◈ 🖐 🄰 Los Tres Alamos s/n 🕙 10am-1pm & 2-6pm Tue-Fri, 2-6pm Sat & Sun 🅆 mercantil.com

---

18

Calama

🄰 C2 🄰 242 miles (390 km) SE of Iquique ✈ El Aeródromo El Loa de Calama 🚌 🄱 J J Latorre 1689; www. mascalama.cl

The industrial city of Calama is the base for visits to the great copper mines of

Did You Know?

Not a single drop of rain fell in Calama between 1570 and 1971.

Chuquicamata. An oasis city in the driest zone on the planet's driest desert, Calama has its roots in pre-Columbian Chile, and derives its name from the Atacameño word *kara ama*, meaning water haven. Though this name seems rather non-sensical now, until the mid-20th century the town was surrounded by the River Loa.

In the 1920s, Calama boomed as a service town and provider of some of the more debauched diversions to pit workers. Today, the city of Calama is fairly unremarkable. It recently experienced an influx of new inhabitants from nearby Chuquicamata, in 2003, after the open-pit

copper mine there was closed for good,.

Calama's single daytime attraction is the **Parque El Loa**, a riverside tourist park featuring a replica of the Colonial church at Chiu-Chiu (p182). The grounds are also the site of the city's Museo Arqueológico y Etnografico Parque El Loa, which houses artifacts belonging to this area's pre-Incan oasis villages.

Parque El Loa

🕙 🄰 Avenida Bernardo O'Higgins s/n 📞 (055) 2845585 🕙 10am-7pm daily

→

A striking sculpture of a pit worker in Calama

19
Chiu-Chiu

⛰C2 ⧉22 miles (36 km) NE of Calama 🚌

Founded by the Spanish around 1610, Chiu-Chiu is an oasis village of whitewashed adobe houses and cactus-wood doors. Visited on tours from Calama *(p181)*, or more usually from San Pedro de Atacama *(p158)*,

The exterior and interior *(inset)* of the Iglesia San Francisco de Chiu-Chiu ↑

the village conserves one of Chile's oldest churches, the Iglesia San Francisco de Chiu-Chiu. This whitewashed adobe church was built in 1674 in the Spanish Colonial style, with two interesting bell towers, walls over 3 ft (1 m) thick, and a well-preserved interior of mini altars and polychrome statues of saints and virgins. The church's small and quaint grounds, protected by a thick perimeter wall, contain a tiny cemetery that is certainly worth exploring.

One block from the main plaza of Chiu-Chiu is the **Museo Geológico de Chiu-Chiu**, which is worth visiting for some interesting rock and fossil exhibits.

Museo Geológico de Chiu-Chiu
📞(09) 9703-8988 🕙10am–1pm & 3–6pm Thu–Mon

EAT

Talatur
Family-run restaurant serving homemade Chilean food. Rabbit features prominently, but visitors can also expect delicious casseroles.

📍Ruta 21 128, Esmeralda 881

⑤⑤⑤

20
Pukará de Lasana

⛰C2 ⧉28 miles (45 km) N of Calama; Pueblo Lasana, Valle Lasana 🕙9:30am–5pm daily

The stone ruins of the pre-Inca Pukará de Lasana occupy a natural promontory that overlooks the green Valle Lasana from within a rocky canyon. The people of the Atacameño civilization (400 BC–AD 1400) erected this fortress from a pre-existing village during a period of war in the 11th century. Today, the well-preserved ruins are a hilly maze of perimeter walls, roofless houses, storehouses, patios, narrow passageways, and fortifications. Incan forces sacked this site in 1447, and converted it into a strategic administrative center for control of the valley. They abandoned it in the 16th century on the arrival of the Spanish to this region.

---

21 Chuquicamata

🅰C2 📍10 miles (16 km) N of Calama; Entrada al Campamento, J.M. Carrera 🕐Tours 2pm Mon–Fri (book in advance; passport needed for entry) 🌐codelco.com

Visited only by guided tour, Chuquicamata – or "Chuqui," as it is affectionately known to locals – is the world's biggest open-pit mine. This huge copper quarry is about 2 miles (3 km) wide, 3 miles (5 km) long, and an impressive 2,300 ft (1,000 m) deep. The mine is to copper what Saudi Arabia is to oil – the commodity accounts for approximately 11 percent of global production, and any blip in the production process here strikes panic in world copper markets. Chile's biggest state company, Codelco, oversees the mine. It employs 20,000 workers, operates 24 hours per day, and is the single biggest contributor to Chile's coffers, bankrolling the country's health and education systems. Each year this hole in the Andes mountains is gouged ever deeper, a phenomenon brought into stunning perspective on one-hour coach tours of the site. Tours pass refineries and crushing and smelting plants to a viewpoint that overlooks the open pit. Here, visitors can peer into the depths of Chuquicamata, and glimpse the giant 394-ton (400-tonne) dump trucks, with 10-ft- (3-m-

→

Bathing in the warm waters of the Termas Baños de Puritama

Did You Know?

A young Che Guevara visited Chuquicamata during his legendary motorcycle trip across South America.

) high wheels, that ascend and descend its terraced walls like worker ants. It is advisable to wear comfortable shoes and choose clothes that cover the arms and legs.

In 2018 the mine performed its last blast at the bottom of the open pit, and its processes are currently transitioning to underground block cave mining. This is a far more efficient and more sustainable method, and is expected to extend the mine for another 50 years. The switch cost an estimated US$5.6 billion, and was part of Codelco's long-term overhaul of and investment in its mines.

22 Termas Baños de Puritama

🅰C2 📍19 miles (30 km) NE of San Pedro de Atacama; Camino al Tatio, Km 32 🚌🕐9am–5:30pm daily 🌐termasdepuritama.cl

A half-day excursion from San Pedro, the Termas Baños de Puritama are terraced hot springs that tumble down a narrow canyon. At 77–86°F (25–30°C), these natural volcanic pools make for perfect bathing. There are changing rooms nearby, and wooden footbridges link the interconnected pools.

> A half-day excursion from San Pedro, the Termas Baños de Puritama are terraced hot springs that tumble down a narrow canyon.

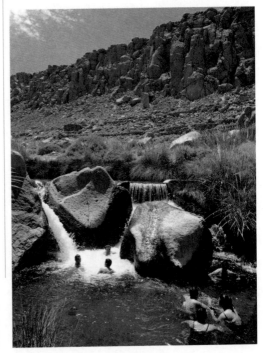

23 ⓜ ⓓ ⓗ

Valle de la Luna

🅰C3 🗺12 miles (19 km) SW of San Pedro de Atacama; Sector 6, Reserva Nacional Los Flamencos

"The Valley of the Moon" is a stark landscape of other-worldly rock formations, salt caves, natural amphitheaters, and vast sand dunes. Set 7,870 ft (2,400 m) above sea level in the Cordillera de Sal (Salt Mountain Range), it is explored via a well-marked circuit. There are a number of caverns en route, so it's best to come prepared with a torch if you'd like to dip into these. The path also includes Las Tres Marias, eroded rock sculptures that resemble three praying women, and the Duna Mayor, the greatest of this valley's massive sand dunes. The valley is well known for its exceptional sunsets, so most tours climb the Duna Mayor at dusk for stupendous views of the Andean peaks and volcanoes washed in indigo, orange, and red tones. The vistas include Volcáns Licancabur and Láscar; the latter being one of Chile's most explosive peaks. It is best to visit this wonderful landscape during the hotter months, from December through February.

24

Geisers de Tatio

🅰C2 🗺74 miles (119 km) E of Calama; Camino a Tatio 🕕6am–5pm daily 🛈www.chile.travel

A natural spectacle, the Geisers de Tatio shoot sky-ward in columns of white vapor at an altitude of 14,200 ft (4,320 m) above sea level. There are some 40 geysers and 70 fumaroles here, each a scar on the surface of a flat geothermic basin that is ringed by rust-colored mountains and pointed volcanoes. Their origin lies in the contact of a cold river with hot, magmatic rock deep underground. This contact causes jets of vapor to stream upward through fissures in the earth's crust and to exit here, in white-vapor streams that rise to a height of 33 ft (10 m) and reach a temperature of 185°F (85°C). It is best to visit the geysers on 4WD excursions that depart from San Pedro

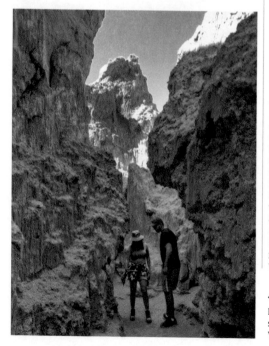

←

Exploring the strangely shaped salt caves of the Valle de la Luna

↑ Dusk falling across the Salar de Atacama, creating a gorgeous purple sky

de Atacama at 4am, reaching the geysers at around daybreak, when they are at their most impressive. Visitors who make this early trip will be able to view the geyser field at its most elemental; hear it groan, grumble, spit, and ultimately, both audibly and visibly exhale. Half-day trips to the Geisers de Tatio end with a dip in sulfur-rich hot springs. Full-day excursions continue to the city of Calama, visiting Caspana, Chiu-Chiu and the Pukará de Lasana, before returning to San Pedro de Atacama.

25
Salar de Tara

🄰D3 🕑62 miles (100 km) E of San Pedro de Atacama; Reserva Nacional Los Flamencos 🛈 Control de CONAF; www.conaf.cl

Adventurous travelers make the arduous yet memorable excursion from San Pedro de Atacama to the Salar de Tara, a salt lake located 14,100 ft (4,300 m) above sea level. Tough roads lead to this breathtaking white spectacle decorated by jewel-like lakes and green vegetation with abundant fauna. Its birdlife includes Chile's three species of flamingo, Andean geese, and horned coots. Herds of vicuña can be seen grazing at the salt pan's edge. Visitors on tours should get the opportunity to see Catedral de Tara, a giant rock wall in the middle of the desert that was once surrounded by an ancient volcanic crater. You can also experience Monjes de la Pacana, which are rock formations sculpted by the erosion of the wind.

26
Salar de Atacama

🄰C3 🕑15 miles (25km) S of San Pedro de Atacama; RN Los Flamencos 🛈 Control de CONAF, Sector Soncor; www.conaf.cl

Occupying 1,160 sq miles (3,000 sq km) of surface area, Salar de Atacama is Chile's largest, and the world's third-largest, salt flat. It lies 7,700 ft (2,350 m) above sea level in a great geological depression between the Domeyko and Andes mountain ranges. The *salar* formed when lakes that originally filled this basin evaporated, leaving a thick coat of silver-gray salt crystals. Not blindingly white like other salt pans in this region, the Salar de Atacama is nevertheless a vision of beauty, with lagoons of intense hues decorating its surface. Laguna Céjar is a brilliantly blue lake whose high salt and lithium content allows bathers to float weightlessly on its surface. Laguna Chaxa has shallow waters, a volcanic backdrop, sure flamingo sightings, and stunning sunsets.

Lying 13,100 ft (4,000 m) above sea level, a short drive east from Salar de Atacama, are the beautiful Laguna Miscanti, Laguna Miñeques, and Laguna Lejía, famous for their birdlife. Also east are Toconao, Peine, and Socaire, oasis villages with early-colonial churches, pre-Incan ruins, and petroglyphs.

> **Laguna Céjar is a brilliantly blue lake whose high salt and lithium content allows bathers to float weightlessly on its surface.**

27 🏃

Cerro Paranal Observatory

🅰 B3 🚗 75 miles (120 km) S of Antofagasta; Cerro Paranal, Ruta B-710 🕐 Tours: 10am & 2pm Sat (book in advance) 🌐 eso.cl

One of the world's most advanced astronomical facilities, the Cerro Paranal Observatory is housed in a futuristic complex of brilliant-white buildings, sharp lines, and curved domes. It stands at 8,500 ft (2,600 m) above sea level atop Cerro Paranal and is overseen by the European Southern Observatory (ESO). Its star attraction is the Very Large Telescope (VLT). One of the world's most powerful optical instruments, the VLT comprises four separate telescopes that combine to form one gigantic lens measuring 650 ft (200 m) in diameter. This lens can define objects four billion times fainter than any that are visible to the naked eye – that is the equivalent of distinguishing car headlights from the surface of the moon.

Did You Know?

Norte Grande comprises 25 percent of Chile's mainland, but is home to just 5 percent of the population.

Fascinating two-hour guided tours follow a presentation on astronomy with visits to the VLT and its control room. Some scenes from the James Bond movie *Quantum of Solace* were shot here.

28

Antofagasta

🅰 B3 🚗 194 miles (313 km) SW of San Pedro de Atacama ✈ Aeropuerto Cerro Moreno 🚉🚌 ℹ Avenida Prat 384; www.municipali dadantofagasta.cl

This historic port-city is the sea outlet for the metals and minerals mined in the Atacama desert. Founded in 1869 as part of Bolivia,

Antofagasta was absorbed by Chile in the War of the Pacific (1879–83) and used to ship silver, nitrates and, from 1915, copper from the great Chuquicamata mine (p183). Chile's most progressive city by the 1930s, it appears today as a slightly grimy place, but some historic charm remains.

Set in the city center, the Neo-Gothic cathedral dates from 1917 and faces the Plaza Colón. The clock tower adorning the plaza was donated in 1910 by the city's English community, and is a tangible reminder of British influence in Antofagasta. Just north of the plaza, the former Customs House, dating from 1869, is home to the **Museo Regional de Antofagasta**. The museum's collection of over 9,000 objects includes fossils from the region, objects salvaged from the old nitrate mines, and period furniture.

At the end of the same road is **Ex-Estación El Ferrocarril de Antofagasta a Bolivia**, the city's former train station. Built in 1873 using British capital, this was the terminus for the Antofagasta-Bolivia railway. Designated a National

→ Domes of the Cerro Paranal Observatory dotting the landscape

Historic Landmark in 1981, it conserves Scottish steam trains, English clocks, and red telephone boxes. Trains carrying copper from the Chuquicamata mine still pass through this station on their way to the port. Also near the port is the Muelle Histórico Salitrero (Nitrates Wharf), which dates from 1872, and the Terminal Pesquero, Antofagasta's rustic fish market.

Facing the Pacific Ocean, some 5 miles (8 km) south of the city center, are the massive stone remnants of a silver refinery dating from 1888–92. Known as the **Ruinas de Huanchaca**, this fascinating and intact site occupies a desert hillside in stepped terraces, and features a steep central staircase, a round tower, narrow passageways, and rows of stone storehouses. The casino opposite the ruins, Enjoy Antofagasta, runs tours (including night tours) for visitors. The casino's glitzy architecture mirrors the ruins with a round tower and terraced facade that lends a quasi-Aztecan symmetry to this site.

A small on-site museum displays geological, archaeological, and anthropological objects, including antique silver-refining machinery.

Museo Regional de Antofagasta

♿🏛 🏠 Balmaceda 2786 ⏰ 9am–5:30pm Tue–Fri, 11am–2:30pm Sat & Sun 🌐 museodeantofagasta.cl

Ex-Estación El Ferrocarril de Antofagasta a Bolivia

🏛 🏠 Bolívar 255 ⏰ 9am–6pm daily 🌐 fcab.cl

Ruinas de Huanchaca

♿🏛 🏠 Avenida Angamos 01606 🚌 From Antofagasta ⏰ 10am–1pm & 2:30–7pm Tue–Sun 🌐 ruinasde huanchaca.cl

---

29 🍴 💻 🏛

La Portada

🗺 C2 🚗 10 miles (16 km) N of Antofagasta; Ruta 5, Lado Norte 🚌 From Antofagasta ⏰ Daily 🌐 conaf.cl

La Portada (The Gateway) is a natural sedimentary arch that faces dramatic coastline. The arch, eroded over seven million years, is visible from a parking area a short distance to its north; however, descending from the unstable headlands to the beach is prohibited. Visitors can explore the small CONAF-run museum on the cliff that overlooks the arch.

↑ Posing by the dramatic natural coastal arch of La Portada

STARGAZING IN THE ATACAMA DESERT

The Atacama desert has some of the world's clearest and skies and most advanced observatories, including facilities at Cerro Mamalluca (p172) and Cerro Paranal. Visitors can travel to the desert as night descends, huddle around a telescope and view the dazzling array of stars. Tours are available in the region, which include guides who can provide information and point out star and planet formations billions of light years away, which means visitors can essentially view the dawn of the universe.

↑ Outside the attractive Neo-Classical Iglesia de San Franciso in Copiapó

30 Copiapó

🅐B4 🏠351 miles (566 km) S of Antofagasta 🚆🚌 🛈Sernatur, Los Carrera 691; www.municipalidad copiapo.cl

The capital of Chile's Atacama (III) region, Copiapó is a low-key city whose attractions are linked to its silver-mining heritage. Silver was first found here in 1832 by the muleteer Juan Godoy. His statue stands in a plaza fronting the Iglesia de San Francisco, an 1872 church with ornate paintings. Chile's first (and now defunct) railway was built in 1851 to take silver from Copiapó to the port at Caldera. Copiapó is centered around a plaza, which is fronted by a wooden cathedral from 1851. The Neo-Classical design of this edifice features an unusual three-tiered bell

tower. Set at the city's western end is its grandest mansion, the Palacio Viña de Cristo, built in 1860 in the Georgian style for a silver baron. The **Museo Mineralógico** and **Museo Regional de Atacama** recount the Atacama region's history and mineral wealth.

There is free admission to the latter site on Sundays. Flash floods and mudflows in early 2015 damaged some of the lovely wooden buildings

on Avenida Manuel Matta that date from the 1800s.

Museo Mineralógico

⊗⊗ 🏠Colipi 333 📞(052) 2206606 🕒9am–12:45pm & 3–5pm Tue–Fri

Museo Regional de Atacama

⊗⊗ 🏠Atacama 98 🕒9am–6:15pm Mon–Fri, 10am–12:15pm & 3–5:45pm Sat, 10am–1:15pm Sun 🌐museodeatacama.cl

31 Caldera

🅐B4 🏠50 miles (80 km) W of Copiapó 🚌 🛈Plaza Carlos Condell; www. caldera.cl

The colorful harbor town of Caldera grew in the late 1800s as a port for shipping silver brought in by the railway from Copiapó. Today, it has a picturesque waterfront of sparkling ocean and sandy beaches where pelicans congregate. On the waterfront, the Terminal Pesquero is the fishermen's harbor and market, where small ma-and-pa eateries serve fresh seafood specialties. Located next to it, the **Museo Paleontológico**, built in 1850, is housed in Caldera's recycled railway station and displays mammoth marine fossils. Its stand out exhibit is the fossilized skull of a bearded whale that lived 10 million years ago.

THE RESCUE OF THE 33 SAN JOSÉ MINERS

On August 5, 2010, 33 miners at the San José gold and copper mine near Copiapó were trapped around 2,300 ft (700 m) underground after a collapse. Their families camped out on the surface, urging the mining company and the authorities to keep searching for their loved ones. Improbably, 17 days later, rescuers found a drillhead with a note attached: "We are fine in the shelter - the 33." The story gained international attention and finally, after 69 days underground, the men were safely brought to the surface on October 13.

Once home to an Italian immigrant family, the red Neo-Classical mansion, **Casa Tornini**, was built in the 1890s. Guided tours in English, German, and Spanish take in the appealing original furniture owned by the family. Occasional art exhibitions are also held here.

Just south of Caldera is northern Chile's most beautiful beach, named **Bahía Inglesa** (English Bay) for the swashbuckling English pirates who dropped anchor here in the 17th century. The long sweep of bleach-white sand is fronted by a turquoise ocean of calm, sheltered waters and blissfully little construction save a smattering of upscale hotels and restaurants.

Museo Paleontológico

⊛ ⊛ 🖾 🖾 Centro Cultural Estación Caldera, Wheelwright s/n 🕐 1–5pm Tue–Fri, 11am–7pm Sat & Sun ⓦ museo-paleontologico-chile.es.tl

Casa Tornini

⊛ ⊛ 🖾 🖾 Paseo Gana 210 📞 (052) 2317930 🕐 Jan & Feb: noon–8pm daily; Mar–Dec: 11:30am–4:30pm

Bahía Inglesa

🖾 4 miles (6 km) S of Caldera
🚌 🛈 Next to Hotel Rocas de Bahía; www.bahia inglesachile.com

Parque Nacional Pan de Azúcar

🅱 B4 🖾 120 miles (194 km) NW of Copiapó; Ruta C-120, Km 27 de Chañaral
ⓦ conaf.cl

Created in 1985 to protect 169 sq miles (438 sq km) of coastal desert, this park has beaches, sheltered coves, and vertiginous sand cliffs. The coastline plays refuge to easily sighted marine fauna. Dolphins, southern sea lions, gulls, Humboldt penguins, cormorants, and pelicans populate the shoreline. Coastal attractions include the offshore Isla Pan de Azúcar, a refuge to penguins and other seabirds that is reached by boat excursion; and Caleta Pan de Azúcar, a picturesque fishermen's hamlet with

Scenic coastline and (inset) Humboldt penguins in the Parque Nacional Pan de Azúcar ↓

EAT

Legado
Popular with journalists during the rescue of 33 miners in 2010 (p188). Today, the ambience is calmer, but food remains sophisticated. Many dishes feature game from across Chile.

🅱 B4 🖾 O'Higgins 12, Copiapó 🕐 Sun
ⓦ legadorestaurant.com

$$⑤

campsites and cabins. Farther inland the flora and fauna includes guanacos, foxes, condors, and over 20 species of cactus. Highlights include the Quebrada del Castillo and Quebrada Pan de Azúcar canyons; and the Mirador and Las Lomitas viewpoints offer vistas of desert and the ocean.

33

Parque Nacional Nevado Tres Cruces

C4 94 miles (151 km) E of Copiapó 8:30am–6pm daily CONAF, Laguna del Negro Francisco; www. conaf.cl

This remote but stunning national park conserves some 228 sq miles (591 sq km) of altiplano wilderness typified by colored lakes, snowy volcanoes, and abundant native fauna. Most visits focus on the northern sector, where Laguna Santa Rosa, an intensely blue saltwater lake, fills a depression ringed by the snowy peaks of the Nevados Tres Cruces massif. Next to the lake, the white Salar de Maricunga is Chile's southernmost salt flat.

Accessed via a 4WD route from Laguna Santa Rosa, the park's southern sector is less visited. Its greatest natural feature is Laguna del Negro Francisco, a lake with mirror-like waters which reflect the pointed cone of Volcán Copiapó and the giant wings of flapping flamingos. Chile's three flamingo species are present on the lakeshore here, part of a wildlife bonanza that features some 30 bird species and easily sighted mammals,

including vicuñas, guanacos, vizcachas, and Andean foxes. Walking trails circle around Laguna Santa Rosa and Laguna del Negro Francisco, where a 12-bed CONAF *refugio* offers lodging and hot showers.

> Most visits focus on the northern sector, where Laguna Santa Rosa, an intensely blue saltwater lake, fills a depression ringed by the snowy peaks of the Nevados Tres Cruces massif.

34

Ovalle

B5 53 miles (86 km) S of La Serena Victoria, esq Independencia; (053) 2622108

The rarely visited but often enjoyed, Valle del Limarí is a fertile area of orchards and farms that feeds much of the arid Norte Chico. The valley's largest settlement is Ovalle, a small city ringed by interesting monochrome peaks. Farmers working in and around the valley sell their fresh produce at Feria Modelo de Ovalle *(p193)*, the city's great food market.

In the city center, the Iglesia de San Vicente Ferrer faces Ovalle's tree-lined plaza. Built in 1888, it has a strikingly tall bell tower and an ornate interior. The city's big draw, however, is the outstanding **Museo del Limarí** which exhibits pre-Hispanic items from the local area and features Chile's most impressive displays of Diaguita ceramics (AD 1000–1536).

Ovalle is a springboard for visits to Valle del Limarí's wineries and villages. West of the city is the picturesque oasis village of Barraza, with narrow adobe streets and a church that dates from 1681. The upright tombs of former priests are encased within its adobe walls. Also in the western sector are the wineries **Viña Tabalí** and **Viña Casa Tamaya**, which open for tours and tastings. The area is best known for its incredible white wine production.

Museo del Limarí

Covarrubias, esq Antofagasta, Ovalle 10am–6pm Tue–Fri, 10am–2pm Sat & Sun museolimari.gob.cl

Viña Casa Tamaya

🏠 Camino Quebrada Seca Km 9, Ovalle 🕐 1–6pm Mon–Fri 🌐 tamayawines.cl

Viña Tabalí

⊗ ⊗ 🏠 Hacienda Santa Rosa de Tabalí, Ruta Valle del Encanto 🕐 8:30am–5pm Sun–Fri, 11am–4pm Sat 🌐 tabali.com

---

35 (M)

Laguna Verde

🅰 C4 🏠 164 miles (265 km) NE of Copiapó 🕐 Oct–Mar
ℹ Sernatur, Los Carrera 691, Copiapó; (052) 2212838

Located high in the Andes, at 13,780 ft (4,200 m) above sea level, Laguna Verde is a breathtaking lake of green and turquoise tones that change hue according to the light and time of day. On the lake's western shore, rustic hot springs provide blissful relaxation. Mighty volcanoes, including El Muerto, Peña Blanca, Incahuasi, Barrancas Blancas, and Vicuñas, encircle the area. Their snowy peaks and the brown, red, and ocher tones of their flanks complete an artist's palette of sharply contrasting colors. However, most of these peaks are challenging and hard to climb. Wildlife in this area includes flamingos, ducks, foxes, and horned coots, all of whom have adapted to live in the extreme temperatures of this desert environment.

Stretching to 22,615 ft (6,893m), Volcán Ojos del Salado towers over the southern basin of Laguna Verde. This is the world's highest active volcano, as well as Chile's highest peak. The climb to its summit is physically challenging but technically undemanding.

Those seeking to climb Ojos del Salado must acquire permits from Chile's foreign ministry. The best time to attempt a climb is between December and late March, and the easiest way up is from the Chilean side (the volcano can also be tackled from Argentina). There are shelters at several levels.

36

Reserva Nacional Pinguino de Humboldt

🅰 B5 🏠 54 miles (87 km) N of La Serena 🕐 8:45am–2pm daily ℹ CONAF, park entrance; www.conaf.cl

Named after the Humboldt penguins that breed here, this 2,195-acre (888-ha) reserve consists of three islands off the rocky coast. It is a popular day trip from La Serena. Almost 10,000 pairs of this vulnerable penguin species nest in the reserve, particularly on Isla de Choros. Zodiac offers boat tours that make landings on the more accessible Isla Damas. For conservation reasons, visitors are advised to stick to the established paths and not to disturb the birds. While on the boat, visitors can hear and smell the sea lion colony that also call this area home. Pods of friendly bottle-nosed dolphins and sea otters are also known to make the occasional appearance.

SHOP

Feria Modelo de Ovalle

Farmers and producers from across the region come to this market to sell their tempting goods. You can easily lose a few hours wandering around the colorful stalls.

🅰 B5 🏠 Cnr of Avenida la Feria and Benavente

↑ A road unfurling toward the pristine turquoise waters of the Laguna Verde

A replica dinosaur in the Monumento Natural Pichasca

37 🏔️ 🚶 🏛️

Monumento Natural Pichasca

🅰️B5 🚗34 miles (55 km) NE of Ovalle, Valle del Limarí 🚌 From Ovalle to 3 miles (5 km) before entrance ⏰8:30am-5:15pm daily 🌐conaf.cl

Rich in paleontological and archaeological finds, the Monumento Natural Pichasca is a site featuring petrified forests of fossilized tree trunks, gigantic dinosaur fossils, and 11,000-year-old rock paintings in ancient lava caves. The area was also a refuge for hunter-gatherers around 8000 BC.

Tours begin at a visitors' center that has displays on the area's fauna and flora, paleontology, and archaeology. From here, a walking trail explores the site, which passes life-size replicas of the gigantic dinosaurs that once roamed this region.

GREAT VIEW
Heading Higher

For mountain views (and a cooler climate), travel 22 miles (35 km) from Monumento Natural Pichasca to Hurtado, an oasis village around 3,940 ft (1,200 m) above sea level.

---

38 🚶 🏛️

Monumento Nacional Valle del Encanto

🅰️B5 🚗16 miles (25 km) SW of Ovalle; D45, Valle del Encanto 🚌 From Ovalle to 3 miles (5 km) from entrance ⏰Jan-Feb: 8:30am-8pm daily; Mar-Dec: 8:30am-6:30pm daily

An ancient ceremonial and hunting ground, this site has Chile's finest collection of El Molle petroglyphs, dating from around AD 700. Viewed from a marked circuit, there are more than 30 petroglyphs, which were etched onto rockfaces using sharp stones. Most are line drawings depicting human, zoomorphic, abstract, and geometric shapes. The human portraits are most interesting: entire families are shown in various poses with fingers pointing upward at the sun or downward, at Mother Earth. The shamans and deities in these carvings are crowned with tiaras and headdresses. The petroglyphs are best seen at noon, when the sharp midday light shows them at their most impressive.

Another highlight of the site is the *piedras tacitas* – slabs of flat rock gouged with large patterns of identical, circular, and deep holes that were probably used as mortars for grinding food and for ceremonial purposes, including the preparation of hallucinogens. There are also smaller, earlier depressions known as cupules, the purpose of which was decorative.

→
Riding down Parque Nacional Bosque Fray Jorge

39 ⊕ ⊗ ⊗

Termas de Socos

⛰ B5 🚗 24 miles (38 km) SW of Ovalle; Panamericana Norte, Km370 🕐 8:30am–7pm daily (spa) 🌐 terma socos.cl

Encircled by rugged and dusty canyons in the Valle del Limarí, Termas de Socos is a family-owned spa retreat open to day and overnight visitors. Its amenities include massage treatments, thermal baths, and an exterior pool that is ringed by various cacti and eucalyptus trees. There is a rustic but refined feel to this place – poolside vistas rise to rocky canyons, wild honey grows in the spa's gardens, and guests are accommodated in comfortable rooms.

For budget travelers, there is a separate campsite with its own thermal baths. Staff run trips to Monumento Nacional Valle del Encanto and Parque Nacional Bosque Fray Jorge.

At night, guests can gaze at the clear, bright stars from the canyon-top observatory.

40 ⊗

Parque Nacional Bosque Fray Jorge

⛰ B5 🚗 56 miles (90 km) W of Ovalle; Km 26 de la Ruta Patrimonial 🕐 9am–4pm daily ℹ CONAF, park entrance; www.conaf.cl

The highlight of this UNESCO biosphere reserve is a relictual Valdivian rain forest – a remnant of the temperate rain forest that cloaked all Norte Chico prior to the southward advancement of the Atacama desert, some 30,000 years ago.

The densest forest occurs on the western slopes of the coastal mountains that reach as high as 1,837 ft (560 m). It owes its continued existence to the high rainfall that hits the mountain peak each year – around 47 inches (120 cm) per year compared with just 4 inches (10 cm) on the semi-arid lowlands directly to the mountain's east. Parque Nacional Bosque Fray Jorge is at its most impressive between October and December, when, after heavy rainfall, the forest floor is carpeted with flowers.

A vehicle route and a 6-mile (10-km) walking trail strike west from the park entrance, where a CONAF center has displays on the area's flora. Overlooking the Pacific, a short boardwalk traverses the lush forest. At mid-morning visitors can see the mist-shrouded rain forest.

> Parque Nacional Bosque Fray Jorge is at its most impressive between October and December, when, after heavy rainfall, the forest floor is carpeted with flowers.

LAKE DISTRICT AND CHILOÉ

Chile's Lake District features emerald forests, smoldering volcanoes, and rivers and waterfalls. South of the district lies Chiloé, a beautiful island archipelago of misty bays, quaint *palafitos*, and historic Jesuit churches. The Lake District is bound to its north by Río Bío-Bío and to its south by the Canal Chacao, the channel that links it to Chiloé.

In pre-Columbian times, the Lake District was populated by Mapuche communities, and Chiloé by the seafaring Chono. Spaniards arrived in 1552 and established what are today the region's largest cities, including Valdivia, Villarrica, and Osorno. Much of the area remained a Mapuche stronghold even after independence, when Chile launched the Araucanian wars to suppress indigenous resistance. The area then opened up to European immigrants, notably German settlers. The indigenous population continued to fight against European occupation, however, and in the 1840s undertook raids on German-speaking settlements. They were later defeated by the Chilean army, and forced to settle on reservations in the region's south.

By the 19th century, railroad construction had sparked agriculture, forestry, and port industries, with the city of Temuco emerging as the Lake District's main commercial center. In the Chiloé archipelago, fishing has become the bedrock of the economy. More recently, a boom in tourism has brought added prosperity to the Lake District and Chiloé, with visitors attracted by the area's spectacular national parks.

LAKE DISTRICT AND CHILOÉ

Must Sees

1. Parque Nacional Conguillío
2. Valdivia
3. Parque Nacional Villarrica
4. Parque Nacional Vicente Pérez Rosales

Experience More

5. Temuco
6. Termas de Malalcahuello
7. Parque Nacional Tolhuaca
8. Ski Center Corralco
9. Puerto Montt
10. Nevados de Sollipulli
11. Lago Caburgua
12. Ojos del Caburgua
13. Villarrica
14. Coñaripe
15. Santuario Cañi
16. Santuario de la Naturaleza Carlos Anwandter
17. Parque Nacional Huerquehue
18. Panguipulli
19. Licán Ray
20. Pucón
21. Reserva Biológica Huilo-Huilo
22. Parque Nacional Puyehue
23. Lago Ranco
24. Termas de Puyehue
25. Osorno
26. Lago Llanquihue
27. Puerto Octay
28. Puerto Varas
29. Frutillar
30. Ancud
31. Monumento Natural Islotes de Puñihuil
32. Dalcahue
33. Parque Nacional Chiloé
34. Castro
35. Curaco de Vélez
36. Achao
37. Chonchi
38. Quellón
39. Parque Tantauco

Pacific

Ocean

CENTRAL VALLEY
p114

Renaico
Angol
Trintre
Collipulli
Mulchén

Volcán Copahue
9,776 ft (2,979 m)

PARQUE NACIONAL TOLHUACA ❼
Victoria

Volcán Tolhuaca
9,203 ft (2,805 m)

❽ **SKI CENTER CORRALCO**
❻ **TERMAS DE MALALCAHUELLO**
❶ **PARQUE NACIONAL CONGUILLIO**

Traiguen
Curacautín

ARAUCANÍA
Lautaro
Cherquenco

Tirúa
△ *Volcán Llaima*
10,253 ft (3,125 m)

Melipeuco

Carahue
TEMUCO ❺
Cunco

Puerto Saavedra
La Araucanía
International Airport ✈
Freire

❿ **NEVADOS DE SOLLIPULLI**
❶❼ **PARQUE NACIONAL HUERQUEHUE**

Puerto Domínguez

Gualpin
LAGO CABURGUA ⓫
OJOS DE CABURGUA ⑫
⑮ **SANTUARIO CAÑI**
VILLARRICA ⑬
⑳
Curarrehue

Mehuín
PUCÓN
LICÁN RAY ⑲
❸ **PARQUE NACIONAL VILLARRICA**
Lanco
Lago Calafquén
⑭ **COÑARIPE**

Pichoy Airport ✈
PANGUIPULLI ⑱

SANTUARIO DE LA NATURALEZA CARLOS ANWANDTER ⑯
Máfil
Riñihue
Lago Panguipulli
Neltume

Valdivia ❷
Los Lagos
Lago Riñihue
㉑ **RESERVA BIOLÓGICA HUILO-HUILO**

Corral
Volcán Mocho Choshuenco
7,923 ft (2,414 m)

Paillaco
LOS LAGOS
Futrono
San Martín de los Andes

La Unión
Lago Ranco
㉓ **LAGO RANCO**
ARGENTINA
Río Bueno
San Pablo
Volcán Puyehue
7,334 ft (2,236 m)

OSORNO ㉕
Lago Puyehue
㉒ **PARQUE NACIONAL PUYEHUE**

Maicolpué
Cañal Bajo Carlos Hott Siebert Airport ✈
Entre Lagos
㉔
△ *Volcán Casablanca*
6,529 ft (1,990 m)

Purranque
PUERTO OCTAY
TERMAS DE PUYEHUE

㉗
Volcán Osorno
8,700 ft (2,652 m)
Bariloche

FRUTILLAR ㉙
㉖ **LAGO LLANQUIHUE**
Petrohué
Volcán Tronador
11,351 ft (3,460 m)

Fresia
❹ **PARQUE NACIONAL VICENTE PÉREZ ROSALES**

Llanquihue
PUERTO VARAS ㉘
Ralún

El Tepual Airport ✈
❾ **PUERTO MONTT**

Maullín
La Arena

Pargua
Calbuco

NORTHERN PATAGONIA
p228

El Bolsón

ANCUD ㉚
Chacao
Golfo de Ancud

MONUMENTO NATURAL ISLOTES DE PUÑIHUIL ㉛
Quemchi
Caleta Gonzalo

Degán
Quicaví

DALCAHUE ㉜
CURACO DE VÉLEZ ㉟
CASTRO ㉞ ㉟
㊱ **ACHAO**
PARQUE NACIONAL CHILOÉ ㉝
Rilán
Esquel

CHONCHI ㊲
Parque Nacional Los Alerces

Aituy
Queilen

Isla Grande de Chiloé
Chaitén
Futaleufú

㊳ **QUELLÓN**

PARQUE TANTAUCO
㊴
Lago Yelcho

Inio
Golfo de Corcovado

0 kilometers 60
0 miles 60

N ↑

PARQUE NACIONAL CONGUILLÍO

⛰F1 **📍74 miles (120 km) E of Temuco** **🚌From Temuco. Taxi from Melipeuco & Curacautín**
ℹCONAF, Sector del Lago Conguillío; Apr-mid-Dec: 8:30am-1pm & 2:30-6pm daily, mid-Dec-Mar: 8:30am-9:30pm daily; www.conaf.cl

Home to araucaria trees, deep canyons, alpine lakes, and native forests, Parque Nacional Conguillío is a prime location for visitors throughout the year. The park offers mountain trails for hikers, deep and plentiful snow for skiers, and an abundance of wildlife for nature lovers.

One of the Lake District's great natural attractions, Parque Nacional Conguillío stretches over 235 sq miles (609 sq km) of volcanic wilderness, crowned by the smoking cone of the 10,253-ft- (3,125-m-) high Volcán Llaima. A diverse, spectacular landscape surrounds this colossal peak and features ancient araucaria forests, rolling sierras, crystalline lakes, and deep valleys scarred by jagged lava flows. The park abounds with rich wildlife, including pumas, smaller wildcats, red and gray foxes, woodpeckers, hawks, and condors. Splendid hiking trails, skiing down volcanic slopes, and boat trips across serene lakes draw a large number of visitors to the park throughout the year.

Exploring the Park

Parque Nacional Conguillío comprises two sectors separated from each other by Volcán Llaima. The western sector, Sector Los Paraguas, offers winter skiing, while the bigger eastern sector, Sector del Lago Conguillío, has great hiking trails including the popular Sendero Sierra Nevada. This sector is served by the gateway towns of Melipeuco in the south and Curacautín in the north. Heavy snowfall usually makes this sector impassable between May and September.

THE WRATH OF VOLCÁN LLAIMA

Smoldering Volcán Llaima is one of Chile's two most explosive volcanoes; the other being Volcán Villarrica (p202). More than 40 eruptions have been recorded since 1640, and Volcán Llaima's lava has shaped Parque Nacional Conguillío's landscape. Eruptions in 2008-9 created 9,800-ft- (3,000-m-) high smoke columns, forced the evacuation of villages, and dumped ash on Argentina. Over the years, lava flows blocked rivers, turning forests into lakes. Today, lava fields scar the earth where lush forests once stood, and dense woods are still visible in the water.

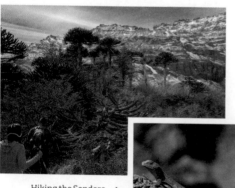

Hiking the Sendero Sierra Nevada ↑

→
Vibrant lizard resting on lava rock

→
Expansive views of the beautiful Lake Conguillío

→

Boats docked alongside the Río Valdivia, near the lively Mercado Fluvial

2

VALDIVIA

⚑ F2 ⛰ 100 miles (162 km) SW of Temuco ✈ 🚌 🚐
ℹ Arturo Prat 555; www.valdivia.cl

Spread along the banks of three rivers, Valdivia was a prized possession of the Spanish, who guarded it with military forts for over 200 years. In 1960, a massive earthquake devastated Valdivia, but today, it is a vibrant city whose lush riverside is fronted by fine museums and 19th-century Teutonic architecture.

①

Mercado Fluvial

⚑ Avenida Arturo Prat s/n
🕒 8am-4pm daily

Set on the banks of the Río Valdivia, Mercado Fluvial, the city's bustling fish market, is a colorful snapshot of coastal Chilean life as well as the prime industry that sustains it. Traders clean the day's catch, while live crabs scuttle about in huge crates and bobbing sea lions bellow for scraps by the water's edge – the scene watched over by hundreds of seabirds. Inexpensive seafood eateries serving local specialties edge the market.

②

Centro Cultural El Austral

⚑ Yungay 733 🕒 10am-1pm & 4-7:15pm Tue-Sun
🌐 centro-cultural-el-austral.negocio.site/

Set in a large, beautifully restored house, Valdivia's Centro Cultural El Austral dates from the period of German settlement in the Lake District. Built in the 1870s for a pioneer family, it was made entirely from local wood in the German chalet style and features a striking Bavarian steeple. The interiors reflect typical living quarters of early German settlers. Dazzlingly furnished, the rooms feature Art Nouveau chandeliers, extravagant wall mirrors, and stately 19th-century European furniture. Other rooms in the building showcase notable works by contemporary artists.

> 💬 **INSIDER TIP**
> **Up All Night**
>
> Head to Valdivia on the third Saturday in February to experience Noche de Valdivia, a festival that includes a fleet of beautifully decorated riverboats, fireworks and flares, and a night of dancing.

④ Museo Histórico y Antropológico Mauricio Van de Maele

🏛 Los Laureles s/n, Isla Teja
🕙 10am-1pm & 2-6pm Tue-Sun 🌐 museosaustral.cl

Adjacent to the Museo de Arte Contemporaneo is the 19th-century mansion and former home of the founder of Chile's first brewery, Karl Anwandter (1801–89). Today, the edifice houses the Museo Histórico y Antropológico Mauricio Van de Maele, whose collection is displayed in a series of themed salons, each depicting different periods in local history, from pre-Columbian times to the 20th century. Each salon has a multilingual information panel that shows historical details about the period that it represents.

Sala de Platería Mapuche has various exhibits showing Mapuche tools and textiles. The stunning jewelry display portrays the indigenous Mapuche's belief in silverware as a symbol of power and prestige. Dedicated to Thomas Cochrane (1775–1860), the Sala Lord Cochrane displays some of his personal belongings. This buccaneering British naval officer led Chile's naval forces during the 1820 attack on Valdivia that ended Royalist resistance in the area. The museum also re-creates a colonial-period lounge embellished with ornate wall hangings, damask tapestry, and a Venetian mirror.

DRINK

El Growler
Sur Chico's best beer place has 15 taps with IPAs, red ales, stouts, and more. Also has great bar food and interesting vegetarian options.

🏛 Saelzer 41 🕙 Noon-2am Mon-Thu, noon-3am Fri-Sat, noon-1am Sun

$$ $⑤$

③ Museo de Arte Contemporaneo

🏛 Los Laureles s/n, Isla Teja
🕙 For renovations until 2021 🌐 macvaldivia.cl

On the banks of the river, a recycled brewery building with a strikingly modern glass facade is the post-Industrial setting for the city's Museo de Arte Contemporaneo, often referred to as MAC. The exhibitions here feature video and installation art as well as paintings, photographs, and sculptures by emerging and established artists, both international and Chilean.

The collection is spread over two floors of abandoned industrial workspace, which is characterized by bare cement flooring and cast-iron columns. These still bear the scars of the devastating earthquake that hit this area in 1960.

The museum building was closed in 2019 for a major restoration program that is anticipated to last two years.

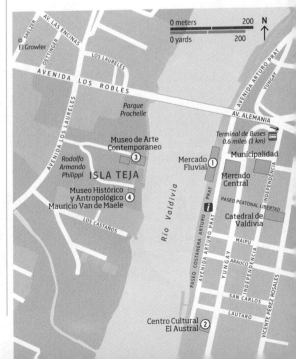

PARQUE NACIONAL VILLARRICA

⬛ F2 ⬛ 5 miles (8 km) SE of Pucón ⬛ Taxi from Pucón ⬛ CONAF, Lincoyán 336, Pucón; www.conaf.cl

The soaring, volcanic peaks of Villarrica, Lanín and Quetrupillán rise high over Parque Nacional Villarrica, one of Chile's most popular national parks. Alongside this fiery triumvirate, the park is home to tranquil lakes and rushing rivers, snowy mountains and lush forests.

Conserving 243 sq miles (629 sq km) of wilderness, Parque Nacional Villarrica extends from south of Pucón to the frontier with Argentina. The 9,341-ft- (2,847-m-) high snow-swathed cone of Volcán Villarrica forms the park's centerpiece, crowning a landscape that embraces two other volcanoes, several small lakes, and forests of southern beech and araucaria. The park provides shelter to a rich array of wildlife, including the rare Chilean shrew opossum. Eruptions in February and March 2015 closed the park until late 2016. Although it has reopened, volatile volcanic activity leaves the park vulnerable to future closures.

Discovering the Park

Parque Nacional Villarrica has three sectors, each with hiking trails and a ranger station. The westernmost sector, accessible from the gateway town of Pucón, features the park's major highlights, including the magnificent Volcán Villarrica. The two sectors to the east are remote, yet beautiful; the park's wildest sector is in the area bordering Argentina.

The snowcapped peaks of the magnificent Volcán Villarrica ↓

2015

The last year that Volcán Villarrica erupted.

The quick brown fox jumps over the lazy dog.

HOUSE OF THE DEVIL

The Mapuche of the area refer to Volcán Villarrica as Rucapillán, or House of the Devil – an apt description for one of Chile's most explosive peaks. It erupted 18 times in the 20th century alone. An explosion in 1971 almost destroyed the nearby village of Coñaripe *(p212)*. It last erupted in 2015, and remains constantly active. Its crater smokes, hisses, and belches, and is one of only a few craters on the globe that has an active lava lake.

↑ Tourists climbing up a snow-covered Volcán Villarrica

→ Hikers exploring the stark terrain of Volcán Villarrica

Volcanoes

Volcán Villarrica

▷ The trek to Volcán Villarrica's steaming crater features a physically challenging but technically undemanding hike through blue-tinged, icy glaciers and a slide down the slopes via glistening snow tunnels. The route has reopened for trekkers after the 2015 volcanic activity.

Volcán Lanín

◁ Located on the border between Chile and Argentina, the snow-topped, cone-shaped Volcán Lanín is the biggest volcano in southern Chile. The spectacular hike from Laguna Abutardes to Lago Quilleihue offers some of the most fabulous vistas of this truly awe-inspiring volcano.

Volcán Quetrupillán

▷ This dormant, snowcapped volcano lies on the border between the Los Rios Region and the La Araucanía Region, neighboring Volcán Villarrica. The volcano's name, Quetrupillán, means "mute devil" in the language of the Mapuche people.

Did You Know?

Charles Darwin witnessed Volcán Osorno's eruption in 1835.

PARQUE NACIONAL VICENTE PÉREZ ROSALES

F2 **NE of Puerto Varas** **From Puerto Montt & Puerto Varas, via Ensenada & Petrohué** **CONAF, Petrohue; www.conaf.cl**

The oldest national park in Chile, Parque Nacional Vicente Pérez Rosales is one of the principal destinations in Los Lagos. The celestial lakes and abundant forests attract horseback riders and swimmers, hikers and nature enthusiasts, while the soaring volcanoes offer outstanding panoramic views and bring skiers to the slopes over the winter period.

Created in 1926, Parque Nacional Vicente Pérez Rosales is one of Chile's most breathtaking parks. Its landscape of lost-world beauty encompasses volcanoes, crystalline lakes and lagoons, gushing waterfalls, and evergreen forests. Its crowning glory is the perfect cone of the active Volcán Osorno. Two more great volcanoes – Tronador and Puntiagudo – pierce the skyline here. They, along with Lago Todos Los Santos and Saltos de Petrohué, protect an abundant bird and mammal life, and offer activities such as boat rides, horseback riding through forests, lava treks, and volcano skiing.

Exploring the Park

Parque Nacional Vicente Pérez Rosales' star sights are concentrated in its western sector, which is served by road and local bus, and is linked to the gateway city Puerto Varas (p218). Located in the western sector are the villages of Ensenada and Petrohué, which offer hotel and campsite accommodations. From Petrohué, catamarans make the daily two-hour trip over the teal-colored waters of the Lago Todos los Santos to the park's eastern sector, called Peulla. This area's eponymous hamlet has two hotels.

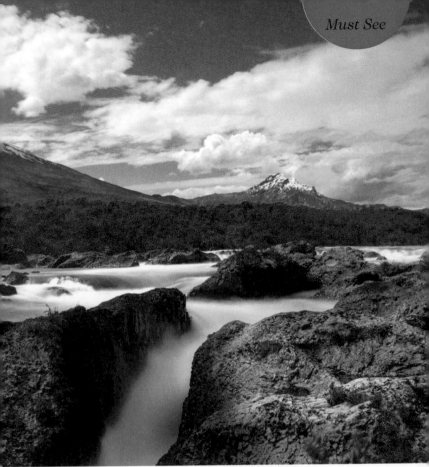

↑ Sweeping views of flora surrounding Volcán Osorno

← Volcán Tronador, seem from the Andean crossing

INSIDER TIP
💬 Cruce de los Lagos

This spectacular crossing over the Andes, between the lake districts of Chile and Argentina, traverses two national parks and four lakes. The full-day journey, beginning at Petrohué, over both land and lakes, ends at Bariloche, Argentina. En route, there are four volcanoes, many great waterfalls, and abundant wildlife.

Wild horses grazing near ↓ Volcán Tronador

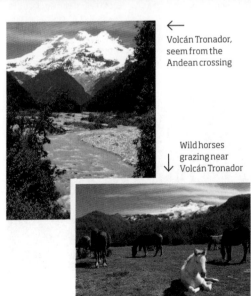

EXPERIENCE MORE

5 Temuco

F2 **385 miles (620 km)
S of Santiago** ✉️ 🏛️ 🚌
ℹ️ **Bulnes 590; www.chile.
travel/temuco**

Set in the former Mapuche
heartland, Temuco traces its
origins to a fortress settlement established during the
19th century – the city itself
was officially founded in
1881. The construction of
the railroad and European
immigration in the 20th
century brought about rapid
growth. Today, Temuco is a
commercial hub with busy
plazas and museums. Famous
for colorful markets attended
by Mapuche traders and
artisans, the city is also an
ideal base for exploring
the natural beauty of the
surrounding countryside.

The **Museo Regional de
la Araucanía** makes a good
place to start wandering the
city. Housed in a 1924 mansion,
this museum records the
often bloody history of Chile's
Araucanía region through a
collection of some 3,000
archaeological, ethnographic,
and historical objects. Among
them is one of the country's
most impressive collections of
Mapuche objects, including
stunning 19th-century weavings and an array of silver
jewelry, heavy necklaces, and
belts. Also on display is a life-
size reconstruction of a *ruca*
(communal thatched house).

A protected hillside, the
**Monumento Natural Cerro
Ñielol** is also of interest. It
harbors a species-rich temperate rain forest that once
covered the Araucanía region.
Walking trails explore native
evergreen woods of coigüe
and arrayan, and lagoons
that provide refuge for an
abundant birdlife. One of the
trails leads to La Patagua del
Armisticio, a site commemorating the signing of an
armistice in 1881 between the
Mapuche and the Chilean
government, by which the
Mapuche ceded territory for
the founding of Temuco. The
hill's crest offers extraordinary
panoramic city vistas.

Shaded by lime, oak, and
palm trees, **Plaza Teodoro
Schmidt** is best known as the
site of the city's Feria Arte.
This important crafts fair, held
each year in February, features
woodcarvings, ceramics, and
weavings made by artisans
from across the country.

Plaza Aníbal Pinto, the
city's main square, is planted

with native trees and exotic
palms, and centered on the
Monumento a la Araucanía, a
bronze-and-stone sculpture
that pays homage to this
area's principal colonizers.
The figure of a robed *machi*
(female Mapuche shaman)
crowns the monument and is
flanked by four other figures –
a Mapuche hunter with a
spear; a Spanish conquistador
with a Christian cross; a 19th-
century soldier; and a settler
farmer. A stylized rock face
symbolizing the Andes forms
the base of the monument.

The **Feria Libre Aníbal Pinto**,
Temuco's rustic open-air market, is a high-energy nexus of
feverish trading and stimulat-
ing smells. Traders here sell
pungent cheese, herbs, spices,
vegetables, and fruit, including
piñones (araucaria nuts),
cochayuyo (dried seaweed),
and *merquen* (smoky, spicy
chili powder), a staple part of
the Mapuche diet. Mapuche
women travel from outlying
districts to sit groups selling
flour, eggs, and *mote* (husked
wheat). Small restaurants in
the center of the market serve
local specialties such as *pastel
de choclo* (beef pie with a

↑ Examining an old engine at the Museo
Nacional Ferroviario Pablo Neruda

↑ Wandering through the pleasant and leafy Plaza Aníbal Pinto

sweetcorn crust) and seafood dishes. More stalls stocking traditional *huaso* hats, stirrups, and spurs ring this market's outer limits.

The **Museo Nacional Ferroviario Pablo Neruda** is Chile's national railway museum and occupies the old headquarters of the country's national railroad, a UNESCO World Heritage Site. Its great attraction is the old Casa de Máquinas (Locomotive Hall), a cavernous oval construction built 1929–43 for the maintenance of locomotives. Today, the hall preserves rows of old trains, such as the Presidential Train, built in Germany in 1920 and used by all Chilean presidents between 1924 and 2004, barring General Pinochet. Tours of the train's opulent interior include the presidential quarters, linked to the First Lady's bedroom via a hidden door. The old Administrative Hall features photographic displays.

The museum is named for Temuco's most celebrated son, Pablo Neruda *(p105)*, whose father was a lifelong employee of the railways. Neruda's many odes to Chile's railroad adorn plaques throughout this large and beautifully curated museum.

Museo Regional de la Araucanía

🏛 🅰 Avenida Alemania 084 🕐 9:30am–5:30pm Tue–Fri, 11am–5pm Sat, 11am–2pm Sun 🅦 museoregional araucania.gob.cl

Monumento Natural Cerro Ñielol

🅰 Avenida Arturo Prat s/n 📞 (045) 2298222 🕐 8am–7pm Mon–Fri, 8am–to 9pm Sat & Sun

Plaza Teodoro Schmidt

🅰 Avenida Arturo Prat

Plaza Aníbal Pinto

🅰 Avenida Arturo Prat, esq Claro Solar

Feria Libre Aníbal Pinto

🅰 Avenida Aníbal Pinto, esq Balmaceda 🕐 8am–6pm Mon–Sat

Museo Nacional Ferroviario Pablo Neruda

🅰 Avenida Barros Arana 0565 🕐 Oct–Mar: 9am–6pm Tue–Fri, 10am–6pm Sat & Sun; Apr–Sep: 9am–6pm Tue–Fri, 10am–6pm Sat, 11am–5pm Sun 🅦 tacb.cl

---

MAPUCHE CULTURE

The Mapuche are the largest indigenous group in Chile, with around 1.5 million people (10 percent of the population) having Mapuche heritage. The biggest communities are in the Lake District, Patagonia, and Santiago. They fiercely resisted the Spanish colonialists and - in the face of entrenched racism, prejudice, and marginalization - continue to struggle against the Chilean state for their rights. Get an insight into Mapuche history and culture - and admire examples of Mapuche craftsmanship (such as the cultrun drums below) - at the Museo de Volcanes near the Salto del Huilo-Huilo *(p215)*.

↑ Ski climbers scaling a snowcapped volcano in the Termas de Malalcahuello

Termas de Malalcahuello

⚑F1 🏠 Ruta Bioceánica 181-CH, Km 86, Región de la Araucanía, Malalcahuello 🚌 🕐 **12pm–11:30pm daily** 🌐 **malalcahuello.cl**

The serene location for the modern spa complex of Termas de Malalcahuello is a lushly forested valley at the foot of the 9,400-ft- (2,865-m-) high Volcán Lonquimay. Both day and overnight visitors are welcome here. On offer are three indoor thermal pools, each filled with mineral-rich water that bubbles up from deep beneath the earth's crust – the temperature of the water ranges from 99° F (37° C) to 109° F (43° C). Floor-to-ceiling windows surround the pools and offer bathers dreamy views of the fertile Lonquimay valley and the snow-covered peak of its volcano. There is also a sun terrace overlooking the valley.

A range of therapeutic treatments are on offer at the resort, while accommodations options include a mountain lodge-style hotel, log cabins, and family-sized bungalows. Local bus services and private transfers connect the Termas de Malalcahuello to the nearby Ski Center Corralco.

EAT

Cotelé
A short drive from Puerto Montt's city center, Cotelé is a top-notch steakhouse, serving perfectly cooked prime cuts along with wines.

⚑F2 🏠 Manfredini 1661, Puerto Montt 📞 **(065) 2278000** 🗓 **Sun**

$$$

Parque Nacional Tolhuaca

⚑F1 🏠 81 miles (130 km) NE of Temuco; Acceso 1, road via village of Inspector Fernández 🚌 🕐 **9am–6pm daily** 🛈 **CONAF office near southeastern entrance to park; www.termasde tolhuaca.cl**

Set in the far north of the Lake District and distant from the region's more traveled routes, the Parque Nacional Tolhuaca conserves a highly scenic area of the Andean foothills across varying altitudes. The park encompasses wild temperate rain forest famous for the prehistoric araucaria (*Araucaria araucana*), also called the monkey-puzzle tree. Attractive trails through the pristine forests offer great bird-watching; among the more easily observed species are the Chilean parakeet, several types of duck, and the Andean condor. Swimming, fishing, and hiking are also popular activities in this park. Tolhuaca's most hiked trail, the Sendero Salto Malleco, skirts the northern shore of Lago Malleco, the park's dominant feature, before crossing native forest to the stunning 164-ft (50-m) Salto Malleco waterfalls.

Another picturesque hike edges along the Laguna Verde, which lies 4,264 ft (1,300 m) above sea level and is ringed by small waterfalls and spindly araucaria woods. Other treks in the area include the Sendero Lagunillas and the Sendero Mesacura. The first is an undemanding climb

→ Moody skies looming over Puerto Montt's waterfront

to a set of mountain lagoons, and the second passes through dense forest. Both are full-day hikes and require advance planning.

Just south of the park lie the thermal pools of Termas Malleco. Located in a canyon, the natural sauna created by the rocks and sulfurous steam provides the ideal spot to relax after a long hike. Formerly known as Termas de Tolhuaca, Malleco has refurbished the facilities of what was once a worn-down hot-springs resort, and is now open for both day use and overnighters.

8 🏂 🖥 🍴 🛍

Ski Center Corralco

🗺 F1 🚠 Volcán Lonquimay, Camino a RN Malalcahuello 🚌 🕐 Mid-Jun-Sep: 9am–5pm Fri–Sun; Oct-mid-Jun: 9am–5pm daily 🌐 corralco. com

The scenic Ski Center Corralco is one of Chile's newest resorts. Skiers can descend Volcán Lonquimay on seven pistes that have a maximum drop of 3,018 ft (920 m). The off-piste opportunities are best suited to experts. There are snowboarding runs as well, and Nordic skiing circuits. In summer, activities include trekking, horseback riding, and mountain-biking.

9

Puerto Montt

🗺 F2 🚠 130 miles (210 km) S of Valdivia 🚉🚌🚢 ✈ San Martín 80; www.chile. travel/puertomontt

The port-city of Puerto Montt is where the Lake District meets the Pacific Ocean. Founded in 1853 on a hillside overlooking the Seno de Reloncaví, the city grew rapidly around its port, which was used to ship grains and alerce timber. Puerto Montt was badly hit by the 1960 earthquake and much of it was rebuilt thereafter. The city is now used strictly as a transit point by most travelers. It is the departure point for south-bound ferries and cruise ships sailing through Chile's fjords.

Built on the site of the city's foundation, Puerto Montt's main plaza is overlooked by the Neo-Classical Iglesia Catedral. Erected in 1856–96, the cathedral is modeled on Greece's iconic Parthenon, with Doric pillars of alerce adorning the facade. One of these columns conceals the city's founding stone.

Located on the waterfront, the raucous **Angelmó Fish Market** is the city's biggest attraction. A whirl of vibrant colors and aromas, the market is a maze of narrow, guttered passageways along which traders sell fish, spices, algae strings, and local delicacies. Wooden stairs climb to numerous small restaurants that serve some of the best seafood platters in the city. On streets bordering the market, craftspeople sell woolens and woodcarvings made from local alerce (also known as Patagonian Cypress).

Angelmó Fish Market
🍴 🚠 Avenida Angelmó s/n 🕐 6am–8pm daily

🔍 HIDDEN GEM
Río Puelo

This valley, 55 miles (90 km) southeast of Puerto Montt, is a wonderful place to hike, horseback-ride, fish, or simply while away a few days amid tranquil lakes, rivers, and rain forests.

STAY

Hostal Andenrose

Located about 20 miles (33 km) southwest of Volcán Lonquimay, this German-run B&B has simple but comfortable rooms. Home-cooked meals are available, and there is a small riverside campground perfect for travelers hoping to stick to a shoestring budget.

🅰F1 🅐Ruta 181, Km 68.5, Curacautín 🆆andenrose.com

$$$

---

volcano's ancient crater, and the 5-sq-mile (12-sq-km) glacier that fills it, are two of the primal elements that are responsible for the formation of the massive Andes mountain range.

Visitors can climb to the crater on a day-long hike that passes through dense forests of araucaria, offering sweeping vistas along the way of the Andean peaks, crystal-line rivers, and countless parasitic craters. For those looking to push themselves further, there is also a two-day trekking circuit, which includes ice-hikes on the glacier. All hikes start at the Nevados de Sollipulli Dome Camp. Situated next to a forested lake on the volcano's northeastern face, this camp comprises six superbly equipped, centrally heated domes. Among the many luxuries found here are hot tubs in the open air.

10 🍴

Nevados de Sollipulli

🅰F2 🅐Nevados de Sollipulli Dome Camp, Camino hacía Carén Alto 🆆sollipulli.cl

There are few places in Chile where travelers can witness nature's powerful geological forces more clearly than at Volcán Sollipulli, part of the Nevados de Sollipulli range, which lies close to Chile's border with Argentina. This

←

Navigating a gaping chasm in Nevados de Sollipulli's glacier

11 🍴 🍽 🏠

Lago Caburgua

🅰F2 🅐76 miles (122 km) SE of Temuco via Pucón 🚌

Ringed by forested mountains, Lago Caburgua is a beautiful crystalline lake that is edged by this region's only white-sand beaches. Thermal activity in the depths of the lake make its waters warmer than those of the district's other lakes. There are a number of popular beaches here, including Playa Negra, a black-sand beach, and Playa Blanca, with its stretch of white, crystallized sand. Boat tours of the lake depart regularly from Playa Negra, from where paddleboats are also available to be rented. A scenic lakeside walk links these two beaches.

A canoeist on Lago Villarrica, overlooked by the Volcán Villarrica ↑

12 🏄 🍽

Ojos del Caburgua

🅰F2 🅐73 miles (117 km) SE of Temuco via Pucón Camino Internacional 7, Km 17 or Km 20 🚌 🕐9am-9pm daily

The waters of Lago Caburgua flow southward and under-ground for 3 miles (5 km) before gushing out to form the Ojos del Caburgua (Eyes of Caburgua). This necklace of aquamarine rock pools lies at the base of cascading waterfalls and is shrouded in pristine forest. Travelers to the site are able to access the pools at a signposted entrance on the main road from Pucón. There is also a second entrance, which lies 2 miles (3 km) north on the same road and offers a more intimate view of the pools, falls, and forest. Keep your eyes peeled; this approach is marked solely by a wooden roadside statue of Christ on the cross.

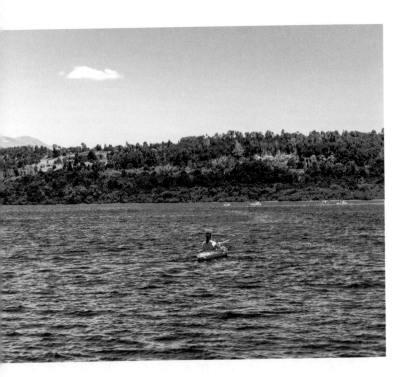

⑬

Villarrica

⚑ F2 ⬚ 54 miles (87 km) SE of Temuco 🚌 ℹ Pedro de Valdivia 1070; www. villarrica.org

Originally founded in 1552 by the Spanish, Villarrica (Rich Town) was named for the abundant gold and silver deposits discovered here. In 1598, the town was razed in a Mapuche uprising and only resettled in 1883. Today, it is a laid-back, family-oriented destination on the western shore of a sapphire lake of the same name and at the foot of the majestic 9,341-ft- (2,847-m-) high Volcán Villarrica. Lago Villarrica, a big attraction in its own right, boasts a charming *costanera* (lakefront promenade), and an attractive black-sand beach, Playa Pucará.

Villarrica's wonderful Mapuche heritage finds expression at the excellent **Museo Arqueológico Municipal Mapuche**, where a range of pre-Columbian exhibits include ceramics and weaponry. Next door to the museum, the Centro Cultural Mapuche features a Mapuche crafts market in the summer months. At the edge of town, the Mirador Canela is a lookout point with great views of the lake and volcano.

Museo Arqueológico Municipal Mapuche

🖉 🕑 ⚑ Pedro de Valdivia 1050 📞 (045) 2415706 🕒 9am-1pm & 2:30-6pm Mon-Fri

---

VOLCÁN LONQUIMAY

North of Villarrica is Volcán Lonquimay, which last erupted on December 25, 1988 (earning it the nickname Navidad). It's great for snowboarding, skiing, and hot springs, but it is also a great place to hike, with three- and five-day circuits around the base of the volcano. More adventurous travelers can climb to the summit – experienced mountaineers could even attempt this during winter (with crampons, ice axes, and a guide).

14

Coñaripe

F2 **83 miles (134 km)
SE of Temuco**

On the eastern shore of
Lago Calafquén, and away
from the region's more
traveled routes, Coñaripe is
a tiny village with a soporific
air and a couple of black-sand
beaches. The area around the
village offers ample opportunities for adventure sports,
including white-water rafting
on the Río San Pedro, and
horseback, mountain-bike,
and trekking trips. Coñaripe
has many accommodations
options for overnight guests;
budget travelers in particular
will enjoy the well-equipped
campsites by the beaches.

The hills around Coñaripe
are dotted with more than a
dozen thermal springs which
are scenic, relaxing, and well
worth visiting. They range
from very basic, rustic pools
to modern hotel-and-spa
complexes. One of the best
among these is the **Termas
Geómetricas**. Nestled within
a forested ravine, this stylish
spa comprises 60 thermal
fountains that gush into
bubbling bathing pools
through a network of wooden
water channels. Visitors simply
walk across the ravine on a
1,476-ft- (450-m-) long
catwalk, and descend via
wooden stairs to the pool
of their choice.

In terms of the overnight
accommodations on offer,
the **Termas Coñaripe** is an
excellent choice. This modern
hotel and spa made of glass
and wood offers indoor and
semi-covered pools, along
with outdoor thermal pools.
A number of other appealing
amenities are available;
guests can slather around in
mud baths and enjoy walks
and horseback rides to nearby
waterfalls and lagoons.

From the Termas Coñaripe,
a rough road leads to the
Parque Nacional Villarrica
(p202), some 11 miles (18 km)
to the north.

Termas Geómetricas
⊛ ⊕ **10 miles (16 km) NE
of Coñaripe** **11am-8pm
Sun-Fri, 9am-11pm Sat**
termasgeometricas.cl

Termas Coñaripe
⊛ ⊕ ⊕ ⊕ **9 miles (15 km)
SE of Coñaripe; Camino
Coñaripe-Liquine, Km 15**
termasconaripe.cl

15 ⊛

Santuario Cañi

F2 **83 miles (134 km)
SE of Temuco via Pucón;
Camino Termas de Huife,
Km 21, Pichares** **24 hrs** **santuario
cani.cl**

Enclosing a lush swath of
temperate Valdivian rain
forest, Santuario Cañi is
home to some of Chile's
oldest stands of araucaria.
A single trail climbs through
forests of southern beech
(*Nothofagus*) to reveal hidden
mountain tarns and, at higher
elevations, pure forests of
araucaria. Together, these
habitats harbor a rich variety
of birdlife and many shy
mammals that are usually
difficult to spot, including the
puma and pudú. The steep

12
The number of lakes in
Chile's Lake District.

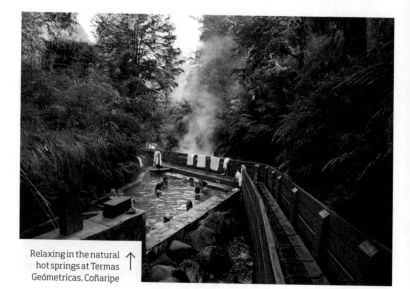

Relaxing in the natural
hot springs at Termas
Geómetricas, Coñaripe ↑

↑ Walking through the trees in the Parque Nacional Huerquehue

6-mile (9-km) trail ends at a lookout point about 5,084 ft (1,550 m) above sea level. This has 360-degree views of the area's four volcanoes – Lanín, Villarrica, Quetrupillán, and Llaima – as well as its three biggest lakes – Caburgua, Villarrica, and Calafquén. Travelers on overnight treks can stay at rustic La Loma and camping grounds.

16 ⟨🅜⟩

Santuario de la Naturaleza Carlos Anwandter

🅰F2 🏠13 miles (21 km) N of Valdivia 🚌 🚹CONAF Valdivia; (063) 2245200

Over 23 sq miles (60 sq km) of wildlife-rich wetlands are protected by the Santuario de la Naturaleza Carlos Anwandter. The origin of these wetlands lies in the aftermath of the 1960 earthquake, when a tsunami submerged the area's forests and cattle pastures. The new ecosystem attracted a variety of birdlife and was recognized as a nature sanctuary in 1981. Over 100 species of birds, such as pelicans and black-necked swans, can be seen here. It is also possible to spot river otters and the coipú, a large aquatic rodent.

17 ⟨🖉⟩

Parque Nacional Huerquehue

🅰F2 🏠94 miles (152 km) SE of Temuco via Pucón; Camino a Caburgua 🚌 🕗8:30am–8pm daily 🚹CONAF Pucón, Lincoyán 336; www.conaf.cl

Created in 1967, the compact Parque Nacional Huerquehue protects around 48 sq miles (124 sq km) of native forest that includes 2,000-year-old araucaria woods. The park has some of the Lake District's best short treks and offers spectacular views of Volcán Villarrica and its surroundings. A must-do trail is the 4-mile (7-km) Sendero Los Lagos, which traverses forests of Chilean yew and beech, skirts five different lakes, and two waterfalls. Along the way there are vistas of the volcano and of Lago Tinquilco, the park's largest body of water. The trail ends at Lago Chico, a small alpine lake surrounded by cliffs. Another spectacular hike is the 10-mile (16-km) round trek to Cerro San Sebastián. From here, you can spot up to eight volcanoes from the height of 6,562 ft (2,000 m) on a clear day.

Between hikes, visitors can enjoy lake swimming and nature-watching. Many species of eagle can be seen, and among the mammals here are the puma; the pudú, the world's smallest deer; and the mouse opossum (*Dromiciops gliroides*), one of the southern Andes' few surviving marsupials.

EAT

Latitude 39
This casual café is run by expat Californians. It offers a diverse menu and a strong selection of craft beers.

🅰F2 🏠Gerónimo de Alderete 324, Pucón 📞(09) 7430-0016 🔒Sun

$⑂$⑂$⑂

La Maga
An Uruguayan-run joint, La Maga takes its decor cues from gaucho style, though the menu makes a few concessions to Chilean tastes, too. Steaks are the main focus here.

🅰F2 🏠Gerónimo de Alderete 276, Pucón 📞(045) 2444277

$⑂$⑂$⑂

THE SIETE LAGOS REGION

South of Pucón, the Siete Lagos (Seven Lakes) is a beautiful region that receives fewer tourists than it should. It is made up of interlinked lakes – six of them in Chile, with another over the border in Argentina – that are surrounded by sleepy villages and soaring mountains. The area is perfect for scenic drives and nature-based activities.

18 Panguipulli

F2 90 miles (145 km) SE of Temuco Bernardo O'Higgins s/n; www.sietelagos.cl

Panguipulli is a popular stop for visitors continuing on to the Reserva Biológica Huilo-Huilo. A pleasant lakeshore destination of brightly painted clapboard houses on hillside streets, the town's biggest attraction is the landmark Iglesia Capuchina. The church was built by German Capuchin missionaries in 1947 and stands on the site of a German mission from the 1890s, and the building is fronted by a latticed facade that is painted red, yellow, and black – the colors of Germany's flag.

Panguipulli and its namesake lake lie at the heart of Chile's Seven Lakes region. These lakes – Calafquén, Pallaifa, Pullinque, Ruñihue, Neltume, Panguipulli, and Pirihueico – are linked to each other by rivers, which together comprise a single hydrological system. A chain of beautiful and generally uncrowded villages face the shores of these lakes. Although it's possible to spend the night in Panguipulli, Pucón is the main springboard for day trips into the Siete Lagos area.

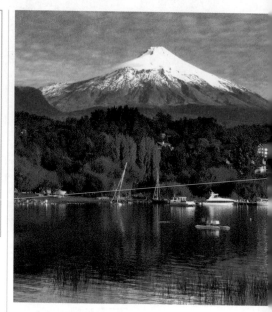

↑ The town of Pucón, overlooked by the snowcapped Villarrica volcano

19 Licán Ray

F2 70 miles (113 km) SE of Temuco General Urrutia, esq Cacique Marichanquin; (045) 243 1516 (Dec-Mar only)

Licán Ray is the main resort on the hauntingly beautiful Lago Calafquén. The village is a quiet oasis, except in February when hordes of people from Santiago arrive to holiday by Lago Calafquén's mist-shrouded warm waters.

There are two beaches at this miniature retreat – Playa Grande and the more picturesque Playa Chica, which is ringed by rolling forested peaks that sweep down to a shore of black volcanic sand. A wooded peninsula divides these two beaches and is crossed by walking paths that ascend to lookout points with great vistas. Catamaran tours of the lake depart from Playa Chica. At the village center, the main plaza is edged by sandy sidewalks and artisans' fairs.

20 Pucón

F2 69 miles (112 km) SE of Temuco O'Higgins 483; www.chile.travel/pucon

On the eastern shore of Lago Villarrica, Pucón is the Lake District's adventure-tourism capital. It was founded in 1883 as a fort settlement at the foot of Volcán Villarrica; today its compact grid of smoothly paved streets caters mostly to the tourism industry. Nestled in an area of natural beauty, Pucón is a base for trips to

 INSIDER TIP
High Hiking

For a physical challenge and a memorable experience, try one of the rock- or volcano-climbing trips with the well-established Pucón-based agency Summit Chile (www.summitchile.org).

nearby hot springs and national parks, and visitors heading out to these areas will find the city's CONAF office helpful. Pucón is also the starting point for many adrenaline-charged activities in the region. It has two black-sand beaches where swimming and water sports are possible: Playa Grande, and the smaller La Poza beach that faces a protected inlet. In summer, boat rides from La Poza are a popular way of touring Lago Villarrica.

㉑ ⊗ 🍴 🍺 🛍️

Reserva Biológica Huilo-Huilo

🅰F2 **🕓130 miles (210 km) SE of Temuco; El Portal, Camino Internacional Panguipulli-Puerto Fuy, Km 56** 🚌 **🆆huilohuilo.com**

Run by a private foundation dedicated to sustainable tourism, Reserva Biológica Huilo-Huilo preserves 232 sq miles (600 sq km) of temperate rain forest that was once the target of large-scale logging. It offers some truly compelling scenery; the most impressive is the Volcán Mocho-Choshuenco, which is in fact two volcanoes bridged by a large glacier. The surrounding landscape comprises glacial lakes and Andean prairies.

There is a range of lodging options, from an upscale mountain lodge in the woods, to more inexpensive accommodations in the small towns of Neltume and Puerto Fuy. These were built in the 1930s to house employees of the logging companies. Puerto Fuy is situated near the lovely Lago Pirihueico and is the starting point for fly-fishing, kayaking, and boating trips.

The reserve's lodge, Montaña Mágica (Magic Mountain), is worth a visit even for non-guests. It rises above the forest like a castle from a fairy tale, and its interior is constructed almost entirely from native woods. Next door is the whimsical Nothofagus Hotel, which looks like a giant treehouse. Activities here are mostly guided and arranged at La Montaña Mágica or at the administration center.

A cascading waterfall within the Reserva
↓ Biológica Huilo-Huilo

These include horseback rides and wildlife observation of reintroduced fauna that once roamed freely here. Travelers looking for more rugged activities will also find ziplining, mountain-biking, trekking excursions, and an impressive range of hiking trails. The premises also house the stunning Museo de los Volcanes, which displays Chile's most extensive collection of silver Mapuche items within a pyramid-like interior.

22

Parque Nacional Puyehue

F2 **116 miles (187 km)** SE of Valdivia; Aguas Calientes **9am-7pm** daily **Centro de Informacion Ambiental, Aguas Calientes; www.conaf.cl/parques**

Famed for its hot springs, Parque Nacional Puyehue is one of Chile's most popular and remote national parks. It covers 412 sq miles (1,067 sq km) of wilderness that encompasses two volcanoes, around 200 craters, and large swaths of evergreen Valdivian rain forest. Close to the park's entrance, in its Aguas Calientes sector, the **Termas Aguas Calientes** is a rustic hot-springs resort featuring sulfur-rich outdoor rock pools edged by forest and tumbling rivers. In the park's Antillanca sector, Volcán Casablanca, rising to a height of 6,529 ft (1,990 m), has one of the Lake District's least demanding ascents. The base is the starting point for several trails, both easy and challenging, that wind through native forests of lenga, ulmo, and coigüe trees. The park is home to a rich and varied birdlife, including hummingbirds, condors, and kingfishers. Hikers can also hear the distinctive chirp of the endemic, onomatopoeically named chucao (*Scelorchilus rubecula*). Among the park's mammals are pumas, foxes, the native and endangered huemul, as well as the tiny, tree-dwelling mouse opossum.

Volcán Casablanca is also the location for the highly rated and popular **Centro de Ski Antillanca**, which operates on the volcano's western wall. Offering excellent off-piste skiing, it features 17 slopes for all levels, snowboard runs, and a maximum drop of

1,640 ft (500 m). The slopes afford panoramic views of the blue skyline pierced by the snowcapped cones of surrounding volcanoes. Services include an equipment rental shop, a ski-school, and a snow park for children. In summer, activities feature mountain-biking, horseback riding, caving, and trekking on the volcano, as well as kayaking and fishing excursions. Snowmobile rides through virgin forest are an added draw during winter months.

In the northern, less trodden sector of the national park, the 7,334-ft (2,236-m) Volcán Puyehue offers a difficult two-day ascent, and is for experienced hikers only. The stunning trails here pass geysers, steaming fumaroles, and gurgling hot springs.

←

Hiking in the Parque Nacional Puyehue, and *(inset)* a resident ringed kingfisher

Termas Aguas Calientes

Km 4 Camino Antillanca
termasaguascalientes.cl

Centro de Ski Antillanca

Volcán Casablanca Jun-Oct: 8am-5:30pm daily antillanca.cl

㉓
Lago Ranco

F2 77 miles (124 km) SE of Valdivia Linares & Concepción; (063) 2491348

Located on the southern shore of the eponymous silver-gray lake, Lago Ranco is a small and quiet village of gravel streets and weatherboard houses. These old, weather-beaten structures encircle the forested shoreline of what is possibly the Lake District's most beautiful body of water. Ringed by craggy Andean peaks, the lake's crystalline, warm waters are perfect for a swim. The village's cultural attraction, **Museo Tringlo Lago Ranco**, displays archaeological and anthropological exhibits, including ancient ceramics.

Museo Tringlo Lago Ranco

Ancud s/n 10am-1pm & 3-5pm daily museoregiondelosrios.cl

㉔
Termas de Puyehue

F2 114 miles (183 km) SE of Valdivia; Ruta 215, Km 76, Puyehue 8am-8pm Mon-Fri, 8am-9pm Sat & Sun puyehue.cl

The five-star spa resort of Termas de Puyehue is the ideal place to soothe aching limbs after long treks in the nearby Parque Nacional Puyehue. Hidden within forests at the edge of the park, this luxurious yet accessible mountain lodge and spa receives both day and overnight guests. It is possible to relax in the therapeutic waters of three large thermal pools – covered, semi-covered, and outdoor – whose temperatures range from a comfortable 22°C (72°F) to a warm 41°C (106°F). There are hot rooms and hydrotherapy pools, and a tempting variety of indulgent treatments that include honey, algae, and herbal massages, as well as sulfur-rich mud baths. The spa has a daily program of children's activities and a well-equipped playroom. Other facilities include two gourmet restaurants, a small art gallery, and outdoor tennis courts. Visitors can enjoy exhilarating horseback rides to the forested shore of the nearby Lago Puyehue, where the spa arranges several water sports for its guests.

㉕
Osorno

F2 66 miles (107 km) S of Valdivia O'Higgins 667; (064) 2234104

Founded in 1558 by García Hurtado de Mendoza, then governor of Chile, the city of Osorno is located at the center of Chile's cattle heartland. The country's biggest cattle market, the Feria

↑ The striking Catedral San Mateo Apóstol in Osorno

Ganadera de Osorno, is held here on Mondays and Fridays.

Although primarily an agricultural city, Osorno offers many attractions. Most striking of these is the Neo-Gothic Catedral San Mateo Apóstol with its massive facade of reinforced concrete and ogival filigree. Built in 1960, it towers over the city's central plaza.

South of the cathedral is the Calle Juan Mackenna, lined with a row of Teutonic-style wooden houses dating from the 19th century, when German settlers arrived at Osorno. A number have been designated national monuments.

A block west of the houses, an elegant 1929 Neo-Classical building is the setting for the **Museo Histórico Municipal**. Its displays trace the city's history chronologically; exhibits include Mapuche pottery and colonial-era weapons.

Osorno is a convenient base for visits to the nearby Parque Nacional Puyehue; travelers are advised to first visit Osorno's CONAF office for information on the park.

Museo Histórico Municipal

M A Matta 809 (064) 2238615 9:30am-5:30pm Mon-Thu, 9:30am-5pm Fri, 2-6pm Sat

---

EAT

La Parrilla de Pepe
Situated at the end of a row of houses built by German pioneers, this spot is an architectural landmark and a reliable grill restaurant.

F2 Mackenna 1095, Osorno (064) 2249653

$ $ $

The peaceful waters of Lago Llanquihue at sunset, with Volcán Osorno in the distance

26 🍴 📷 🏛

Lago Llanquihue

⚑F2 **⌖99 miles (160 km) SE of Valdivia** 🚌

Resembling a small sea in its size, the breathtakingly beautiful Lago Llanquihue is South America's third-largest natural lake. It covers a surface area of 338 sq miles (875 sq km), plunges to a depth of 1,148 ft (350 m), and its crystal blue waters are bound by Volcán Osorno and Volcán Calbuco. The Mapuche believed this lake and its dominions to be a realm of monsters and evil spirits. The Spanish discovered it in 1552,

but it was not until the arrival of German immigrants in the 19th century that Europeans finally colonized the lake's shores. Since then, Llanquihue has been the German heartland of the Lake District and is today fronted by steepled Bavarian towns.

27

Puerto Octay

⚑F2 **⌖99 miles (160 km) SE of Valdivia** 🚌 **ℹ German Wulf s/n; www.turismo puertoctay.si**

Set on the northern shore of Lago Llanquihue, Puerto Octay was founded in 1852 by German immigrants and grew into an important lake port. Today, it is a charming holiday destination with streets of well-conserved Germanic architecture. Occupying an old settler's house, the excellent **Museo El Colono** exhibits period objects. Another noteworthy building is the 1907-built Iglesia Parroquial, constructed in a simple Gothic style.

Puerto Octay faces the peaks of three volcanoes – Calbuco, Puntiagudo, and Osorno. Each is visible from the town's main beach, Playa La Baja, a stretch of volcanic black sand fringed by pine and eucalyptus forests.

Museo El Colono

🎟 🕐 **⚑Avenida Independencia 591** **⌚10:15am–1pm & 3–5pm daily** 🌐 **museo elcolono.jimdo.com**

28

Puerto Varas

⚑F2 **⌖118 miles (190 km) S of Valdivia** ✈🚌 **🌐puertovaras.org**

Fronting the southern shores of Lago Llanquihue, Puerto Varas is the biggest town on the lake. It was founded in 1854 by German immigrants, and pioneer-era homes can still be seen on the streets. The town's most remarkable Teutonic building, the **Iglesia Sagrado Corazón de Jesús**, was built in 1915–18 as a to-scale replica of a church in Germany's Black Forest. Made entirely from wood, its Baroque interior has two cupolas, built to the maximum height possible without metal supports.

The town is popular for various adventure sports, and visitors can also trek to Volcán Osorno, and hike in Parque Vicente Perez-Rosales (p204).

During winter, the locals celebrate the seasonal rains with the traditional Rain Festival. The most popular of the town's black-sand beaches is Playa de Puerto Chico, with views of Volcán Osorno.

GERMANIC DISTRICT

In 1845, the Chilean government passed the Badlands Law, which aimed to undermine Mapuche control of the Lake District. Some 150 German Catholic families accepted Chile's invitation to colonize the area; more followed, fleeing persecution in their home country. German settlers founded three towns - Puerto Octay, Frutillar, and Puerto Varas. These became a German heartland.

Iglesia Sagrado Corazón de Jesús
🏠 Verbo Divino, esq San Francisco ⏰ Hours vary

29
Frutillar

🗺 F2 🚗 105 miles (170 km) SE of Valdivia 🚌
ℹ Philippi & O'Higgins; www.frutillar.com

Said to be the Lake District's loveliest town, Frutillar was founded in 1856 by German colonists on the western shore of Lago Llanquihue. The town's Frutillar Bajo (Lower Frutillar) district has stunning views of Volcán Osorno, and its shores are lined by a mix of hotels, crafts markets, restaurants, and old Germanic architecture. The **Museo Colonial Alemán** stands in landscaped gardens and re-creates the pioneer era with life-size buildings furnished with period objects.

On the waterfront, the Teatro del Lago Sur is a contemporary theater venue and site of the Semana Musical de Frutillar, a ten-day music festival. At the town's northern edge, the **Reserva Forestal**

→

A Germanic wooden house located in Frutillar

Edmundo Winkler preserves Valdivian rain forest. A path here climbs to a lookout point with lake and volcano views.

Museo Colonial Alemán
🏠 Avenida Vicente Pérez Rosales, esq Arturo Prat, Frutillar Bajo ⏰ 10am–6pm daily 🌐 museosaustral.cl

Reserva Forestal Edmundo Winkler
🏠 Calle Caupolicán s/n, Frutillar Bajo ⏰ 8am–7pm Mon–Fri (winter: to 5pm)

30

Ancud

F3 **54 miles (87 km) S of Puerto Montt; Isla Grande** **Libertad 665; www.ancud.cl**

A picturesque fishing town, Ancud is the first stop for most visitors crossing the Canal de Chacao, from the Lake District to Chiloé.

The town was set up by the Spanish in 1768 as a fort settlement on the Bahía de Ancud, a tongue of water dotted with fishing boats, edged by algae-strewn beaches and colorful houses, and ringed by emerald hills. This compact town is easily explored on foot. Its coastal Avenida Salvador Allende runs parallel to the bay, which is overlooked by the ruins of **Fuerte San Antonio**. This Spanish fort marks the site where Royalist forces made their last stand in Chile's War of Independence in 1826. An obelisk at the fort commemorates the Spanish Crown's final defeat. Beneath rocky cliffs nearby is Playa Arena Gruesa, a horseshoe-shaped beach and bathing spot.

In the town itself, **Museo Regional de Ancud** in the central plaza displays archaeological and ethnographic exhibits. It includes an ornate collection of 17th- and 18th-century Jesuit artifacts; carved

figures from Chilote mythology; and a life-size replica of *Goleta Ancud*, the Ancud-built schooner that carried the first Chilean settlers to the Strait of Magellan in 1843. Adjacent to the museum is the town's cathedral, whose shingled exterior resembles the facade of a typical Chilote home. Visitors can also explore the scale models of Chiloé's 16 unique churches at Centro de Visitantes Inmaculada. To find out more about the archipelago's churches, visit the Centro de Visitantes de las Iglesias de Chiloé, a visitor center with a number of exhibits that provide information on the area's history and architecture.

Fuerte San Antonio

Cochrane esq San Antonio **9am-9pm daily**

MYTHS AND FOLKLORE OF CHILOÉ

Folktales and myths have long enriched Chilote life, with stories handed across generations through oral tradition. Goddesses who protect the land, a lascivious forest dweller who tricks adolescent girls into surrendering their virginity, and a serpent that sucks the lifeblood from a household; these are just a few of the benevolent and evil beings believed by the islanders to roam Chiloé. The origin of these tales lies in Mapuche legend and its later blurring with Spanish superstition and Roman Catholic beliefs. The archipelago's landscape forms an ideal background; mist-shrouded bays, silent forests, and frequent bad weather are all evocative of fantastical worlds.

Museo Regional de Ancud

Libertad 370 **10am-5:30pm Tue-Fri, 10am-1:30pm Sat & Sun** **museoancud.gob.cl**

31

Monumento Natural Islotes de Puñihuil

E3 **17 miles (27 km) W of Ancud** **11:30am-8pm daily** **pinguineraschiloe.cl**

Three rocky islets of volcanic origin, the Monumento Natural Islotes de Puñihuil are refuge to colonies of Humboldt and

Magellanic penguins that nest here each year. These islets are among the world's few places where the vulnerable Humboldt shares the same habitat as its close Magellanic relative. Small-boat excursions depart from Bahía Puñihuil on Isla Grande's northwestern coast to observe the penguins and other fauna. This includes marine otters, which scramble across the black rock at the water's edge; red-legged cormorants, agile flyers that can be seen dive-bombing the water for crustaceans; flightless steamer ducks; and two species of oystercatchers.

↑ Walking along a boardwalk trail through the Parque Nacional Chiloé

㉜
Dalcahue

🅰F3 **📍17 miles (28 km) NE of Castro** **🚌** **🌐dalcahue.cl**

Located on the eastern coast of Isla Grande, the town of Dalcahue faces the smaller islands of the Chiloé archipelago. Dalcahue was not founded on any particular date; it evolved from the 1700s onward as a stop on the Jesuits' Circular Mission – annual trips made by the Jesuits across Chiloé.
The town's chief draw is the

↓ The life-size monument to *Goleta Ancud*, standing in the town of Ancud

UNESCO-protected Iglesia Dalcahue, a Neo-Gothic structure built in 1903 on the site of the Jesuits' original mission. Close to it, the Museo Cultural de Dalcahue has local historical exhibits. There is also a wooden dining hall on the waterfront that features the best of Chilote food.

Dalcahue is also a sales hub for craftsmen from the nearby islands, who arrive daily by boat to offer their wares at the artisans' market.

㉝ 🎿
Parque Nacional Chiloé

🅰E3 **📍32 miles (52 km) W of Castro; Sector Chanquín, Cucao** **🚌** **🕐9am-7pm daily** **ℹ️CONAF, Gamboa 424, Castro; www.conaf.cl**

The scenic Parque Nacional Chiloé is fringed by the Pacific Ocean on its west and by Chile's coastal mountain range on its east. In between, it protects over 164 sq miles (426 sq km) of indigenous forest, including Chile's southernmost forests of alerce. Parque Nacional Chiloé has abundant wildlife and its coastal sections harbor colo-

nies of southern sea lions, Magellanic and Humboldt penguins, and seabirds.

Most visits to the park focus on the southern sector, where the Cucao village offers rustic accommodations close by the park entrance. The village is the trailhead for the Chanquín-Cole Cole Trail, which skirts past a stretch of the Pacific coastline, marked by white beaches, big surf, and sand dunes edged by native forest. At the end of the trail, members of a Huilliche community organize horseback rides through the verdant woods.

The park's northern sector, although less visited, has forests of greater size and density. Here, the outstanding Castro-Abtao Trek crosses through thick alerce forest and ends at the Pacific Ocean.

> **Parque Nacional Chiloé has abundant wildlife and its coastal sections harbor colonies of southern sea lions, Magellanic and Humboldt penguins, and seabirds.**

34

CASTRO

⬛ F3 🏠 48 miles (77 km) S of Ancud 🚌 ℹ️ Plaza de Armas; www.municastro.cl

An island gem, Castro is an inevitable stop on any visit to the archipelago. It was founded by the Spanish in 1567 on a hill overlooking the mist-swathed Fiordo Castro. Today, it is a picturesque destination of hilly lanes, gorgeous sea views, and historic *palafitos*.

① 🤿 Ⓜ️

Museo Regional de Castro

🏠 Esmeralda 255
🕐 9:30am-1pm & 3-6pm Mon-Fri, 9:30-1pm Sat
🌐 museodecastro.cl

This small museum traces Chiloé's history from the arrival of hunter-gatherer groups at the archipelago – around 6,000 years ago – to modern times. Historical objects and information panels record the islands' colonization by the Chono and Huilliche communities; the subsequent Spanish conquest during the 16th century; and the primary role played by Chiloé as a Royalist stronghold during Chile's War of Independence (1810–18). The exhibits on modern history feature photographs of the destruction caused by the 1960 earthquake and tsunami, which affected coastal villages throughout the archipelago.

---

②

Iglesia San Francisco

🏠 Plaza de Armas
🕐 9:30am-12:30pm & 3:30-6:30pm Mon-Sat, 3:30-6:30pm Sun
🌐 iglesiadecastro.cl

Without a doubt Chiloé's most iconic landmark, the beautiful, sunshine-colored Iglesia San Francisco is an extraordinary work of local craftsmanship. A UNESCO-protected building, it was designed by Italian architect Eduardo Provasoli in 1910 to replace an older church that burned down. Constructed entirely from native woods such as cypress, alerce, and coigüe, the church is finished in flamboyant polychrome fashion. The edifice's striking Neo-Gothic facade is clad with sheets of corrugated tin, painted gold and purple, and features two 130-ft- (40-m)- high bell towers. For decades, these towers were used to guide ships arriving at the port and today their status as Castro's tallest structures is protected by law. The church's vaulted interior is ornamented with opulent religious imagery and the altar, pulpit, and confessional boxes are exquisitely hand-carved from native woods by local artisans. It also has colorful stained-glass windows.

> 💬 INSIDER TIP
> **Feria Yumbel Market**
>
> A craft and food market northwest of Castro city center, Feria Yumbel is an excellent place to buy traditional Chilote woolen jumpers, hats, socks, and other items of clothing.

↑ Brightly painted wooden *palafitos* along the shores of Fiordo Castro

These wonderfully picturesque homes are constructed from local woods and painted in vibrant colors. Each *palafito* has two facades: one facing the street and the other over-looking the water. Exquisite examples of vernacular archi-tecture, the *palafitos* were originally built in the 19th century for local fishermen, who would moor their boats in the water before climbing a wooden ladder to their family home.

Prior to the 1960 earth-quake, the *palafitos* lined most of Isla Grande's eastern shore. However, following the earthquake their numbers have greatly reduced and they are now concentrated on Castro's coastal Avenida Pedro Montt, Calle Lillo, and Calle Ernesto Riquelme, with particularly splendid examples on the northern approach to Castro. Experience Castro by staying in one of the *palafitos* that have been restored and converted into luxurious guesthouses and boutique hotels.

③

Palafitos

🅰 Shore of Fiordo Castro

Castro's pastel-hued *palafitos*, the city's favorite postcard image, are traditional wooden houses built on stilts along the edge of the Fiordo Castro.

④

Museo de Arte Moderno Chiloé

🅰 Galvarino Riveros s/n, Parque Municipal 🕐 Only during exhibitions; check website for details 🌐 mamchiloe.cl

Housed in a former grain warehouse, this excellent con-temporary art museum sits atop a windswept hillside that offers spectacular views of the city. It showcases a wide range of styles such as installation, graffiti, and digital art. The permanent collection also includes works by well-known Chilean artists Arturo Duclos and Ricardo Yrarrázaval.

Many of the museum's dis-plays make use of indigenous materials such as sheep's wool. It also explores local themes that emphasize Chiloé's identity as distinct from that of mainland Chile.

EAT

Travesía
Come here for traditional Chilote food with a modern, global twist. If you enjoy the food, pick up a copy of the chef's cookbook.

🅰 Eusebio Lillo 188
☎ (065) 2630137
🕐 Sun eve

⑤⑤⑤

La Brújula del Cuerpo
On Plaza de Armas, this lively, low-cost café serves simple, tasty meals, including sandwiches, soups, burgers, ice cream, and set lunches.

🅰 O'Higgins 308 🕐 (065) 2633229

⑤⑤⑤

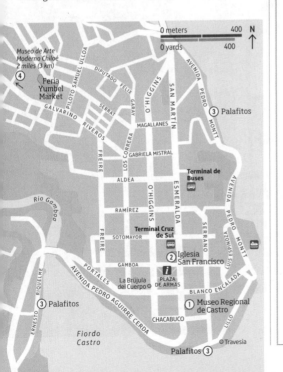

JESUIT CHURCHES IN CHILOÉ

In 1608, Jesuit priests arrived at Chiloé to evangelize the indigenous Huilliche. They established the Circular Mission and built wooden churches. The construction represented a new form of religious architecture – the Chilote School – whose roots lay in the Jesuit architecture of 17th-century central Europe. Over 60 churches survive; some were rebuilt in the 18th and 19th centuries after fires or earthquakes. Sixteen of them constitute a UNESCO World Heritage Site.

CHURCH ARCHITECTURE

Chiloté churches have key characteristics, all of which can be seen in Achao's Iglesia Santa María de Loreto (p226), also known as the Iglesia de Achao. One of the distinctive aspects of the architecture of the churches, as seen with the Iglesia de San Francisco, are the unmistakable bell towers and symmetrical facades. The bell tower of Santa María is typical, soaring above the center of the facade, lending the building its symmetrical design. Rising up from a rectangular base, the octagonal tower is crowned by a cross, which acts as a beacon for fishermen and sailors. Windows sit along the church's portico and side walls, providing light to the interior.

↑ The bright yellow and purple facade of Iglesia de San Francisco

The symmetrical wooden interior of Iglesia Santa María de Loreto ↑

ENTRANCE DESIGN

The entrances of Chiloté churches may have a columned and arched arcade in the Neo-Gothic or Neo-Classical style, as seen in Iglesia de Dalcahue. The Jesuits laid out squares in front of entrances for religious processions.

CHURCH INTERIORS

The interior of Chiloté churches can be simple and austere or highly decorative. A vaulted ceiling covers the central nave, as in Iglesia de Castro. This elegant feature might be brightly painted or left bare. At the heart of the church is the long nave. Wooden columns, set in stone and carved from trunks of native trees, separate this part from two lateral naves. Only the central nave reaches the back of the church and the altar. The altar table, crafted from native alerce, cypress, and mañío trunks and richly decorated with Catholic imagery, stands at the church's northern end.

THE JESUITS' CIRCULAR MISSION

Jesuit priests faced one major obstacle to the evangelization of Chiloé: the exceptional isolation of its islands and of its Huilliche pop-ulations. In an effort to overcome this, the Jesuits made annual round-trips of the archipelago by sea. On this Circular Mission, priests disembarked at each indigenous settlement, converted its people, deposited a layman for continued spiritual assistance, and returned the following year. The Jesuits built a church at each new mission – there were 200 constructed overall – around which villages grew. After the Jesuits were removed and expelled from the Spanish New World in 1767, Franciscans continued the Circular Mission.

←
The distinctive exterior of Iglesia Santa María de Loreto

35

Curaco de Vélez

⛰F3 ⏱23 miles (37 km) E of Castro 🚌🚐 **ℹ Entrada a Curaco de Vélez, Plazoleta la Amistad; www.curacodevelez.cl**

From Dalcahue *(p225)*, boats cross the Canal Dalcahue – part of the Mar Interior (Inner Sea) that separates Chiloé from mainland Chile – to reach Isla de Quinchao, an island dotted with tiny coastal villages. Facing the canal on this island is the pretty village

↑ The painted façade and *(inset)* wooden interior of the protected Iglesia de Chonchi

of Curaco de Vélez, the smallest settlement in the Chiloé archipelago. Its origins can be traced to the 1600s, when Jesuit priests first dropped anchor here on their missionary route. Although the town's original Jesuit church was destroyed in a fire in 1971, a wealth of century-old vernacular architecture can still be seen. Calle Errázuriz is lined with gray wooden houses clad in alerce tiles in the typical Chilote style. These stand as a testament to Curaco de Vélez's prosperous past, when forestry brought wealth and fine craftsmanship. Today, life revolves around a small plaza where the Museo Municipal de Curaco de Vélez has displays on the town's local history. The plaza backs onto a dramatic sweep of shell-strewn beach facing the narrow stretch of sea. Colonies of black-necked swans dot the water's surface in summer. Isla de Quinchao is also visited for its old Jesuit churches, historic wooden houses, seafood restaurants, and crafts markets.

36

Achao

⛰F3 ⏱28 miles (45 km) E of Castro 🚌ℹ **Amunátegui s/n, Plaza de Armas**

Nestled on Isla de Quinchao's eastern coast, the small town of Achao makes for a good half-day visit. Iglesia Santa María de Loreto, the archipelago's oldest church, is the single surviving structure from the Jesuits' original mission. Built in 1754, it fronts the town's main plaza and is a completely wooden structure: even the pegs and nails used in its construction are made of wood. The vaulted interior features Baroque columns and a beautifully carved altar and pulpit. The church's Neo-Classical facade is clad in alerce tiles in the traditional Chilote style. Also facing the plaza, the **Museo de Achao** has engaging exhibits on the Chono, the nomadic people who colonized Chiloé in the pre-Columbian era, and bright displays of Chilote weavings.

Museo de Achao

⊛ 🏠 Amunátegui 014
🕙 10am–6pm daily

37
Chonchi

🅰 F3 🏠 14 miles (23 km) S of Castro 🚌 🚆 ℹ️ Centenario, esq Sgto Candelaria

Referred to as the City of Three Floors for its abrupt topography, Chonchi is actually a hillside village overlooking a scenic bay on Isla Grande. The town, seen by Jesuit priests as a beachhead from where they could evangelize the archipelago's southern zones, evolved around the Jesuits' Circular Mission in the 17th century.

In the late 19th century, Chonchi reached its commercial peak as a major timber port and wooden buildings still line its gravel streets. Dating from 1883, the Iglesia de Chonchi is one of 16 UNESCO-protected churches on the archipelago. Also of interest, the **Museo de las Tradiciones Chonchinas** is housed in a large family mansion that was built for a rich logging baron in 1910. Inside,

the museum re-creates the rooms of a typical pioneer-era Chilote home.

Museo de las Tradiciones Chonchinas

⊛⊛🕙 🏠 Centenario 116
☏ (065) 2672802 🕙 9:30am–1:30pm & 2:30–6pm Mon–Fri, 9:30am–1:30pm Sat

---

38
Quellón

🅰 F3 🏠 62 miles (99 km) S of Castro 🚌 🚆 ℹ️ 22 de Mayo 251; (065) 2683500

A commercial fishing port, Quellón is a departure hub for ferries bound for destinations along the Carretera Austral. It is also the official end point of the great Pan-American highway. Visitors can use Quellón as a jumping-off point to visit the southern sector of Parque Tantauco, though this requires booking in advance.

In the town itself, the **Museo Inchin Cuivi Ant** is of interest, with exhibits on Chilote technology and history, and sculptural representations of Chiloé's mythological figures (p220).

Museo Inchin Cuivi Ant

🏠 Avenida Juan Ladrilleros 225 ☏ (065) 2681901
🕙 10am–6pm daily

FESTIVAL COSTUMBRISTA CHILOTE

A vibrant celebration of Chilote culture, this festival is Chiloé's biggest annual event, and is held in towns and villages across the archipelago during January and February. Festivities feature folk music and dance, food and drink, craft fairs, and demonstrations of traditional island activities. Ask at a tourist information office for details on what's happening when.

39
Parque Tantauco

🅰 E3 🏠 45 miles (73 km) SW of Castro 🚌 🚆 🚆 ➕ ℹ️ Pan-american Sur 1826, Castro; www.parquetantauco.cl

Created by business tycoon and former president of Chile Sebastián Piñera, this 456-sq-mile (1180-sq-km) private nature reserve sits in the southwest corner of Chiloé. It is among the world's 35 biodiversity hotspots and is home to a variety of flora and fauna, including Darwin foxes and pudú deer. The park has an excellent infrastructure with its well-kept trails, camping huts, and designated campsites. Only a limited number of visitors are allowed in the park at any one time.

Tantauco is divided into two halves; the northern section can be reached via several weekly buses from Quellón in summer, while the southern section is accessed via a small plane from Castro, or by boat from Quellón to Caleta Inio.

Visitors can choose from a two-day loop trek around the Caleta Inio Peninsula or from a three- to eight-day trek within the park. Several tour companies in Castro organize flights and treks into the park.

↑ Colorful fishing boats crowding the commercial port of Quellón

NORTHERN PATAGONIA

Thinly populated Northern Patagonia is home to some of the continent's wildest country, including Chile's most scenic highway, the Carretera Austral. The region embraces glaciers and icebergs, rugged Andean pinnacles, and large forest reserves.

The fjords, forests, and steppes of Northern Patagonia were originally inhabited by a handful of Tehuelche hunter-gatherers and Kawéskar fisherfolk. During the 16th and 17th centuries, few Europeans penetrated the area, apart from Jesuit missionaries based in Chiloé, and some British seafarers and scientists such as John Byron (1723–86) and Charles Darwin (1809–82). Following independence, Chile was slow to colonize Northern Patagonia, and it was not until 1903 that a huge land grant for sheep ranching and forestry provided the impetus for economic growth in the region. The grant was made by the Chilean government to private agricultural companies in and around the regional capital of Coyhaique. The resulting change in land use led initially to large-scale fires, deforestation, and erosion that closed up Puerto Aisén, the area's main port, at a time when nearly all transportation was seaborne. Road access began to be established in the 1970s with the construction of the Carretera Austral.

Northern Patagonia's many national parks conserve old native forests, wild rivers, rugged peaks, and waterfalls. Explored via ferry routes and road trips, these are ideal for activities, from white-water rafting to fly-fishing and trekking.

NORTHERN PATAGONIA

Must Sees

1 Parque Nacional Pumalín
2 Futaleufú
3 Parque Nacional Queulat
4 Parque Nacional Laguna San Rafael

Experience More

5 Chaitén
6 Palena
7 Melinka
8 Hornopirén
9 Puyuhuapi
10 Puyuhuapi Lodge & Spa
11 Puerto Cisnes
12 Puerto Chacabuco
13 Puerto Edén
14 Cochrane
15 Coyhaique
16 Parque Aiken del Sur
17 Reserva Nacional Río Simpson
18 Reserva Nacional Cerro Castillo
19 Reserva Nacional Lago Jeinemeni
20 Chile Chico
21 Caleta Tortel
22 Río Baker
23 Villa O'Higgins

NORTHERN PATAGONIA

Pacific Ocean

0 kilometers 100
0 miles 100

N
↑

LAKE DISTRICT AND CHILOÉ
p194

El Tepual Airport
Puerto Montt

Ancud

Isla Grande de Chiloé

Chonchi

Quellón

Inio

Parque Nacional Hornopirén

8 **HORNOPIRÉN**

Isla Llancahué

LOS LAGOS

1 **PARQUE NACIONAL PUMALÍN**

Caleta Gonzálo

Santa Barbara

CHAITÉN 5

Volcán Chaitén 3,681 ft (1,121 m)

Parque Nacional Corcovado

Lago Yelcho

Villa Santa Lucía

2 **FUTALEUFÚ**

Puerto Ramírez

6 **PALENA**

✈ Alto Palena Airport

La Junta

Melinka Airport **7** **MELINKA**

Lago Rosselot

Lago Verde

PUYUHUAPI 9

PUYUHUAPI LODGE & SPA 10 **3** **PARQUE NACIONAL QUEULAT**

La Tapera

Parque Nacional Isla Magdalena

11

Villa Amengual

PUERTO CISNES

Puerto Aisén

RESERVA NACIONAL RÍO SIMPSON

Archipiélago de los Chonos

PUERTO CHACABUCO 12 **16**

17 **15** **COYHAIQUE**

PARQUE AIKEN DEL SUR

Balmaceda Airport

✈ Balmaceda

Volcán Hudson 6,250 ft (1,905 m)

Reserva Nacional las Guaitecas

AISÉN

18 **RESERVA NACIONAL CERRO CASTILLO**

Villa Cerro Castillo

Puerto Ingeniero Ibáñez

Río Exploradores

Puerto Murta

Monte San Valentín 13,314 ft (4,058 m)

Puerto Tranquilo

Lago General Carrera

20 **CHILE CHICO**

✈ Chile Chico Airport

Lago Bertrand

Puerto Guadal

19 **RESERVA NACIONAL LAGO JEINEMENI**

PARQUE NACIONAL LAGUNA SAN RAFAEL 4

Golfo de Penas

Campo de Hielo Norte

Puerto Bertrand

COCHRANE 14 **✈ Cochrane Airport**

22 **RÍO BAKER**

Cerro San Lorenzo 12,158 ft (3,705 m)

CALETA TORTEL 21

Puerto Yungay

Reserva Nacional Katalalixar

Parque Nacional Bernardo O'Higgins

Campo de Hielo Sur

VILLA O'HIGGINS 23

Lago O'Higgins

PUERTO EDÉN 13

MAGALLANES

Isla Wellington

SOUTHERN PATAGONIA AND TIERRA DEL FUEGO
p248

El Maitén

Cushamen

Paso del Sapo

Esquel **✈ Esquel Airport**

Colan Conhué

Tecka

Gobernador Costa

Lago Palena

Los Tamariscos

Alto Río Senguer

Facundo

El Puma

El Puma

Bajo Caracoles

Las Horquetas

Lago Strobel

Río Chico

Gobernador Gregores

Lago Cardiel

A R G E N T I N A

Tres Lagos

①

PARQUE NACIONAL PUMALÍN

⚠ F3 ⓘ 82 miles (132 km) S of Puerto Montt; Caleta Gonzalo 🚌 From Hornopirén: Jan & Feb only ℹ Klenner 299, Puerto Varas; www.parquepumalin.cl

Spanning almost 1,550 sq miles (4,020 sq km) of temperate rain forests, deep fjords, and rugged mountains, Parque Nacional Pumalín is an exhilarating place to hike, with a network of trails, campsites, and cabins.

Founded in 1991 by the late US environmentalist Doug Tompkins, Pumalín was the world's largest privately owned reserve until it became a national park in 2018. A series of hiking trails start from the main road in the southern sector of the park and snake through its pristine landscapes. There are also trails in the less-visited northern and Amarillo sectors; most of them are relatively short but some are challenging. A number of hot springs make ideal places for relaxing after a tough day's trekking.

TOP 3 PUMALÍN HIKES

Sendero Cascadas
1 mile (1.5 km); easy.
A short and straight-forward walk that features a trio of beautiful waterfalls.

Sendero Laguna Tronador
3 miles (5 km); challenging.
A rewarding hike that provides views of the Michinmahuida volcano and finishes at the eponymous lake.

Sendero Ventisquero El Amarillo
12 miles (20 km); fairly challenging.
This largely flat hike takes you to the foot of the incredible Michinmahuida glacier.

Michinmahuida volcano viewed through the trees, Parque Nacional Pumalín ↓

1 Pumalín is home to a number of waterfalls. These can be enjoyed along walking trails.

2 There is a campsite by Lago Blanco, which offers spectacular views of the lake.

3 A guide talking to a group of walkers on the Alerce trail, just one of the park's many walking routes.

TOMPKINS CONSERVATION

Doug Tompkins (1943–2015), co-founder of North Face, and his wife Kris, former CEO of outdoor clothing company Patagonia, spent more than 25 years conserving huge sections of Chile and Argentina. Their work in Chile started in 1991 with the purchase of a large tract of land that became Parque Pumalín. They first faced resistance from locals but opening the park up to the public, and their commitment to conservation, helped shift opinions. Doug tragically died in 2015, but Kris continues their work. In 2018, their NGO, Tompkins Conservation, made the largest donation of land by a private owner to a state in South American history.

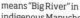

② FUTALEUFÚ

⚑ F3 **⚑ 96 miles (154 km) SE of Chaitén** 🚌
ℹ️ O'Higgins 536; www.futaleufu.cl

Nestled in a secluded and picturesque valley, close to the Argentine border, is the town of Futaleufú. Though charming, it's mainly known for its eponymous river, which is one of the best in the world for white-water rafting and kayaking.

The pretty town of Futaleufú, home to pastel-colored houses, is part of the 19-sq-mile (49-sq-km) Reserva Nacional Futaleufú. This region is thick with verdant forests and numerous species of animals, including the endangered huemul deer. There are plenty of opportunities for hiking, horseback riding, mountain biking, and fishing around the town.

The town is a popular base for adventure-sport lovers, thanks to the Río Futaleufú and its impressive Class IV and V rapids. The calmer sections of the river are suitable for novice rafters and kayakers, who can also try the less demanding Río Azul and Río Espolón nearby. Meanwhile, sea kayaking and canyoning are possible on and around Lago Yelcho.

BIG RIVER

The name Futaleufú means "Big River" in indigenous Mapuche, and locals refer to the valley as "un paisaje pintado por Dios" – a landscape painted by God. Its natural beauty aside, the Río Futaleufú has developed an international reputation for white-water rafting and kayaking. Several well-regarded operators in the town offer half-, full- and multi-day trips, including Bochinche Expediciones *(www.bochinchex. com)*, Expediciones Chile *(www.exchile. com)*, and Condorfu *(www.condorfu.cl)*. They are experienced at taking beginners out on the river, though you need to have a good level of fitness and be a confident swimmer.

←
Kayaking on the choppy waters of Río Futaleufú

↓ A huemul deer, also known as a South Andean deer

💬 INSIDER TIP
Cross into Argentina

If you want to cross the border into Argentina, there are several weekly buses from Futaleufú to the city of Esquel and the town of Trevelín.

↑ Photographing
Patagonia's majestic
Río Futaleufú

Did You Know?

In the 19th century, the Ventisquero Colgante stretched to the sea; today it's 5 miles (8 km) away.

③ 🏞️ 🗓️

PARQUE NACIONAL QUEULAT

🅰️ F4 📍 269 miles (434 km) SE of Puerto Montt 🚍 ℹ️ CONAF, Sector Ventisquero Colgante, Carretera Austral 🌐 conaf.cl

This far-flung national park is magnificent, thanks to its sinuous fjords, forested cliff-sides, dramatic waterfalls, and epic glaciers – most spectacularly the hanging Ventisquero Colgante glacier. Head to Queulat to experience the great outdoors via various hiking trails.

Covering some of Northern Patagonia's most rugged terrain, Parque Nacional Queulat's dense rain forests, limpid lakes, clear trout streams, and steep mountains span more than 5,800 sq miles (15,000 sq km). Altitudes in the park vary significantly – from sea level up to 7,300 ft (2,255 m), where precipitation falls as snow.

←

Walking across the Sendero Río Guillermo suspension bridge

TOP 4 QUEULAT TRAILS

Sendero Ventisquero Colgante
2 miles (3 km); easy.
One of the most popular short hikes in the park, offering awesome views of the glacier and the icy lake below.

Sendero Laguna Los Pumas
6 miles (10 km); fairly easy.
This Angostura sector trail climbs through forests to the Los Pumas lagoon.

Sendero Aluvión
0.5 miles (1 km); easy.
A pleasant stroll through a forested area of the Ventisquero Colgante sector that is rich in birdlife.

Salto Padre García Trail
0.2 miles (0.3 km); easy.
This short walk descends 500 ft (150 m) to a lovely waterfall.

↑ The lush landscape of the park, and *(inset)* the park's hanging glacier

Although Parque Nacional Queulat fronts the Carretera Austral (Southern Highway), its trackless back country is generally left unexplored.

Exploring the Park

The central Ventisquero Colgante sector is the most popular part of the park, with good hiking routes. From the visitor center, a couple of trails offer breathtaking views of the Ventisquero Colgante hanging glacier. From this mass of solid ice, waterfalls plunge into the jade-colored Laguna Témpanos (Iceberg Lake; in spite of the name, there are no icebergs). The lake can be reached via the Sendero Río Guillermo, a 1,969-ft- (600-m-) long route that crosses a suspension bridge over the river from which it takes its name. In the northern Angostura sector of the park, Lago Risopatrón is a popular point for fly-fishing. The southern sector is known as Portezuelo Queulat and, though less visited, it is well worth exploring.

↑ A Magellanic woodpecker residing in Parque Nacional Queulat

237

4

PARQUE NACIONAL LAGUNA SAN RAFAEL

F4 **118 miles (190 km) SW of Coyhaique** **conaf.cl**

This is one of Chile's largest protected areas, sprawling across 6,730 sq miles (17,420 sq km), and a UNESCO World Biosphere Reserve. Almost half of the park is covered by the spectacular Campo de Hielo Norte, the second-largest ice sheet in the southern hemisphere, outside of Antarctica.

The Campo de Hielo Norte (Northern Patagonian Ice Field) embraces the towering Monte San Valentín, which at 13,314 ft (4,058 m) is the highest summit in Patagonia. This ice field feeds more than 18 glaciers, including the 200-ft- (60-m-) high Ventisquero San Rafael. From the face of this receding glacier, massive chunks of blue ice spill into the Laguna San Rafael below. Tour operators arrange sailing excursions to the glacier through a maze of fjords and channels. While the larger tour boats usually keep a safe distance from the glacier, passengers can often jump in an inflatable dinghy for a closer look. You can also take the plane ride over the park for breathtaking panoramas of the ice field.

A boat sitting in front of the Northern Patagonian Ice Field, and *(inset)* a resident leopard seal ↓

↑ Watching the tumbling Las Cascadas in Parque Nacional Laguna San Rafael

KAYAKING AND TREKKING

While boat trips might be the classic way to explore the Parque Nacional Laguna San Rafael region, there are also other more adventurous activities on offer. AguaHielo Expediciones *(www.aguahielo.cl)* runs challenging but exhilarating multi-day sea kayaking trips that take in the San Rafael glacier. Out of the water, Patagonia Adventure Expeditions *(www.patagonia adventureexpeditions.com)* runs adventurous ice-trekking tours on and around the Campo de Hielo Norte, which last from five to ten days; while not often technically demanding, the tours do require excellent fitness levels.

Did You Know?

John Byron, grandfather of poet Lord Byron, was shipwrecked here in 1742.

EXPERIENCE MORE

⑤ Chaitén

🅰F3 🏠100 miles (160 km) S of Puerto Montt ✈ 🚌 ⛴

Located along Chile's Ruta 7, better known as the Carretera Austral (p245), the Patagonian town of Chaitén was popular for its scenic blend of seaside and sierra until the Volcán Chaitén, barely 6 miles (10 km) away, erupted on May 2, 2008. This catastrophe was followed by massive flooding, which swept many houses off their foundations and buried several other houses in soggy ash.

A government attempt to relocate the dishomed residents proved unpopular, however, and many of them returned to the town. In spite of the volcano's presence, the area continues to attract many visitors with its hiking options and the nearby El Amarillo hot springs.

Ferries from Puerto Montt and the Chiloé archipelago arrive at Chaitén's port.

⑥ Palena

🅰F3 🏠160 miles (257 km) SE of Puerto Montt 🚌
ℹ️ O'Higgins 740; www. municipalidadpalena.cl

The village of Palena, close to the Argentine border, is named for the river that flows past it. It is notable for the Rodeo de Palena, which showcases Chile's huaso heritage. The main event at this rodeo involves costumed huasos on horseback, trying to pin a calf to a padded ring.

The Sendero de Chile, a network of trails across Chile, passes through Palena en route to the little-known Reserva Nacional Lago Palena, from where the road continues to the Argentine border.

Did You Know?

Chilean pirate Pedro Ñancúpel was finally captured in Melinka in 1886.

⑦ Melinka

🅰F3 🏠171 miles (276 km) SW of Puerto Montt ✈ ⛴

Off the mainland west of Palena, the Guaitecas archipelago comprises several tiny islands. Of these, Isla Ascensión is home to the fishing village of Melinka, the archipelago's main settlement. The village overlooks Golfo de Corcovado, known for its sizable blue whale population; these are often visible from shore. Melinka has some simple but comfortable lodgings and a few small eateries.

⑧ Hornopirén

🅰F3 🏠73 miles (117 km) S of Puerto Montt 🚌 ⛴

Scenically set on the edge of a serene fjord, Hornopirén is named for the towering,

A boat moored in the shallows of the glassy fjord bordering Hornopirén

↑ Colorful wool hanging from beams in the Alfombras de Puyuhuapi factory

EAT

Martín Pescador
Housed in a rustic wooden building, this popular spot focuses on well-prepared local ingredients. Salmon features prominently, but you can also expect dishes such as king crab quiche and house-made gnocchi.

🅰F3 🄰Balmaceda 603, Futaleufú
📞(065) 2721279

$$$

5,150-ft- (1,570-m-) high Volcán Hornopirén that looms over the town. Hornopirén has been prosperous since the 19th century, despite being hard hit by the Volcán Chaitén eruption in 2008. Today, it is the gateway to Parque Nacional Hornopirén, 7 miles (12 km) to the northwest, which offers good wildlife-watching and hiking. Local launches docked at the ferry port take visitors to hot-spring pools nearby, and harborside vendors sell fresh fish.

9
Puyuhuapi

🅰F3 🄰269 miles (434 km) SE of Puerto Montt 🚌 🛈 Otto Übel s/n; (067) 2325244

Sitting on the edge of a scenic fjord, Puyuhuapi, unlike the newer settlements along the Carretera Austral, was founded by German immigrants from the Sudetenland (later, part of Czechoslovakia) in the 1930s. As a result, many houses in this area are distinctly Teutonic in style and the traditions of early settlers are still kept alive by the residents. Along with the building of wooden boats, artisanal fishery constitutes the main economic activity of

the village. It's known for the **Alfombras de Puyuhuapi**, a family-owned factory that produces custom-made carpets for export. Set up in 1945 by German textile engineer Walter Hopperdietzel, the factory (open for tours on request) employs women from the archipelago of Chiloé to weave a range of exquisite hand-knotted woolen carpets. Unique vertical looms are used to create these beautiful rugs.

Puyuhuapi also serves as an ideal base for those who want to explore nearby destinations such as the Parque Nacional Queulat (p236) and the adjacent Reserva Nacional Lago Rosselot. Also in the vicinity are the hot springs of the luxurious Puyuhuapi Lodge & Spa (p242). The place

also offers activities such as trekking, horseback riding, and boat rides.

Located 4 miles (6 km) south of Puyuhuapi, the **Termas Ventisquero de Puyuhuapi** has four thermal pools overlooking the sound, basic changing rooms, and a café.

Alfombras de Puyuhuapi
♿💲 🄰Aisén s/n 🕐10am-1:30pm & 3-6:30pm Mon-Sat
🌐puyuhuapi.com

Termas Ventisquero de Puyuhuapi
♿💲 🄰Carretera Austral Sur Km 6 🕐9am-11pm daily
🌐termasventisquero puyuhuapi.cl

SAILING THE FJORDS OF NORTHERN PATAGONIA

The three-day voyage from Puerto Montt (p209) south to Puerto Natales (p258) aboard the M/V Edén is one of Northern Patagonia's top attractions. The journey passes through innumerable fjords, channels, and thousands of uninhabited islands; from the deck, passengers can admire an electrifying landscape - dense rain forests, serene lakes, massive glaciers, and snowcapped mountains. It is also possible to spot some wildlife, including the odd colony of sea lions and pods of dolphins. Entertainment on board includes talks on natural history and screenings of Chilean documentaries. The ferry passes the fishing village of Melinka and the fjord town of Puerto Eden, home to a few remaining indigenous Yamana people.

←

Tranquil setting of Puyuhuapi Lodge & Spa, perched by the water's edge

10 (icons)

Puyuhuapi Lodge & Spa

🅰F4 🚗277 miles (447 km) SE of Puerto Montt; Bahía Dorita s/n 🚢 🌐puyuhuapilodge.com

In a country that is well known for its hot-springs resorts, Puyuhuapi Lodge & Spa is one of the top choices. Located in a secluded and exceptional spot on the western side of the gorgeous Seno Ventisquero inlet—a place where the water from the sea, waterfalls, and thermal springs converges—the lodge blends smoothly into the fern- and flower-filled rain forest.

Puyuhuapi Lodge & Spa welcomes overnight guests

HIDDEN GEM
Puerto Raul Marin Balmaceda

North of Puyuhuapi Lodge & Spa is this gorgeous river island. Accessed by car ferry, the little-visited fishing village is one of the region's prettiest and well worth the detour.

---

and day guests during the off season. The complex is made up of charming units, the facades of which recall the shingled houses often seen on the islands of Chiloé. Rooms at the lodge feature polished wooden interiors and face the Bahía Dorita. Day visitors have access to three outdoor thermal pools and a café, while hotel guests can also use the heated indoor pool and enjoy a wide range of therapies and treatments.

An interesting variety of package options are available for overnight guests. These include a number of outdoor activities such as hiking through the Parque Nacional Queulat (p236), fly-fishing on the nearby rivers, and a visit to the village of Puyuhuapi (p241) and its famous carpet factory. Most stays conclude with a day trip south to Parque Nacional Laguna San Rafael (p238), sailing on the high-speed catamaran Patagonia Express, which passes through serene fjords and canals. The boat then returns north to Puerto Chacabuco, from where the lodge's guests are transferred to Coyhaique (p244) and its airport at Balmaceda.

11

Puerto Cisnes

🅰F4 🚗320 miles (520 km) SE of Puerto Montt 🚌 ℹSotomayor s/n; (09) 7663-7208

Sitting at the mouth of the eponymous river, Puerto Cisnes was founded in 1929 as a humble lumber factory. Today it is a pretty fishing village, with colorful boats lining its waterfront. The wooden Neo-Classical Biblioteca Pública Genaro Godoy, the village library, is a notable landmark. Its facade is adorned with figurines from Greek mythology. Puerto Cisnes is also the access point to the Parque Nacional Isla Magdalena, and local fishermen shuttle visitors to this lushly forested park.

On the Carretera Austral, immediately east of the turnoff to Puerto Cisnes, is the Viaducto Piedra El Gato, a remarkable engineering achievement. Here the highway runs parallel to the river along the face of a nearly vertical granite pitch. There are several viewpoints on each approach to the viaduct that allow motorists to admire the structure and the landscape.

⑫ Puerto Chacabuco

🅰F4 📍37 miles (60 km) W of Coyhaique 🚌🚢

Located on the shores of an attractive natural harbor, Puerto Chacabuco is a small but lively port town, and the center of a thriving fishing industry. It superseded nearby Puerto Aisén as the Aisén region's main port in the 1940s; by this time, deforestation of Patagonia's forests had filled Río Aisén's outlet with sediments that made it impossible to anchor at Puerto Aisén.

Today, Puerto Chacabuco serves as the gateway to appealing nearby sights such as Parque Aiken del Sur (p244) and Parque Nacional Laguna San Rafael (p238).

⑬ Puerto Edén

🅰F5 📍272 miles (438 km) SW of Coyhaique 🚢

On Isla Wellington, in one of the rainiest sectors of the Pacific fjords, the town of Puerto Edén owes its origin to an air force initiative that contemplated a stop for seaplanes between Puerto Montt (p209) and Punta Arenas

↑ Guanacos roaming in the Reserva Nacional Lago Tamango

(p256). However, the site soon became the last outpost of Kawéskar hunter-gatherers, who settled here after the air force abandoned it. Today, Puerto Edén is home to the few surviving members of the Kawéskar community, who have re-created some of their traditional shelters. It is possible to purchase a sample of their crafts here. Weather and schedule permitting, the town is a stop for Skorpios cruise ships and Navimag ferries that sail out of Puerto Natales (p258); on ferry and cruise ship days, a lively market is held in the town.

⑭ Cochrane

🅰F4 📍119 miles (192 km) S of Coyhaique 🚐🚌 ℹ️ **Dr Steffen and Esmeralda; www.cochranepatagonia.cl**

Situated at the western edge of the eponymous lake, the tidy town of Cochrane is the last service center on the Carretera Austral (also known as the Southern Highway). Visitors, notably motorists, will find the highway's last gasoline station here. Cochrane is also the gateway to the **Reserva Nacional Lago Tamango**, which is situated 4 miles (6 km) northeast of town and is a major sanctuary for the endangered huemul deer. Many other native species are also found in the beautiful reserve, which sprawls across nearly 7 acres (3 ha). From the entrance, hiking trails run to Laguna Tamnaguito, Laguna Elefantina, and up Cerro Tamango. It is also possible to hike directly from this reserve to Valle Chacabuco in Parque Nacional Patagonia.

Reserva Nacional Lago Tamango

📍4 miles (6 km) E of Cochrane; CONAF, Río Nef 417 🌐 conaf.cl

STAY

Casa Ludwig
The attic rooms at the German-Chilean B&B are a good bet for budget travelers.

🅰F3 📍Avenida Übel 202, Puerto Puyuhuapi 🌐casaludwig.cl

💲💲💲

El Pangue
Stay either in a hotel or freestanding cabañas here, both with an informal vibe.

🅰F3 📍Carretera Austral, Km 240, Puerto Puyuhuapi 🌐elpangue.cl

💲💲💲

Nómades Hotel Boutique
This bijou option overlooks the river and has gorgeous, Patagonia-inspired interiors.

🅰F4 📍Avenida Baquedano 84, Coyhaique 🌐nomadeshotel.com

💲💲💲

Hostal Salamandras
A family-run hostel with good-value dorms and private rooms.

🅰F4 📍Teniente Vidal, Km 1.5, Coyhaique 🌐salamandras.cl

💲💲💲

Robinson Crusoe Deep Patagonia
An ideal base for those exploring the Southern Patagonia Ice Field.

🅰F5 📍Carretera Austral, Km 1240, Villa O'Higgins 🌐robinsoncrusoe.com

💲💲💲

15

Coyhaique

F4 ⌂ 286 miles (461 km) SE of Puerto Montt 🚌 ℹ Bulnes 35; www.coyhaique.cl

Capital of Chile's Aisén region, and Northern Patagonia's only sizable city, Coyhaique is a labyrinth of concentric roads that encircle the pentagonal Plaza de Armas and change names on every other block. Despite this bewildering orientation, Coyhaique offers the region's best tourist infrastructure and easy access to destinations such as Lago Elizalde and the Reserva Nacional Río Simpson.

Though Coyhaique has no major attractions, it is the only major town on the Carretera Austral that has a vibrant dining scene. Those who wish to explore the Carretera Austral can find rental cars in town. Visitors who are headed north or south should take the opportunity to withdraw money from ATMs while in the city.

Just beyond the city limits, the **Reserva Nacional Coyhaique** is a 10-sq-mile

Simpson River Valley, within the Reserva Nacional Río Simpson ↓

(27-sq-km) park with hiking trails through forests of coigüe and lenga. It has a campground and offers great panoramas of the city and its environs.

Reserva Nacional Coyhaique

⊛ Ruta 7 Norte 🕗 8:30am–5:30pm Mon–Sat 🌐 conaf.cl

---

16 🚲 🥾 🍴

Parque Aiken del Sur

F4 ⌂ 54 miles (87 km) SW of Coyhaique 🚌 Reservations required ℹ J.M. Carrera 50, Puerto Chacabuco; www.loberiasdelsur.cl

The privately owned nature reserve and botanical garden of Parque Aiken del Sur covers a densely forested area of 1 sq mile (3 sq km). It has four good hiking trails featuring information panels and viewpoints that offer some spectacular views, as well as an arboretum with a number of helpfully labeled plant species. Completing the trails takes around two hours at a reasonably leisurely pace. Parque Aiken is under the same ownership as Puerto Chacabuco's Hotel Loberías del Sur, which

organizes guided trips to the park. Tours end with a *parrillada* lunch – a typical Patagonian barbecue – and enjoyable folkloric entertainment that includes performances of Chile's national dance, the *cueca*.

EAT

Mamma Gaucha

This pizzeria dishes up thin-crust offerings with creative toppings. It also has a selection of craft beers, and artwork that pays tribute to the region's gaucho heritage.

F4 Paseo Horn 47, Coyhaique 📞 (067) 2210721 🗓 Sun

$$$

La Casona

Housed in a spacious converted residence, this is a reliable, no fuss restaurant that serves tasty Chilean food, with standout seafood dishes.

F4 Obispo Vielmo 77, Coyhaique 📞 (067) 2238894

$$$

Trekking across the Reserva Nacional Cerro Castillo's craggy landscape

17

Reserva Nacional Río Simpson

F4 **15 miles (25 km) W of Coyhaique** **8:30am–5:30pm Mon–Sat** **CONAF, Ruta 240, Km 37; www.conaf.cl**

Straddling both the Carretera Austral and the Río Simpson are the wooded mountains of the Reserva Nacional Río Simpson. This reserve protects over 256 sq miles (426 sq km), characterized by deep canyons, gushing waterfalls and forests of tepa, coigüe, and lenga. The park is also an important sanctuary for the pudú and the endangered huemul deer.

CONAF's visitor center has a small natural history museum that offers interesting information on native flora and fauna. A short trail leads from the center to the attractive Cascada La Vírgen waterfall, which is encircled by wild ferns and shrubs.

18

Reserva Nacional Cerro Castillo

F4 **28 miles (45 km) S of Coyhaique**

Covering over 517 sq miles (1,340 sq km) of rugged Andean landscape, Reserva Nacional Cerro Castillo is named for the impressive 8,465-ft- (2,581-m-) high Cerro Castillo, which crowns this reserve. A popular destination for hikers, the reserve offers several nature trails that snake through forests of lenga and around cascading waterfalls and icy glaciers. Wildlife spotted on these hikes includes the huemul, puma, and fox.

The reserve's big attraction is a four-day trek through dense vegetation that ends at the tiny hamlet of Villa Cerro Castillo. Just south from this village is **Alero de las Manos**, a natural rock shelter that is home to spectacular pre-Columbian paintings that date from 3,000 years ago.

Situated along the northern border of Reserva Nacional Cerro Castillo, Lago Elizalde is a narrow lake that stretches for 15 miles (25 km), but is less than a mile (2 km) wide at any point. It is a popular spot for fishing, sailing, and kayaking.

Southeast of the reserve, the port town of Puerto Ingeniero Ibáñez sits at the edge of Chile's largest lake, Lago General Carrera. Noted for its orchards, the town is frequented by travelers wishing to take the ferry across the lake to Chile Chico (p246).

Alero de las Manos
3 miles (5 km) S of Villa Cerro Castillo **10am–6pm daily**

DRIVING THE CARRETERA AUSTRAL

Chile's Route 7 was constructed under the dictatorship to connect remote communities. It passed through Patagonia, running from Puerto Montt (p209) to Villa O'Higgins (p247). A regular car is fine for most of the Carretera Austral, though a 4WD is useful for side trips around Patagonia. Most towns along the road have petrol stations, but it's worth filling up regularly, just in case. Bring a spare tire and all the gear you need to attach it, as well as water, food, a sleeping bag, and a first aid kit, plus a supply of cash, as ATMs are rare in this region.

↑ The striking configuration of handprints within the Cueva de las Manos

19

Reserva Nacional Lago Jeinemeni

🅰F4 🅰89 miles (143 km) SE of Coyhaique; Blest Gana 121, Chile Chico
🆆conaf.cl

Hugging the Argentine border, and accessible only by high-clearance vehicles, the Reserva Nacional Lago Jeinemeni is an enormous 622-sq-mile (1,600-sq-km) sanctuary named for its lake, which is popular with fly-fishers. The reserve is located 32 miles (52 km) southwest of Chile Chico and is linked to Valle Chacabuco by a three- day hiking traverse. Encompassing four ecosystems, including steppe, evergreen forest and deciduous forests, it's home to such wildlife as flamingoes.

🔍 HIDDEN GEM
Handy Art

Located in the Reserva Nacional Lago Jeinemeni is Cueva de las Manos, or "Cave of the Hands". The rock face inside the cave is covered with red handprints, believed to have been made by the region's Tehuelche people thousands of years ago.

20

Chile Chico

🅰F4 🅰68 miles (110 km) SE of Coyhaique 🔳🚌🚤
🛈O'Higgins 192; www.chilechico.cl

Close to the Argentine border, Chile Chico is part of a fruit-growing belt near Lago General Carrera. The town can either be approached by a scenic and precipitous road from the Carreta Austral, or via an equally exciting ferry ride across the vast, electric-blue lake.

Chile Chico dates from 1909, when Argentines crossed over to settle in this area. It became briefly famous in 1917, when the colonizers faced the ranchers in the War of Chile Chico. In 1991, the eruption of Volcán Hudson nearly smothered the area's apple and pear orchards. This past and a comprehensive overview of the area's natural history are well documented in the **Museo de la Casa de Cultura**, part of which occupies the grounded *Los Andes* steamer, which once toured the lake.

Museo de la Casa de Cultura

🏠Calle O'Higgins and Lautaro 📞(067) 2411355
🕗8am-7pm Mon-Sat

21

Caleta Tortel

🅰F5 🅰172 km (277 miles) SW of Coyhaique 🚌

Located on an inlet off the Río Baker's Fiordo Mitchell, Caleta Tortel is arguably Patagonia's most picturesque village. The settlement was unreachable by road until 2003. It still has no streets as such, but rather boardwalks and staircases that link its bayside *palafitos* (overwater bungalows). These home-steads show the influence of the folk architecture of the Chiloé archipelago. Most of the buildings are made of guaiteca cypress, the world's southernmost conifer species.

In recent years, the tourism industry has grown, with more basic guesthouses and motorized boat trips to Glaciar Steffens and Glaciar Montt, which is part of Parque Nacional Bernardo O'Higgins (p259). Hiking and horseback riding can also be arranged.

The village is also an ideal base for visiting the nearby Reserva Nacional Katalalixar, which can also be reached by basic motor launches.

㉒
Río Baker

F5 **146 miles (235 km) S of Coyhaique** 🚌

Flowing between Caleta Tortel and Lago Bertrand, the 116-mile- (170-km-) long Río Baker is Chile's largest river in terms of volume. Owing to its flow, and the mountainous terrain through which it runs, this wild and scenic river has long been a candidate for a massive hydro-electric project; however, the river has not been dammed due to environmental concerns. The area just south of Puerto Bertrand, especially at the stunning confluence of the Baker and the Río Nef, is a paradise for campers, hikers, rafters, fly-fishers, and other recreationists. Rafting trips can be arranged in tiny Puerto Bertrand, north of Cochrane (p243).

㉓
Villa O'Higgins

F5 **204 miles (328 km) S of Coyhaique** ✈🚌🚢
Carretera Austral 267; www.villaohiggins.com

Beyond Cochrane, services are nearly non-existent on the last 120 miles (200 km) of the Carretera Austral. A free ferry shuttle from Puerto Yungay – near the Río Bravo – takes visitors to the last stretch of the highway, which terminates at Villa O'Higgins.

This village dates from 1966 and is named for the Chilean hero Bernardo O'Higgins (p259). The village has grown thanks to the arrival of the Carretera Austral (p245) in 1999 and the tourism this has brought with it. Surrounded by wild mountain scenery, and within sight of the Campo del Hielo Sur (Southern Ice Field), Villa O'Higgins offers ample hiking trails, including part of the Sendero de Chile, an ongoing project that connects major trails across the country. It is a popular destination for cyclists and trekkers who wish to cross over to Argentina's El Chaltén. Enthusiasts can take the La Quetru catamaran from Villa O'Higgins across Lago O'Higgins to the border post of Candelario Mansilla, hike for 13 miles (21 km), and then take the ferry across Argentina's Lago del Desierto.

Did you Know?

The area around Villa O'Higgins was the site of a short-lived English settlement from 1914 to 1916.

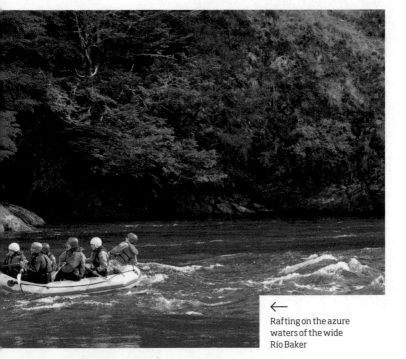

← Rafting on the azure waters of the wide Río Baker

SOUTHERN PATAGONIA AND TIERRA DEL FUEGO

An archipelagic labyrinth, Southern Patagonia is a dramatic wilderness of emerald fjords, rugged peaks, and windswept prairies. Separated from the mainland by the Strait of Magellan, Tierra del Fuego stretches across largely unpopulated territory to Cape Horn, the tip of South America. The original inhabitants of Southern Patagonia and Tierra del Fuego were the Ona, Yamana, Tehuelche, and Alacaluf (Kawéskar) communities, who are now greatly reduced in number.

In 1520, Portuguese navigator Ferdinand Magellan became the first European to discover the area. However, permanent settlements were not established until the 19th century, when missionaries, adventurers, and merchants arrived from Spain, Britain, Croatia, and northern Chile.

The late 19th century witnessed a rise in prosperity as a result of sheep ranching. A thriving shipping industry also developed, benefiting from the navigable Strait of Magellan, which served as a passage between the Pacific and Atlantic until the opening of the Panama Canal in 1914. Today, sheep farming, along with oil extraction and tourism, are the mainstays of the economy.

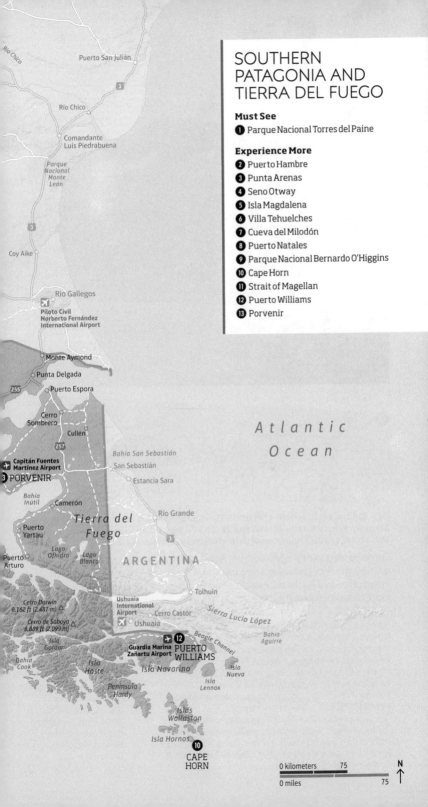

SOUTHERN PATAGONIA AND TIERRA DEL FUEGO

Must See

1 Parque Nacional Torres del Paine

Experience More

2 Puerto Hambre
3 Punta Arenas
4 Seno Otway
5 Isla Magdalena
6 Villa Tehuelches
7 Cueva del Milodón
8 Puerto Natales
9 Parque Nacional Bernardo O'Higgins
10 Cape Horn
11 Strait of Magellan
12 Puerto Williams
13 Porvenir

Atlantic Ocean

Río Chico
Puerto San Julián
Río Chico
Comandante Luis Piedrabuena
Parque Nacional Monte León
Coy Aike
Río Gallegos
Piloto Civil Norberto Fernández International Airport
Monte Aymond
Punta Delgada
Puerto Espora
Cerro Sombrero
Cullén
Capitán Fuentes Martínez Airport
13 PORVENIR
Bahía Inútil
Camerón
Puerto Yartau
Puerto Arturo
Lago Ofhidro
Lago Blanco
Bahía San Sebastián
San Sebastián
Estancia Sara
Río Grande
Tierra del Fuego
ARGENTINA
Tolhuin
Cerro Darwin 8,162 ft (2,487 m)
Cerro de Saboya 6,889 ft (2,099 m)
Ushuaia International Airport
Cerro Castor
Ushuaia
Sierra Lucio López
Isla Gordon
Guardia Marina Zañartu Airport
12 PUERTO WILLIAMS
Isla Navarino
Bahía Cook
Isla Hoste
Isla Nueva
Isla Lennox
Península Hardy
Bahía Aguirre
Beagle Channel
Islas Wollaston
Isla Hornos
10 CAPE HORN

0 kilometers 75
0 miles 75

N

1

PARQUE NACIONAL TORRES DEL PAINE

△F6 △43 miles (70 km) NW of Puerto Natales ✈From Punta Arenas 🚌from Punta Arenas or Puerto Natales 🚢Navimag ℹCONAF Administration Headquarters: Lago del Toro sector, southern entrance of park; www.parquetorresdelpaine.cl

Encompassing sweeping mountains, almost vertical soaring granite pillars, dazzling glaciers, glistening azure lakes, and sprawling emerald forests, Parque Nacional Torres del Paine is undoubtably one of South America's most beautiful national parks.

Torres del Paine (Towers of Blue) is a UNESCO World Biosphere Reserve. It is named for the Paine massif, a cluster of meta-morphic ridges and needles between the Southern Patagonian Ice Field and the Patagonian steppe. The name itself is a mix of Spanish and indigenous Patagonian words: *paine* being the Tehuelche term for blue, a color frequently seen throughout the area in the form of turquoise glaciers, icebergs, rivers, and lakes. The park is Chile's trekking mecca, with numerous day hikes as well as three- to ten-day backpacking routes. The national park is dominated by the Paine massif, which includes the Cuernos formation of mountains, the Torres del Paine peaks, and the park's highest summit – the 10,006-ft- (3,050-m-) high Cerro Paine Grande.

> **INSIDER TIP**
> **When to Visit**
>
> The park is busiest during the Jan–Feb summer months, while temperatures can plummet well below zero during the winter (Jun–Sep), so the best times to visit are Oct–Dec and Mar–Apr.

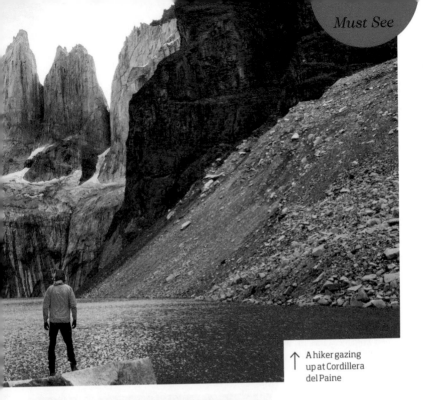

↑ A hiker gazing up at Cordillera del Paine

↑ Guanacos can be spotted on Torres del Paine's grassy tundra

Apart from rugged peaks, there are many other microclimates and geological features throughout the park. These include glaciers, granite spires, beech forests, lakes, and steppe, and can be explored by foot, by vehicle, aboard a catamaran, or on horseback. The park offers a series of camp-grounds and *refugios*, in addition to several hotels (*p225*).

The southern road from Puerto Natales is the most beautiful route into the park, and leads to the CONAF Administration Headquarters. This center gives a compulsory talk on park safety and provides general information about the park. It also has educational displays on the flora, fauna, and geological features of the sanctuary. A small kiosk sells maps, books, and sundry items.

WILDLIFE WATCH

Although best known for its spectacular scenery and dazzling landscapes, Parque Nacional Torres del Paine is also incredibly biodiverse, as shown by the classification as a UNESCO World Biosphere Reserve. There are 25 species of mammals, most notably grey and red foxes, guanacos, hard-to-spot huemuls (an endangered deer) and pumas. The park is even richer in birdlife: there are around 120 species, including Andean condors, Chilean flamingos, Magellanic woodpeckers, black-chested buzzard-eagles and Darwin's rheas (large flightless birds that are similar to ostriches and emus).

EXPLORING PARQUE NACIONAL TORRES DEL PAINE

Access to the park is by road from Punta Arenas or Puerto Natales, or by boat along the Río Serrano. There are three entrances, all manned by CONAF ranger stations. Within its boundaries, 155 miles (250 km) of the sanctuary is covered by marked trails. The longest is the Circuito Grande, a hike that requires six to eight days and takes visitors to the Paine massif, passing by the lakes of Paine, Dickson, and Grey. There are also trails to Lago Paine, the Torres peaks, and the Valle del Francés, which are combined into one hike, named The W after its shape.

The W

A medium-difficult trail, The W is the most popular multiday trek. Most trekkers begin at the Las Torres, a ranch-style complex with campgrounds, hostels, and a hotel, the Hotel Las Torres. The seven- to eight-hour roundtrip hike to the iconic Torres del Paine is strenuous, first traversing the beech forests of the Valle Ascencio and ending with a steep, 45-minute hike up a boulder field to the Torres, three stunning granite towers that rise in front of a glacial tarn. The W continues from Hotel Las Torres along the shores of the turquoise Lago Nordenskjold and skirting the flank of the park's famous two-toned Cuernos. About 7 miles (11 km) along this route are the hostel and campgrounds of Refugio Los Cuernos. Trekkers may spend the night here or, if camping, continue onward 4 miles (6 km) to the Valle del Francés and its Campamento Italiano. The trail up and into the Valle del Francés is about 5 miles (8 km), climbing high into the valley ringed with granite peaks and sweeping views of the Patagonian steppe. From the base of the Valle del Francés, it is some 5 miles (8 km) to the Refugio Paine Grande and campground and to the docking area for a catamaran that crosses Lago Pehoé to the Pudeto sector. The trail then heads north for the final leg of The W, 7 miles (11 km) to Refugio Grey. Visitors can arrange trekking excursions to Glaciar Grey. Most trekkers return to Lago Pehoé and take the catamaran to Pudeto, from where transportation is available to Puerto Natales.

Circuito Grande

For a thorough exploration of the park, hikers should consider the Circuito

TOP 3 SHORTER HIKES

Mirador las Torres
11 miles (17 km): This popular trail ends with superb views of the park's famous granite *Torres* (towers).

Mirador Zapata
9 miles (15 km): A rewarding hike starting at the southern shore of Lago Grey and passing glaciers and waterfalls. Good wildlife-watching opportunities.

Mirador Ferrier
1.2 miles (2 km): A steep trail leads up to Mirador Ferrier, where there are views of glaciers, lakes, and mountains.

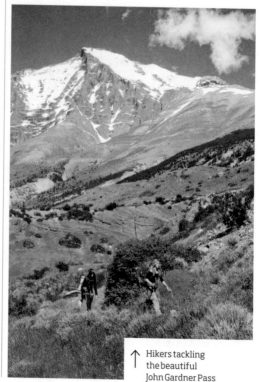

↑ Hikers tackling the beautiful John Gardner Pass

↑ The dazzling ice-blue shards of Glacier Grey

Grande (Big Circuit Trail), which circles the Paine massif and takes roughly six to eight days. The trail is often undertaken counter-clockwise, starting at Hotel Las Torres or the Laguna Amarga ranger station. The Hotel Las Torres trail begins with a four-hour hike through the Valle Ascencio to Campamento Seron. It continues for 12 miles (19 km) to Refugio Dickson, which offers views of Glaciar Dickson. The trail grows increasingly strenuous. About 6 miles (9 km) through forest and swampy terrain from Refugio Dickson lies the campground Los Perros. The 7-mile (12-km) climb to John Gardner Pass can be difficult during bad weather. It's advisable to wait a few days when crossing, particularly if there are dangerous winds. Views of the Glaciar Grey and the Southern Ice Field from the pass are the highlights. Hikers can stay at the wonderful Campamento Paso, as the next 6 miles (10 km) to Refugio Grey are quite difficult. Hikers are then advised to trek from Refugio Grey to Lago Pehoé, for the journey to Puerto Natales.

Sendero Pingo-Zapata

This infrequently visited trail is good for bird-watching, and has an easy-medium difficulty level. The trail begins at the Lago Grey CONAF station and follows the Río Pingo passed views of the western granite walls of the Paine massif. After about five hours, visitors arrive at the Campamento Zapata, with a decrepit refugio, and a half-hour later to a lookout point to view Glaciar Zapata and its rows of glacial moraine.

Glaciar Grey

Although its receding rate has increased, Glaciar Grey is still one of the largest and most easily accessed glaciers in Patagonia. The icebergs that break off from the glacier float to the end of Lago Grey. These can be seen along a short walk on flat beach from the Grey sector's ranger station, near Refugio Grey. At the end of the beach, reached by a half-hour walk, a peninsula with a viewing platform offers vistas of Glaciar Grey in the distance. A popular journey here is aboard the catamaran *Grey II*, which leaves Refugio Grey twice daily and sails to the face of the glacier in summer.

← Admiring the view from an outcrop on the edge of Punta Arenas

EXPERIENCE MORE

②
Puerto Hambre

🅰 G7 🚗 36 miles (58 km) S of Punta Arenas
🕘 9:30am–6:30pm daily
🌐 parquedelestrecho.cl

The first attempt to establish a settlement on the Strait of Magellan took place in 1584 when a Spanish captain left several hundred colonists about 20 miles (50 km) south of Punta Arenas. He called the settlement Rey Felipe, but it was changed to Puerto Hambre (Port Hunger) in 1587 by British captain Thomas Cavendish, who landed here to find just one survivor – the rest had starved or succumbed to the elements. The traces of these ruins are now considered a national monument.

About 2 miles (3 km) to the south is the national monument Fuerte Bulnes, set up in 1843 by colonists from Chiloé who were later transplanted to present-day Punta Arenas in 1848. This became the second, and first successful colonization of the strait, and the site offers an interesting look into the colonists' lives.

③
Punta Arenas

🅰 G7 🚗 153 miles (247 km) S of Puerto Natales ✈🚌
ℹ Lautaro Navarro 999; www.puntaarenas.cl

The capital of the Magallanes region, Punta Arenas was initially a penal colony and a disciplinary center for military personnel. In the late 19th and early 20th centuries, it drew thousands of Europeans escaping World War I and seeking fortunes in sheep ranching, gold and coal mining, and the shipping industry. Today, the best place to begin exploring the town is at the Plaza Muñoz Gamero, the main square, with the Magellan Monument at its center. The ritual is for visitors to kiss the toe of the Tehuelche statue on the monument, for good luck or, as legend goes, to ensure they return to Punta Arenas.

Travelers can appreciate the staggering wealth of the Braun-Menéndez family – owners of mammoth ranching operations in the early 20th century – at the **Museo Regional Braun Menéndez**. Dating from 1903, the edifice is preserved with its original furniture and finery, which was imported from Europe. The museum also features a room dedicated to the ethnographic history of the region. Another mansion of the Braun-Menéndez family, the Palacio Sara Braun, can be seen on Plaza Muñoz Gamero, and is home to a hotel.

Also of interest is the **Museo Regional Salesiano Maggiorino** Borgatello, which was founded in 1893 and charts the history, ecology, and anthropology of the Magallanes region. Displays include stuffed local fauna, pickled marine life, and geological samples collected by Salesian missionaries of the early 20th century, as well as ethnographic exhibits relating to the Kawéskar and Selk'nam peoples, and a floor devoted to the industrial history of Punta Arenas.

The **Cementerio Municipal Sara Braun** is the site of many tombs belonging to Punta Arenas' powerful families, along with the graves of immigrants from Scotland and Croatia. On the northwest side of the cemetery, the Indiecito (Little Indian) statue represents deceased indigenous groups and is a totem for good luck.

Located on the banks of Magellan Strait, **Nao Victoria Museum** features replica ships of the great explorers of this region. Visitors can climb aboard Darwin's HMS *Beagle*, and Magellan's *Nao Victoria*, but most impressive is the replica of the lifeboat used by Ernest Shackleton and his men while navigating the Antarctic Ocean.

Museo Regional Braun Menéndez

📍 H. de Magallanes 949 🕐 10:30am–2pm Mon & Wed–Sun 🌐 museodemagallanes.gob.cl

Museo Regional Salesiano Maggiorino Borgatello

📍 Ave M. Bulnes & Maipú 🕐 10am–12:30pm & 3–5:30pm Tue–Sat 🌐 museomaggiorinoborgatello.cl

Cementerio Municipal Sara Braun

📍 Avenida M. Bulnes & Rómulo Correa 📞 (061) 221 2777 🕐 7:30am–8pm daily

Nao Victoria Museum

📍 Off Ruta 9 🕐 9am–6pm daily 🌐 naovictoria.cl

4

Seno Otway

📍 G6 📍 40 miles (65 km) N of Punta Arenas 🕐 Mid-Oct–Mar: 8am–6:30pm daily 🌐 turisotway.cl

This penguin rookery is a delightful half-day tour from Punta Arenas. Every year between November and March, some 2,500 pairs of Magellanic penguins come to burrow nests here before heading north to Argentina or the south-central Chilean coast. The 110-acre (45-ha) reserve features roped walkways and lookout platforms, and a souvenir store.

5

Isla Magdalena

📍 G6 📍 22 miles (35 km) NE of Punta Arenas 🚢 comapa.com

The 2-hour boat trip to Isla Magdalena is worth the effort with the island hosting up to 60,000 breeding pairs of Magellanic penguins. Each pair produces two chicks November–March, bringing the population to some 240,000 penguins. A roped walkway runs across the area, and an old lighthouse acts as a ranger and research station. Adult penguins take turns guarding the nest and fishing, and visitors can watch the birds waddling along narrow paths to and from the sea, passing just inches from them.

EAT

Damiana Elena

In a Magellanic house, this spot has a great wine list and menu.

📍 G7 📍 Magallanes 341, Punta Arenas 📞 (061) 2222818 🕐 Sun, Mon

$$ ⑤⑤⑤ $$

Afrigonia

The menu here combines Zambian and Chilean flavors; try the shrimp and scallop curry.

📍 F6 📍 Eberhard 343, Puerto Natales 📞 (061) 2412877

⑤⑤⑤

El Living

This vegetarian café-restaurant serves up hearty meals, with a book exchange on site.

📍 F6 📍 Arturo Prat 156, Puerto Natales 📞 (061) 2411140 🕐 Sun

⑤⑤⑤

DRINK

La Taberna del Club de la Unión

A characterful bar in the basement of the Palacio Sara Braun.

📍 G7 📍 Plaza Muñoz Gamero 716, Punta Arenas 📞 (061) 224 1317

↑ Magellanic penguins posturing on the shore of Isla Magdalena

6

Villa Tehuelches

🅰 G6 🄰 96 miles (154 km) SE of Puerto Natales 🚌

The pocket-sized outpost of Villa Tehuelches was founded in 1967 as a service center for the regional population. This village is famous for the annual Festival de la Esquila, or Shearing Festival, which draws hundreds of people from across Patagonia and features rodeos, sheep-shearing competitions, and lamb barbecues.

7

Cueva del Milodón

🅰 F6 🄰 15 miles (24 km) NW of Puerto Natales 🚌 🄾 Oct–Apr: 8am–7pm daily; May–Sep: 8:30am–6pm daily 🆆 cuevadelmilodon.cl

Arguably the most important paleontological and archaeological site in Southern Patagonia, the Cueva del Milodón is named for the now-extinct ground sloth, or milodón (Mylodon darwinii), whose partial remains were discovered here by Hermann

Did You Know?

A scrap of milodón skin provided the inspiration for Bruce Chatwin's epic travelog *In Patagonia*.

Eberhard in 1895. The milodón, measuring up to 10 ft (3 m) in height and weighing around 400 pounds (181 kg), roamed Patagonia until the Pleistocene period, about 10,000 years ago. Today, a replica of this sloth dominates the cave entrance, and its fossil remains are displayed in a visitors' center.

8

Puerto Natales

🅰 F6 🄰 1,268 miles (2,040 km) S of Santiago ✈🚌🚢 🄸 Pedro Montt 19; www.torresdelpaine.com

Puerto Natales is a windswept town backed by the Sierra Dorotea range. The town overlooks the Seno Última Esperanza (Last Hope Sound) – so called because this was the site that Spanish explorer Juan Ladrilleros considered his last hope while attempting to locate the Strait of Magellan in 1557. The region was originally inhabited by the indigenous Tehuelche and Kawéskar tribes; the present town was only founded in 1911 when a sheep-ranching boom led to an influx of European immigrants, as well as of people from the Chiloé archipelago. Today, the economy of Puerto Natales is primarily based on its flourishing tourism industry.

The town's **Museo Histórico Municipal** features displays of antique tools and household items, as well as photographs of the vanished Kawéskar and Aonikenk indigenous communities. The main road, Avenida Pedro Montt, affords splendid views of glacier-topped peaks and the aqua sound, which is dotted with cormorants, black-necked swans, and other birds.

Puerto Natales serves as the main gateway to Southern Patagonia's famous Parque Nacional Torres del Paine (p252), and caters to numerous travelers who stop here en route to the park. Several tour operators offer activities such

↑ The overhanging lip of paleontological site Cueva del Milodón

↑ Epic Glaciar Balmaceda, Parque Nacional Bernardo O'Higgins

as ice trekking, cruises to a glacier, and horseback riding.

Situated 6 miles (10 km) from Puerto Natales, Mirador Dorotea is a moderate trek of 2,625 ft (800 m). After crossing the forest, visitors can enjoy breathtaking views from the summit of Puerto Natales, surrounding mountains, and the glacial valley. The excursion can also be done on horseback, which includes a traditional late-afternoon *once* (high-tea) with a local family. A small admission fee may apply.

Just north of Puerto Natales is Puerto Bories, a small housing community and site of the Frígorifico Bories, an old sheep-processing plant that was part of the Sociedad Explotadora de Tierra del Fuego, once Patagonia's largest sheep-ranching operation. Today, the Frígorifico Bories is a national monument and has been converted into the region's finest hotel.

A short distance northwest of Puerto Prat, Estancia Puerto Consuelo was founded by German immigrant Hermann Eberhard. One of the earliest ranches in Chilean Patagonia, the *estancia* offers stunning views of Parque Nacional Torres del Paine and enjoyable activities around the site.

Museo Histórico Municipal
◎ ♿ 🏛 Manuel Bulnes 285
🕙 8am–7pm Mon–Fri, 10am–1pm & 3–7pm Sat 🌐 registro
museoschile.cl

 9

Parque Nacional Bernardo O'Higgins

🗺 F6 🚗 90 miles (145 km) NW of Puerto Natales 🚤
ℹ CONAF, Manuel Baquedano 847, Puerto Natales; www.conaf.cl

Created in 1969, Parque Nacional Bernardo O'Higgins is bordered on the east by the mammoth ice field Campo de Hielo Sur and comprises a maze of small islands, fjords, and channels. It is Chile's largest national park, but the lack of land access also makes it one of the least visited. The park is reached on a full-day catamaran cruise from Puerto Natales. Retracing the 16th-century voyage of Juan Ladrilleros through the Seno Última Esperanza, the trip offers spectacular views and includes a visit to the hanging Glaciar Balmaceda and a short trek to the iceberg-laden lagoon of Glaciar Serrano. From the lagoon, kayaks and dinghies navigate up the Río Serrano through a little-known route marked by untrammeled scenery of glaciers, peaks, and dense forest, and ends at Parque Nacional Torres del Paine administration center. This trip can also be made in the opposite direction from Torres del Paine.

BERNARDO O'HIGGINS

Born in Chillán, Bernardo O'Higgins (1778–1842) was the illegitimate son of an Irish officer in the Spanish army and a local woman. His father rose to be Viceroy of Peru, and Bernardo was educated in Europe, where he met revolutionaries intent on Spain's overthrow in Latin America. By 1814, O'Higgins was heading Chile's independence struggle, and eventually became the post-Independence leader.

STAY

The Singular Patagonia

Transformed from a crumbling slaughter-house, this top-end hotel has glorious views of Last Hope Sound.

🅰F6 🏠Puerto Bories s/n, Puerto Natales 🌐thesingular.com

$$$

Bories House

This Anglo-Chilean enterprise has turned a traditional *estancia* into a modern hotel, with a welcoming fire blazing in the dining room.

🅰F6 🏠Puerto Bories 13-B, Puerto Natales 🌐borieshouse.com

$$$

Lakutaia Lodge

A luxury lodge located right on the Beagle Channel, this is a great base for outdoor activities in the area.

🅰H7 🏠Seno Lauta s/n, Puerto Williams 🌐lakutaia.cl

$$$

Exploring Cape Horn, the most southerly point of the Americas ↑

⑩ Cape Horn

🅰H7 🏠437 miles (703 km) SE of Punta Arenas 🚌🚢

The southernmost "point" of the Americas, Cape Horn, or the Horn as it is often called, actually comprises a group of islands that form the Parque Nacional Cabo de Hornos. Cape Horn was discovered by Europeans during a Dutch sailing expedition in 1616 and named for the town of Hoorn in the Netherlands. From the 18th century until the opening of the Panama Canal in 1914, it served as an important trade route for cargo ships.

The waters around the Cape Horn islands are among the most treacherous in the world, due in particular to the williwaws, blasts of wind that appear out of nowhere. Inhospitable sailing conditions make it difficult to reach the very tip, and Isla Hornos, to its northwest, is usually as far as people can go. Moss-covered Isla Hornos is home to the Monumento al Navegante Solitario, which honors sailors who died while sailing around the Horn. The island has a rich birdlife, and dolphins and whales can be seen offshore.

⑪ Strait of Magellan

🅰G7 🏠62 miles (100 km) S of Punta Arenas 🚢

A navigable sea route linking the Atlantic with the Pacific Ocean, this strait is named for Ferdinand Magellan, the first European to discover the passage in 1520. It separates Tierra del Fuego from the Chilean mainland, and offers a safer route for ships rounding the South American continent than the Drake Passage farther south. Until the opening of the Panama Canal, the Strait of Magellan served as the principal route for steam ships traveling between Europe and the Americas.

The strait is a breeding and feeding ground for humpback whales, sea lions, and other marine fauna during summer months. Breeding colonies are easily spotted at Isla Carlos III, near the strait's western entrance. The waters surrounding the island comprise the 259-sq-mile (670-sq-km) Parque Marino Francisco Coloane, Chile's first marine reserve. Whale-watching boat trips to Isla Carlos III include a stop at the Cabo San Isidro, which has a lighthouse dating from 1904. Once used to guide ships through the Strait, the lighthouse has now been converted into a comfortable lodge with a small museum that charts the history of the region's indigenous groups such as the Selk'nam and Yamana communities.

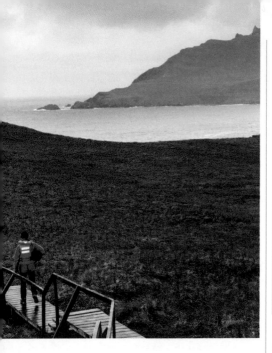

mausoleums in the shade of cypress trees pruned into cylindrical shapes. On Avenida Manuel Senoret, Parque del Recuerdo displays antique machinery and vehicles from the 19th century, while the Plaza de las Américas features a monument constructed to commemorate the Selk'nam people, the original inhabitants of the region.

Museo Municipal Fernando Cordero Rusque

🚶 🖐 🏠 Padre Mario Zavattaro 402 🕿 (061) 2581800 🕐 8am–5:15pm Mon-Thu, 8am–4:15pm Fri, 10am–4pm Sat, Sun & hols

⑫ Puerto Williams

🅰 H7 🏠 182 miles (293 km) SE of Punta Arenas
➕ 🚌 🌐 ptowilliams.cl

The solitary town on Isla Navarino, Puerto Williams is the capital of the Magallanes and Chilean Antarctic region, and the southernmost town in the world. Founded in 1953 as a Chilean naval base, it was later named Puerto Williams in honor of Irish-born officer Juan Williams, who captured the Strait of Magellan for Chile in 1843. The town is backed by the granite peaks of Dientes de Navarino, a rugged area that offers some of south Chile's most challenging trekking. The town's main attraction, the Museo Martín Gusinde, is dedicated to an Austrian anthropologist and clergyman (1886–1969) who did significant research on the region's indigenous Yamana and Selk'nam communities.

Just east of Puerto Williams, Villa Ukika is home to the few surviving members of the Yamana community.

⑬ Porvenir

🅰 G7 🏠 25 miles (40 km) SE of Punta Arenas ➕ 🚢 🚌
🌐 muniporvenir.cl

Windswept Porvenir first grew as an outpost for miners working in the Baquedano mountain range during a local gold rush in the mid-19th century. During the 20th-century boom in wool production, the town acted as a service center for the region's sheep *estancias*. Today, Porvenir is the capital of the Tierra del Fuego province, and its main highlight is the **Museo Municipal Fernando Cordero Rusque**. The museum has archaeological and anthropological exhibits on the indigenous cultures that once inhabited the region. North of the museum, the Cementerio Municipal features antique

→

A monument honoring the Selk'nam people standing in Porvenir

VISITING ARGENTINA

In a few hours, travelers to Chile's Parque Nacional Torres del Paine can visit the Argentine town El Calafate, a tourism-oriented town that forms the base for visits to the Glaciar Perito Moreno and Los Glaciares National Park. Cruise ship passengers can stop over in the Argentine port-city of Ushuaia, a phenomenally beautiful town backed by jagged peaks.

Parque Nacional Los Glaciares

▲ 227 miles (336 km) NW of Puerto Natales; 50 miles (80 km) W of El Calafate
✈ El Calafate 🚌 El Calafate
🛈 Avenida del Libertador 1302, El Calafate; www.losglaciares.com

Created in 1937, Parque Nacional Los Glaciares is an add-on destination favored by many of the travelers to Parque Nacional Torres del Paine, as there are two border crossings in close proximity. Named after the mesmerising glaciers that cascade down from the Southern Ice Field, this reserve is Argentina's second-largest national park and a trekking and climbing mecca.

The park, which is for the most part inaccessible, covers 1.6 million acres of rugged mountains, turquoise lakes, glaciers, and thundering rivers. Dominating the whole park is the Fitz Roy massif, a towering cluster of granite needles. Trekkers to this area can take part in camping-based trips over days, or they can opt to go on shorter day hikes that last between two and six hours. Trips begin at the mountain village of El Chaltén, which is a collection of hotels and restaurants that sprang up in the 1990s along the Río Las Vueltas.

The major crowd-puller at Parque Nacional Los Glaciares is the Glaciar Perito Moreno, which flows roughly 18 miles (29 km) before making contact with a peninsula that provides visitors with ideal lookout points from which to view the glacial marvel. The glacier is one of the few in Patagonia that is not receding, although it cannot grow far either as its terminus is obstructed by land. Every several years, pressure that has built up from the ice's contact with land causes the glacier to calve in a crashing fury, a sight travelers aspire to see when visiting this park.

Several agencies offer trekking tours which take visitors on the glacier with crampons and sturdy ropes, nature walks, and boat rides some of the other neighboring glaciers of Upsala and Spegazzini and around floating icebergs.

Los Glaciares is accessed from El Calafate, which is a tourism-based town on the shore of Lago Argentino, a five-hour drive from Puerto Natales, Chile. Old estancias (sheep ranches) here have been converted into hotels and restaurants and give visitors a little taste of Patagonian gaucho life and gaucho culture.

INSIDER TIP
Road trip

Various companies rent out four-wheel drives and other off-road vehicles. Why not crisscross southbound between Chile and Argentina, allowing you to see more of the beautiful landscape.

↓ Tourist capturing the ice-blue shards of Glaciar Perito Moreno

← Sea lions relaxing
on the Beagle Channel,
near Ushuaia

foxes, or the island's scourge,
the Canadian beaver, which
was introduced in the 1940s
to harvest pelts.

④ 🔌 🍽 🖥 🛍
Cerro Castor

📍 16 miles (26 km) NE of
Ushuaia; Ruta Nacional 3,
Km 3047 ☎ (02901) 499301
✈ 🚌 from Ushuaia
🕐 Mid-Jun–mid-Oct
🌐 cerrocastor.com

The base of Argentina's
southernmost ski resort is
just 640 ft (195 m) above
sea level, with the highest
elevation at 3,468 ft (1,057 m),
yet Cerro Castor receives
prodigious snowfall. The
retreat consists of the Castor
Ski Lodge, with 15 rustic-chic
cabins, four restaurants, and
four mountain cafés. It has
nearly 1,500 acres (607 ha)
of skiable terrain, 2,630 ft
(800 m) of vertical drop,
a snowpark, and seven lifts.
Numerous activities are on
offer, including ski and
culinary events that extend
throughout the season.

②
Ushuaia

📍 351 miles (564 km) SE of
El Calafate ✈ 🚌 ℹ Avenida
Prefectura Naval 470;
www.turismoushuaia.com

Ushuaia is Argentina's southernmost city. and the jumping
off point for Antarctica trips.
It is a wildlife-watching destination. Boat companies offer
penguin and sea-lion spotting
tours on the Beagle Channel.

The city is named in the
language of the region's first
indigenous inhabitants, the
Yamana; Ushuaia translates
as the Bay Leading West. It
was established as the capital
of Tierra del Fuego in 1904.
British missionaries settled
the area in the mid 1800s.
In 1896, President Julio
Argentino Roca founded
a penal colony here for
criminals and political
prisoners from the north and
Buenos Aires. The colony not
only served as a means of
hiding away society's most
dangerous criminals, it
also established a strong
Argentine presence in the
region of Tierra del Fuego.
The prison was shut down in
1947 and now houses the
Museo Marítimo y Presidio,
which has a vast collection of
historical, nautical, scientific,
and cultural exhibits from
around the area.

③ 🔌 🖥 🛍
Parque Nacional
Tierra del Fuego

📍 8 miles (11 km) N of
Ushuaia 🚌 from Ushuaia.
ℹ Ruta Nacional 3, Km
3047; www.parques
nacionales.gob.ar

Parque Nacional Tierra del
Fuego was Argentina's first
coastal national park. It is still
popular with Ushuaia locals as
an area offering trails, bird-
watching, and trout fishing.
Pedestrian paths and longer
hikes pass through thick
forest and past dark-water
turbales (peat bogs). Visitors
may see guanacos and red

Palm trees on the incredible Anakena Beach

EASTER ISLAND AND ROBINSON CRUSOE ISLAND

Chile's borders extend over two of the planet's most isolated, remote, and exotic islands. Easter Island, known as Rapa Nui to its inhabitants, is visited for its moai statues, world-renowned icons of archaeology, and remnants of a vanished society. Closer to mainland, Robinson Crusoe Island is the site of one of the greatest adventure sagas.

Five hours from the mainland by plane, Easter Island is a volcanic triangle whose culture, despite its political link to Chile, is more Polynesian than Latin American. The original settlers island-hopped their way across the Western Pacific and arrived at Rapa Nui around AD 1000. What they lacked in numbers they made up for with ingenuity and creativity, carving monuments that have since made the island famous. Restored to their original platforms, the moai attract thousands each year.

Robinson Crusoe Island is part of the Juan Fernández archipelago. The island takes its name from the Daniel Defoe novel *Robinson Crusoe*, which was inspired by the story of 18th-century Scotsman Alexander Selkirk.

EASTER ISLAND AND ROBINSON CRUSOE ISLAND

Must Sees
1. Rano Raraku
2. Ahu Tongariki

Experience More
3. Hanga Roa
4. Rano Kau and Orongo
5. Ahu Vinapu
6. Ahu Akivi
7. Ana Te Pahu
8. Playa Anakena
9. Península Poike
10. San Juan Bautista
11. Sendero Salsipuedes
12. Cueva Robinson
13. Mirador Selkirk
14. Plazoleta El Yunque

EASTER ISLAND
AND ROBINSON
CRUSOE ISLAND

Easter
Island

Robinson
Crusoe Island

❶ ⊛ ⊛

RANO RARAKU

⌂ 11 miles (18 km) E of Hanga Roa 🛈 Ranger station and rangers on-site : www.conaf.cl

Among Easter Island's most breathtaking features are the *moai*-studded slopes of Rano Raraku; some 400 of the striking monolithic statues built by the Rapa Nui people can be seen here today. The site is also home to Crater Lake, an enormous prehistoric volcanic crater overlooking the Pacific Ocean.

Here, long before the arrival of Europeans, Rapa Nui carvers crafted their massive statues from volcanic tuff and, with substantial effort, freed them from the quarry to be transported across the island. These are seen standing or toppled beside their *ahu* (ceremonial platforms). While they differ in detail, they have much in common.

Rano Raraku is one of the most popular sites on Easter Island, so aim to arrive for opening time or stay until closing time. Entry to the site is covered by a general ticket, which you buy at the airport on arrival; you can't book a visit to Rano Raraku ahead of time.

Crater Lake

The vast center of Rano Raraku is occupied by a serene lake. The crater can be reached through a gap in the western end of this site, and the CONAF-built trails around the crater's outer slopes are the only way to explore the area. East of Tukuturi (*p271*) are the basalt foundations of many *hare paenga*, thatched boat-shaped houses that were reserved for priests.

Moai statues dotting the slopes of Rano Raraku, Easter Island ↑

Timeline

c 300,000 years ago

The crater of Rano Raraku is formed by a volcanic eruption.

600– 900 AD

The first human settlers arrive on Easter Island from Polynesia. They soon start carving *moai*.

1050– 1680 AD

The high point of *moai* construction at Rano Raraku.

1774

Captain James Cook reports that many statues have been toppled. Increasing numbers of *moai* are knocked from their *ahus* over the following years.

1950s

Many of the toppled *moai* are restored to their *ahus*.

MOAI STATUES OF RANO RARAKU

Moai are the highly stylized monolithic statues for which Rapa Nui has become famous. Carved from tuff (compacted volcanic ash), and ranging from 6 ft (2 m) to 65 ft (20 m) in height, there are around 400 completed *moai* on the island today, as well as many others that were never finished, notably at Rano Raraku. They represent important ancestors and were erected to watch over and protect their respective kin-groups. The earliest *moai* are believed to have been carved around 600–900 AD.

HINARIRU

Located on one of the lower points of the trail, the much-photographed, 13-ft (4-m) high Hinariru is also called the moai with the twisted neck, in reference to its bulging base. According to various folktales, Hinariru was the brother-in-law of Hotu Motu'a, legendary leader of the first island settlers, and perhaps also the master who brought the *moai* to the island.

EL GIGANTE

Climbing to the upper slopes of Rano Raraku, the trail reaches El Gigante. As its name implies, at 65 ft (20 m), El Gigante the largest *moai* ever carved. Unfinished and still attached to the bedrock, its estimated weight is around 270 tons (240 tonnes).

↑ Hinariru with his twisting body and a neighbor in the background

Did You Know?

A single *moai* took a team of 5 to 6 men about a year to finish.

PIROPIRO

Just west of Hinariru, on the main path that runs to the quarry, is another 13-ft- (4-m-) high *moai* known as Piropiro. This name means "bad smell" as signified in the *moai* having a prominent nose. About 22 ft (7 m) of its body is buried beneath volcanic soil.

TUKUTURI

The fenced-off Tukuturi is different from other *moai*. It is the site's singular kneeling, bearded *moai* with a complete (if seemingly unfinished) body, and apparently mimics the posture of Polynesian ceremonial singers. According to American archaeologist Joanne van Tilburg, it may be the last *moai* ever made, with links to the Birdman cult.

KO KONA HE ROA

The *moai* known as Ko Kona He Roa, which stands very closely to a second *moai*, bears evidence of European contact in the image of a three-masted sailing ship roughly etched on its trunk. This carving could well depict the sailing ship of Dutch explorer Jacob Roggeveen, who landed at Easter Island in 1722 and reportedly encountered some 2,000 inhabitants.

TAI HARE ATUA

This is understood to be the first *moai* on the island as shown in the statue's rudimentary style. It has been left abandoned, as if the carvers were disappointed with their work.

→

Ko Kona He Roa with petroglyphs showing a ship on his torso

←

Admiring El Gigante, carved into the rock face, Rano Raraku

> ## THE STATUE-CARVERS
>
> Craftsmen were revered members of society, exempt from food production and supported by other farmers and fishermen. But the balance was tipped when statues became more ambitious, requiring more skill and hands. Overpopulation and deforestation – wood was needed for rollers to transport the statues – meant the island fell into anarchy.

2

AHU TONGARIKI

⌂ 12 miles (20 km) W of Hanga Roa 🚌 From Hanga Roa
🕐 Dawn until 6pm ℹ️ No toilets or food services for visitors

On the southeast coast of Easter Island you'll find the iconic and otherworldly sight of Ahu Tongariki. These 15 fascinating and towering *moai* statues are gravely lined up on a 720-ft- (220-m-) long ceremonial platform – or *ahu* – which is the largest platform on the island.

Like most of the other *moai* on the island, the 15 giant statues at Ahu Tongariki were toppled during the civil wars of the 19th century. The site suffered further damage in 1960 when a 9.5-magnitude earthquake struck the Chilean mainland, triggering a massive tsunami that subsequently hit Easter Island. The *ahu* and fallen *moai* were washed further inland and experienced considerable damage in the process. It was only in 1996, after a five-year restoration project, that the archaelogical site was returned to its former glory. The restoration work cost a whopping US$2 million, which was covered by the government of Japan following a heartfelt TV appearance by the governor of Easter Island.

Note that this site is part of the Rapa Nui National Park, which covers most of Easter Island. You will pay your park entry fee at the airport on arrival, and this includes entry to all sites.

> PICTURE PERFECT
> **Ahu Tongariki's Maoi**
>
> An essential souvenir for anyone visiting Easter Island is a snap of the *maoi* at sunrise (check online for timing). You'll need to be up and out early to get the best vantage point - you won't be the only one with this idea.

The impressive *maoi* of Ahu Tongariki, backed by the Pacific Ocean ↓

① A rock at Ahu Tongariki includes a petroglyph of a tuna fish.

② After the tsunami, archaeologist Claudio Cristino sought to return the *maoi* to their rightful place. This photograph shows work taking place at the site in 1992.

③ The site's *maoi* were restored by archaeologists after a tsunami in 1960.

Did You Know?

At the site's entrance is the "traveling *moai*," which toured Japan after the tsunami.

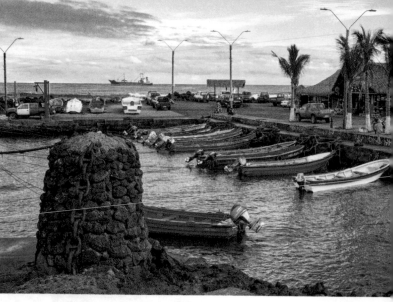

EXPERIENCE MORE

③

Hanga Roa

🏠 2,340 miles (3,765 km)
NW of Santiago ✈ ℹ
Avenida Policarpo Toro, at
Tuu Maheke; (032) 2100255

Easter Island's only permanent
settlement, Hanga Roa is a
sprawling subtropical village
housing nearly all of the
island's inhabitants. Most of
its wide streets are lined with
compact homes fronted
by gardens. The population
is mainly Polynesian but
there are also expatriates –
from mainland Chile – who
participate in the island's
growing tourism industry.
The village is a hub for visitors
who come to enjoy the area's
unique attractions, including
a sophisticated cuisine that
blends varios interesting and
fresh ingredients with South
Pacific touches.

TAPATI RAPA NUI

Easter Island's biggest annual
event for the past 30 years,
Tapati Rapa Nui, has filled the
streets of Hanga Roa with
folkloric music, dance, and
competitive events. Cele-
brated during the first two
weeks of February, the
festival is a chance for
islanders to showcase their
skills and crafts. Tapati Rapa
Nui focuses on tradition and
identity, despite the use of
imported elements such as
drums and guitars.

④

Rano Kau and Orongo

🏠 3 miles (5 km) S of Hanga
Roa; Sector Orongo ⏰ 9am–
7pm daily

Part of a national park, the
water-filled crater of Rano Kau
is Easter Island's most striking
natural sight – the panorama
from its rim, with the seemingly endless Pacific Ocean on
the horizon, is one of the most
unforgettable sights of the
island. Descending into the
crater is no longer permitted,
but walking around its rim
is a true top-of-the-world
experience. On the crater's
southwest side, the ceremonial village at Orongo is a
complex of 53 houses that
were linked to this island's
Birdman sect in the 18th and
19th centuries. The sect gets
its name from the Birdman, an
influential post whose incum-
bent was chosen each year
(p277). Visitors to this historic
and fragile site are requested
not to leave the marked path
or enter the houses, which

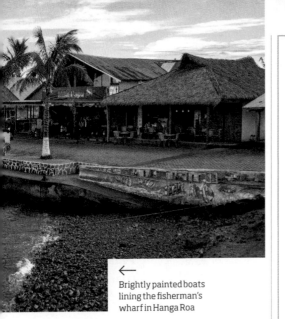

Brightly painted boats lining the fisherman's wharf in Hanga Roa

EAT

Au Bout du Monde
A Belgian-restaurant with seafood dishes, homemade pasta, and chocolate mousse.

🏠 Policarpo Toro s/n, Hanga Roa 📞(032) 2552060 🕒 Tue

$$$

DRINK

Te Moana
Enjoy a sunset cocktail or beer (try the Tahitian lager Hinano), in a prime location looking out over the sea.

🏠 Av Policarpo Toro s/n, Hanga Roa 📞(032) 2551578 🕒 Sun

consist of overlapping slabs and earth, with doors so low that entering them would require crawling.

Rano Kau and Orongo are reached by a road that passes the west end of Mataveri airport. However, it is also possible to hike there, and back, on the Te Ara O Te Ao footpath that starts at Ana Kai Tangata; this route is closely associated with the Birdman rituals. The admission fee for Rano Kau, collected by CONAF, is also valid for entry to Rano Raraku (p268).

fossilized palm, believed to be evidence of island settlement around AD 1300. Theory holds that the tree became extinct as islanders cleared woods to make space for erecting *moai*.

6
Ahu Akivi

📍 4 miles (6 km) NE of Hanga Roa; Sector Akivi

With seven standing *moai*, restored in 1960 by American anthropologist William Mulloy

and his Chilean colleague Gonzalo Figueroa García-Huidobro, Ahu Akivi is one of few inland *ahu* (stone platforms) and, unlike most other *ahus*, its *moai* look toward the sea. They also look toward the platform's ceremonial center and, during both equinoxes, directly into the setting sun.

5
Ahu Vinapu

📍 2 miles (3 km) NE of Rano Kau; Sector Orongo

Ahu Vinapu was once mistakenly held to be proof of South American influence on Easter Island, because its closely fitted stones superficially resemble Incan sites in Peru. The site actually consists of three separate platforms, whose *moai* tumbled over in conflicts during the 18th and 19th centuries. The site is also known for the discovery of

↑ Standing on the rim of Rano Kau, a spectacular volcanic crater

↑ A tree growing from inside the Ana Te Pahu cavern

7 Ana Te Pahu

🏠 4 miles (6 km) NE of Hanga Roa; Sector Ahu Akivi

Today, much of Easter Island's food is imported from the mainland, but before this became an option, the islanders used lava tube caves called *manavai*, or sunken gardens, to grow their produce. These tunnel-like caves formed when rock solidified around a flowing stream of molten lava, which had resulted from the regular volanic activity that gave rise to Easter Island in the first place. Ana Te Pahu is one such lava tube cave – the largest cavern on the island.

Owing to the total absence of surface streams on Easter Island's porous volcanic terrain, large-scale agriculture has always been a challenge. The humid microclimate and relatively deep soils in the caves permitted the cultivation of crops; these are still grown in Ana Te Pahu and in similar sites around the island. Visitors can easily descend into the cave to explore, but a flashlight is necessary.

8 Playa Anakena

🏠 10 miles (16 km) NE of Hanga Roa; Sector Anakena

On the northeastern shores of Rapa Nui, Playa Anakena is the island's only broad sandy beach and, with its tall palms and turquoise waters, it is almost a caricature of a South Pacific idyll. The beach is a perfect spot for swimming and sunbathing. It also has barbecue pits, picnic tables, changing rooms, and several snack bars that make it the most popular choice with locals for a day's outing.

According to Easter Island's oral tradition, Playa Anakena is the place where the first Polynesian settlers, under chief Hotu Motu'a, landed. Anakena has one thing that no part of Polynesia can match – the seven standing *moai* of Ahu Nau Nau, four of them with *pukao* (topknots) that were restored in 1979 under the direction of island archaeologist Sergio Rapu. Two of these *moai* are badly damaged, but the remainder are in excellent condition. Also on the same beach, slightly to the south, is the smaller Ahu Ature

→ Palm-dotted Playa Anakena, and *(inset)* seven somber *moai* of Ahu Nau Nau

Huki with a single *moai*. This was re-erected in 1956 by Norwegian explorer Thor Heyerdahl, with the help of a group of islanders.

From Anakena, it is possible to hike around the little-visited north coast, returning to Hanga Roa *(p274)* via two other sites – Ahu Tepeu and Ahu Tahai. However, this is a full day's trip and demands an early start. Since there is an absence of shade along the shore, be sure to carry plenty of water.

9 Península Poike

🏠 13 miles (21 km) NE of Hanga Roa; Sector Poike

The peninsula at the island's eastern end takes its name from Volcán Poike, which is the oldest volcano on the island and marks this area's highest point. In pre-European times there was a village here, and petroglyphs from the period include a turtle, a tuna fish, and a Birdman. The area also has fascinating landmarks associated with legends of the island. Key among these is a 2-mile- (3-km-) long westerly "ditch," believed to mark a line of defensive fortifications during a war between rival clans.

On the peninsula's southwestern edge is Poike's most stunning asset – Ahu Tongariki (p268). With its 15 moai, which stand with their backs to the Pacific Ocean, it is the island's largest platform, and arguably the most important megalithic monument in all of Polynesia.

LEGEND OF THE BIRDMAN

Around the 16th century, Rapa Nui's culture, rooted in ancestor worship, was replaced by a system of beliefs known as *makemake*, named after the creator god. One of this new sect's key customs was an annual competition held to elect the Tangata Manu (Birdman), who held a position of power on the island. Each of the contestants would sponsor an islander, a *hopu*, whose task was to scramble down the slope of Rano Kau, swim through shark-infested waters to the islet of Motu Nui, and retrieve the egg of a sooty tern. The sponsor of the first *hopu* to return would become that year's Birdman.

10

San Juan Bautista

🏠 472 miles (759 km) W of Santiago 🛬 From Santiago 🚢 From Valparaíso ℹ️ Larraín Alcalde s/n; www.comunajuanfernandez.cl

Robinson Crusoe Island's only permanent settlement, San Juan Bautista is nestled on the curving shoreline of the scenic Bahía Cumberland. The waters around it are part of a 187,000-sq-mile (301,000-sq-km) marine reserve that was created in 2015 to protect the area around Robinson Crusoe Island and its neighbours.

Located just south of the village plaza, atop a hill, the

←

The village of San Juan Bautista on Robinson Crusoe Island

small Fuerte Santa Barbara dates from 1770. This stone fort was constructed by the Spanish in response to the presence of the British in the South Pacific. It was rebuilt in 1974, but the fort's several cannons, pointing at the harbor, still stand here.

Next to the fort, the Cuevas de los Patriotas (Caves of the Patriots) was where, in the early 19th century, the Spanish held Chilean leaders who had been fighting for independence. At the village's western end, the Cementerio San Juan Bautista is home to the tombs of early settlers, as well as those of German sailors who stayed on the island after the scuttling of the *Dresden* in 1915. This battleship had been cornered by the British navy in the Bahía Cumberland.

Since the tsunami of 2010, a disaster that was unleashed by a massive earthquake and ultimately claimed eight lives, the **Casa de Cultura Alfredo de Rodt**, named for an early Swiss settler, shares space with **CONAF**'s national park information office.

Casa de Cultura Alfredo de Rodt/CONAF

🏠 Vicente González 130 🕐 8am–1pm & 2–6pm Mon–Fri

1966

The year that Más a Tierra was renamed Robinson Crusoe Island.

11

Sendero Salsipuedes

🏠 1 mile (2 km) W of San Juan Bautista 🌐 conaf.cl

Starting at Calle La Pólvora, just west of San Juan Bautista, the Sendero Salsipuedes is a nature trail with multiple switchbacks. The path snakes through dense vegetation and verdant forests of acacia, eucalyptus, Montrey cypress, Montrey pine, and the native murtilla before culminating at the jagged Salsipuedes ridge. The views from here are exceptional and include sweeping panoramas of San Juan Bautista and of the blue waters of Bahía Cumberland that surround the village.

12

Cueva Robinson

🏠 2 miles (3 km) NW of San Juan Bautista by boat; Puerto Inglés 🚢 🌐 conaf.cl

From the Salsipuedes ridge, a steep pathway descends to the beach at Puerto Inglés

↑ Mirador Selkirk, with the curve of Bahía Cumberland seen below

and to the Cueva Robinson, claimed to be the site of Alexander Selkirk's shelter (*see box*). This precipitous approach can be dangerous, and it is necessary to hire the services of a local guide. While there is no clear evidence that Selkirk inhabited this cave, a replica of his supposed refuge dominates the site. From 1995 onward, American treasure hunter Bernard Keiser spent several years in this area, searching for a massive, 18th-century Spanish treasure, allegedly found by the British and then re-hidden here.

⑬ 〈⊠〉

Mirador Selkirk

⌂ 2 miles (3 km) S of San Juan Bautista 𝕨 conaf.cl

A popular hiking destination, Mirador Selkirk is the saddle from where the castaway Alexander Selkirk watched for the ship that would rescue him from his lonely exile. The trek to this lookout starts at the southern end of San Juan Bautista's central plaza and climbs steeply through an eroded zone. As the trail gains altitude, it passes through thick endemic rain forest, studded with towering tree ferns, before culminating at the saddle. It is also possible to start the hike from Mirador Selkirk all the way to the airstrip. Visitors can ask the local fishermen to drop them

off in the morning and hike back to San Juan Bautista.

Two metal plaques on the saddle, one placed by the Royal Navy in 1868 and the other by a distant relative in 1983, commemorate Selkirk's exile. The site offers great views over Bahía Cumberland and San Juan Bautista. To the south, the landscape changes dramatically from dense rain forest to desert at Tierras Blancas, where the rugged shoreline provides habitat for the endemic Juan Fernández fur seal, *Arctocephalus philippii*.

---

⑭ 〈⊠〉 〈⊠〉

Plazoleta El Yunque

⌂ 2 miles (3 km) S of San Juan Bautista 𝕨 conaf.cl

Starting at San Juan Bautista's power plant, a southbound

road turns into a gentle nature trail that leads to the Plazoleta El Yunque, a serene forest clearing with a campsite. The site is also the spot where Hugo Weber, a German survivor of the *Dresden* sinking, built a house – the dilapidated foundations of which are still visible today.

There is a steep and challenging hike that begins at the Plazoleta El Yunque and traverses dense forest to reach the saddle of El Camote, which offers sweeping views of the island. Farther ahead, a more strenuous hike culminates at Cerro El Yunque (The Anvil Hill), which, at 3,002 ft (915 m), is the highest point on Robinson Crusoe Island, as well as being one of the most visited. Diverse wildlife can be seen here; CONAF organizes guides for those who wish to undertake this hike.

ALEXANDER SELKIRK

Scotsman Alexander Selkirk – who inspired Daniel Defoe's *Robinson Crusoe* (1719) – was abandoned on Isla Más a Tierra in 1704, after he complained about the seaworthiness of his ship, *Cinque Ports*. Selkirk subsisted on feral goats, fish, and plants, clothed himself with animal skins, and stayed hidden from Spanish vessels until his rescue in 1709 by a British privateering ship. As Selkirk had predicted, the vessel sank within a month of his being put ashore, and most of its crew tragically drowned.

NEED TO KNOW

Before You Go...................................282

Getting Around.................................284

Practical Information..........................288

BEFORE YOU GO

Forward planning is essential to any successful trip. Be prepared for all eventualities by considering the following points before you travel.

AT A GLANCE

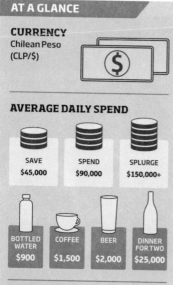

CURRENCY
Chilean Peso
(CLP/$)

AVERAGE DAILY SPEND

SAVE	SPEND	SPLURGE
$45,000	$90,000	$150,000+

BOTTLED WATER	COFFEE	BEER	DINNER FOR TWO
$900	$1,500	$2,000	$25,000

ESSENTIAL PHRASES

Hello	Hola
Goodbye	Adiós
Please	Por favor
Thank you	Gracias
Do you speak English?	¿Habla inglés?
I don't understand	No entiendo

ELECTRICITY SUPPLY

Standard voltage is 220 volts. Power sockets are type L, fitting two-pronged plugs.

Passports and Visas

Citizens of most countries, including the UK, US, Australia, Canada, South Africa, New Zealand, and all EU countries do not require visas for stays of up to 90 days. A reciprocity charge (arrival tax) of US$117 is charged on arrival at Santiago airport to all citizens of Australia. On arrival, visitors are given a tourist card, valid for 90 days, which can be extended for another 90 days for US$100 and must be surrendered when departing Chile. Visit the **Ministry of Foreign Affairs** website for more information.
Ministry of Foreign Affairs
W chile.gob.cl/chile/en

Travel Safety Information

Visitors can get up-to-date travel safety information from the **UK Foreign and Commonwealth Office**, the **US Department of State**, and the **Australian Department of Foreign Affairs and Trade**.
Australia
W smartraveller.gov.au
UK
W gov.uk/foreign-travel-advice
US
W travel.state.gov

Customs Information

Gifts up to the value of US$300 are allowed into Chile. No fresh fruit or agricultural products can be imported. The northernmost cities of Arica and Iquique, and southern Magellanes, have duty-free zones, so there are occasional internal customs checks when visitors are traveling from those regions. An individual is permitted to carry the following into Chile for personal use:
Tobacco products 400 cigarettes and 17 oz (500 g) of pipe tobacco and 50 cigars.
Alcohol 2.5 liters of alcoholic beverages.
Cash If you plan to enter or leave Chile with US$10,000 or more in cash (or the equivalent in other currencies), you must declare it to the customs authorities.

Insurance

It is wise to take out an insurance policy covering theft, loss of belongings, medical problems, cancellation, and delays.

Vaccinations

There are no inoculations required to visit Chile. However, the Centers for Disease Control and Prevention and World Health Organization both recommend that travelers are vaccinated against hepatitis A and tetanus.

Money

The currency in Chile is the Chilean peso. Many hotels and tour companies also accept US dollars, but it is best to carry pesos especially if you plan to visit more rural locations. All major credit and debit cards are widely accepted, although certain budget accommodations and restaurants may only take cash. ATMs are found in major towns and cities and most charge a fee of around $2–3 per transaction. Prepaid currency cards are increasing in popularity.

Booking Accommodations

Chile has a huge range of accommodations from budget hostels and local *hostales* to luxury hotels and resorts. Online booking is prevalent but tourist offices can also help locate local options. Most cities and major tourist areas offer plenty of accommodations, which visitors should be able to book all year round, although it may be worth booking in advance during high season. Chile has many campgrounds in national parks and areas of natural beauty, which should be booked in advance during the high season.

Travelers with Specific Needs

While facilities for visitors with specific needs are improving, they are still inadequate. New public buildings are required to provide wheelchair access but only the larger hotels are likely to be fully accessible or even have lifts. Wheelchair ramps and disabled toilets are rare and public transportation can be quite complicated, although Santiago is better equipped.

Operators such as **Accessible Holidays**, **Korke**, and **Wheel the World** are able to make special arrangements should visitors need them.

Accessible Holidays
w disabledholidays.com
Korke
w korke.com
Wheel the World
w gowheeltheworld.com

Language

Spanish is the official language, albeit with a distinctive accent and vocabulary that differs from other South American dialects. Some indigenous people, such as the Mapuche, Aymara, and Quechua, speak their own language among themselves but know Spanish too. The level of English is increasing rapidly, especially in the main tourist areas.

Closures

Afternoons Many shops and services are closed between 1pm and 3pm.
Mondays Some museums and tourist attractions are closed for the day.
Weekends Most shops and businesses are open for limited hours on Sundays; banks are closed on Saturday and Sunday.
Public holidays Banks and government offices are closed all day. Some shops and attractions close early or for the entire day.

PUBLIC HOLIDAYS	
Jan 1	New Year's Day
Mar/Apr	Easter
May 1	Labor Day/May Day
May 21	Navy Day
end Jun	Feast of St. Peter & St. Paul
Jul 16	Our Lady of Mount Carmel
Aug 15	Assumption of Mary
Sep 18	Independence Day
mid-Oct	Columbus Day
Nov 1	All Saints Day
Dec 1	Immaculate Conception
Dec 25	Christmas Day

GETTING AROUND

Whether you are visiting for a short city break or rural retreat, discover how best to reach your destination and travel like a pro.

AT A GLANCE

TRANSPORTATION COSTS

SANTIAGO

$710

Single bus journey

ANTOFAGASTA

$300

Single bus journey

VALPARAÍSO

$350

Single bus journey

TOP TIP
Avoid on-the-spot fines – be sure to stamp your ticket to validate your journey.

SPEED LIMITS

HIGHWAYS

75 mph (120 km/h)

COUNTRY ROADS

60 mph (100 km/h)

URBAN AREAS

30 mph (50 km/h)

Arriving by Air

Most visitors arrive at Aeropuerto Internacional Arturo Merino Benítez, 10 miles (16 km) north-west of Santiago. There are connections to the city by bus, shuttle, and taxi, as well as domestic flights. Other airports only receive flights from neighboring countries, but Aeropuerto Mataveri on Easter Island has flights from Tahiti and Australia. Chile's main airline, with direct flights from North America, Australasia, and Europe, is **LATAM**. **Air France**, **Iberia**, and **KLM** operate direct flights from Europe; **American Airlines**, **Delta**, and **Air Canada** fly directly from North America, and **Qantas** from Australia.

Air Canada
W aircanada.com
Air France
W airfrance.com
American Airlines
W aa.com
Delta
W delta.com
Iberia
W iberia.com
KLM
W klm.com
LATAM
W latam.com
Qantas
W qantas.com.au

Domestic Air Travel

Many travelers move between the regions of Chile by air. Flying is also the only way to reach Easter Island. There are domestic airports, served by LATAM and independent airlines, the biggest of which is **Sky Airline**. Smaller regional airlines, such as **DAP**, which serves parts of Patagonia, often face cancellations due to bad weather during winter in the south.

DAP
W dapairline.com
JetSmart
W jetsmart.com
Sky Airline
W skyairline.com

GETTING TO AND FROM THE AIRPORT

Airport	Distance to city	Taxi Fare	Public Transportation	Journey Time
Santiago	11 miles/17 km	$8,500	Bus	30 mins
La Serena	3 miles/5 km	$3,000	Micro	10 mins
Copiapó	33 miles/52 km	$27,000	Bus	45 mins
Antofagasta	16 miles/26 km	$14,000	Micro	30 mins
Iquique	25 miles/40 km	$18,000	Bus	45 mins
Arica	12 miles/18 km	$8,000	Micro	20 mins
Concepción	3 miles/5 km	$3,500	Bus	15 mins
Puerto Montt	10 miles/16 km	$7,000	Bus	20 mins
Castro	12 miles/18 km	$8,000	Bus	45 mins
Punta Arenas	13 miles/21 km	$6,500	Bus	30 mins
Hanga Roa	1 mile/1.5 km	$7,000	N/A	10 mins

Train Travel

Chile's once extensive railroad network, originally used for transporting minerals, has shrunk and no public services operate north of Santiago. Indeed, the only currently viable services on the state railway **EFE** run from the capital through the Central Valley to Rancagua, San Fernando, Talca, and Chillán, although there are plans for a new high-speed service from Santiago to Valparaíso.

EFE
W efe.cl

Ferry Travel

In Chile's far south, beyond Puerto Montt, a well developed ferry network negotiates the intricate patchwork of inlets, fjords, and islands that constitute Patagonia, providing a scenic alternative to plane and bus travel. There are also ferry connections along the Chiloé archipelago and the Carretera Austral. Companies such as **Andina del Sud**, **Transbordadora Austral Broom**, **Naviera Austral**, **TransMarChilay**, and **Navimag** may prove useful.

Andina del Sud
W andinadelsud.com
Naviera Austral
W navieraaustral.cl
Navimag
W navimag.com
Transbordadora Austral Broom
W tabsa.cl
TransMarChilay
W transmarchilay.cl

Bus Travel

International Bus Travel
A number of bus routes connect Chile with neighboring countries. Connections with Argentina include Valparaíso/Santiago to Mendoza, Puerto Montt/Osorno to Bariloche, Puntas Arenas to Rio Gallegos, and La Serena to San Juan. There are crossings between Chile and Bolivia: Arica via the high Lauca National Park to La Paz, and San Pedro de Atacama to Uyuni on the Bolivian salt flats. The most frequently used and least challenging crossing is from Arica to Tacna in Peru, where connections to Arequipa and other destinations are available.

FERRY ROUTES

Petrohué to Puella	5 hrs
Puerto Montt to Chacabuco	24 hrs
Puerto Montt to Laguna San Rafel	4 days
Puerto Montt to Chaltén	10 hrs
Puerto Montt to Puerto Natales	3 days
Punta Arenas to Porvenir	2 hrs 30 min
Punta Arenas to Puerto Williams	32 hrs
Quellón to Chaltén	5 hrs

REGIONAL BUS JOURNEY PLANNER

Plotting the main bus routes according to journey time, this map provides a handy reference for travelling between Chile's main towns and cities. The times given reflect the fastest and most direct routes available.

Key

••• Main bus routes

Antofagasta to San Pedro de Atacama	4 hrs 30 mins
Antofagasta to Iquique	6 hrs
Concepción to Puerto Montt	10 hrs
Iquique to Arica	5 hrs
Puerto Montt to Castro	3 hrs
Puerto Montt to Coyhaique	18 hrs
Puerto Montt to Punta Arenas	24 hrs
Santiago to Valparaíso	1 hr 45 mins
Santiago to La Serena	6 hrs 30 mins
Santiago to Copiapó	11 hrs 30 mins
Santiago to Antofagasta	19 hrs
Santiago to Concepción	6 hrs

Regional Bus Travel

With an extensive network of routes operated by private companies, the bus is the most efficient and widely used means of transportation. **TurBus** and **Pullman Bus** are the largest nationwide companies, and are complemented by several regional operators.

Standards are quite high, with three classes offering increasing comfort levels: the *clásico* has normal semireclining seats; the *semicama* offers more legroom and the seats recline further; and the *salon cama* contains much wider seats, which recline almost horizontally. All have on-board toilets and the more luxurious usually offer free water, soft drinks, and the occasional light snack.

Prices are relatively low because of intense competition – tickets cost in the region of $1,500–2,000 per hour of travel on a basic bus, with luxury services costing up to three or four times more. Booking in advance is advisable, especially on popular routes. Visitors can book using comparison sites such as **Recorrido**, the bus company's own website, and at bus stations. Cities and larger towns often have several bus stations, with dedicated depots for larger companies, while other towns have huge integrated terminals.

Pullman Bus
w pullmanbus.cl
Recorrido
w recorrido.cl
TurBus
w turbus.cl

Public Transportation

The main form of public transportation in towns and cities is local buses, supplemented by *micros* and *colectivos*. Only Santiago has a fully developed metro system, although there is a single-line overground train between Valparaíso and Viña del Mar. In Santiago, when using the **Transantiago**, you must use the electronic Tarjeta Bip! card, named for the noise it makes. You can buy and top up these cards at machines or ticket windows found in all stations and major bus depots. Fares are flat but vary according to the time of day. Outside Santiago, travelers must pay for local transportation with cash.

Many buses have a plastic box to deposit money, so you need to have the exact fare, while others have a conductor on board.

Transantiago
w transantiago.cl

Metro

The **Santiago Metro** system is modern, clean, and generally safe. The network consists of six intersecting lines covering major transportation hubs (excluding the airport) and most places of interest. Trains run 6:30am–11pm on weekdays and 8:30am–10:30pm on weekends.

Santiago Metro
w metro.cl

City Buses

Santiago has an extensive bus network that is useful for reaching places not covered by the metro. Buses are modern and comfortable but can get crowded during rush hour, when the heavy traffic means they can also move slowly.

Colectivos

These shared taxis ply set routes for fixed fares that are often not much higher than local bus fares. The destination is usually displayed on a board on the roof, and taxis depart when full. Mainly used for travel within urban areas, they sometimes connect outlying towns and villages.

Micros

Local bus services are supplemented by these numbered minibuses, which can be useful for reaching some destinations not covered by the official network.

Taxis

Taxis are found in all Chilean cities and towns. They are black with yellow roofs; a light in the windscreen's top right-hand corner indicates availability. Fares are low, at $130 per 655 ft (200 m) on top of the initial $300 charge. Radio taxis are more expensive, with a $2,000 call-out charge, followed by a quote for each destination. Taxi apps, such as Uber and Beat, are popular in Santiago and spreading to other cities. Small-town and rural taxis are rarely metered, so get an idea of the going rate and be prepared to bargain; although not frequent, rip-offs of unsuspecting tourists do sometimes occur.

Driving

Most visitors use planes or buses to get around the country, but the public transportation network to many national parks and other areas of natural beauty is limited or non-existent. If visitors want to avoid an organized tour, car rental is the only alternative.

Driving in Chile

There is currently a four-lane highway from La Serena in the Norte Chico to Puerto Montt at the top of Patagonia, and well-surfaced roads in all but the most remote parts of the country. The main highways are all toll roads and around Santiago they require an electronic or daily fee permit, which can be bought online at **Servipag**.

Driving the country's famed Gringo Trail will take you through spectacular scenery on some-times narrow but well-paved roads. Much of the southerly Carretera Austral has loose gravel and blind curves in places, so care is required. The off-the-beaten-track parts of the Atacama Desert, most national parks, and the high-altitude altiplano are best negotiated in a locally rented jeep or 4WD vehicle.

Servipag
w servipag.com

Car Rental

International rental companies such as Avis and Hertz have affiliates in all major cities and some smaller towns and tourist hubs. There are also local companies, including **Lys**, **Free Rent a Car**, and **Seelmann**, which offer cheaper rates. Unlimited mileage is the rule but prices are generally higher than in the US or Europe.

Drivers must be at least 21 years old and have a valid driving license, passport, and credit card. In theory an international licence is required but that is hardly ever enforced, although it can help avoid bureaucratic problems if you are stopped by the police. The rental company must provide the vehicle's ownership documents. Insurance policies have deductibles as high as 20 percent of the vehicle's value. Crossborder rentals need power of attorney and additional insurance.

Free Rent a Car
w freerentacar.cl
Lys
w lys.cl
Seelmann
w seelmann.cl

Rules of the Road

Driving is on the right and passengers are required by law to wear seat belts. There are strict penalties for drunk driving. On the Carretera Austral, drivers must carry warning triangles, a fire extinguisher and a first-aid kit.

Cycling

Bikes can be rented in most towns and tourist centers but those intent on some serious cycling are advised to bring their own cycle, a repair kit, and spares. Naturally, you should wear a helmet; it is, in fact, illegal not to. The greatest danger comes from careless drivers, so luminous and reflective gear is essential.

PRACTICAL
INFORMATION

A little local know-how goes a long way in Chile. Here you will find all the essential advice and information you will need during your stay.

AT A GLANCE

EMERGENCY NUMBERS

GENERAL EMERGENCY	AMBULANCE
113	**131**

FIRE DEPARTMENT	POLICE
132	**133**

TIME ZONE
CST/CLST. Daylight saving time runs from the first Sunday in September to the first Sunday in April.

TAP WATER
Unless otherwise stated, tap water is safe to drink in Chile, apart from in the Atacama Desert region.

TIPPING

Waiter	10 percent
Hotel Porter	$500
Housekeeping	Not expected
Concierge	$500
Taxi Driver	Not expected

Personal Security

Chile is one of the safest countries in South America, possibly the safest. Violent crime against foreign travelers is extremely rare. That is not to say that petty theft does not exist, especially in parts of Santiago, Valparaíso, and transit towns such as Arica, Calama, and Puerto Montt, where extra vigilance is advisable. Naturally, you should take the usual precautions with your valuables around busy stations and on public transportation, but you are unlikely encounter any of the tricks used to rip off tourists in other countries.

Health

Chile has high standards of public health and excellent hospitals in the larger towns and cities. No inoculations are required and there are no endemic diseases to be concerned about. There have been very few cases of tourists developing infections from diseases such as dengue fever, Chagas' disease, and hantavirus disease, which have occasionally broken out. Given the wealth of adventure activities on offer, trauma injuries are the most common cause for requiring medical treatment and thus it is wise to be covered against such eventualities by taking out travel insurance.

As the northern and central Andes contain some of the highest elevations in the western hemisphere, you should be aware of the danger of altitude sickness (AMS). Symptoms include headaches, nausea, fatigue, dizziness, and dehydration. The best precaution is to acclimatize by gradually increasing altitudes and if you do start showing symptoms, retreat back down to lower ground immediately.

Alcohol, Smoking, and Drugs

A range of alcohol is available throughout Chile, which is unsurprising for a country renowned for the quality of its red wine and signature pisco sour. Consequently, it is part of the culture, although you do not generally see people drinking to excess in the same way as in some

Western countries, and public inebriation is generally frowned upon. A fairly high percentage of Chileans smoke tobacco but the laws banning the habit from all enclosed public areas, including restaurants and bars, are strictly adhered to. Unlike some other South American countries, almost all recreational drugs are illegal as well as socially unacceptable. There's a confusing statute that small amounts of cannabis can be consumed in private homes but not in any public places, including hotels. This effectively renders the practice impractical to travelers and it is best to refrain, as penalties can be harsh.

ID

Both Chilean nationals and foreigners are officially required to carry ID, so it's advisable to keep your passport with you at all times.

Visiting Churches and Cathedrals

Modest dress is advisable when visiting churches and other places of religious significance. This means no shorts or skirts above the knee, nor sleeveless tops.

Local Customs

Chile is a moderately conservative country and the Catholic Church still exerts a great deal of influence here. Chileans value courtesy and are polite in their dealings with strangers, so rudeness does not go down well.

LGBT+ Safety

Due to the somewhat conservative nature of Chilean society, public displays of affection by same-sex couples are viewed unfavorably outside of Santiago, so discretion is advisable. However, the government has passed strict anti-discrimatory laws in recent years, and there is very little chance of encountering homophobic violence.

Cell Phones and Wi-Fi

Local SIM cards can easily be purchased for your cell phone for use within the country, although you need to register online first; the Spanish-only **Multibanda** site has more information. Pre-paid phone cards usually offer the best rates for international dialing, and are best bought in the larger cities and tourist centers.

Multibanda
W multibanda.cl

Post

Post offices, easily identified by the blue Correos sign, are generally open 9am–5pm during the week, with some large branches operating longer hours and on Saturday.

Taxes and Refunds

Chile has a hidden tax called IVA, equivalent to VAT, of 19 percent on all goods and services. This is included in the quoted price, with a couple of exceptions. Some hotels don't include IVA in their room prices, instead adding it at the end, so always check. Tourists are exempt from IVA if paying for rooms in US dollars but may need to ask for the discount. Car rental companies rarely include IVA in their prices.

Discount Cards

Valid youth and student ID cards allow visitors discounted or free entry to museums and other tourist sites. Santiago's **Costanera Center** offers foreigners an easily obtainable discount card.

Costanera Center
W costaneracenter.cl

WEBSITES AND APPS

Chile Travel
chile.travel is the country's official tourism website.

CONAF
conaf.cl has the best national parks information, although only in Spanish.

Chile 360
This app offers incredible 360-degree images, videos, and maps of sights.

Recorrido
This is a handy app for comparing bus companies and booking tickets.

INDEX

Page numbers in **bold** refer to main entries

A

Accommodation see Hotels
Achao **226-7**
Adventure sports **26-7**
Aguirre, Francisco de
  Catwedral de La Serena 169
  Plaza de Armas (La Serena) 168
  Pukará de Quitor 160
Ahu Akivi **275**
Ahu Tongariki **272-3**
Ahu Vinapu **275**
Airports 285
Air travel **284-5**
Alcohol **288-9**
  customs information 282
Aldea de Tulor (Norte Grande) **160, 184**
Aldunate, Manuel 70, 72-3
Alero de las Manos 245
Alessandri, Arturo 89
Algarrobo **133**
Allende, Isabel, House of the Spirits, The 39
Allende, Salvador 48, 105
  Cementerio General (Santiago) 104
  Museo de la Solidaridad Salvador Allende (Santiago) **94**
  statue of 72
Almagro, Diego de 44
Alpacas **35**
Altitude sickness (AMS) **167**, 288
Ambulances 288
Amusement parks
  Fantasilandia (Santiago) **93**
Ana Te Pahu **276**
Ancud **220**
Antofagasta **186-7**
Antúnez Xañartu, Nemesio **31**, 126
Anwandter, Karl 201
Apoquindo 110
Apps 289
Aravena, Alejandro **37**
Architecture **36-7**
  Jesuit churches in Chiloé **224-5**
Argentina 234, **262-3**
Argentino Roca, Julio 263
Arica **154-6**
Art **30-31**
  street art (Valparaíso) **127**
  see also Museums and galleries
Arteaga, Gerardo 93
Arts and crafts see Crafts
Assler, Federico 108

Astronomy 11

Astronomy 11
  Atacama Desert **187**
  Cerro Mamalluca Observatory **174-5**
  Cerro Paranal Observatory **186**
  Observatorio del Pangue **175**
  Planetario USACH (Santiago) **92**
Atacama Desert **37**
  Desierto Florido **169**
  stargazing **187**
Atacameño civilization 182-3, 184
Avenida del Mar (La Serena) **171**
Aylwin, Patricio 48, 49

B

Baburizza, Pascual 123
Bachelet, Michelle 48, **49**
Badlands Law (1845) 218
Bahía Inglesa 189
Balmaceda, José Manuel 108
Bannen, Germán 108
Bar Inglés (Valparaíso) **120**
Bar La Playa (Valparaíso) **120**
Barrio Brasil (Santiago) **92-3**
Barrio Concha y Toro (Santiago) **95**
Barrio Dieciocho (Santiago) **95**
Barrio Lastarría (Santiago) **79**
Barrio París-Londres (Santiago) **74**
Barrio Patronato (Santiago) **106-7**
Barrios, Gracia **31**, 126
Barrio Vitacura (Santiago) **111**
Bars
  Easter Island and Robinson Crusoe Island 275
  Lake District and Chiloé 201
  Norte Grande and Norte Chico 161
  Santiago 78, 109
  Southern Patagonia and Tierra del Fuego 257
  Valparaíso 125
Bascuñán, Raquel 110
Basilica de los Sacramentinos (Santiago) **96**
Basilica y Museo de la Merced (Santiago) **77**
Batacura 111
Bauer, Alfonso 172
Beaches
  Bahía Inglesa 189
  Iquique **165**
  Norte Grande and Norte Chico 154
Bear Story (film) 61
Beckett, Andy, Pinochet in Piccadilly 39
Benmayor, Samy 78

C

Bernardo O'Higgins, Parque Nacional **259**
Biblioteca de Santiago **91**
Biblioteca Nacional (Santiago) **76**
Bicycles 287
Bieregel, Federico 107
Birdman 274, **277**
Birds
  condors **34**
  Isla Magdalena **257**
  Lago Vichuquén 144
  Laguna Verde 191
  Monumento Natural Islotes de Puñihuil **220-21**
  penguins **34-5**
  Reserva Nacional Altos de Lircay 143
  Reserva Nacional Pinguino de Humboldt **191**
  Salar de Tara 185
  Seno Otway **257**
  see also National parks
Blue whale **35**
Boats
  ferries 286, 287
  Nao Victoria Museum (Punta Arenas) 257
  Parque Quinta Normal (Santiago) 89
  sailing the fjords of Northern Patagonia **241**
Bolaño, Roberto, Savage Detectives, The 39
Bolsa de Comercio (Santiago) **75**
Bontá, Marco A. 80
Bookworms, Chile and Easter Island for **38-9**
Bosque Fray Jorge, Parque Nacional **193**
Botero, Fernando 80
Brandy
  pisco **175**
Braun-Menéndez family 256
Brown, Ricardo 68
Brunet des Baines, Claude François 76
Buses
  bus journey planner 285
  international buses 286
  long-distance buses 286
  micros (minibuses) 287
  Santiago 286
Byron, John 239

C

Cabezas, Rodrigo 78
Cachagua **133**
Cafés
  café con piernas (coffee with legs) **71**
  Confitería Torres (Santiago) **92**
Cajón del Maipo **139**

Calama **181**
Caldera **188-9**
Caleta Tortel **246-7**
Calle Esmeralda (Valparaíso) **122**
Calle Prat (Valparaíso) **122**
Camino del Inca **177**
Camping, wild 216
Cancillería (Santiago) **72**
Cape Horn **260**
Cardoen, Carlos 141
Carpets
    Alfombras de Puyuhuapi 241
Carreterra Austral **245**
Cars
    car rental 287
    driving 287
    driving the Carreterra Austral **245**
    speed limits 284
    see also Tours
Cartagena **132**
Casablanca Valley **130**
Casa Colorada (Santiago) **71**, 83
Casa de Cultura Alfredo de Rodt (San Juan Bautista) 278
Casa de la Ciudadanía Montecarmelo (Santiago) **108**
Casa Incaica (San Pedro de Atacama) **158-9**
Casa Museo Isla Negra (Valparaíso) **128-9**
Casa Museo La Chascona (Santiago) **105**
Casino Español (Iquique) **164-5**
Caspana **180-81**
Castro **222-3**
    palafitos **36**
Catarpe **160**
Catedral de La Serena **169**
Catedral de San Marcos (Arica) **154-5**
Catedral Metropolitana (Santiago) **68**, 83
Cathedrals see Churches and cathedrals
Cavalle-Coll, Aristide de 127
Cavendish, Captain Thomas 256
Caves
    Ana Te Pahu **276**
    Cueva del Milodón **258**
    Valle de la Luna 184
Cazotte, Teresa 95
Cementerio Católico (Valparaíso) **124-5**
Cementerio Disidentes (Valparaíso) **124-5**
Cementerio General (Santiago) **104**
Cementario Municipal Sara Braun (Punta Arenas) 256-7
Central Valley 17, **115-49**
    hotels 122, 133, 140, 145
    map 116-17
    restaurants 121, 131, 135, 142, 147
    skiing 139
    tour **148-9**
    wines 13, **28**

Centro Cultural El Austral (Valdivia) **200**
Centro Cultural Estación Mapocho (Santiago) **80-81**
Centro Cultural Palacio La Moneda (Santiago) **73**
Cerro Castor **263**
Cerro Dragón (Iquique) **162-3**
Cerro Mamalluca Observatory **174-5**
Cerro Paranal Observatory **186**
Cerro Pintados **180**
Cerro Santa Lucía (Santiago) **78**
Cervantes, Miguel de 165
Chaitén **240**
Charles V, Emperor 78
Chatwin, Bruce **39**
Chile Chico **246**
Chillán **144-5**
Chiloé
    Jesuit churches in Chiloé 12, 36, **224-5**
    Parque Nacional **221**
    see also Lake District and Chiloé
Chinchorro culture 44
    mummies **41**, **157**
    Museo Arqueológico San Miguel de Azapa 156
    Museo de Sitio Colón 10 (Arica) **155**
Chiu-Chiu **182**
Chonchi **227**
Chuquicamata **183**
Churches and cathedrals 289
    Basilica de la Merced (Santiago) **77**
    Basilica de los Sacramentos (Santiago) **96**
    Catedral de La Serena **169**
    Catedral de San Marcos (Arica) **154-5**
    Catedral Metropolitana (Santiago) **68**, 83
    Iglesia Anglicana San Pablo (Valparaíso) **124**
    Iglesia de los Sagrados Corazones (Valparaíso) **126-7**
    Iglesia de San Francisco (La Serena) **170**
    Iglesia de San Gerónimo de Poconchile **176**
    Iglesia de Santo Domingo (Santiago) **80**
    Iglesia Luterana de la Santa Cruz (Valparaíso) **124**
    Iglesia Sagrado Corazón de Jesús (Puerto Varas) 218, 219
    Iglesia San Agustín (Santiago) **76-7**
    Iglesia San Francisco (Castro) **222**
    Iglesia y Convento de San Francisco (Santiago) **74-5**
    Iglesia y Convento de San Francisco (Valparaíso) **127**

Churches and cathedrals (cont.).
    Jesuit churches in Chiloé 12, 36, **224-5**
    Santuario de la Tirana 179
Cicarelli, Alejandro 89
Cienfuegos, Gonzalo 78
Cinema **61**
Closures 283
Club de la Unión (Santiago) **77**
Club Hípico (Santiago) **96-7**
Coal mines
    Lota **147**
Cochamó Valley 33
Cochiguazhas **175**
Cochrane **243**
Cochrane, Lord Thomas 71, 119, 201
Colchagua Valley wineries tour **148-9**
Colectivos (shared taxis) 287
Collado, Sebastian 125
Coñaripe **212**
Concepción **146**
Concha y Toro, Enrique 95
Condors **34**
Confitería Torres (Santiago) **92**
Congreso Nacional (Valparaíso) **127**
Conguillío, Parque Nacional **198-9**
Cook, Captain James 45, 269
Copiapó **188**
Copper mines
    Calama 181
    Chuquicamata **183**
    El Teniente **138**
Correo Central (Santiago) **68**, 83
Cousiño, Luis 97
Cousiño family 94, 147
Coyhaique **244**
Crafts
    Poblado Artesanal (Arica) **155**
Crater Lake **268**
Credit cards 283
Crime 288
Cristo Redentor **135**
Cruce de los Lagos **205**
Cruz Montt, Alberto 77
Cueva del Milodón **258**
Cueva Robinson **278-9**
Curaco de Vélez **226**
Curanto **29**
Currency 282, 283
Customs information 282
Cycling 287

D

Dalcahue **221**
Dalí, Salvador 91, 105
Dario, Rubén 118
Darwin, Charles **39**, 46
    La Campana **137**
    Termas de Cauquenes 138
    Volcán Osorno 204
Debit cards 283
Defoe, Daniel, *Robinson Crusoe* 279

De Gaulle, Charles 72, 94
Desierto Florido **169**
Dientes de Navarino 32
Dinosaurs 96
Monumento Natural Pichasca **192**
Disabled travellers 283
"Disappeared"
Museo de la Memoria y los Derechos Humanos (Santiago) 41, **90**
Discount cards 289
Diving **27**
Doctors 288
Domeyko, Ignacio 170
Donoso, José, *Curfew* 39
Doyere, Emilio 70, 71
Drake, Sir Francis 76
Drinks *see* Bars; Food and drink
Driving *see* Cars
Drugs 289
Duclos, Arturo 223

E

Earthquake (2010) **146**
Easter Island and Robinson Crusoe Island 11, 19, **265-79**
bars 275
hiking 33
history **45**, 47
map 266-7
restaurants 275
Eberhard, Hermann 258, 259
Edificio de la Aduana (Valparaíso) **118**
Edwards-Ross family 124, 125
Egidio Meléndez, Luis 72
Egneau, Juan 108
Eiffel, Gustave 80
Catedral de San Marcos (Arica) 154-5
Ex-Aduana (Arica) 156
El Chacal de Nahueltoro (film) 61
Electricity supply 282
El Gigante **270**
El Gigante de Atacama **177**
El Mercurio de Valparaíso **124**
El Teniente **138**
Emergency numbers 288
Enoteca Wine Museum (Santiago) 103
Entertainment
Santiago **60-61**
Escuela de México (Chillán) 145
Ex-Aduana (Arica) **156**
Ex Congreso Nacional (Santiago) **70**, 82

F

Fantasilandia (Santiago) **93**
Fantastic Woman, A (film) 61
Fashion
Museo de la Moda (Santiago) **110**
Ferham, J. Eduardo 68

Feria Yumbel Market (Castro) 222
Fernández, Juan 45
Ferries 286, 287
Festivals and events **42-3**
Festival Costumbrista Chilote **227**
Festival de La Tirana **179**
Noche de Valdivia 200
Tapati Rapa Nui **274**
Figueroa García-Huidobro, Gonzalo 275
Films **61**
Fire services 288
Fjords
Northern Patagonia **241**
Flowers
Desierto Florido **169**
Food and drink **28-9**
pisco **175**
Santiago **58-9**
see also Bars; Markets; Restaurants; Wines
Fortresses
Fuerte San Antonio (Ancud) 220
pukarás and the Camino del Inca **177**
Frutillar **219**
Fuente, Gregorio de la 146
Funicular, Valparaíso **120**
Futaleufú 10, **234-5**

G

Galleries *see* Museums and galleries
Garcia Postigo, Gustavo 76
Gardens *see* Parks and gardens
Garrido Falcón, Don Julio 73
Garzón, Báltazar 49
Gay, Claudio 88
Gazitúa, Francisco 104
Geisers de Tatio 184
Generación del Trece 80
Geoglifos de Cerro Sagrado 157
Geoglyphs *see* Rock art
Germans in Lake District and Chiloé **218**
Gil de Castro, José 79
Glaciers
Glaciar Grey **255**
Nevados de Sollipulli **210**
Parque Nacional Laguna San Rafael **238-9**
Parque Nacional Los Glaciares **262**
Gloria (film) 61
Godoy, Juan 188
González Cortés, Ricardo 95
González Videla, Gabriel 171
Histórico Gabriel González Videla (La Serena) 168-9
Gran Torre Santiago **110**
Grupo Signo 80, 126
Guerrero, Xavier 145

Guevara, Che 183
Motorcycle Diaries, The 39
Gusinde, Martin 261

H

Hacienda Los Lingues **140**
Hanga Roa **274**
Health care 288
Henault, Lucien 76
Herbage, Juan 169
Heyerdahl, Thor 276
Hiking **32-3**
high hiking 214
Reserva Nacional Altos de Lircay 143
Sendero Salsipuedes **278**
see also National parks
Hinariru **270**
Historic buildings
Cancillería (Santiago) **72**
Casa Colorada (Santiago) **71**, 83
Casa de la Cultura (Rancagua) 137
Casa Incaica (San Pedro de Atacama) **158-9**
Casa Tornini (Caldera) 189
Casino Español (Iquique) **164-5**
Centro Cultural Estación Mapocho (Santiago) **80-81**
Club de la Unión (Santiago) **77**
Confitería Torres (Santiago) **92**
Correo Central (Santiago) **68**, 83
Edificio de la Aduana (Valparaíso) **118**
Ex-Aduana (Arica) **156**
Ex Congreso Nacional (Santiago) **70**, 82
Municipalidad de Santiago **69**, 83
Palacio Alhambra (Santiago) **72-3**
Palacio Astoreca (Iquique) **162**
Palacio Baburizza (Valparaíso) **123**
Palacio Cousiño (Santiago) **94-5**
Palacio de la Justicia (Valparaíso) **121**
Palacio de La Moneda (Santiago) **72**
Palacio de la Real Audiencia (Santiago) **68-9**, 83
Palacio de los Tribunales de Justicia (Santiago) **71**, 82
Palacio Edificio Íñiguez (Santiago) 94
Palacio Errázuriz (Santiago) 94
Palacio Irarrázabal (Santiago) 94
Palacio Vergara (Viña del Mar) 130
Posada del Corregidor (Santiago) **81**
see also Churches and cathedrals

History **40-41**, **44-9**
Hitachi, Prince of Japan 103
Holzmann, Ernesto 74
Hopperdietzel, Walter 241
Hornopirén **240-41**
Horse racing
Club Hípico (Santiago) **96-7**
Hospitals 288
Hotels
booking 283
Central Valley 122, 133, 140, 145
Lake District and Chiloé 210, 215, 219, 226
Norte Grande and Norte Chico 155, 161, 163, 167, 182
Northern Patagonia 243
Santiago 74, 97, 104
Southern Patagonia and Tierra del Fuego 255, 260
Hot springs *see* Spas and hot springs
Hotu Motu'a 276
Huerquehue, Parque Nacional **213**
Huidobro, Vicente 95, 132
Humberstone 37, **178**
Hurtado 192
Hurtado de Mendoza, Garcia 217

I

Ibañez del Campo, Carlos 89
ID 289
Iglesia Anglicana San Pablo (Valparaíso) **124**
Iglesia de los Sagrados Corazones (Valparaíso) **126-7**
Iglesia de San Francisco (La Serena) **170**
Iglesia de San Gerónimo de Poconchile **176**
Iglesia de San Pedro de Atacama **158**
Iglesia de Santo Domingo (Santiago) **80**
Iglesia Luterana de la Santa Cruz (Valparaíso) **124**
Iglesia San Agustín (Santiago) **76-7**
Iglesia San Francisco (Castro) **222**
Iglesia y Convento de San Francisco (Santiago) **74-5**
Iglesia y Convento de San Francisco (Valparaíso) **127**
Incas **45**
pukarás and the Camino del Inca **177**
Indigenous cultures **31**, **45**
Insurance 283
Internet access 289
Iquique **162-5**
beaches **165**
Isla Dawson **261**
Isla Magdalena **257**

Itineraries
2 days in Santiago 57
2 weeks in Chile and Easter Island 21-3
7 days in Chile and Easter Island 24-5

J

Jara, Victor 104
Jardín Japonés (Santiago) 103
Jardín Mapulemu (Santiago) 103
Jecquier, Emilio
Bolsa de Comercio (Santiago) **75**
Centro Cultural Estación Mapocho (Santiago) 80
Museo Nacional de Bellas Artes (Santiago) 79
Jesuits
Jesuit churches in Chiloé 12, 36, **224-5**
The Jesuit's Circular Mission **225**
Juan Fernández Island 45
Jufré del Águila, Don Melchor 140

K

Kayaks **26**
Parque Nacional Laguna San Rafael **239**
Keiser, Bernard 279
Ko Kona He Roa **271**

L

La Campana, Parque Nacional **137**
Ladrilleros, Juan 258
Lago Caburga **210**
Lago Llanquihue **218**
Lago Ranco **217**
Lagos, Ricardo 73
Lago Vichuquén **144**
Laguna del Laja, Parque Nacional **147**
Laguna San Rafael, Parque Nacional **238-9**
Laguna Verde **191**
Lagunillas 139
Lake District and Chiloé 18, **195-227**
bars 201
hiking 33
hotels 210, 215, 219, 226
hot springs 11
map 196-7
myths and folklore **220**
restaurants 206, 208, 213, 217, 223
Landscape 12
Language 282, 283
La Portada **187**
La Quintrala 134
Larrain Bravo, Ricardo 95, 96
Larraín Garcia-Moreno, Sergio **67**

Las Condes (Santiago) **111**
La Sebastiana (Valparaíso) **125**
La Serena 40, **168-71**
Lathoud, Paul 94
La Tirana **179**
La Tirana, Festival de **179**
Lauca, Parque Nacional 33, **166-7**
La Vega (Santiago) 29, **106**
Legend of the Birdman **277**
Lehuedé, Pedro 107
Le Paige, Gustavo 159, 161
Letelier, Orlando 104
LGBT+
safety 289
venues in Bellavista (Santiago) **107**
Libraries
Biblioteca de Santiago **91**
Biblioteca Nacional (Santiago) **76**
Licán Ray **214**
Lira, Pedro 89, 91
Literature **38-9**
Llamas **35**
Llico 144
Lloyd, William 124
Local customs 289
Los Andes **135**
Los Glaciares, Parque Nacional **262**
Lota **147**
Luco, Barros 92
Lukas (Renzo Antonio Pecchenino Raggi) 125
Casa Mirador de Lukas (Valparaíso) 123

M

MAC Espacio Quinta Normal (Santiago) **89**
Machiacao y Bianchi 95
Magellan, Ferdinand **45**, 260
Mamiña Hot Springs **179**
Maps
Argentina 263
Arica 155
bus journey planner 285
Castro 223
Central Valley 116-17
Chile 15
Colchagua Valley 148-9
Easter Island and Robinson Crusoe Island 266-7
Iquique 163
Lake District and Chiloé 196-7
La Serena 169
Norte Grande and Norte Chico 152-3
Northeast of Santiago Centro 100-101
Northern Patagonia 230-31
San Pedro de Atacama 159
Santiago 52-3
Santiago: Plaza de Armas and Santiago Centro 64-5, 82-3

Maps (cont.)
 Santiago: West of Santiago
  Centro 86–7
 South America 14
 Southern Patagonia and
  Tierra del Fuego 250–51
 Valdivia 201
 Valle de Elqui 173
 Valparaíso 119
Mapuche culture 45, **207**
 arts and crafts **31**
 Museo Regional de la
  Araucanía (Temuco) 206
 Pacification of the Araucania
  47
Marin, Gladys 104
Marin, Hugo 80
Markets **29**
 Angelmó Fish Market 209
 Feria Libre Aníbal Pinto
  (Temuco) 206–7
 Feria Yumbel Market (Castro)
  222
 La Vega (Santiago) 29, **106**
 Mercado Central (Santiago)
  29, **81**
 Mercado Chillán 145
 Mercado Fluvial (Valdivia)
  200
Matta, Roberto **31**
 Museo a Cielo Abierto
  (Valparaíso) 126
 Museo de la Solidaridad
  Salvador Allende
  (Santiago) 94
 Museo Nacional de Bellas
  Artes (Santiago) 79
 Palacio Astoreca (Iquique)
  162
Matte Bello, Rebeca **31**, 79
Matucana 100 (Santiago) **92**
Maule **142–3**
Melinka **240**
Mercado Central (Santiago) 29,
 81
Mercado Fluvial (Valdivia) **200**
Meteorites
 Museo del Meteorito (San
  Pedro de Atacama) **160**
Metro
 Santiago 286
Micros (minibuses) 287
Mines
 Calama 181
 Chuquicamata **183**
 El Teniente **138**
 Humberstone 178
 Lota **147**
 Museo Mineralógico (La
  Serena) **170–71**
 rescue of the 33 San José
  miners **188**
 Santa Laura **178**
Mirador Selkirk **279**
Miró, Joan 94, 105
Mistral, Gabriela **38**, 79
 Iglesia y Convento de San
  Francisco (Santiago) 75

Mistral, Gabriela (cont.)
 Museo de Sitio Casa-Escuela
  Gabriela Mistral
  (Montegrande) 173
 Museo Gabriela Mistral
  (Vicuña) 172
 Museo Pedagógico Gabriela
  Mistral (Santiago) 90
Moai
 Ahu Akivi **275**
 Ahu Tongariki **272–3**
 Península Poike 277
 Playa Anakena 276
 Rano Raraku **268–71**
Mobile phones 289
Monckeberg, Gustavo 95
Money 282, 283
Montegrande **173**
Monumento Nacional Manos de
 Cerro Castillo 246
Monumento Nacional Valle del
 Encanto **192**
Monumento Natural Cerro Ñielol
 206, 207
Monumento Natural El Morado
 139
Monumento Natural Islotes de
 Puñihuil **220–21**
Monumento Natural Pichasca
 192
Mori, Camilo 107
Morro de Arica **154**
Muelle Prat (Valparaíso) **121**
Mulloy, William 275
Mummies, Chinchorro **41**, **157**
 Museo Arqueológico San
  Miguel de Azapa 156
 Museo de Sitio Colón 10
  (Arica) **155**
Municipalidad de Santiago **69**,
 83
Murals
 Museo a Cielo Abierto
  (Valparaíso) **126**
Museums and galleries **30–31**
 Ballenera de Quintay 132–3
 Barrio Vitacura (Santiago) 111
 Casa Mirador de Lukas
  (Valparaíso) 123
 Casa Museo Isla Negra
  (Valparaíso) **128–9**
 Casa Museo La Chascona
  (Santiago) **105**
 Centro Cultural El Austral
  (Valdivia) **200**
 Centro Cultural Palacio La
  Moneda (Santiago) **73**
 Enoteca Wine Museum
  (Santiago) 103
 La Sebastiana (Valparaíso)
  125
 MAC Espacio Quinta Normal
  (Santiago) **89**
 Matucana 100 (Santiago) **92**
 Museo a Cielo Abierto
  (Valparaíso) **126**
 Museo Arqueológico (La
  Serena) **170**

Museums and galleries (cont.)
 Museo Arqueológico de los
  Andes 135
 Museo Arqueológico Gustavo
  Le Paige (San Pedro de
  Atacama) **159**
 Museo Arqueológico
  Municipale Mapuche
  (Villarrica) 211
 Museo Arqueológico San
  Miguel de Azapa **156–7**
 Museo Artequín (Santiago)
  91
 Museo Casa El Solar de los
  Madariaga (Vicuña) 172, 173
 Museo Chileno de Arte
  Precolombino (Santiago)
  41, **66–7**, 82
 Museo Colonial Alemán
  (Frutillar) 219
 Museo de Achao 226–7
 Museo de Arqueología e
  Historia Francisco Fonck
  (Viña del Mar) 131
 Museo de Arte
  Contemporaneo (Santiago)
  80
 Museo de Arte
  Contemporaneo (Valdivia)
  201
 Museo de Arte Moderno
  Chiloé (Castro) **223**
 Museo de Artes Decorativas
  (Santiago) **104–5**
 Museo de Artes Visuales
  (Santiago) **78–9**
 Museo de Ciencia y
  Tecnología (Santiago) **89**
 Museo de Colchagua (Santa
  Cruz) 141
 Museo de Historia Natural de
  Valparaíso **126**
 Museo de la Casa de Cultura
  (Chile Chico) 246
 Museo de la Memoria y los
  Derechos Humanos
  (Santiago) 41, **90**
 Museo de la Merced
  (Santiago) **77**
 Museo de la Moda (Santiago)
  110
 Museo de la Solidaridad
  Salvador Allende
  (Santiago) **94**
 Museo de las Tradiciones
  Chonchinas (Chonchi) 227
 Museo del Limari (Ovalle) 190
 Museo del Meteorito (San
  Pedro de Atacama) **160**
 Museo de Pica 180
 Museo de Sitio Casa-Escuela
  Gabriela Mistral
  (Montegrande) 173
 Museo de Sitio Colón 10
  (Arica) **155**
 Museo de Tajamares **109**
 Museo El Colono (Puerto
  Octay) 218

Museums and galleries (cont.)
Museo Etnográfico (Caspana)
181
Museo Ferroviario (Santiago)
89
Museo Gabriela Mistral
(Vicuña) 172
Museo Geológico de
Chiu-Chiu 182
Museo Histórico de Lota 147
Museo Histórico Municipal
(Osorno) 217
Museo Histórico Municipal
(Puerto Natales) 258, 259
Museo Histórico Religioso del
Antiguo Monasterio del
Espíritu Santu (Los Andes)
135
Museo Histórico y
Antropológico Maurici Van
de Maele (Valdivia) **201**
Museo Inchin Cuivi Ant
(Quellón) 227
Museo Marítimo Nacional
Valparaíso **119**
Museo Mineralógico (Copiapó)
188
Museo Mineralógico (La
Serena) **170-71**
Museo Municipal Fernando
Cordero Rusque (Porvenir)
261
Museo Nacional de Bellas
Artes (Santiago) **79**
Museo Nacional de Historia
Natural (Santiago) 89
Museo Nacional Ferroviario
Pablo Neruda (Temuco)
207
Museo Paleontológico
(Caldera) 189
Museo Pedagógico Gabriela
Mistral (Santiago) **90**
Museo Ralli (Santiago) **105**
Museo Regional (Iquique) **165**
Museo Regional Braun
Menéndez (Punta Arenas)
256, 257
Museo Regional de Ancud
220
Museo Regional de
Antofagasta 186, 187
Museo Regional de Atacama
(Copiapó) 188
Museo Regional de Castro
222
Museo Regional de la
Araucanía (Temuco) 206,
207
Museo Regional de Rancagua
137
Museo Regional Salesiano
Maggiorino Borgatello
(Punta Arenas) 256, 257
Museo Tringlo Lago Ranco
217
Nao Victoria Museum (Punta
Arenas) 257

Museums and galleries (cont.)
Palacio Alhambra (Santiago)
72-3
Palacio Baburizza (Valparaíso)
123
Palacio Cousiño (Santiago)
94-5
Palacio Rioja (Viña del Mar)
131
Posada del Corregidor
(Santiago) **81**
Santiago **61**
Myths and folklore
Chiloé **220**
Legend of the Birdman **277**

N

Ñancúpel, Pedro 240
Napoleon I, Emperor 46
National parks
Bernardo O'Higgins **259**
Bosque Fray Jorge **193**
Chiloé **221**
Conguillío **198-9**
Huerquehue **213**
La Campana **137**
Laguna del Laja **147**
Laguna San Rafael **238-9**
Lauca 33, **166-7**
Los Glaciares **262**
Nevado Tres Cruces **190**
Pan de Azúcar **189**
Pumalín 33, **232-3**
Puyehue **216-17**
Queulat 33, **236-7**
Radal Siete Tazas **144**
Tierra del Fuego **263**
Tolhuaca **208-9**
Torres del Paine 13, 32, **252-5**
Vicente Pérez Rosales **204-5**
Villarrica **202-3**
Volcán Isluga **178-9**
Neruda, Jan 105
Neruda, Pablo **38**, **105**
Casa Museo Isla Negra
(Valparaíso) **128-9**
Casa Museo La Chascona
(Santiago) **105**
La Sebastiana (Valparaíso)
125
Museo Nacional Ferroviario
Pablo Neruda (Temuco) 207
Nevados de Chillán **145**
Nevados de Sollipulli **210**
Nevado Tres Cruces, Parque
Nacional **190**
No (film) 61
Noche de Valdivia 200
Norte Grande and Norte Chico
17, **151-93**
bars 161
beaches 154
hotels 155, 161, 163, 167, 182
map 152-3
restaurants 156, 159, 164,
171, 174, 185, 191
shopping 193

Northeast of Santiago Centro
55, **99-111**
map 100-101
Northern Patagonia 18, **229-47**
hotels 243
map 230-31
restaurants 241, 244
sailing the fjords of Northern
Patagonia **241**

O

Observatories *see* Astronomy
Observatorio del Pangue **175**
O'Higgins, Bernardo 46, **259**
Battle of Rancagua 136
Casa Colorada (Santiago) 71
Cementerio General
(Santiago) 104
Chillán 144
Concepción 146
Museo de Colchagua (Santa
Cruz) 141
Museo Marítimo Nacional
Valparaíso 119
Palacio de la Real Audiencia
(Santiago) 69
Parque Bernardo O'Higgins
(Santiago) **97**
Plaza Bulnes (Santiago) 73
Termas de Cauquenes 138
Villa O'Higgins 247
Ojos del Caburgua **210**
Olvin, Marta 108
Orongo **274-5**
Osorno **217**
Ovalle **190-91**

P

Pacification of the Araucania
(1861-83) 47
Palacio Alhambra (Santiago)
72-3
Palacio Astoreca (Iquique) **162**
Palacio Baburizza (Valparaíso)
123
Palacio Carrasco (Viña del Mar)
131
Palacio Cousiño (Santiago) **94-5**
Palacio de la Justicia (Valparaíso)
121
Palacio de La Moneda (Santiago)
72
Palacio de la Real Audiencia
(Santiago) **68-9**, 83
Palacio de los Tribunales de
Justicia (Santiago) **71**, 82
Palacio Edificio Íñiguez
(Santiago) 94
Palacio Errázuriz (Santiago) 94
Palacio Irarrázabal (Santiago) 94
Palacio Lyon (Valparaíso) **126**
Palacio Rioja (Viña del Mar) 131
Palafitos (Castro) **222-3**
Palena **240**
Pan de Azúcar, Parque Nacional
189

Panguipulli **214**
Papudo **134**
Paragliding **26**
　Cerro Dragón (Iquique) **162-3**
Parks and gardens
　Cerro Santa Lucía (Santiago)
　　78
　Ex Congreso Nacional
　　(Santiago) 70
　Jardín Botánico Nacional (Viña
　　del Mar) 131
　Jardín Japonés (Santiago) 103
　Jardín Mapulemu (Santiago)
　　103
　Parque Balmaceda (Santiago)
　　108
　Parque Bernardo O'Higgins
　　(Santiago) **97**
　Parque de las Esculturas
　　(Santiago) **108**
　Parque El Loa (Calama) 181
　Parque Metropolitano de
　　Santiago **102-3**
　Parque Quinta Normal
　　(Santiago) **88-9**
Parque Aiken del Sur **244**
Parque Nacional *see* National
　parks
Parque Tantauco **227**
Parra, Violeta 104
Paseo Ahumada (Santiago) **70**,
　82
Paseo Gervasoni (Valparaíso)
　123
Paseo Huérfanos (Santiago) **70**,
　82
Paso del Agua Negra **174**
Passports 282, 289
Patagonia *see* Northern
　Patagonia; Southern
　Patagonia and Tierra del
　Fuego
Patio Bellavista (Santiago) **107**
Pecchenino Raggi, Renzo
　Antonio *see* Lukas
Pelli, César 110
Penguins **34-5**
　Isla Magdalena **257**
　Reserva Nacional Pinguino de
　　Humboldt **191**
　Seno Otway **257**
Península Poike **276-7**
Personal security 288
Petroglyphs *see* Rock art
Pharmacies 288
Philip III, King of Spain 140
Phones 289
Pica **180**
Pichilemu 13, **142**
Picq, Henri 91
Piñera, Sebastián 49, 106, 227
Pinochet, Augusto 48, 49
　Barrio París-Londres
　　(Santiago) 74
　Congreso Nacional
　　(Valparaíso) 127
　Ex Congreso Nacional
　　(Santiago) 70

Pinochet, Augusto (cont.)
　Plaza Bulnes (Santiago) 73
　southernmost prison 261
Piropiro **271**
Pirque **138**
Piscina Antilén (Santiago) 103
Pisco **175**
　Destilería Pisco Mistral (Pisco
　　Elqui) 173
　Planta Capel (Vicuña) 172, 173
Pisco Elqui **173**
Pizarro, Francisco 44
Planetario USACH (Santiago) **92**
Playa Anakena **276**
Plaza, Nicanor 76
Plaza Aníbal Pinto (Temuco)
　206, 207
Plaza Aníbal Pinto (Valparaíso)
　122
Plaza Arturo Prat (Iquique) **164**
Plaza Bulnes (Santiago) **73**
Plaza Camilo Mori (Santiago)
　107
Plaza Caupolicán (Santiago) 102
Plaza de Armas (La Serena)
　168-9
Plaza de Armas and Santiago
　Centro 54, **63-97**
　map 64-5
　walk **82-3**
Plaza Echaurren (Valparaíso)
　118
Plaza Mulato Gil de Castro
　(Santiago) 79
Plaza Sotomayor (Valparaíso)
　120
Plaza Teodoro Schmidt
　(Temuco) 206, 207
Plazoleta El Yunque **279**
Poblado Artesanal (Arica) **155**
Police 288
Portillo **136**
Porvenir **261**
Posada del Corregidor
　(Santiago) **81**
Postal services 289
Prat, Arturo 119, 120, 164
Prehistoric sites **44**
　Aldea de Tulor **160**, **184**
　Cueva del Milodón **258**
　Monumento Nacional Valle
　　del Encanto **192**
　Monumento Natural Pichasca
　　192
　Pukará de Lasana **182-3**
　see also Rock art
Prison, southernmost **261**
Protests (2019) **106**
Provasoli, Eduardo 222
Providencia (Santiago) **109**
Public holidays 283
Public transport 284, 286-7
Pucón **214-15**
Pueblo Los Dominicos
　(Santiago) **110**
Puerto Chacabuco **243**
Puerto Cisnes **242**
Puerto Edén **243**

Puerto Hambre 40, **256**
Puerto Montt **209**
Puerto Natales **258-9**
Puerto Octay **218**
Puerto Raul Marin Balmaceda
　242
Puerto Varas **218-19**
Puerto Williams 32, **261**
Pukará de Lasana **182-3**
Pukará de Quitor **160**
Pukarás and the Camino del Inca
　177
Pumalín, Parque Nacional 33,
　232-3
Punta Arenas 40, **256-7**
Putre **176**
Puyuhuapi **241**
Puyuhuapi Lodge & Spa **242**
Puyehue, Parque Nacional
　216-17

Q

Quellón **227**
Queulat, Parque Nacional 33,
　236-7
Quintay **132-3**
Quiroga, Rodrigo de 77

R

Radal Siete Tazas, Parque
　Nacional **144**
Rafting *see* White-water rafting
Railways *see* Train travel
Rancagua **136-7**
Rano Raraku **268-71**
Rao Kau **274-5**
Rapanui people 47
Rapu, Sergio 276
Recanati, Harry 105
Rescue of the 33 San José
　miners (2010) **188**
Reserva Biológica Huilo-Huilo
　215
Reserva Forestal Edmundo
　Winkler (Frutillar) 219
Reserva Nacional
　Altos de Lircay **143**
　Cerro Castillo **245**
　Coyhaique 244
　Lago Jeinemeni **246**
　Lago Tamango 243
　Las Vicuñas **176-7**
　Pinguino de Humboldt **191**
　Río Clarillo 139
　Río de los Cipreses **140-41**
　Río Simpson **245**
Restaurants
　Central Valley 121, 131, 135,
　　142, 147
　Easter Island and Robinson
　　Crusoe Island 275
　Lake District and Chiloé 206,
　　208, 213, 217, 223
　Norte Grande and Norte Chico
　　156, 159, 161, 164, 171, 174,
　　185, 191

Restaurants (cont.)
Patagonia 241, 244
Santiago 58, 69, 91, 109
Southern Patagonia and
Tierra del Fuego 257
see also Bars; Food and drink
Río Baker **247**
Rio Puelo 209
Robinson Crusoe (Defoe) 45
Robinson Crusoe Island **278-9**
map 266-7
Rock art
Alero de las Manos 245
Cerro Pintados **180**
El Gigante de Atacama **177**
geoglyphs **41**
Geoglifos de Cerro Sagrado
157
Monumento Nacional Manos
de Cerro Castillo 246
Monumento Nacional Valle
del Encanto **192**
Monumento Natural Pichasca
192
Península Poike 277
Rodeo **141**
Roggeveen, Jacob 45
Rojas, Román 168
Ross-Edwards, Agustín 142
Route of Parks (Ruta de los
Parques) **32**
Rules of the road 287
Ruta de los Parques (Route of
Parks) **32**

S

Saavedra, Juan de 118
Safety
LGBT+ safety 289
personal security 288
travel safety advice 282
Sailing the fjords of Northern
Patagonia **241**
Salar de Atacama **185**
Salar de Tara **185**
Salt
Salar de Atacama **185**
Salar de Tara **185**
Valle de la Luna **184**
Saltos del Laja **146**
San José miners, rescue **188**
San Juan Bautista **278**
San Martín, José 71
San Miguel de Azapa **156**
San Pedro de Atacama **158-61**
Santa Cruz **141**, 148
Santa Laura 37, **178**
Santiago 12, 16, **50-111**
architecture **36**
art and culture **60-61**
bars 78, 109
food and drink 28, **58-9**
hotels 74, 97, 104
itinerary 57
map 52-3
markets **29**
modern art **31**

Santiago (cont.)
Northeast of Santiago Centro
55, **99-111**
Plaza de Armas and Santiago
Centro 54, **63-97**
public transport 286-7
restaurants 58, 69, 91, 109
shopping 70
walk **82-3**
West of Santiago Centro 55,
85-97
Santuario Cañi **212-13**
Santuario de la Naturaleza
Carlos Anwandter **213**
Santuario de la Naturaleza
Cascada de las Animas 139
Selkirk, Alexander 45, **279**
Sendero Salsipuedes **278**
Seno Otway **257**
Sewell **132**
Sharp, Bartholomew 169, 170
Shopping
Norte Grande and Norte Chico
193
Santiago 70
taxes and refunds 289
Siegel, Alberto 70, 95
Siete Lagos (Seven Lakes) **214**
Silver
Copiapó 188
Ruinas de Huanchaca
(Antofagasta) 187
Siqueiros, David Alfaro 145
Skiing
Central Valley 139
Centro de Ski Antillanca 216,
217
Cerro Castor **263**
Lagunillas 139
Nevados de Chillán **145**
Portillo **136**
Ski Center Corralco **209**
Smith Solar, Josué 72, 96
Smoking 288-9
Sotomayor, Carlos **31**
South America
map 14
Southern Patagonia and Tierra
del Fuego 19, **249-63**
bars 257
hiking in Tierra del Fuego 32
hotels 255, 260
map 250-51
restaurants 257
Spanish colonizers **45-6**
Spas and hot springs 11
Cocha Resbaladero (Pica) 180
Mamiña Hot Springs **179**
Nevados de Chillán **145**
Parque Nacional Tolhuaca 209
Puyahuapi Lodge & Spa **242**
Termas Aguas Calientes 216,
217
Termas Baños de Puritama
183
Termas Coñaripe 212
Termas de Cauquenes **138**
Termas de Jahuel **136**

Spas and hot springs (cont.)
Termas de Malalcahuello **208**
Termas de Panimávida **142**
Termas de Puyehue **217**
Termas de Quinamávida 142
Termas de Socos **193**
Termas Geómetricas
(Coñaripe) 212
Termas Valle de Colina 139
Termas Ventisquero de
Puyahuapi 241
Specific needs, travellers with
283
Speed limits 284
Stargazing see Astronomy
Statues see Moai
Strait of Magellan **260**
Street art
Santiago **60**
Valparaíso **127**
Stuardo, Carlos 90
Suarez, Inés de 77
Subways
Santiago 286
Surfing
Llico 144
Pichilemu 13, **142**
Swimming pools
Parque Quinta Normal
(Santiago) 89
Piscina Antilén (Santiago) 103

T

Tai Hare Atua **271**
Tapati Rapa Nui **274**
Tap water 288
Taxes 289
Taxis 287
colectivos (shared taxis) 287
Teatro Municipal (Iquique) **163**
Teatro Municipal (Santiago) **76**
Telescopes see Astronomy
Temuco **206**
Termas Baños de Puritama **183**
Termas de Cauquenes **138**
Termas de Jahuel **136**
Termas de Malalcahuello **208**
Termas de Panimávida **142**
Termas de Puyehue **217**
Termas de Socos **193**
Terminal Pesquero (Arica) **156**
Theater
Centro Gabriela Mistral
(Santiago) 79
Teatro Municipal (Iquique) **163**
Teatro Municipal (Santiago)
76
Thrill seekers **26-7**
Tickets, public transport 286
Tierra del Fuego, Parque
Nacional **263**
see also Southern Patagonia
and Tierra del Fuego
Time zone 288
Tipping 288
Tobacco products, customs
information 282

Toesca, Joaquin **69**
  Basilica de la Merced
    (Santiago) 77
  Iglesia de Santo Domingo
    (Santiago) 80
  tajamares 109
Tolhuaca, Parque Nacional
  208-9
Tomé, Lota **147**
Tompkins, Doug 232-3
Tompkins Conservation
  233
Toro y Zambrano, Dom Mateo
  de 71
Torrecilla, Antonio 165
Torres del Paine, Parque
  Nacional 13, 32, **252-5**
Tours
  Colchagua Valley driving tour
    148-9
Train travel 286
  Ex-Estacion El Ferrocarril de
    Antofagasta a Bolivia 186,
    187
  Museo Ferroviario (Santiago)
    89
  Museo Nacional Ferroviario
    Pablo Neruda (Temuco)
    207
  Tren Sabores del Valle (Santa
    Cruz) 141
Travel **284-7**
Travel safety advice 282
Trekking *see* Hiking
Trolebuses (trolleybuses)
  Valparaíso **119**
Tukuturi **271**

U

Undurraga, Cristián 73
UNESCO World Biosphere
  Reserves
  Parque Nacional Bosque Fray
    Jorge **193**
  Parque Nacional La Campana
    137
  Parque Nacional Laguna San
    Rafael **238-9**
  Parque Nacional Torres del
    Paine **252-5**
UNESCO World Heritage Sites
  Humberstone **178**
  Iglesia Dalcahue 221
  Iglesia de Chonchi 227
  Iglesia San Francisco
    (Castro) **222**
  Jesuit churches in Chiloé 12,
    36, **224-5**
  Museo Nacional Ferroviario
    Pablo Neruda (Temuco)
    207
  Santa Laura **178**
  Sewell **132**
  Valparaíso 118
Urrutia, Matilde 105,
  128-9
Ushuaia **263**

V

Vaccinations 283
Valdivia **200-201**
Valdivia, Pedro de 45, 83
  Casa Incaica (San Pedro de
    Atacama) 158
  Cerro Santa Lucía 78
  Iglesia y Convento de San
    Francisco (Santiago) 75
Valle de Cachapoal **138**
Valle de Curicó **141**
Valle de Elqui **172-5**
Valle de la Luna **184**
Valle de la Muerte **161**
Valparaíso 10, **118-29**
  architecture **37**
  bars 125
  map 119
  street art **127**
Vasconcelos, Juan de los Santos
  80
Verdi, Giuseppe 76
Vergara, José Francisco 125,
  130
Vicente Pérez Rosales, Parque
  Nacional **204-5**
Victoria, Queen of England 124
Vicuña **172**
Vicuña, Pedro Felix 124
Vicuña Mackenna, Benjamin 78
Vicuñas **35**
Villa O'Higgins **247**
Villarrica **211**
Villarrica, Parque Nacional **202-3**
Villa Tehuelches **258**
Viña del Mar **130-31**
Vineyards *see* Wines
Visas 282
Vivaceta, Fermín 75, 76, 81
Volcán Isluga, Parque Nacional
  178-9
Volcanoes **27**
  Colcán Llaima **198**
  Laguna Verde 191
  Nevados de Sollipulli **210**
  Parque Nacional Vicente
    Pérez Rosales **204-5**
  Parque Nacional Villarrica
    202-3
  Parque Nacional Volcán Isluga
    178-9
  Reserva Nacional Las Vicuñas
    176-7
  Volcán Lanín **203**
  Volcán Lonquimay **211**
  Volcán Quetrupillán **203**
  Volcán Villarrica 202, **203**

W

Walks
  Plaza de Armas (Santiago)
    82-3
  see also Hiking
War of the Pacific (1879-83) 46,
  165
Water, drinking 288

Waterfalls
  Ojos del Caburgua **210**
  Parque Nacional Pumalín 233
  Parque Nacional Radal Siete
    Tazas 144
  Saltos del Laja **146**
Weber, Hugo 279
Websites 289
Well, Thomas 124
West of Santiago Centro 55,
  85-97
  map 86-7
Whales **35**
  Ballenera de Quintay 132-3
  blue whale **35**
Wheelwright, William 118
Whitewater rafting 10, 26
  Futaleufú **234**
Wi-Fi 289
Wild camping 216
Wildlife **34-5**
  Parque Aiken del Sur **244**
  Parque Tantauco **227**
  Reserva Nacional Coyhaique
    244
  Reserva Nacional Lago
    Tamango 243
  Reserva Nacional Las Vicuñas
    176-7
  Reserva Nacional Río
    Simpson **245**
  Santuario de la Naturaleza
    Carlos Anwandter **213**
  Strait of Magellan 260
  see also Birds; National parks
Williams, Juan 261
Williamson-Balfour Company 47
Wines
  antique wineries of Pirque **138**
  Casablanca Valley **130**
  Central Valley 13, **28**
  Colchagua Valley tour **148-9**
  Enoteca Wine Museum
    (Santiago) 103
  Gillmore Winery (Maule) 142-3
  Hacienda Los Lingues **140**
  Maule **142-3**
  Ruta del Vino Curicó 141
  Santiago 59
  Valle de Cachapoal **138**
  Via Wines (Maule) 143
  Viña Balduzzi (Maule) 142, 143
  Viña Casa Tamaya (Ovalle)
    190, 191
  Viña Corral Victoria (Maule)
    142, 143
  Viña Tabalí (Ovalle) 190, 191
Writers **38-9**

Y

Yarur, Juan 110
Yrarrázaval, Ricardo 223

Z

Zanelli, Ottorino 123
Zapallar **134-5**

PHRASE BOOK

Chileans themselves sometimes apologize for speaking bad Spanish, and anyone who has learned the language elsewhere may find it a challenge. Still, it is fairer to say that, given the country's geographical isolation, Spanish simply developed differently here. Additionally, because of Mapuche influence, there are many non-standard words, and pronunciation can also be difficult.

Chileans often omit the terminal "s," making it difficult for outsiders to distinguish singular from plural, and sometimes even the internal "s." On the tongue of a Chilean, for instance, las escuelas (the schools) may sound more like "la ecuela." Similarly, Anglicisms such as "show" sound more like "cho" in local speech.

In everyday informal speech, Chileans may also use non-standard verb forms. For instance, second-person familiar verbs often end in an accented "í," as in "¿Querí?" (Do you want?) rather than the conventional "¿Quieres?".

SOME SPECIAL CHILEAN WORDS

carrete	kahrehteh	party
chupe	choopeh	a seafood stew
completo	kohmplehtoh	Chilean hot dog
copa	kohpah	glass (of wine)
galería	gahlehree-ah	shopping mall
oficina	ohfeeseenah	office; in the Atacama nitrate-mining towns
parcela	pahrsaylah	country home or small farm
parrilla	pahreeyah	grill restaurant
paseo	pahsayoh	pedestrian mall

IN AN EMERGENCY

Help!	¡Socorro!	sokorro
Stop!	¡Pare!	pareh
Call a doctor!	¡Llamen un médico!	yamen oon mehdeeko
Call an ambulance	¡Llamen a una ambulancia	yamen a oona amboolans-ya
Police!	¡Policía!	poleesee-a
I've been robbed	Me robaron	meh robaron
Where is the nearest hospital?	¿Dónde queda el hospital más cercano?	dondeh keda el ospeetal mas sairkano
Could you help me?	¿Me puede ayudar?	meh pwedeh a-yoodar

COMMUNICATION ESSENTIALS

Yes	Sí	see
No	No	no
Please	Por favor	por fabor
Pardon me	Perdone	pairdoneh
Excuse me	Disculpe	deeskoolpeh
I'm sorry	Lo siento	lo s-yento
Thanks	Gracias	gras-yas
Hello!	¡Hola!	o-la
Good morning	Buenos días	bwenos dee-as
Good afternoon	Buenas tardes	bwenas tardes
Good evening	Buenas noches	bwenas noches
Night	Noche	nocheh
Morning	Mañana	man-yana
Tomorrow	Mañana	man-yana

Yesterday	Ayer	a-yair
Here	Acá	aka
What?	¿Cómo?	komo
When?	¿Cuándo?	kwando
Where?	¿Dónde?	dondeh
Why?	¿Por qué?	por keh
How are you?	¿Cómo está?	komo estah
Very well, thank you	Muy bien, gracias	mwee byen gras-yas
Pleased to meet you	Encantado/a/ mucho gusto	enkantad o/a/ moocho goosto

USEFUL PHRASES

That's great!	¡Qué bien!	keh b-yen
Do you speak English?	¿Habla usted Ingles?	abla oo-sted eenglehs
I don't understand	No entiendo	no ent-yendo
Could you speak more slowly?	¿Puede hablar más despacio?	pwedeh ablar mas despas-yo
I agree/okay	De acuerdo/bueno	deh akwairdo/ bweno
Let's go!	¡Vámonos!	bamonos
How do I get to/ which way to...?	¿Cómo se llega a...?/¿Por dónde e va a...?	komo se llega a/por dondeh seh ba a

USEFUL WORDS

large	grande	grandeh
small	pequeño	peken-yo
hot	caliente	kal-yenteh
cold	frío	free-o
good	bueno	bweno
bad	malo	malo
sufficient	suficiente	soofees-yenteh
open	abierto	ab-yairto
closed	cerrado	serrah-do
entrance	entrada	entrada
exit	salida	saleeda
full	lleno	yeno
right	derecha	dairehcha
left	izquierda	eesk-yairda
straight on	derecho	dehrehcho
above	arriba	arreeba
quickly	rápido	rahpidoh
early	temprano	temprahno
late	tarde	tardeh
now	ahora	a-ora
soon	pronto	pronto
less	menos	menos
much	mucho	moocho
in front of	delante	delanteh
opposite	enfrente	enfrenteh
behind	detrás	detrahs
second floor	segundo piso	segoondo peeso
ground floor	primer piso	preemair peeso
bar	bar	bar
discoteque	boliche	bohleecheh
lift/elevator	ascensor	asensor
bathroom	baño	ban-yo
toilet paper	papel higiénico	papel eeh-yeneeka
bribe	coima	koyma
girl/woman	mina	meena
women	mujeres	moohaires
men	hombres	ombres
child (boy/girl)	niño/niña	neen-yo, neen-yah
camera	cámara	kamara

batteries	pilas	peelas
passport	pasaporte	pasaporteh
visa	visa	beesa
tourist card	tarjeta turística	tarheta tooreesteeka
driver's license	licencia de conducir	leesensyah de condooseer
thief	ladrón	lahdrohn
cop	carabinero	ka-ra-bin-air-oh
money	dinero	deenehroh
lazy	flojo	flohoh
mess	lío	lee-oh
shanty town	callampa	kayahmpah
to eat	comer	koh-mehr
to steal	robar	rohbahr
to back away	arrugar	ahroogahr
to put up with	soportar	sohportahr
No way	¡De ningun manera!	Day neengoonah manehra

HEALTH

I don't feel well	No me siento bien	No meh s-yento been
I have a stomach ache/ headache.	Me duele el estómago/ la cabeza	meh dweleh el estohmago/ la kabesa
He/she is ill	Está enfermo/a	esta enfairmo/a
I need to rest	Necesito decansar	neseseeto deskansar

POST OFFICES AND BANKS

I'm looking for a... bureau de change	Busco una... casa de cambio	boosko oona kasa deh kamb-yo
What is the dollar rate?	¿A cuánto está el dólar?	a kwantoh esta el dohlar
I want to send a	Quiero enviar una	k-yairo en-vyar-oona
letter	carta	karta
postcard	postal	postal
stamp	estampilla	estampee-ya
withdraw money	sacar dinero	sakar deenairo

SHOPPING

I would like...	Me gustaría...	meh goostaree-a
I want...	Quiero...	k-yairo
Do you have any...?	¿Tiene...?	t-yeneh
How much is it?	¿Cuánto cuesta?	kwanto kwesta
What time do you open/close?	¿A qué hora abre/ cierra?	a ke ora abreh/ s-yairra
May I pay with a credit card?	¿Puedo pagar con tarjeta de crédito?	pwedo pagar kon tarheta deh kredeeto
expensive	caro	karo

SIGHTSEEING

beach	playa	pla-ya
castle, fortress	castillo	kastee-yo
guide	guía	gee-a
hamlet	aldea	ahdayah
motorway	autopista	owtopeesta
neighborhood	barrio	bahreeoh
road	carretera	karretaira
street	calle	ka-yeh
tourist bureau	oficina de turismo	ofeeseena deh tooreesmo
town hall	municipalidad	mooneeseepaleedad

GETTING AROUND

When does it leave?	¿A qué hora sale?	a keh ora saleh

When does the next train/bus leave for...?	¿A qué hora sale el próximo tren/ autobús a...?	a keh ora saleh el prokseemo tren/ owtoboos a
Could you call a taxi for me?	¿Me puede llamar un taxi?	meh pwedeh yamar oon taksee
departure gate	puerta de embarque	pwairta deh embarkeh
boarding pass	tarjeta de embarque	tarheta deh e embarkeh
customs	aduana	adwana
fare	tarifa	tareefa
insurance	seguro	segooro
car hire	alquiler de autos	alkeelair deh owtos
bicycle	bicicleta	beeseekleta
gas station	estación de servicio	estas-yon deh serveeseeoh
garage	garage	garaheh
I have a flat tire	Se me pinchó un neumático	seh meh peencho un nayoomahtikoh

STAYING IN A HOTEL

I have a reservation	Tengo una reserva	Tengo oona rresairba
Is there a room available?	¿Hay habitación disponible?	I ahbitahseeohn deesponeeble
single/double room	habitación single/ doble	abeetas-yohn senglay/dobleh
twin room	habitación con camas gemelas	abeetas-yon kon kamas hemelas
shower	ducha	doocha
bathtub	tina	teenah
I want to be woken up at...	Necesito que me despierten a las...	neseseeto keh meh desp-yairten a las
hot water	agua caliente	agwa lak-yenteh
cold water	agua fría	agwa free-yah
soap	jabón	habohn
towel	toalla	to-a-ya
key	llave	yabeh

EATING OUT

I am a vegetarian	Soy vegetariano	soy behetar-yano
fixed price	precio fijo	pres-yo feeho
glass	vaso	baso
cup	taza	tahsah
cutlery	cubiertos	koob-yairtos
Can I see the menu, please?	¿Puedo ver la carta, por favor?	pwedoh vair la carta, por fabor
The check, please	la cuenta, por favor	la kwenta por fabor
I would like a glass of water	Me gustaría un vaso de agua	meh goostaree-a oon baso deh agwa
breakfast	desayuno	desa-yoono
lunch	almuerzo	almwairso
dinner	cena	saynah

MENU DECODER

parrillada	pahreeyada	mixed grill
lomo	lohmoh	beefsteak
lomo a la pimienta	lohomo ah la peemee-entah	pepper steak
lomo vetado	lohmoh vehtadoh	ribeye
lomo liso	lohmoh leesoh	sirloin
barros luco	bahros lookoh	beef sandwich with melted cheese
cazuela de vacuno	kahswaylah de vahkoonoh	beef and vegetable stew
cazuela de ave	kahswaylah de ahvay	chicken and vegetable stew
centolla	sentoyah	king crab

pebre	*pehbray*	Chilean salsa
chorizo	*chohreezoh*	pork sausage
choripán	*choreepan*	pork sausage in a bun
churrasco	*choorrasko*	thin boneless steak on bread
cola de mono	*kohlah de mono*	aperitif of coffee, milk, and liqueur
curanto	*kooranhntoh*	stew of shellfish, meat, and potatoes
lúcuma	*lookoohmah*	eggfruit
mollejas	*moyehas*	sweetbreads
pastel de choclo	*pahstel deh chohcloh*	sweet corn pie
plateada	*plahte-ahda*	stewed beef and vegetables
terremoto	*tairehmohtoh*	cocktail of white wine, Fernet, and pineapple ice cream
humita	*oomeeta*	mashed sweet corn mixed with onion and milk
arroz	*arrohs*	rice
atún	*atoon*	tuna
azúcar	*asookar*	sugar
bacalao	*bakala-o*	cod
camarones	*kamarones*	shrimp
carne	*karneh*	beef
cebolla	*sebo-ya*	onion
chirimoya	*cheereemoyah*	custard apple
huevo	*webo*	egg
jugo	*hoogo*	fruit juice
langosta	*langosta*	lobster
leche	*lecheh*	milk
mantequilla	*mantekee-ya*	butter
marisco	*mareesko*	shellfish
pan	*pan*	bread
papas	*papas*	potatoes
pescado	*peskado*	fish
pimienta dulce	*peemee-entah doolsay*	sweet pepper
pollo	*po-yo*	chicken
postre	*postreh*	dessert
roseta	*rroseta*	bread roll
sal	*sal*	salt
salsa	*salsa*	sauce
sopa	*sopa*	soup
té	*teh*	tea
vinagre	*beenagreh*	vinegar
zapallito	*sapa-yeeto*	squash

TIME

minute	**minuto**	*meenootoh*
hour	**hora**	*ora*
half an hour	**media hora**	*med-ya ora*
quarter of an hour	**un cuarto**	*oon kwarto*
Monday	**lunes**	*loones*
Tuesday	**martes**	*martes*
Wednesday	**miércoles**	*m-yairkoles*
Thursday	**jueves**	*hwebes*
Friday	**viernes**	*b-yairnes*
Saturday	**sábado**	*sabado*
Sunday	**domingo**	*domeengo*
January	**enero**	*enairo*
February	**febrero**	*febrairo*

March	**marzo**	*marso*
April	**abril**	*abreel*
May	**mayo**	*ma-yo*
June	**junio**	*hoon-yo*
July	**julio**	*hool-yo*
August	**agosto**	*agosto*
September	**septiembre**	*sept-yembreh*
October	**octubre**	*oktoobreh*
November	**noviembre**	*nob-yembreh*
December	**diciembre**	*dees-yembreh*

NUMBERS

0	**cero**	*sairo*
1	**uno**	*oono*
2	**dos**	*dos*
3	**tres**	*tres*
4	**cuatro**	*kwatro*
5	**cinco**	*seenko*
6	**seis**	*says*
7	**siete**	*s-yeteh*
8	**ocho**	*ocho*
9	**nueve**	*nwebeh*
10	**diez**	*d-yes*
11	**once**	*onseh*
12	**doce**	*doseh*
13	**trece**	*treseh*
14	**catorce**	*katorseh*
15	**quince**	*keenseh*
16	**dieciséis**	*d-yeseesays*
17	**diecisiete**	*d-yesees-yeteh*
18	**dieciocho**	*d-yes-yocho*
19	**diecinueve**	*d-yeseenwebeh*
20	**veinte**	*baynteh*
30	**treinta**	*traynta*
40	**cuarenta**	*kwarenta*
50	**cincuenta**	*seenkwenta*
60	**sesenta**	*sesenta*
70	**setenta**	*setenta*
80	**ochenta**	*ochenta*
90	**noventa**	*nobenta*
100	**cien**	*s-yen*
500	**quinientos**	*keen-yentos*
1000	**mil**	*meel*
first	**primero/a**	*preemairo/a*
second	**segundo/a**	*segoondo/a*
third	**tercero/a**	*tairsairo/a*
fourth	**cuarto/a**	*kwarto/a*
fifth	**quinto/a**	*keento/a*
sixth	**sexto/a**	*seksto/a*
seventh	**séptimo/a**	*septeemo/a*
eighth	**octavo/a**	*oktabo/a*
ninth	**noveno/a**	*nobeno/a*
tenth	**décimo/a**	*deseemo/a*

ACKNOWLEDGMENTS

The publisher would like to thank the following for their kind permission to reproduce their photographs:

Key: a-above; b-below/bottom; c-centre; f-far; l-left; r-right; t-top

123RF.com: Antonio Abrignani 45clb.

4Corners: Guido Cozzi 192–3b.

akg-images: 46cr; Album / Oronoz 45tr; 46tl; historic-maps 45tl.

Alamy Stock Photo: age fotostock / Tolo Balaguer 221tr, 225cl, 226t, / Gábor Kovács 200–201t, / Dave Stamboulis 235; Albertoloyo 178–9b; Sally Anderson 67clb; Arco Images GmbH / G. Lacz 189crb; Al Argueta 25tr, 68t; Sven Arved 27t; B.O'Kane 58–9b; Krys Bailey 238cr; Joao Barcelos 234br; Norman Barrett 156bl; Aaron Beck 164tl; Hal Beral / VWPics 270cra, 271ca; Bildagentur-online / Begsteiger 181br; BIOSPHOTO / Jean-Claude Malausa 33cl, 133tr, 137b; Blickwinkel / Hummel 237br; Tibor Bognar 55t, 69bl, 72tl, 84–5; Michele Burgess 24tl, 41crb, 157br; byvalet 24cra, 70b; Cal Sport Media 108–9t; Cannon Photography LLC / BrownWCannonIII 27b, 268–9b; Blanca Saenz de Castilllo 204–5t; Cavan / Aurora Photos / Tim Martin 16c, 50–51; Cephas Picture Library / Matt Wilson 28–9t; Chris Schmid Photography 272–3b; Jan A. Csernoch 167tr; Cultura Creative Ltd / Ben Pipe Photography 20t; Ian Dagnall / Graffiti by Gabriel Eduardo Maulen Muñoz 105tr; Danita Delimont / DanitaDelimont.com / Walter Bibikow 172–3b, 224cra, / Fredrik Norrsell 246–7b; David Noton Photography 148bl; Chile DesConocido 124tl; Design Pics Inc / Destinations / Deddeda 26–7b, / Peter Langer 94cr; DGB 279br; Doleesi 161tr; Reiner Elsen 76tl; Everett Collection Inc / © Sony Pictures Classics / Ron Harvey 61br; FerrizFrames 32br; Constanza Flores 8clb; Florilegius 45cr, 47cb, 269tr; Folio Images / Felix Oppenheim 10clb; Galopin 43tr; Jorge Garrido 56cr; David Gee 259br; Diego Grandi 104b; Granger Historical Picture Archive / NYC 47tr, 105br; Mark Green 11br; Marcel Gross 10ca, 34–5t; Have Camera Will Travel | Central & South America 59br; hemis.fr / Walter Bibikow 171cra, / De Winter - Van Rossem 184–5t; Heritage Image Partnership Ltd / Index 44bc, / Werner Forman Archive / N.J Saunders 269tl; Cindy Hopkins 22cla; Ian Dagnall 12–13b; Image Professionals GmbH / Enno Kapitza 208t; imageBROKER / Christian Handl 192t, / Christian Heinrich 233tr, / Martina Katz 43crb, / Karol Kozlowski 40–41b, / Michael Runkel 27cl, / Stefan Schurr 129t, / Harald von Radebrecht 243bl; incamerastock / ICP 45cla; John Warburton-Lee Photography / Paul Harris 59tr; Jon Arnold Images Ltd 20bl, / Walter Bibikow 158–9b, 224–5b, 255t; Paul Kennedy / Street Art Bellavista Sunflower Energy by Gonzalo Matiz Salinas 30–31b; Keystone Press / Keystone Pictures USA 48tl; Ivan Konar 246tl; Russell Kord 17tl, 109bl, 114–15; MARKA / maurizio virgili 167ca; Stefano Politi Markovina 38–9t; mauritius images GmbH / Stefano

Paterna 55bl, 83tl, 98–9, / Jutta Ulmer 212b; mikecranephotography.com 213t; MJ Photography 274–5t; Ashot Mnatsakanyan 89br; Raquel Mogado 242t; Gianni Muratore 43tl; National Geographic Image Collection / Babak Tafreshi 11t; National Geographic Image Collection / Nigel Hicks 216br, / Maria Stenzel 18cb, 228–9, / Dave Yoder 160tl; The Natural History Museum 46br, 137tr; Nature Picture Library / Merryn Thomas 25cla; Francisco Negroni 211br; Niebrugge Images 72–3b; M. Timothy O'Keefe 110tl; Panther Media GmbH / braeumer 276bc; Stefano Paterna 254br; Pictorial Press Ltd 48cb; Maurizio Polese 28bl; Porky Pies Photography 257bl; Prisma Archivo 46–7t; Mauricio Quevedo 179tr; Ricardo Ribas 164–5b; Jeremy Richards 278–9t; Robertharding 168–9b, / Jordan Banks 56crb, / Geoff Renner 273tr, / Yadid Levy 30–31t, 78b, / Street art by Izak One ft Henruz, 2013 93b; Pep Roig 236bl, 241tl; Francisco Javier Ramos Rosellon 130t; RP Images / SrA Sarah Mattison 136cra; Michael Runkel 135br; Philip Scalia 36tr, 60–61b; Cristian Silva 119cr; David South 180tc; South America 226cra; Marina Spironetti 20crb, 183br; Dave Stamboulis 120cla; Jose Luis Stephens 56t, 97tr; Johnny Stockshooter 122bl; Keren Su / China Span 184bl; Sueddeutsche Zeitung Photo / Jose Giribas 40t, 41cla, 89cl, 90b, 125crb; Tetra Images / Henryk Sadura 256t; Markus Thomenius 162–3t; Toniflap 67crb; travelbild.com 278bl; Universal Images Group North America LLC / DeAgostini / DEA Picture Library 31crb; UPI 49clb; Lucas Vallecillos 23tr, 66–7t, 160–61b, 177br; Ivan Vdovin 220–21b; Simon Vine 203tr; Shiona Webster 203cra; WENN Rights Ltd 49bc; Leon Werdinger 26tl; Andreas Werth 13br, 233cra; Westend61 GmbH / Stefan Schütz 32–3t, 239tl, 245t; Karin De Winter 167cra; Wim Wiskerke 67br; Xinhua / © Jorge Villegas 42cla; Alessandro Zappalorto 182cra; Zoonar GmbH / Barbara Boensch 170bl.

AWL Images: Walter Bibikow 187t; Karol Kozlowski 2–3, 25tl, 56bl, 71t, 79tr, 92t, 276tl; John Warburton-Lee 275br; Alex Robinson 260–61t.

Bridgeman Images: Archivio Arici / Graziano Arici 38bl; Sophie Bassouls 39cla; Look and Learn 45crb; Photo Josse 46clb.

Depositphotos Inc: pierivb 4; tjalex4life@gmail.com 17cb, 150–51; Toniflap 215b.

Dorling Kindersley: Demetrio Carrasco 31cla; Nigel Hicks 207br.

Dreamstime.com: Hernan Perez Aguirre 132b; Hoang Bao Nguyen / Street Art by Aibar 22–3ca; Albertoloyo 176–7t; Antonella865 182t; Pierre-yves Babelon 122–3t; Rui Baião 42cr; Bigapplestock 125b; Lukas Bischoff 54c, 62–3; Larisa Blinova 210–11t; David Brooks 58tr; Byvalet 39b, 244b; Dmitry Chulov 176bl; Danflcreativo 88–9t; Ionut David 19t, 248–9; Francisco Javier Espuny 96b; Marcelo Vildosola Garrigo 188tl; Diego Grandi 8–9b, 22tl, 36–7b, 42cl, 77b, 91tl, 102–3t, 106–7b, 118–19t,

Penguin
Random
House

Main Contributors Shafik Meghji, Steph Dyson, Nick Edwards, Wayne Bernhardson, Declan McGarvey, Kristina Schreck

Senior Editor Alison McGill

Senior Designer Tania Da Silva Gomes

Project Editors Lucy Richards, Ioan Marc Jones

Project Art Editor Jordan Lambley

Designers Stuti Tiwari Bhatia, Bharti Karakoti, Meghna Barua, Priyanka Thakur

Factcheckers Nick Edwards, Maria Edwards

Editors Amy Braddon, Laure Gysemans, Lydia Halliday, Rachel Laidler, Jackie Staddon, Rachel Thompson, Ankita Awasthi Tröger

Proofreader Kathryn Glendenning

Indexer Hilary Bird

Senior Picture Researcher Ellen Root

Picture Research Sumita Khatwani, Vagisha Pushp, Rituraj Singh, Flora Spens

Illustrators Chinglemba Chingtham, Surat Kumar Mantoo, Arun Pottirayil, T. Gautam Trivedi

Senior Cartographic Editor Casper Morris

Cartography Subhashree Bharati, Uma Bhattacharya, Rajesh Chhibber, Simonetta Giori

Jacket Designers Jordan Lambley, Bess Daly

Jacket Picture Research Susie Watters

Senior DTP Designer Jason Little

DTP Designer Tanveer Zaidi

Technical Prepress Manager Tom Morse

Image Retouching Steve Crozier

Producer Kariss Ainsworth

Managing Editor Rachel Fox

Managing Art Editor Bess Daly

Art Director Maxine Pedliham

Publishing Director Georgina Dee

Hampshire County Library

C016936092

A & H

918.304666

LI483567

06-Aug-2020

£15.99

9780241411490

Chile and Easter Island Revise

6321375

The information in this DK Eyewitness Travel Guide is checked regularly.
Every effort has been made to ensure that this book is as up-to-date as possible at the time of going to press. Some details, however, such as telephone numbers, opening hours, prices, gallery hanging arrangements and travel information, are liable to change. The publishers cannot accept responsibility for any consequences arising from the use of this book, nor for any material on third party websites, and cannot guarantee that any website address in this book will be a suitable source of travel information. We value the views and suggestions of our readers very highly. Please write to: Publisher, DK Eyewitness Travel Guides, Dorling Kindersley, 80 Strand, London, WC2R 0RL, UK, or email: travelguides@dk.com

First edition 2011

Published in Great Britain by Dorling Kindersley Limited, 80 Strand, London, WC2R 0RL

Published in the United States by DK Publishing, 1450 Broadway, Suite 801, New York, NY 10018

Copyright © 2011, 2020 Dorling Kindersley Limited
A Penguin Random House Company
20 21 22 23 10 9 8 7 6 5 4 3 2 1

A CIP catalog record for this book is available from the British Library.

A catalog record for this book is available from the Library of Congress.

ISSN: 1542 1554
ISBN: 978 0 2414 1149 0

Printed and bound in Malaysia

www.dk.com